D. W. GRIFFITH
AND THE ORIGINS OF
AMERICAN NARRATIVE FILM

D. W. Griffith (with Henry Walthall) demonstrates a gesture in *Judith of Bethulia* (1913). Frame enlargement from film's outtakes, courtesy of the Museum of Modern Art.

D. W. Griffith and the Origins of American Narrative Film

THE EARLY YEARS AT BIOGRAPH

TOM GUNNING

UNIVERSITY OF ILLINOIS PRESS
Urbana and Chicago

Society for Cinema Studies annual dissertation award winner.

Illini Books edition, 1994

© 1991 by the Board of Trustees of the University of Illinois
Manufactured in the United States of America
P 5 4 3 2

This book is printed on acid-free paper.

Library of Congress Cataloging-in-Publication Data

Gunning, Tom, 1949–
    D. W. Griffith and the origins of American narrative film : the
early years at Biograph / Tom Gunning.
        p.   cm.
    Includes bibliographical references and index.
    ISBN 0-252-06366-X (alk. paper)
    1. Griffith, D. W. (David Wark), 1875–1948—Criticism and
interpretation. 2. Motion pictures—United States—History.
3. Biograph Company.   I. Title.
PN1998.3.G76G8   1991
791.43′0233′092—dc20   90-37588
                                                  CIP

Dedicated to
the memory of Jay Leyda (1910–88)
and to the ongoing inspiration of Eileen Bowser.

A major work will either establish the genre or
abolish it; and the perfect work will do both.
—Walter Benjamin,
The Origins of German Tragic Drama

Contents

Acknowledgments

A project such as this one, undertaken for more than a decade, has incurred more debts than can be noted here. However, some of these are so evident that it would be more than ordinary rudeness not to make some mention. First must be my thesis committee at New York University, beginning with my advisor, the late Jay Leyda, and followed closely by Eileen Bowser, William Simon, Robert Sklar, and Janet Staiger. Professor Leyda was in every sense the inspiration of this work, and if it has caught some small measure of his spirit, I am deeply proud. Next must come the readers for the Society for Cinema Studies Dissertation Award, John Belton, Tania Modelski, and David Cook, and the readers for the University of Illinois Press, David Desser and Joyce Jesionowski. Jesionowski also made this volume's frame enlargements. And special thanks to Judith McCulloh, executive editor at the Press, and Mary Giles for her careful and insightful editing of the manuscript.

A variety of archives and their staffs have been helpful, especially the Motion Picture Division of the Library of Congress, for providing access to the Paper Print Collection, with special thanks to Paul Spehr and Pat Lough-ney. The Film Department of the Museum of Modern Art has been so supportive of my work that I almost feel that it is my second home. Special thanks to Charles Silver and Ron Magliozzi at the Film Study Center, Jon Gartenberg, assistant curator, Robert Summers, formerly in film circulation, and, once again, in another capacity, Eileen Bowser, curator. I would like to thank the staff of the Library of Performing Arts at Lincoln Center and the staff at the archives of the Edison National Historical Site, as well as the Study Center at the Department of Cinema Studies of New York University.

The 1978 Brighton Project organized by the International Federation of Film Archives had a decisive impact on this work, and I wish to thank David Francis of the British Film Institute and, again, Eileen Bowser who made it possible, as well as the participants in that project, particularly, Barry Salt, Charles Musser, Jon Gartenberg, Martin Sopocy, David Levy, John Fell, and my friend and colleague, André Gaudreault.

A large number of intellectual debts must be acknowledged, with Jay Leyda again primary. Almost of equal importance are Noel Burch, although I am sure he will disagree with much that is said herein; André Gaudreault for his thoughts on narratology and early film; Charles Musser for his pioneering work on both film discourse and industry organization in early American cinema; Jean Mottett for pointing out the need for a theoretical grounding for this project and for putting me in contact with contemporary French theorists (particularly Jacques Aumont); Ron Mottram for our early discussions of Biograph; Brooks McNamara for insight into melodrama, vaudeville, and other forms of popular entertainment; Ted Perry for early guidance in the research materials available for early film; Annette Michelson for convincing me that she should not be the advisor for my thesis but providing a model for insightful film viewing that has inflected all my work; Russell Merritt for inspiration through the quality of his own work on Griffith, supplemented by a number of discussions; Marcel Ohms for inviting me to the Conference on Early French Cinema at Perpignon in 1984; Miriam Hansen for her unique sense of reading early film against the grain; Steven Higgins for his careful research advice; Paolo Cherchi Usai for inviting me to the Giornate del Cinema Muto and his love of nitrate; Richard Abel for his knowledge of early French film; Adam Simon for conversation about the cinema of attractions; Dana Polan for his support of the project and comments on cutting it; John Belton for his insights into the sexual orientation of Florence Lawrence's fans; and, once again, Eileen Bowser for more than I can list here.

Personal debts are owed to Allison Denny and Phillipe Browning, who word-processed the original dissertation; SUNY/Purchase for approving a paid leave during which the final stages of the work were completed; and Claribel Cone, Mary Hadley Gunning, and my wife Deborah for their support.

Introduction

I N 1940 a young filing clerk at the Library of Congress, whose interests in theater and literature made him consider his job as more than a menial task, found references to a series of paper films stored in a neglected vault of the Library. Curious about what these copyright records were, Howard Lamarr Walls went to the librarian of Congress, the poet Archibald MacLeish, and requested the key. The vault's lock was discovered to be so corroded that the key was useless, and the lock had to be removed. Once open, the vault revealed not only stacks of photographic stills, but also the rolls of paper films that had piqued Walls's curiosity. Examining a few rolls he recognized names from the earliest period of film history: Thomas Edison, American Mutoscope, and Biograph.

What Walls rediscovered was a series of copyright documents of an unique sort. At the turn of the century, film was such a new means of expression that it was not covered by existing copyright legislation. However, film manufacturers (in particular, Thomas Edison) very much desired the legal protection that copyright could give their productions, which otherwise could easily be copied and distributed by other companies. An Edison employee hit upon the idea of transferring every photographic frame of a film onto bromide paper and sending the resulting roll of paper to the Library of Congress, where it could be copyrighted as a still photograph. The clerk who received the first such Edison submission decided that there was no reason a photograph could not be three-fourths of an inch wide and a hundred feet long, and duly recorded the copyright. Until 1912, when the copyright law was amended to include motion pictures, the creation and filing of "paper prints" was the primary way motion picture companies legally protected their products.

What were intended and preserved simply as legal records were recognized by Walls as unique historical and aesthetic documents. Because nitrate film stock (on which nearly all films were printed and photographed until the 1940s) had a volatile and short-lived chemical makeup, original prints of films from this period have largely disappeared. For many early films (including most of the films discussed in this book) these paper rolls are the only surviving versions. Walls, with the support of MacLeish (and such interested government figures as Harry Truman), realized that he had material that could reconstruct the themes and methods of the beginning of American filmmaking. The task of making these paper records into projectable films was achieved by Kemp Niver with the support of the Academy of Motion Picture Arts and Sciences in the 1950s, treating the rolls of dried and fragile paper and then re-photographing them onto 16mm film. Presently, the Paper Print Collection is once again being photographed, this time onto 35mm film, with greatly enhanced image quality.[1]

All history begins with traces, and these unusual legal documents on paper rolls form the primary basis of this book. In film history, as Michele Lagny[2] has pointed out, the traces, the films themselves, are the goal rather than the means of a reconstruction. However, historical investigation always trans- forms the traces it deals with as it tries to understand them, and film history is no exception. Through the efforts of these men, the films were able to be projected, put into motion, and brought to life as the photographic records of men and women long dead, re-animating action performed (and probably forgotten) long ago.

If I begin this introduction with this rather romantic and archetypal tale of the discovery of buried treasure (with its science fiction complement in Niver's resurrection of the dead material into the illusion of life through cinema), it is because I find it exemplary of the tasks of film history. Although the survival of the paper prints was a sine qua non for the recovery of early American film history, physical survival alone was not sufficient. It took the imagination of Walls to be able to see them differently, not as essentially useless legal records but as the remains of films, and clear the way for their study as works of art and evidences of film history.[3] History is never simply the surviving records of the past, but always a creative and imaginative act of trying to understand the past, a belief that it says something to us.

This book derives from an ongoing curiosity about what these early films can tell us. The Paper Print Collection includes a nearly complete run of the films made by the American Mutoscope and Biograph Company from 1900 to 1910, including nearly all the films directed by D. W. Griffith from 1908 to 1909 which form the concern of this book. Study of this unique collection of film reveals, to paraphrase L. P. Hartley, that "they made films differently then." These films demand our attention for both their alien qualities and those that seem familiar. This book tries to deal with those differences and similarities as revealed by the films themselves.

This is also a book about change. The first two decades of film production in the United States (from its commercial introduction in 1894 to the triumph of full-length features in 1914) was one of almost continuous transformation. Toward the end of the period, from 1908 to 1913, David Wark Griffith directed nearly five hundred one- and two-reel films for the American Muto-scope and Biograph (or as it was re-named in 1910, simply, Biograph) Company. These films have gathered through the decades a nearly legendary reputation, described by film historians as films that changed film history. According to this view, if American film came to age with D. W. Griffith's 1915 film *The Birth of a Nation*, these films were the stages on the way to maturity.

However it is only recently that film historians have bothered to look at the films carefully. The pioneer historians, such as Terry Ramsaye, Lewis Jacobs, Georges Sadoul, and Jean Mitry, who studied the origins of narrative film before the availability of the Paper Print Collection, relied almost entirely on written accounts of the films or on their own memories. Their descriptions of films are filled with inaccuracies because of the inadequate materials available to them. But contemporary historians are no longer in this position. Through the resources of the Library of Congress and the film archives of the Museum of Modern Art, all but a handful of the films Griffith made for the Biograph Company are readily available for viewing.[4]

A number of scholars have made use of these films, notably Russell Merritt in his 1970 dissertation on Griffith's work from 1908–15, Kemp Niver in his 1971 book *D. W. Griffith: His Biograph Films in Perspective*, and Roberta Pearson in her dissertation on performance style in Griffith's Biograph films and Joyce Jesionowski in her study of Griffith's dramatic structure, *Thinking in Pictures*.[5] My focus is somewhat different from that of these scholars although there is some overlap: to analyze the narrative structure of these films closely and to place them in a historical context. This context is both vertical and horizontal: on the one hand, I try to determine their place in relation to the development of narrative form in film history before Griffith; and on the other hand I attempt to relate them to the transformations occurring in the film industry during their production. To allow close scrutiny of a number of films, I have restricted my work to the years 1908–9, which I believe witnessed the greatest transformation in Griffith's narrative form, as well as an important upheaval in the American film industry—the creation of the Motion Picture Patents Company.

But it is not only my use of the films themselves that separate this work from the pioneer approaches to Griffith's Biograph films. Concepts of both narrative structure and historical analysis changed radically in film study during the 1980s. Models of film history based on presuppositions of progress or a natural maturing process have been severely questioned. Likewise, investigation of the nature of film narrative has called for new theoretical precision. A new understanding of Griffith's Biograph films demands a whole new framework for thinking about film history and the way narrative operates in film. Both these tasks have been essential to my work.

This work, therefore, includes a theory of film narrative which, although tailored to my needs in approaching Griffith's first Biograph films, discusses film narrative on a broader basis. My narratology is primarily based in thinkers that come out of the structuralist school, such as Tzvetan Todorov and Gérard Genette. Although the presence of a theoretical concern in what is essentially a historical work may seem dismaying to some readers, I consider it essential to a new understanding of the history of American narrative film. Too often the nature of narrative is simply assumed in film history, or its discussion relegated to the theoreticians. I strongly believe that history and theory must proceed in tandem in film study, with the methods of one supplementing the undertakings of the other.

The most fruitful place of fusion for these disciplines comes in an analysis of individual films, an analysis which is aware of both the historical nature of these films and able to use theoretical concepts to explore their structure. Therefore it is the analysis of specific films that forms the center of my work. Viewed as historical objects and as structural complexes, these films are also understood as works of art, showing individuality and uniqueness as well as historical significance and theoretical functions. It was a fascination with Griffith's Biograph films that first drew me to this project. And I hope that history and theory will help to explicate that fascination rather than reduce it.

For the reader familiar with recent work in film study, it is perhaps less my theoretical section that may seem unfamiliar than my primary task, a historical investigation of the Biograph films. There is no question that film history has been a poor relation in the serious work undertaken in film study in the 1980s. Undoubtedly this derives from the preference for synchronic analysis of texts that the authority of the structuralist method brought to film study, and the consequent suspicion of the empirical methods and models of causality associated with historical study. However, even within the structuralist movement there has been a growing concern about the dangers involved in hermetically enclosing the text, and a recognition that the way a text operates involves a reference outside itself to processes of enunciation and reception.

If film history remains underdeveloped in comparison to work in textual analysis and theory, it is partly because its tasks are awesome. To maintain the insights provided by structuralist analysis while at the same time exploring the individual text in relation to the other signifying systems of a culture may seem a process doomed by its delicacy on one hand and its scope on the other. American film study has seen a number of exemplary forays into the re-thinking of film history. Two works are particularly noteworthy for their clarity and challenges: *Film History: Theory and Practice* by Robert C. Allen and Douglas Gomery (1985) and *The Classical Hollywood Cinema: Film Style and Mode of Production to 1960* by David Bordwell, Janet Staiger, and Kristin Thompson (1985). Both works are the fruit of collaboration and draw on nearly a decade of research by their respective authors. Although the disserta-tion on which my book is based was basically completed before the publication of these books, my work is fundamentally in concert with their attempt to introduce into film history some of the theoretical precision found in textual analysis. I share with these authors a belief that the analysis of film texts needs to be founded historically, desperately needs, in David Bordwell's words "to specify the historical conditions that have controlled and shaped textual processes."[6] It is my hope that this work can help establish a newly defined project for film history, one which includes an understanding of the historical contexts of film production and a close analysis of the films themselves.[7]

One of the first tasks of the film historian must be the construction of a historical succession of styles. In the fifth thesis of his discussion of literary history, "Literary History as a Challenge to Literary Theory," the literary theorist and historian Hans Robert Jauss declares, "one must insert the individ-ual work into its 'literary series' to recognize its historical position and signifi-cance in the context of the experience of literature."[8] This task has long been recognized in the histories of other art forms, but has been strangely ignored in film history, largely because filmic discourse has only recently been subjected to close scrutiny. Further, the discussion of early film history has been domi-nated by a model of the progressive attainment of a natural cinematic language which was understood as existing ahistorically.

A historical succession of art styles bases itself in transformations. It is the transformation represented by the films made by Griffith for the Biograph Company from 1908–9 that will be discussed herein. The films will be placed in appropriate historical series, demonstrating (primarily) how they are differ-ent from the films that preceded them and (to a lesser extent) how they relate to the films that followed them. Although I am deliberately dealing herein with a rather small slice of historical time (although a large number of films— Griffith directed more than two hundred films in these two years), a historical treatment of the period involves consideration of the decade of film history that preceded it, as well as anticipating the move into feature filmmaking in the decade that followed. The brief period negotiates an enormous transforma-tion between the two periods on either side of it.

The crux of this transformation lies precisely in Griffith's approach to narrative form. While the legendary approach to D. W. Griffith portrays him as an inventor of cinematic techniques (most frequently of the close-up, and occasionally of parallel editing), even pioneer historians such as Lewis Jacobs, Georges Sadoul, and Jean Mitry were aware that Griffith introduced no new techniques to filmmaking. What then was Griffith's contribution? From Terry Ramsaye through to Christian Metz, historians and theorists have agreed that Griffith was instrumental in a transformation of how films told stories.

Therefore a theoretical treatment of narrative proves essential to an investigation of this claim. It is necessary to determine the functions of narration in film in order to determine precisely exactly what transformations occurred during 1908–9. In defining Griffith's film narration, I will also differentiate it from the narrative styles of the films that precede him, and theoretical definitions will allow the construction of a historical succession of styles.

Therefore, an essential aspect of this work is not only revising the concept of Griffith's early Biograph films, but also the understanding of the films that preceded Griffith. Here again contemporary historians are in a better position than their forebears. Although the films made before 1908 that have survived by no means represent a complete sample, the Paper Print Collection and recent efforts by the film archives of the International Federation of Film Archives (FIAF) have not only preserved a large number of early films but have also labored to make them accessible to scholars.[9] We now have a better sense than ever before of the cinema that preceded Griffith.

This new availability of films has been matched by a reexamination by a number of scholars, including André Gaudreault, Ben Brewster, Miriam Hansen, Kristin Thompson, Charles Musser, Eileen Bowser, Barry Salt, Jon Gartenberg, and Noel Burch. They have overturned simplistic understandings of pre–Griffith cinema as a primitive period limited to a simple reproduction of either reality or theatrical performances. Early cinema can now be understood (and it was primarily Burch who pioneered this understanding) as not simply an elementary stage of cinematic evolution, the infancy of an art form, but as a period that possessed a different conception of space, time, and narrative form from the way in which these issues were approached in the later classical cinema.

I maintain that early cinema did not see its main task as the presentation of narratives. This does not mean that there were not early films that told stories, but that this task was secondary, at least until about 1904. The transformation that occurs in films around 1908 derives from reorienting film style to a clear focus on the task of storytelling and characterization. In this work I will describe the move from what I call a "cinema of attractions," which was more interested in the display of curiosities, to a cinema of narrative integration which subordinates film form to the development of stories and characters. It is this move to a cinema of narrative integration that Griffith's first films exemplify.

At the same time, my concern with narrative form in these Biograph films does not exhaust the historical horizons of this work. This transformation from a cinema of attractions to one of narrative integration does not rest simply on the interior form of these films. The years 1908–9 witnessed a radical reorganization of the American film industry. These two transformations are interrelated. Just as my treatment of the filmmakers who preceded Griffith will modify claims for his innovative force, so consideration of the production context for his Biograph films will limit viewing him as the unique source of these transformations. Changes in the film industry brought new conceptions of the film as commodity and of the sort of audience for whom films were made. These new conceptions had direct impact on Griffith's films.

My historical investigation of the Biograph films therefore involves interrogating these films from a number of angles. Although these angles are distinguishable, it is the way they converge in the individual films that fascinates me. Therefore, the greatest part of this narrative is accorded to a close examination of the films themselves, including a discussion of their esthetic forms. But alongside this "interior" treatment of the films, I will investigate the context of their production—their existence as industrial products and the economic and industrial changes and strategies that shaped them. Such events of industrial history as the formation of the Motion Picture Patents Company and the Biograph Company's position in this industrial organization redefined the nature of the film commodity.

The context of these films' production directly relates to another context, that of their reception: their methods of exhibition, the makeup of their audiences, the way they were reviewed and discussed in the trade journals, and how they were viewed by the political reformers who turned their attention to films around this time. The ways films were received were shaped in part by the way producers defined their commodities and, in turn, producers were influenced by the reception films received from various segments of American society. And both these elements inflected the interior forms of the films themselves.

Although one of my purposes is to show the interrelation among these three areas—the films, the industry that produced them, and the society that received them—they do not form a strictly interlocking pattern in which one area fully explains or determines another. Avoiding both a purely esthetic investigation of the films (such as Jesionowski's) or a narrowly determinist historical approach, I hope to develop a topology in which each area exerts pressure on, and encounters responses from, the others. I maintain that D. W. Griffith's filmmaking is not simply the result of an inspired genius, but rather a response to a series of pressures from the film industry and film's evolving role in American society. At the same time, Griffith's place within a historical series of film style reveals both his inheritance and transformation of the relatively brief (but remarkably vital) stretch of film history that preceded him. Although in some ways the forms he used were shaped by forces beyond his creation, nonetheless Griffith's response, the films he directed, have the uniqueness and ultimately the inexhaustible nature of individual works of art.

Working from the surviving films—physically fragile, but esthetically powerful traces—a historical investigation of Griffith's films tries to understand them by showing the conditions to which they respond. It is my belief that a full understanding of these conditions enriches the films, rather than reducing them to pawns in an impersonal historical destiny. A careful penetration into their esthetic forms likewise endows our historical understanding of the period with the relief and depth demanded by the ongoing fascination exerted by these images and stories from the beginning of our century.

The fragility, and ultimately the persistence, of film history was brought home to me in a personal way as I completed this refashioning of my Ph.D. dissertation into book form by the death of three men whose intellectual presence threads its way throughout. They were three of the finest film historians that this discipline is ever likely to see: Jay Leyda, Jean Mitry, and George C. Pratt. My work owes many debts to them, only a few of which are the sort that can be acknowledged in notes. Professor Leyda was truly my mentor in undertaking this work, both as inspiration and as my dissertation advisor. What is valuable herein I owe to him. Mitry most frequently plays the role of noble opponent, the clearest and most valuable representative of a view of Griffith that I wish to modify. And although I never met Pratt, his personal encouragement of my work on Griffith, and the world he opened by making me aware of the treasure-trove of information available in trade journals, shaped many of my conclusions. Equally important to my personal sense of debt is my sense of the awesome legacy these men left a new generation of film historians. They are some of the last historians for whom early cinema was still a living memory and not simply an archival experience. I know what this work owes to their passion and their wisdom. I hope it can continue their mastery of the historian's task to renew and rediscover the images of the past.

Notes

1. This account of the rediscovery of the Paper Print Collection comes partly from Kemp Niver, *Early Motion Pictures: The Paper Print Collection in the Library of Congress,* ed. Bebe Bergstrom (Washington, D.C.: Library of Congress, 1985), pp. vii–xv. But my primary source was a conversation with Patrick Loughney, who generously shared with me the research he undertook for his dissertation, "A Descriptive Analysis of the Library of Congress Paper Print Collection and Related Copyright Materials," George Washington University, 1988.

2. Michele Lagny, "L'histoire, auxiliare du cinéma, le cinéma, auxiliaire de l'histioire," in *Histoire du cinéma: Nouvelle approaches,* ed. J. Aumont, A. Gaudreault, and M. Marie (Paris: Publication de la Sorbonne, 1989).

3. The study not only of the Paper Print Collection, but also of other copyright records in the Library of Congress as documents in the history of early film has been recently undertaken by Patrick Loughney in both his dissertation and in "In the Beginning Was the Word, Six Pre-Griffith Motion Picture Scenarios," IRIS 2, no. 1 (1984): 17–31.

4. For the period covered herein, all the films released by the Biograph Company have been preserved in the Library of Congress Paper Print Collection, with the exception of *The Winning Coat* (March 2, 1908), *Tender Hearts* (June 15, 17, 1909), and *The Friend of the Family* (May 17, 19, 19, 1909). *The Brahma Diamond* (January 14, 15, 1909) and *One Night and Then . . .* (December 30, 1909) have been preserved only in fragmentary form. However, this does not necessarily mean that these paper prints are always exactly like the films that were shown on their release. In some instances the shots were copied onto paper out of order, and comparison with existing prints from other sources occasionally reveals that a shot was left out of the copyright version. But, for the most part, the paper prints do present the films as they were shown in 1909. The visual quality of the prints, given their process of reproduction, is not very high, so unfortunately qualities of texture and clarity are often obscured. This seems to be minimized in the new 35mm prints being made from them.

Prints do exist from 1909 from other sources, primarily those preserved at the Museum of Modern Art, where a print of *Tender Hearts,* missing from the Library of Congress, is preserved. I have examined all projection prints at the Museum of Modern Art and at points done a careful comparison of the prints for variations. The Library of Congress collection remained my primary source, with the museum collection serving as supplement.

5. Peter Gutman has also published a series of articles that pay careful attention to the scope and details of Griffith's Biograph production in *Classic Images* 89 (n.d.), unfortunately a publication that is difficult to obtain.

6. David Bordwell, Janet Staiger, and Kristin Thompson, *The Classical Hollywood Cinema: Film Style and Mode of Production to* (New York: Columbia University Press, 1985), p. xiv.

7. Although there are differences in our assumptions and methods, I feel that Miriam Hansen's work on early film represents the same attention to the unique text of individual films, its place in an historical horizon, and the responsibilities of the act of reading and interpretation that I call for here. Hansen's *Babel and Babylon: Spectatorship and Figuration in American Silent Film* (Cambridge: Harvard University Press, 1990), raises new challenges and sets new standards for the writing of film history.

8. Hans Robert Jauss, *Towards an Aesthetic of Reception,* trans. Timothy Bahti (Minneapolis: University of Minnesota Press, 1982), p. 32.

9. The 1978 FIAF Brighton Conference on Narrative Film from 1900–1907 was instrumental in a re-thinking of early film history, directly stimulating the work of the scholars I have mentioned. The ongoing interest of David Francis at the National Film Archives in London and of Eileen Bowser at the Museum of Modern Art in New York has also been invaluable in making early films available to scholars.

1

Theory and History: Narrative Discourse and the Narrator System

C AN FILM theory and film history interact in a treatment of a specific historical series of films? Because my intention is to deal with Griffith's Biograph films as both esthetic works and industrial products, esthetic forms as well as modes of production, distribution and exhibition are essential to this work. But I am trying to do more than apply two different approaches to these films, critical on the one hand and industrial economic and social on the other. Because I maintain that the change in narrative form that one can trace through the early Biograph films can in part be understood as a response to changes within the film industry and its role in American society, I also want these different approaches to intersect. To demonstrate a change in narrative form, I must define with theoretical precision the way narrative operates in film. To show the relation of this interior change to the broader horizons of the film industry and social discourse about film, I must have a model of how that industry was structured and a concept of how these interior and exterior structures effect each other.

Can a structural approach to the narrative discourse of films intersect with a treatment of the industrial and social context of their production, or do they cancel each other out with different methods and conceptions of what a film is? There is a potential tension between my textual analysis of films and my consideration of their larger context. My basic conceptions of textual analysis are drawn from the tradition of literary structualism (Todorov and Genette, in particular). This tradition, particularly in its founding phase, tended to approach literary texts as closed systems. The founding concept of structural linguistics, Fernand de Saussure's understanding of the linguistic sign, short-circuits the reference that language bears to an extra-linguistic reality. For Saussure, the linguistic sign "unites not a thing and a name, but a concept and a sound image."[1] Labeled respectively the *signified* and the *signifier*, these elements form a closed system in which the signified is not identical to the "thing out there," to which it refers, but is an entirely linguistic entity.[2] Application of this principle to literature (or film) would seem to define it as a similarly closed system in which social forces outside the text could not be invoked to explain the operation of the system. Insulated from social forces through its constitution as a closed system, a structuralist view of a film text seems utterly at odds with a historical approach.

But even structuralists have begun to question the principle that their analysis must exclude any consideration of social phenomena. The concept of the closed text has been broadly questioned without sacrificing the idea of a text as a coherent system. Tzvetan Todorov, for example, has found that any treatment of texts must move through a sea of discourses that surrounds and penetrates them. Instead of a nontextual exterior reality, the social context provides yet another form of discourse. "Life" declares Todorov, "is a bio-graphy, the world a socio-graph, and we never reach an 'extra-symbolic' or 'prelinguistic' state." A full understanding of a text involves opening it to a series of other discourses as we move, as Todorov puts it, "from one discourse to another, from the text to the text."[3] An understanding of film in relation to social and ideological history can be seen as a movement from the filmic discourse of an individual text to the economic or ideological discourse that penetrates it. Opening up a filmic text to a broader context does not necessarily move from representation to reality or from cause to effect. Rather, it traces relations between, as Raymond Williams puts it, different signifying systems of a culture.[4] Furthermore, if we are dealing with language as discourse rather than a lexical system of signs, we are already moving beyond closed systems (without, however, ignoring signifying practices). In the linguist Emile Benveniste's consideration of the enunciation of the *enoncé* (the actual instance of discourse, such as the act of speaking), language opens up once more to the function of production and reference. As Paul Ricoeur has said, "In the phenomenon of the sentence, language passes outside of itself."[5] A historical approach to works of art requires a dual focus which acknowledges their esthetic identity but is also attuned to their function as social discourse.

Rigorous textual analysis is vital to the social history of film. Likewise, understanding film's relation to a culture's signifying systems is necessary for insightful textual analysis. This interrelation is delicate, however, and must be made with caution. Mechanistic ideas of causality are to be avoided. It should not be claimed that, for example, the Motion Picture Patents Company issued a particular directive and, presto, Griffith's *A Drunkard's Reformation* (1909) appeared. Many aspects of Griffith's filmic discourse are immanent to the filmic system. The most sophisticated attempts to place art works within a social context have emphasized the subtle mediations that relate such works to their social and ideological backgrounds and have drawn upon semiotic or formalist understanding of the discourse of art. Raymond Williams avoids describing the influence of economic forces on cultural production as a complete determinism, seeing it rather as "setting limits and exerting pressures."[6] M. M. Bakhtin and P. M. Medvedev's pioneering attempt at a sociological poetics likewise maintained that a social approach to art should never lose sight of the unique qualities of the work as art, and warned against drawing simplistic relations between base and superstructure, such as declaring "a poem's rhymes and stanzas are fitted together according to economic causality."[7]

In recent years, at least in film study, it is more often art's function as social action that has been overlooked. All too often art's unique discourse has been approached as if it were a private language. Considering film divorced from not only its social context but also from the context of its industrial production has severely limited the historical usefulness of textual analysis. Williams points out that such textual analysis privileges the consuming of a text over a consideration of its production: "The real social conditions of production were in any case neglected because they were believed to be at best secondary. The true relation was seen always as between the taste, the sensibility or the training of the reader and this isolated work, this object 'as in itself it really is,' as most people came to put it."[8] While the reception of a film, both by contemporary film analysts and contemporaneous audiences, must always claim the attention of film historians, this reception is not an atemporal isolated individual delectation, but a historical process open to the processes of social discourse.

Christian Metz's concept of the "cinematic institution" makes a clear interrelation between the "exterior" film industry and the "interior" structures such as narrative form. For Metz, the film industry rests upon a definition of the spectator contained within the film text. He states that "the cinematic institution is not just the cinema industry . . . it is also the mental machinery—another industry—which spectators accustomed to the cinema have internalized historically and which has adapted them to the consumption of films."[9] The outer aspect of the "cinematic institution," which Metz defines as "the financial investment in cinematic undertakings, the material manufacture of films, their distribution, their hire to cinemas,"[10] is founded upon an inner aspect, targeting a particular type of spectator. The film text's address to its spectator meshes with the industrial processes of production, distribution, and exhibition. Both rest upon a definition of the film experience and together define that experience. Analysis of films reveals their address to the spectator, while an exploration of the industrial context shows how that address was defined and exploited technologically and economically.

The historical context of films extends beyond texts to two spheres. First, individual films relate to the film industry which produced, distributed, and exhibited them. Second, these specific cinematic modes of production relate to the larger forces of social history. This work attempts a thorough consideration of only the first sphere. However, the relations I draw between films and their industrial context provide an opening to broader social horizons. Such issues as film censorship or the use of populist rhetoric and temperance themes in Biograph films indicate the routes further studies might take.

The transformation of the film industry in 1908–9 provided a new definition of the film commodity, a new image for film. This new understanding of the film commodity had impact (without absolutely determining) on the changes in filmic discourse which Griffith exemplifies. How a film was produced, how it was sold, who its audience was, and how it was distributed and exhibited all underwent radical change. And these changes provoke responses, interior transformations, in film form. Returning to Todorov's comments about moving from one discourse to another, the broader context for Griffith's films that I trace in this work could be described as the new discourse about film that appeared in 1908–9.

This new discourse took several forms, the first of which was primarily economic. A struggle for domination of the film industry took place that ended in the formation of the Motion Picture Patents Company (MPPC), the first American film trust. The company that employed Griffith, the American Mutoscope and Biograph Company, was at the center of the struggle, first as an excluded party, then as a full partner. New policies in production, distribution, and exhibition instituted by the MPPC provide a detailed ideological discourse about the nature of film. The discussions of film contained in the emerging trade journals also provide an important discourse redefining the image of film. The statements of public officials on such issues as film censorship reveal the extent to which this image was accepted or rejected by the legal representatives of society. Changes in modes of exhibition—the types of theaters where films were shown and the sorts of programs in which they were included—indicate how audiences were expected to receive films through a reorientation of the film-viewing experience. But the films themselves take center stage in my work. Through a close analysis of a number of Griffith's films from the beginning of his career I will both open these films to their historical context and pay full attention to the intricacies of their esthetic structures. Rather than cancelling out, these two processes complete each other.

A close examination of the first films D. W. Griffith made for the Biograph Company reveals a transformation in the narrative form of film. This transformation was part of a wide-ranging change in the way films were made, shown, and the social role they assumed. In no way is it simply the result of a single visionary filmmaker "inventing" a new cinematic language. Griffith's films both responded to and affected a broad transformation of film in American culture.

But to truly understand and be able to describe this transformation we must tackle a series of definitions. If these films display a transformation in narrative form, the nature of narrative in general and narrative in film needs definition. Therefore this historical work needs to linger over concerns that are more frequently thought of as theoretical. Perhaps this theoretical labor will provide a path through a thicket of subtle distinctions rather than create an intellectual jungle of its own.

In investigating narrative, we are hardly faced with a chartless wilderness. The nature of narrative has been a theoretical topic since theoretical investigations began and has been particularly scrutinized in recent decades. But we can begin with basic observations. The structure of the word *storytelling* provides a starting point for definition—its essentially double nature involving both a story to be told and the telling of that story.

The work of the literary critic Gérard Genette has focused precisely on narrative discourse, the *telling* of storytelling, and will form my recurrent reference. Genette distinguishes three different meanings for the term *narrative* (*recit* in French). First, narrative can refer to the actual language of a text that tells a story, as Seymour Chatman puts it, "the means by which the [narrative] content is communicated."[11] The second meaning of narrative refers to the content communicated by the discourse, "the succession of events, real or fictitious, that are the subject of this discourse" and which could be studied "without regard to the medium, linguistic or other" in which they are expressed. The third meaning refers to the event of "someone recounting something, the act of narrating in itself."[12] Genette analyzes narrative from these three perspectives: the means of expression, the events conveyed by these means, and the act of enunciation that expresses them.

Genette proposes the term *story* for the content conveyed by a narrative. The term *narrative* he reserves for the first meaning of the term, "the signifier, statement, discourse or narrative text itself" which communicates the story. The act of telling a story, producing a narrative, Genette terms *narrating.*[13] I shall use Genette's terms with a slight modification. To avoid the equivocal term *narrative,* I shall call the means of expression of a story *narrative discourse,* a term Gennette often uses for the same concept. Genette's description of narrative discourse in literature provides a model for my treatment of Griffith, although my discussion is tailored to the demands of film rather than literature and to the requirements of a specific body of work.

My work on Griffith will not focus primarily on the analysis of story, but on narrative discourse. However, as Genette points out, the analysis of narrative discourse "implies a study of relationships," and to describe any one of the three aspects of narrative necessarily involves the others.[14] The logic of story can shape narrative discourse, marking how it begins, develops, and ends. Therefore some attention to the basic structure or logic of story is called for. Todorov, revising the Aristotelean beginning, middle, and end, offers the following useful definition of story structure (or in his terms *plot*): "The minimal complete plot consists in the passage from one equilibrium to another. An 'ideal' narrative begins with a stable situation which is disturbed by some power or force. There results a state of disequilibrium: by the action of a force directed in the opposite direction, the equilibrium is re-established; the second equilibrium is similar to the first, but the two are never identical."[15] As David Bordwell has pointed out, this equilibrium model corresponds to the "canonical story format," the story pattern most easily recognized and comprehended within our culture.[16] It also corresponds to the stories found in the majority of Griffith's Biograph films.

Narrative discourse is precisely the text itself—the actual arrangement of signifiers that communicate the story—words in literature, moving images and written titles in silent films. It is only through this means of expression that we come in contact with either story or the act of narrating. The story is an imaginary construction that the spectator or reader creates while reading the narrative discourse of the actual text. Likewise, access to the act of narrating (in written literature and in film, at least) is dependent on the traces of telling that exist in the text. The text itself, words, images, or both, is all that we have, and discussions of the other aspects of narrative must begin from the text and refer back to it.[17]

Within narrative discourse Genette defines three functions that relate to either story or the act of narration. The first two relate narrative discourse to story. The first of these is tense, which deals with the temporal relations between narrative discourse and story.[18] Narrative discourse can manipulate the temporal order and form of story events. This temporal patterning shapes and arranges the story, involving the reader or spectator in an often-complex activity of reconstruction. Within tense, Genette describes three principle manipulations of story events. The first, dealing with the succession of events in a narrative, is order. The second, duration, deals with the compression or extension of events within a narrative, while the third, frequency, describes the possibility of multiple retellings of a single event.

The second function of narrative discourse defined by Genette, mood, also relates the discourse to the story it tells. Controlling the reader's access to the events of the story, mood corresponds in many ways to what Anglo-American criticism has called point of view, the narration's perspective of the story told. Genette feels that "one can tell *more* or tell *less* what one tells, and can tell it *according to one point of view or another.*" Mood indicates the way the narrative discourse operates as a sort of screen between reader or spectator and the story as it unfolds: "the narrative can furnish the reader with more or fewer details, and in a more or less direct way, and can thus seem (to adopt a common and convenient spatial metaphor, which is not to be taken literally) to keep at a greater or lesser *distance* from what it tells."[19] This perspective on the action may correspond to the viewpoint of a particular character within the story, in which case we say the narrative adopts the character's point of view.

The last of Genette's categories, voice, deals with the relation between narrative discourse and the act of narrating—the traces of telling left in the text through which we sense a storyteller addressing an implied or real audience.[20] In literature this aspect would not only include such determinations as the person of the narrator (the familiar, first-, or third-person narrator), but also a wider range of means to reflect the act of narrating in the text, for example, the temporal relation between the story and the act of telling it, and a variety of ways in which the narrator asserts its presence.

My use of Genette comes from an appreciation of his precision and systematic analysis, rather than a belief that all film theory must be founded in linguistic or literary concepts. But are Genette's concepts applicable to film analysis, and if so, what sort of transformations must they undergo? More fundamentally, should the terms *narrative* and *narration* be restricted to literature and verbal language? We speak quite commonly of narrative film, and even narrative dance, painting, and pantomime. What allows this concept to cross between diverse media?

The answer lies in the double nature of storytelling, its division into the story constructed by the reader or viewer and the specific discourse that tells the story. I strongly endorse André Gaudreault's statement, "Any message by means of which any story whatsoever is communicated can rightfully be considered as a narrative."[21] Any communication of a story will be composed of Genette's triad of story, narrative discourse, and act of narrating. Because his narrative functions of tense, mood, and voice describe the interrelations between these universal aspects of narrative, I believe they apply to any narrative media.[22] But the task remains of describing film's specific narrative discourse. Genette clearly states that although story can be studied "without regard to the medium, linguistic or otherwise . . .,"[23] narrative discourse (because it exists in actual text) cannot be divorced from its specific medium.

Fundamental differences between literature and film rush to meet us. These differences derive from the noncommensurable nature of the types of signs each medium employs. Whereas literature is never directly iconic, film, as a series of photographic representational signs, is. This aspect of the filmic sign gives it a unique narrative status. While in language, as Genette points out (using the vocabulary of the Anglo-American tradition of Lubbock and

Booth), "Showing can only be a *way of telling*,"[24] film in contrast can show more immediately than it can tell.

But across the chasm between showing and telling the two narrative discourses seem to signal each other. Certain literary narratives have sought to give the impression of "showing" in spite of their lack of film's direct access to the visual. In literature the impression (or as Genette would put it, the illusion) of showing is the result of a narrator's consciously chosen and carefully devised strategy. Genette notes that a narrator may seem to abdicate the role of choosing only the most significant elements and instead gather a number of "useless and contingent" details in order to give the impression of showing.[25]

In film, this excess of mimesis over meaning appears automatically with the photographic image. Although a filmmaker can make images relatively abstract, they will still contain a plethora of information compared to a verbal description. For example, the first films that the Lumière brothers shot in the open air seem much more detailed and realistic than those the Edison Company shot against the dark background of the "Black Maria." But even Edison's films are crowded with the excess of photographic reality. Automatically present are details of posture, costuming, and gesture whose verbal description would overwhelm a written text (e.g., in Edison's kinetoscope film of Annie Oakley, her expression, the way she swings her rifle, the fringe on her costume, the puffs of smoke that seem to issue from the glass balls she shoots, etc.). Film *shows* automatically, recording a world of contingent events and unimportant details.

This dominance of showing over telling is the concealed reef over which the concept of the filmic narrator sails in peril. Does a film "tell" a story? Filmic discourse has an ability to appear nearly neutral. A single shot can seem to show a great deal while telling very little about it. If we approach film as a narrative form which presents stories to an audience, it nonetheless would be foolish to ignore a unique quality of its narrative discourse—its inherent photographic tendency toward mimesis, toward the representation of a world from which the filmic narrator can seem to be absent.

However, this aspect of film does not destroy the concept of the filmic narrator; rather it defines its role. The primary task of the filmic narrator must be to overcome the initial resistance of the photographic material to telling by creating a hierarchy of narratively important elements within a mass of contingent details. Through filmic discourse, these images of the world become addressed to the spectator, moving from natural phenomenon to cultural products, meanings arranged for a spectator. The filmic narrator shapes and defines visual meanings.

This is partly accomplished by a fourth aspect of narrative discourse that I will add to Genette's triad of story, discourse, and the act of narrating—

narrativization. This is less an aspect separate from the other three than a term for the bond among them, and one that takes on particular importance in film. Defined by Stephen Heath, narrativization is precisely what holds Genette's three aspects of narrative together.[26] The process of narrativization binds narrative discourse to story and rules the narrator's address to the spectator. It organizes discourse to tell a story, binding its elements into this single process. In this process the energies of a film are channeled toward the explication of a story, and through this channeling create and define a situation for the spectator.[27]

The concept of narrativization focuses the transformation of showing into telling, film's bending of its excessive realism to narrative purposes. Narrativization, which would be something of a tautology in a literary text where the signs are naturally predisposed to telling, regulates the balance between mimetic and narrative functions in the filmic sign. According to Heath, narrativization "seek[s] to maintain a tight balance between the photographic image as a reproduction of reality and the narrative as the sense, the intelligibility, of that reality." The narrative discourse of a film "picks up—indicating by framing, shot angle, lighting, dialogue mention, musical underscoring, and so on—the notable elements . . . ,"[28] thus carving a story out of a photographed reality.

Film's innate tendency toward mimesis becomes a sign of narrative realism, naturalizing the process of storytelling as the inclusion of apparently useless detail does in verbal narrative. Simultaneously the process of narrativization delivers a sense to this realism, through filmic discourse which "picks up" and selects precisely those meanings necessary for the story to be told. In this way the filmic image, without losing (indeed, using) its capacity for showing, defines its unique way of telling.

The narrative discourse of film involves a unique transaction between showing and telling. The photographic image clearly possesses a unique ability to show. But how do films pick up and indicate the significant elements within this detailed and contingent reality and endow them with a narrative meaning? What is it that tells the story in a narrative film? What are the marks within the film (or to use David Bordwell's more psychological and dynamic term, the cues)[29] by which the film conveys its story to the viewer?

Describing the narrative discourse of film must involve cutting up the filmic text so that its dynamic forces are exposed. Of course a narrative text functions as a whole, and analysis only untangles the synthesis that makes it work. I believe film's narrative discourse can best be described as the interrelation of three different levels that interrelate and express narrative information: the pro-filmic, the enframed image, and the process of editing.[30] I do not claim that they function in isolation, nor do I construct a hierarchy of importance, although I will show that some levels perform some tasks more economically than others. Although I will primarily deal with these levels as they are perceived by viewers, it is not irrelevant that they roughly correspond to the essential stages of film production as well: the periods of before, during, and after shooting.

The pro-filmic refers to everything placed in front of the camera to be filmed. It includes such things as the actors (and therefore casting decisions and performance style), lighting, set design, selection of locations, and selection of props. Strictly speaking, pro-filmic elements do not appear on the screen except through the next level of discourse, their capture on film as enframed images. However film viewers see the images on the screen as images of things, and the selection of the things that make up the image plays an extremely important role in conveying narrative information. Every film makes a selection of elements based on a preexisting set of possibilities (this actor and performance style rather than that one; that sort of set design rather than another). Therefore, as narrative discourse the pro-filmic embodies a series of choices and reveals a narrative intention behind the choices. The viewer receives the results of these choices and makes inferences based on them.

Gaudreault, who in his book *Du Litteraire au filmique* (1988) has largely adopted my schema of filmic discourse, describes the manipulation by the narrator of the pro-filmic as "mise-en-scene," referring particularly to the theatrical sense of this term.[31] Too often ignored in narrative theories, the pro-filmic plays an important role in narrative discourse.[32] Many of Griffith's innovations in filmic discourse lay in this area (e.g., the "restraint in expression" in acting style mentioned in his New York *Dramatic Mirror* advertisement).

The second level of filmic discourse is what I call the *enframed image*. At this level of filmic discourse the pro-filmic is transformed from preexistent events and objects into images on celluloid. The process is far from neutral. Placing an image within a frame entails arranging composition and spatial relations. The act of filming transforms the pro-filmic into a two-dimensional image, filmed from a particular point of view, framed within the camera aperture that geometrically defines the borders of the image. The whole host of formal devices that derive from the effects of perspective, selection of camera distance and angle, framing for composition, and the effects of movement within a frame determine specific choices available within this level of discourse. Whether on a conscious or preconscious level the viewer recognizes this construction of the image as a powerful narrative cue. Gaudreault borrows a term from Eisenstein, *mise-en-cadre*, the placement within the frame, to describe the activity responsible for this level of discourse.[33] New approaches in this level of filmic discourse, such as the role of composition in revealing characters's moods, are also seen in Griffith's Biograph work.

The enframed image can also involve a number of other procedures including setting exposure, control of focus, selection of lenses or film stocks with different properties, manipulations of camera speed, and placing devices in front of the lens (such as Bitzer's vignette-masking diaphragms). Camera movement also falls into this category. Putting the frame itself into motion, camera movement can be a powerful device, creating a strong sense of an intervening narrator and strongly marked narrative cues. I also include in this category the processes of filming that involve re-photography and are carried out after the principle photography, such as split screens, superimpositions, and matting processes.

The third level of filmic discourse consists of editing. In most production practices this occurs after the act of filming and involves the cutting and selection of shots as well as their assembly into syntagmas. This process of combination is stressed by Gaudreault's terminology for the activity of editing, the neologism *mise-en-chain*.[34] In Genette's enumeration of the functions of narrative discourse, one seems particularly suited to this level of discourse— that of tense. Tense deals with the differences that can arise between the temporality of events as presented in narrative discourse and their time relations within the story being told. The single unedited shot, outside of an edited sequence, allows few differentiations between the time of narrative discourse and that of story.[35] This is evident in temporal order, because it is only through editing that a flashback or flashforward can be clearly signified. There have been attempts to create temporal disjunctions within a single shot, as in *A Love in Germany* (Wadja, 1984) or the opening of *Him and Me* (Benning, 1982), but these remain rarities and involve imitations of editing processes through camera movement. Likewise, the temporal relations between narrative discourse and story that Genette groups under duration, such as summary, elipsis, or narrative pauses all have clear equivalents in editing processes, with only awkward semi-equivalents within the single shot.[36] Finally to the extent that the temporal relations that Genette groups under frequency can appear in film (e.g., the repetitive account of a single event, as in the multiple presentations of the rape in *Rashomon*), they seem strongly dependent on editing.

The particular suppleness of editing comes from the discontinuity between shots that allows articulation between them, including the temporal differentiations mentioned previously. But spatial articulations are equally important in the process of editing, such as the synthetic space created by continuity editing or the disjunctions of space that occur in other editing styles. Spatial articulations are less defined in literature than in film. They represent an element of the filmic narrator that has no direct equivalent in Genette's treatment of literary narrative discourse. However spatial figures in film tend to be closely interelated with temporal articulations, and I will generally deal with them together.

In the history of film theory, discussions of the "essential nature" of film have often focused on editing. These have ranged from the proclamation of the supremacy of editing by the early Soviet theorists, through its deemphasis in the work of Bazin, to the reevaluation by theorists such as Marie Ropars-Wuilleumier and Gaudreault.[37] While editing represents a particularly supple level of filmic discourse, I maintain that all three levels must be considered in describing film's narrative discourse. As Bordwell has written, "all film techniques, even those involving the 'profilmic event,' function narrationally, constructing the story world for specific effects."[38]

The emphasis on editing in my analysis of Griffith therefore derives from Griffith's individual and historical situation rather than theoretical privileg-ing. Production during this period favored editing over, for example, an elaborate system of camera movement such as appears in some film production after the 1930s. However, historical and technical determinants are not the sole factor. During the same period as Griffith's Biograph career, Louis Feuillade, as well as other directors at Gaumont, such as Léonce Perret and Georges Monca, created a narrative style less dependent on editing, favoring elements such as composition and lighting. The emphatic role of editing in Griffith's filmmaking must partly derive from his own choices. The importance of editing in this work therefore derives from the films I am discussing.

Each of these levels integrates the one before, transforming it as it does so. Their effect on a spectator is generally due to their interrelation, and I separate them for analysis. These three aspects of filmic discourse—the pro-filmic, the enframed image, and editing—almost always work in concert and represent the mediation between story and spectator in film. They are how films "tell" stories. Taken together, they constitute the filmic narrator.

Because film's narrative discourse represents the actual text of a film—its existence as a series of filmic images—no narrative film can exist except through its narrative discourse. It logically follows that every narrative film has a filmic narrator embodied by this discourse. The three levels of filmic discourse are not optional ornaments of style. They form the very mode of existence for any narrative film. But within a specific film, the particular stance and tone of its filmic narrator is determined by choices made within the levels of filmic discourse. Therefore the filmic narrator appears in a wide range of forms determined by specific choices within and among the three levels of filmic discourse (e.g., expressionist set design, high angle of camera, and match cutting). Relating these choices to the functions of narrative discourse that Genette lays out allows us to distinguish different types of filmic narrators. However, even if a certain type of narrator has a tendency to give the impression that "events seem to narrate themselves" without the intervention of a narrator (what the linguist Emile Benveniste calls *histoire*),[39] the narrator can never disappear entirely but can only be concealed. As Todorov writes, "Events never 'tell themselves'; the act of verbalization is irreducible."[40]

I would assert that the same is true in film. Although what has been termed "classical film narrative" labors to present the illusion of a direct presentation of events, this is always a labor of concealment, the construction of an illusion. As Paul Ricoeur has said of the ideology of literary transparency from which the classical style of film arises, "the rhetoric of dissimulation, the summit of the rhetoric of fiction, must not fool the critic, even if it may fool the reader."[41] As we shall see, Griffith plays an ambiguous role in the establishment of this classical style.

If the marks of enunciation in filmic discourse (which reveal the hand of the narrator) can only be camouflaged and not eradicated, we can establish a range of filmic narrators stretching from the apparent "invisibility" of the classical Hollywood film to the heavily rhetorical montage of, for example, Eisenstein—and it is significant that Griffith is often cited as a seminal influence on both extremes. Arranged synchronically, different degrees of assertiveness in the narrative discourse of films could distinguish among the narrative styles of different filmmakers, different cultures, or simply different films. Arranged diachronically, such differences could provide a historical view of the development of film narrative.

While narrative discourse embodies the telling of a story by a filmic narrator, the process of narration involves an interrelation between a narrator and what semioticians call a "narratee."[42] The dynamic aspect of this interaction should be stressed. Although implied by Genette, the role of the narratee has been discussed more explicitly by American film theorists whose concern with the activity of the viewer gives Genette's model a more dynamic twist.[43]

Edward Branigan, in *Point of View in the Cinema*, defines narration as an *activity*. This activity involves more than Genette's act of narrating because it involves the reader or viewer as well as the narrator. As Branigan puts it, narration is "a dialectical process between narrator and reader *through which* is realized a narrative."[44] We have already caught sight of this activity in the simple fact that the reader or viewer constructs (or reconstructs) the story from the narrative discourse of the text. Bordwell's attempt to describe film narration through the concepts of Constructivist psychology similarly foregrounds the spectator's activity. According to Bordwell the spectator uses cues within the narrative texts "to make assumptions, draw inferences about current story events, and frame and test hypotheses about prior and upcoming events."[45]

Although my approach differs from Bordwell and Branigan's, I fully agree with their vision of an active spectator who contributes to the construction of the narrative. Their focus on the dynamic interaction between narrative discourse and reader or viewer allows me to specify that film's narrative discourse does not overpower a passive spectator but provides patterns within films that provoke active mental responses and set in motion the range of cognitive processes Bordwell describes. A particular narrative discourse addresses a spectator in a particular way, eliciting specific sorts of activities. The change Griffith brings to the way films are narrated is at the same time a change in the way films are viewed. Along with a new sort of filmic narrator, Griffith's transformation of filmic discourse constructs a new sort of spectator for film. Or to put it in a way that gives the spectator due, the spectator constructs a new sort of film experience as cued by Griffith's narrative discourse.

Both Branigan and Bordwell stress the role of the spectator at the expense of the narrator. In fact, they reject this term, preferring impersonal rubics, Branigan opting for "activity of narration"[46] and Bordwell for "narration." Their discomfort with the term *narrator* is in part understandable and methodologically useful and in part disturbing. Both authors stress the impersonal, text-immanent nature of narrative discourse and describe the narrator as an "anthropomorphic fiction."[47] It is theoretically important to avoid identifying a narrator with a biological person such as the author. Narrative discourse is made up of words and images, not flesh and blood. Such theoretical precisions are necessary to maintain the integrity of the esthetic text. I will occasionally use the term *narrative discourse* rather than *narrator* in order to stress that I am dealing with images and their construction rather than a person.

However, the depersonalization of narrative discourse brings its own theoretical blindspot that distorts the way films are received by spectators, and the way they function within history and society. Bordwell particularly seems to set aside the fact that in our perception of films we are aware of them as products, as entities manufactured by human beings with evident purposes and designs upon us. In spite of his emphasis on the spectator's role he distorts the address that films level at audiences. The alert and active spectator proposed by Bordwell's psychological description must realize that these images come from *somewhere*. When Bordwell declares that his theory of narration "presupposes a perceiver, but not a sender, of a message,"[48] one wonders what sort of message this is—and in what universe a receiver can respond to a message without wondering about a sender.

The limits of this depersonalization become particularly clear when Bordwell sets his model of narration in motion. What he has excluded in theory re-emerges in his practice. For Bordwell, narration can be "self conscious," can "voluntarily restrict itself," "refuse to mark," or can "flaunt its ability"[49]— to take only a few examples which indicate that he cannot avoid speaking of this impersonal function as volitional and endowed with something very much like human consciousness. Bordwell grounds some of his objection to the concept of the narrator in the transparency of the classical style, claiming that classical films are not endowed with a perceptible narrator, although certain modernist films do signal that the "spectator should construct a narrator." Only certain exceptional films therefore possess narrators, and even this sort of narrator "does not create the narration" but is constructed by the spectator.[50]

Bordwell's theory is not irrational; the narrative discourse of film with its tendency toward showing does possess a transparent quality that verbal discourse lacks. And certainly the narrator as the embodiment of narrative discourse does not stand outside the text. The narrator communicates to the spectator only through the spectator's engagement with the narrative discourse, so in a sense the spectator does construct the narrator, just as he or she does the story, from the narrative discourse. But storytelling implies a storyteller as surely as it does a story. We must be careful in describing the nature of this teller, this narrator.

In films and literature, the narrator is not a flesh-and-blood entity. The narrator, in my understanding of the term, is a theoretical entity, as divorced from an actual person as Bordwell's spectator is from a particular viewer. But preserving the more personal term *narrator* not only avoids academic abstraction but also responds to the experience a reader or spectator has of being addressed by a story. This address can be described by the volitional activities that slip back in Bordwell's window of praxis after being barred at his theoretical door. We receive a text as though it were saying something to us, as though, in the words of my colleague Robert Stein, it has designs on us. We experience it as an intentional object, designed to have certain effects on us.[51] More than a random set of cues, the narrator embodies the design organizing narrative discourse, the intentions which unify its effects. It corresponds to that force in narrative that Peter Brooks calls plot or plotting, "the design and intention of narrative, what shapes a story and gives it a certain direction or intent of meaning."[52] These designs do not exist outside the text but are evident in the rhetorical arrangement of its devices. The more active term *narrator* stresses that this discourse, to paraphrase Brooks, involves force as well as form. It is not only constructed by the reader or spectator, but also addresses and affects him or her through specific devices. Thus in describing film's narrative discourse I have described each level as activities which arrange and organize material in order to address a spectator. No narrative film exists, even the "transparent" films of the classical style, without making such an address.

Another reason for maintaining the term *narrator* is that although it is theoretically separate from the author and processes of production that created the work, it does provide, in the words of Ricoeur, the image of the author within the text. As a series of intentions it recalls the narrative's nature as a unified manufactured object, the product of human labor. As Ricoeur asserts, "the reader does not ascribe this unification to the rules of composition alone but extends it to the choices and to the norms that make the text, precisely, the work of some speaker, hence a work produced by someone and not by nature."[53] Bordwell's theory tends to occult the spectator's perception of a film as something produced. It belongs to the tendency Raymond Williams attacked of dealing with art works solely from the point of view of consumption, ignoring the process of production.[54] Griffith's films address us through their narrative discourse, which creates the sense of an intervening figure who has arranged the images on the screen in a particular manner with specific social consequences. The concept of the filmic narrator helps us relate filmic form to broader contexts.

How does one relate this series of theoretical definitions to my historical task of describing the narrative form of Griffith's first Biograph films and their place in the larger history of narrative form in film as a whole? The chapters that follow show that this theoretical discussion, far from being removed from the tasks of history, allows me to describe Griffith's place in film history with a new precision. I have called the approach to storytelling that Griffith develops in his first films the *narrator system,* the system of filmic devices through which Griffith centers on the task of narration.

What sort of entity is the narrator system? It is an abstraction from the films that Griffith directed in his first years at Biograph which describes Griffith's systematic approach to narrative form. It is not the only approach to narrative form found in his first films. As the chapters that deal with specific films will show, Griffith developed the narrator system gradually, and for awhile it jockeyed for prominence with other approaches. Further, the narrator system, although specific to Griffith, appeared within an international change in narrative form which occurred during the years 1908–13.

The narrator system is one particular synthesis of filmic discourse occurring in the general move to a cinema of narrative integration. During this period filmmakers began to center their work on the task of storytelling. This constitutes the chief intention of the narrator system as well, but it remains the narrative form of a particular filmmaker and production company. Much of what I will say about the narrator system applies as well to the cinema of narrative integration, but not everything. The extreme importance of parallel editing in the narrator system, for instance, was influential on other filmmakers of the period but is by no means universal. However the particularity of the narrator system comes less from its deviations from the norms of cinema of narrative integration than from its extreme expression of them. With Griffith, the emphasis on the tasks of storytelling is brought to a particular intensity.

Genette's analysis of narrative discourse provides a specific outline of the way the narrator system performs its narrative tasks. However, my use of Genette's categories in analyzing Griffith's Biograph films involves an immense simplification. Genette's basic categories offer a comprehensive narrative analysis. However, the application of the categories is extremely limited in comparison to Genette's own work. By no means all the aspects which Genette discusses in his analysis of Proust will find their equivalent in my description of the narrator system. Tense, mood, and voice as found in Griffith are far from the complicated and subtle examples Genette draws from *The Remembrance of Things Past.*

The narrator system takes on a series of tasks in the realm of tense. As I stated earlier, the issues involved in tense in the cinema are expressed most easily through editing. Assembling several shots allows temporal relations that are elusive in the single unedited shot. Tense in film involves the temporal marking of shots in relation to each other. This is not restricted to such situations as flashbacks or elipses between shots. Even the creation of a continuity of time over two shots involves temporal marking because continuity of time in an edited sequence is a synthetic product not at all identical to the time in which events are actually filmed. The temporal marking of the relation between any two shots forms the basis of tense in film.

Before Griffith, temporal relations between shots were often extremely ambiguous. During the period of Griffith's filmmaking at Biograph this temporal ambiguity nearly disappeared, and the rules of temporal continuity over shots were established. Griffith's parallel editing also marked temporal and spatial relations quite specifically in contrast to the ambiguous temporality of earlier cinema. The narrator system, therefore, establishes temporal marking unambiguously, conveying continuity and simultaneity within a variety of spatial relations.

I will primarily deal with the aspect of mood in the narrator system through Griffith's approach to characterization. Although Genette does not privilege this aspect over others in mood, its key role in differentiating Griffith from earlier filmmakers makes it central to the narrator system. The access that Griffith allows us to characters' emotions and motivations for their actions define his particular development of an authorial point of view.

Although it is tempting to see the films of Porter, Méliès, and other early filmmakers as bereft of character psychology, they contain some signs of characterization. However, these are primarily restricted to pro-filmic elements such as performance, costuming, and make-up. The narrator system conveys characterization by the other levels of filmic discourse as well, such as composition and editing. In addition, Griffith transformed the pro-filmic signs of characterization. Performance, make-up, and casting changed enormously under Griffith while other pro-filmic elements such as the selection of props and settings took on new psychological significance.

Griffith's narrative discourse expressed a range of moral judgments on his characters, an intervening narratorial function that belongs to Genette's category of voice. These moral judgments take a more blatant form than the examples of authorial presence Genette analyzes in the work of Proust. If primitive, they nonetheless assert the narrator's presence through commenting on the story. Although there are tendencies toward asserting a judgment in compositional schemes in Griffith's Biograph films, editing predominantly plays this role in the narrator system. A contrast established through juxtaposing shots expresses most of Griffith's moral judgments.

Each of these aspects of the narrator system can be further specified in terms of their narrativization, their direct expression of story. These devices played important roles in the film industry's desire to fashion films on the model of the respectable forms of the novel and drama. The temporal marking of shots exemplified by parallel editing finds its fusing with story—its narrativization—in the technique of suspense. As the original "master of suspense" in film narrative, Griffith demonstrated the hold of his narrative discourse on both story and spectator with his famous last-minute rescues.

The approach to characterization in the narrator system asserts its hold on story through an expression of psychology, the portrayal of mental acts such as memories or emotional reactions, which then provide motivations for characters' actions and decisions. A number of figures of the narrator system convey characters' memories, concerns, or fears. These mental or emotional states play crucial narrative roles in Griffith's filmmaking in contrast to earlier filmmakers. Although performances in early cinema represent a variety of emotional states, characterization rarely played a determinate role in the story. In Griffith's early Biograph films, the psychology of characters—their motivations and decisions—frequently determined the turning point of a story and were emphasized through filmic discourse.

Of course we are dealing with psychology of a rather elementary sort. The narrator system does not provide the analysis of character psychology found in the nineteenth-century novel, even in its more popular versions. And the ways in which Griffith conveyed the subjectivity of characters, while presaging the point-of-view shot and memory flashback of later cinema, still stop short of these later figures. Nonetheless the narrator system centers filmic discourse and narrative development much more strongly on the psychological motivation of characters than earlier cinema.

As I already indicated, the voice of the filmic narrator in Griffith's films asserts its relation to story primarily through an expression of moral judgment.

Voice is narrativized and ideologized as the voice of morality. The role of morality in Griffith's narrativization is pervasive and determines the construction of story as well, so that narrative resolution frequently involves a fablelike moral. But morality in Griffith's Biograph films is not restricted to the triumph of virtue over vice in the story (which certainly appears in films before him), but rather in a filmic discourse which expresses judgments on proper and improper behavior.

Suspense, psychology, and morality: although they do not exhaust all aspects of the narrator system these concepts do plot its cardinal points. But where does D. W. Griffith figure into the scheme?

Notes

1. John Lyons, *Introduction to Theoretical Linguistics* (Cambridge: Cambridge University Press, 1971), p. 66. See also Ferdinand de Saussure, *Course in General Linguistics,* ed. Charles Bally and Albert Sechehaye in collaboration with Albert Riedlinger, trans. Wade Baskin (New York: McGraw-Hill, 1966), pp. 77–100.

2. See Paul Ricoeur, *Interpretation Theory: Discourse and the Surplus of Meaning* (Fort Worth: Texas Christian University Press, 1976), pp. 5–6.

3. Tvtezan Todorov, *Introduction to Poetics,* trans. Richard Howard (Minneapolis: University of Minnesota Press, 1981), pp. 60–61.

4. Raymond Williams, *The Sociology of Culture* (New York: Schocken Books, 1982), particularly pp. 12–13.

5. Paul Ricoeur, *The Rule of Metaphor: Multi-disciplinary Studies of the Creation of Meaning in Language,* trans. Robert Czerny, Kathleen McLaughlin, and John Costello (Toronto: University of Toronto Press, 1977), p. 74.

6. Raymond Williams, "Base and Superstructure in Marxist Cultural Theory," in *Problems in Materialism and Culture: Selected Essays* (London: NLB, Verso Editions, 1980), p. 32.

7. M. M. Bakhtin and P. M. Medvedev, *The Formal Method in Literary Scholarship: A Critical Introduction to Sociological Poetics,* trans. Wlad Godzich (Cambridge: Harvard University Press, 1985), pp. 27, 15.

8. Williams, "Base and Superstructure," p. 46.

9. Christian Metz, *The Imaginary Signifier: Psychoanalysis and the Cinema,* trans. Celia Britton et al. (Bloomington: Indiana University Press, 1982), p. 7.

10. Metz, *The Imaginary Signifier,* p. 8.

11. Seymour Chatman, *Story and Discourse: Narrative Structure in Fiction and Film* (Ithaca: Cornell University Press, 1978), p. 19.

12. Gérard Genette, *Narrative Discourse: An Essay in Method,* trans. Jane E. Lewin (Ithaca: Cornell University Press, 1980), pp. 25–27.

13. Genette, *Narrative Discourse,* p. 27.

14. Ibid., pp. 27, 29.

15. Todorov, *Introduction to Poetics,* p. 38.

16. David Bordwell, *Narration in the Fiction Film* (Madison: University of Wisconsin Press, 1985), p. 35.

17. Genette, *Narrative Discourse,* pp. 28–29.

18. Ibid., p. 31.

19. Ibid., pp. 161–62.

20. Ibid., p. 31.

21. André Gaudreault, *Du Litteraire au filmique: System du récit* (Paris: Meridiens Klincksieck, 1988), p. 84 (my translation).

22. See letter from Genette quoted in Gaudreault, *Du Litteraire,* p. 29 (footnote), which states in part: "Personally, I favor more and more a narrow definition of narrative, *haplé diégésis,* a statement of actions by a narrator who expresses the actions by verbal means (oral or written) and in this sense a theatrical or filmic narrative does not exist for me" (my translation). I am indebted to Gaudreault's work, including his dissertation, which he was kind enough to make available. Although some of my conclusions differ from his, I am constantly in debt to his thoroughness and clarity in approaching the issue.

23. Genette, *Narrative Discourse,* p. 25.

24. Ibid., p. 166.

25. Ibid.

26. See, Stephen Heath, *Questions of Cinema* (Bloomington: Indiana University Press, 1981), pp. 107–8 and passim.

27. Heath, *Questions of Cinema,* p. 109.

28. Ibid., p. 122. Heath's understanding of narrativization is dependent on the Lacanian theory of the constitution of the subject and the Althusserian theory of ideology. If I am bypassing a complete discussion of these issues in relation to Griffith's work, it is because I find the constant circulating of various film texts through this system to be a time-consuming process often undertaken at the expense of other essential issues. For those who would claim that no historical treatment of this material is valid without such an approach, I can only say that I am aware of these methods of analysis, and have certainly, but not exclusively, been influenced by them.

29. Bordwell, *Narration,* pp. 31–33.

30. This schema does not deal with the important issue of sound in film, which is not relevant to the films I examine herein, and would have to be approached as a fourth level, itself in need of subdividing.

31. Gaudreault, *Du Litteraire,* p. 199.

32. However both David Bordwell and George M. Wilson accord the pro-filmic considerable attention in their respective works, *Narration in the Fiction Film,* and *Narration in Light: Studies in Cinematic Point of View* (Baltimore: Johns Hopkins University Press, 1986).

33. Gaudreault, *Du Littaire,* p. 199.

34. Ibid.

35. See Genette, *Narrative Discourse,* p. 35. There are exceptions to this, however, that do not relate to Griffith's Biograph films but should be included theoretically. Within the level of the enframed image, which corresponds to the production stage of shooting and re-photography, there is the possibility of slow or fast motion, created by shooting or printing, which sets up a differentiation between story time and discourse time. Likewise, the soundtrack can set up a host of temporal relations, most obviously through voice-over, which are not described herein. This seems another indication

that sound would operate as a fourth level of filmic discourse, with strong roles in all three of Genette's aspects of narrative discourse.

36. Ibid., pp. 86–112.

37. See, Gaudreault, *Du Littaire*, pp. 105–15, and Marie-Claire Ropars-Wuilleumier, "Function du montage dans la constitution du récit au cinema," *Revue des sciences humanies* 36 (Jan.–March 1971): 51–52.

38. Bordwell, *Narration*, p. 12.

39. Emil Benveniste, *Problems in General Linguistics* (Coral Gables: University of Miami Press, 1970), p. 208.

40. Todorov, *Introduction*, p. 39.

41. Paul Ricoeur, *Time and Narrative*, trans. Kathleen Blamey and David Pellauer (Chicago: University of Chicago Press, 1988), vol. 3, p. 161.

42. Todorov, *Introduction*, p. 40.

43. And in spite of his own apparent confusion on this matter, (see, for example, *Narration*, p. 63), the narratee corresponds precisely to Bordwell's conception of the spectator, "a hypothetical entity executing the operations relevant to constructing a story out of the film's representations," ibid., p. 30.

44. Edward R. Branigan, *Point of View in the Cinema: A Theory of Narration and Subjectivity in Classical Film* (Amsterdam: Mouton Publishers, 1984), p. 39.

45. Bordwell, *Narration*, p. 39.

46. Branigan, *Point of View*, p. 40.

47. Ibid.; Bordwell, *Narration*, p. 62.

48. Bordwell, *Narration*, p. 62.

49. Ibid., pp. 58, 65, 89, 146.

50. Ibid., p. 62.

51. I use the term *intentional* in its phenomenological meaning indicating a product of human consciousness, rather than its psychological meaning. I am not claiming that a particular definable intention lies behind every narrative, or that criticism should reconstruct this intention. This would lead of course to the intentional fallacy. The intention behind a narrative as an intentional object may remain unspecified, its very vagueness drawing a response from the reader or spectator.

52. Peter Brooks, *Reading for the Plot: Design and Intention in Narrative* (New York: Random House, 1984), p. xi.

53. Ricoeur, *Time and Narrative*, vol. 3, p. 162.

54. Bordwell's own historical work pioneered a new serious consideration of the process of production. However I find a contradiction between his theoretical apparatus and his important scholarly work on production modes. Likewise, the brilliance of his analysis of the narrative discourse of films in *Narration in the Fiction Film* seems unencumbered by what I consider his theoretical weak spot, because intentionality actually reemerges in his specific analyses.

2

D. W. Griffith: Historical Figure, Film Director, and Ideological Shadow

A CCORDING TO the theory of narrative laid out in the preceding chapter, a reader or spectator constructs a story from a narrative text. The storyteller—the narrator—is also constructed from the particular mode of address the text employs. But these constructions are not flights of the reader's vivid imagination. The cues to the story, the rhetorical devices which reveal the stance of the narrator, are in the text for the reader to uncover and respond to. Although the reader has a degree of freedom and interpretation, the text exerts its own force and designs.

This is not unlike the situation of the historian who, working from documents, uncovers an essential plot as well as its chief movers.[1] In this chapter I will try to uncover the transformation in narrative film that occurred during Griffith's Biograph career and discuss who (or what) precisely D. W. Griffith was in relation to this transformation. However the historian is perhaps closer to the literary critic than the reader of narratives because this process of reconstruction must be hyperconscious, submitted to critical probing. The historian unmakes stories as much as creates them, dissolving apparently coherent narratives into tangles of contradictory evidence and differing interpretations.

We begin once again with traces, with the discourses that precede us. D. W. Griffith was not only a biological person, now dead, but also the director of films that have survived him as well as a figure described in the discourse of film historians. I will not deal primarily with the biographical person that was D. W. Griffith, but with his roles as film director and almost legendary figure in film history.[2]

As dissolvers of stories, historians are particularly hard on legends (except those they create, presumably for future historians to destroy). Part of the motivation for this work is to confront traditional accounts of Griffith's early film career with the films that have survived. All traditional accounts of Griffith's work at Biograph privilege it as a turning point in the history of American film. But traditional accounts of Griffith's work are erroneous in their details, particularly in their descriptions of Griffith's key films.

The accounts of Griffith's Biograph films given by Lewis Jacobs, Georges Sadoul, and Jean Mitry are filled with descriptions that do not correspond with the actual films. Based primarily on written documents rather than on the films themselves, these errors in description are still recycled in textbooks on film history.[3] Jacobs's description of Griffith's first films is derived primarily from Linda Arvidson's [Mrs. D. W. Griffith's] memoir, *When the Movies Were Young,* and contains a number of inaccuracies in its description of films. Specifically, his accounts of *For Love of Gold* (1908), *After Many Years* (1908), and *The Lonely Villa* (1909) are erroneous.[4] Sadoul, relying heavily on Jacobs, repeats many of these errors,[5] as does Mitry, who adds misdescriptions of *The Adventures of Dollie* (1908) and *Pippa Passes.*[6] This mass of misinformation about an important period of film history demands to be rectified.

But if the traditional accounts of Griffith's first films are filled with errors, they nonetheless provide the founding description of the transformation in film style Griffith is supposed to inaugurate. In spite of the inaccuracies these accounts often contain—Griffith as the inventor of nearly all film techniques, from the closeup to parallel editing—and the ideological blind spots they often entail—ignoring other films and filmmakers, and a reliance on the "great man" theory of history—the evolution of the traditional account of Griffith's innovation is in itself revealing.

Griffith's advertisement in the New York *Dramatic Mirror* in December 1913 provides a natural starting point. Having just left the Biograph Company and apparently advertising for a job, Griffith claimed credit for "revolutionizing Motion Picture drama and founding the modern technique of the art." The text of the advertisement listed Griffith's innovations as "The large or closeup figures, distant views as represented first in Ramona, the 'switchback', sustained suspense, the 'fade out', and restraint of expression, raising motion picture acting to the higher plane which has won for it recognition as a genuine art."[7] To dismiss this claim to a revolutionary role in film art as mere press agentry is too simple. Resume padding or statement of fact, it provides one of the first accounts that presents Griffith as a prime mover in a transformation of filmmaking.

Although Griffith continued to assert the importance of his early work in film in interviews and authorized biographies, the earliest influential statement of his role in the evolution of film language by a film historian can be found in the work of the chronicler of the legendary history of American film, Terry

Ramsaye. *A Million and One Nights: A History of the Motion Picture* (1926) provided an early and influential formulation of Griffith's role. Ramsaye claimed a number of innovations for Griffith, such as the use of close-ups for dramatic accents or fade-outs for punctuation. But he also introduced the view of Griffith as master of the "syntax of film narration," pointing out his manipulations of sequence for suspense. Ramsaye presented the first, albeit somewhat off-hand, vision of Griffith as a master of film language. According to Ramsaye, "The motion picture spent the years up to 1908 learning its letters. Now, with Griffith, it was studying screen grammar and pictorial rhetoric."[8] While Ramsaye was hardly a semiotician, his comparisons of Griffith's technique to grammar, syntax, and rhetoric had widespread impact on the way Griffith's place in film history was conceived.

Jacobs's *The Rise of the American Film* (1939), attempted to describe in more detailed terms the revolution Griffith inaugurated in film narrative. As in Ramsaye's statement, one sees the influence of Griffith's *Dramatic Mirror* notice (which was reproduced on page 117 of *The Rise of the American Film*) as Jacobs lists the new elements Griffith introduced: the full shot, the medium shot, the close-up, the pan shot, the moving camera, the spot-iris, the mask, and the fade. But making something explicit that Ramsay implied, and undoubtedly influenced by the Soviet films of the twenties and their emphasis on montage, Jacobs placed more emphasis on the role editing played in Griffith's films: "an awareness of tempo and the device of parallel and intercutting, which greatly expanded and enriched the internal structure of movie art."[9]

Perhaps most influential was Jacobs's description of how these innovations allowed Griffith "to catch and control the emotions of the spectator." For Jacobs, this control over the spectator signaled a rejection of theatrical technique, declaring that although Griffith "was himself a former actor and playwright, he repudiated theatrical conventions and evolved a method of expression peculiar to the screen."[10]

Jacobs's descriptions of Griffith's historical role had great influence. It is echoed with more subtlety, and a greater awareness of earlier appearances of Griffith's "innovations," by Sadoul in *Histoire generale du cinéma* when he contrasts Griffith's style to that of Méliès:

> He [Méliès] had used editing, camera movement, superimposition, overlapping dissolves, and close-ups, but he treated them only as theatrical *tricks*, magical effects of stagecraft. Griffith, drawing on the still very rudimentary discoveries of the English school after 1902, transformed these tricks from magical effects to means of dramatic expression. The chase had already broken the screen's identification with a scene played in a single set. Griffith, profiting from his experience filming in both natural exteriors and in the studio, used the camera as a dramatic element.[11]

The separation of Griffith's style from the theatrical inheritance of early cinema (exemplified for Sadoul by Méliès) is stressed by Sadoul as well, and more carefully defined than in Jacobs. For Sadoul, Griffith's stylistic innovation shattered the theatrical unity of space by introducing a ubiquity of the camera and a unity of action.[12] Sadoul indicates that this nontheatrical freedom in time and space was the result of Griffith's development of editing.

Mitry brings perhaps the greatest subtlety both historically and theoretically to this traditional view of Griffith, while following the basic contours laid out by Jacobs and Sadoul. Mitry defines Griffith's mastery of editing in terms of a liberation from the theatricality of most films which preceded him. This nontheatrical conception of film allowed Griffith to "stage action in a space no longer limited by the narrow confines of the stage. The shot could include a larger or smaller space, according to the dramatic necessities and intensities of the event portrayed." This breakdown of space through a variable framing and angle of vision, Mitry claimed, "situated the spectator in the center of the action, among the characters of the drama, *within* dramatic space."[13]

Mitry shows a new historical precision by avoiding claims that Griffith "invented" the close-up, but rather defines Griffith's innovation as a new conception of the technique. According to Mitry, Griffith was the first to make the close-up a means of expression by raising it to the level of a sign.[14] Griffith's new approach to filmic narrative based on signs represents for Mitry, as well, a decisive break with the theatrical model "to whose strict reproduction film had at first been confined."[15]

The classical interpretation of Griffith's impact on film narrative, particularly as formulated by Mitry, has become a component of contemporary theory through its adoption by Christian Metz. Metz derives his understanding of the evolution of early film narrative from Mitry, but rewrites its terminology from a semiotic perspective: "[I]t was Griffith's role to define and to stabilize— we would say, to codify—the *function* of these different procedures in relation to the filmic *narrative,* and thereby unify them up to a certain point in a coherent 'syntax' (note that it would be better to use the term *syntagmatic category:* Jean Mitry himself avoids the word *syntax*). . . . Thus, it was in a single motion that the cinema became narrative and took over some of the attributes of a language."[16]

Metz likewise reworks the classical account of Griffith's liberation of film from theatrical tradition into semiological terms. In Metz's terms cinema's encounter with narrativity involved an addition to film's photographic reproduction of "a second complex of codified constructions, something 'beyond' the image."[17] This second level beyond the image corresponds to the new mastery of filmic "language" described by earlier historians.

In spite of important modification over the years, it is not difficult to summarize the recurrent themes in these formulations of Griffith's role in film history. This view of Griffith claims that, although there had been significant development in film before him, Griffith introduced a broad transformation based on the introduction of a number of new filmic elements, the most important of which was a new exploration of the potentials of editing. This transformation has generally been defined as a liberation of film from its dependence on theater. With Griffith, film develops its own "language" — from Ramsaye's "syntax," "rhetoric," and "grammar," through Jacobs's and Sadoul's "means of expression," to the more precise formulation of Mitry's "raising to the level of a sign," and finally Metz's semiological "second complex of codified constructions." This new language rests on a spatial freedom unavailable to the theater, a mobility of point of view and an analysis of space through editing, exemplified by the use of the close-up. In this new series of "syntagmatic categories," shots no longer represent the spatial whole of the theatrical proscenium, but form chains of images, syntagmas in which individual shots depend upon their relation to other shots in the chain for their meaning, as opposed to the theatrical tradition of discontinuous tableaux that relied primarily upon their analogic qualities to communicate meaning to the spectator.

Much can be learned from this account of Griffith's role in film history. It is not my purpose simply to jettison the way Griffith has been approached for decades, which has influenced even my own point of view. That Griffith does represent a fundamental transformation in filmmaking, and that editing plays a key role in this transformation, cannot be denied. But the traditional account also presents obstacles for a historical understanding of Griffith and the transformation of film discourse in which he took part. First, it distorts the work of the filmmakers who preceded Griffith by claiming their films primarily reproduced theatrical modes of representation. Second, it oversimplifies the roots of Griffith's stylistic innovations by describing them as a revolt against theatrical methods. Rather than a conflict between an outmoded theatricality and a discovery of the essential possibilities of film, this transformation can more accurately be understood as a transformation from a cinema of attractions to one based on narrative integration.

The filmmakers that preceded Griffith did not simply record theatrical presentations. Investigation of the "narrative tradition" of early film shows that, particularly before 1907, filmmakers drew relatively little from the legitimate theater.[18] Comic strips, magic-lantern narratives, illustrated song slides, stereographs, newspaper accounts, and illustrations of current events, popular songs, and political cartoons played more important roles in the development of early cinema narratives than dramatic theatrical plays.

These nontheatrical visual sources not only supplied many of the themes or stories for early films, but also influenced their narrative discourse. As works by John L. Fell, Charles Musser, Martin Sopocy, and myself have indicated, the tradition of the magic-lantern narrative in particular provided models for a visual narrative continuity that had a strong effect on the representation of time and space in early film, often differing considerably from anything found in theater of the time.[19] To a lesser extent the same claim could be made for the comic strip.

Furthermore until the beginning of the nickelodeon period (approximately 1904–5) actuality filmmaking (pp. 216–17) made up the majority of American productions and seemed to be particularly popular in the vaudeville houses that formed the major exhibition outlets. Actuality films owed very little to the methods of theatricality. As David Levy has shown, the continuity of action and representation of space and time in actuality films contrasted sharply to theatrical practice. This nontheatrical style also exerted a strong influence on fiction filmmaking.[20]

Furthermore, the term *theatricality* is dangerously unspecific and ahistorical. What sort of theater is being referred to? Film drew on a variety of theatrical forms in the early twentieth century, some quite opposed to the unity of space and point of view we associate with the dramatic theater. The most important theatrical influence on film before Griffith was vaudeville. The variety format of unrelated acts and the lack of dramatic unity differ sharply from the legitimate theater. The primary dramatic sources for early film came from melodrama and fairy pantomimes—theatrical traditions that emphasized visual effects rather than dialogue, and whose fluid approach to space and time ignored the basic unities of classical theater.[21]

Certainly theatricality played a role in film before Griffith, but we must question its absolute hegemony and its monolithic nature. Approaching the films themselves, theatricality can be a useful concept if it is stylistically defined. The elements of early film that Sadoul and Mitry relate to theatricality may be summarized as composition within the frame that recalls the theatrical proscenium, with considerable space above the head of figures; significant distance between the performance space of the actor and the camera; frontality of the camera in relation to performers and set; use of artificial theatrical sets, often two-dimensional "flats"; and narrative as a succession of individual scenes (tableaux), each covered by a single shot. All of these elements are important in fiction films preceding Griffith, and also in some of his earliest films. However, such elements frequently occur alongside elements from nontheatrical traditions. Edwin S. Porter's *The Execution of Czolgosz with Panorama of Auburn Prison* (1901), for example, juxtaposes a theatrically conceived reenactment of the execution of McKinley's assassin with an actuality panorama of the Auburn, New York, State Prison where the execution took place (pp. 00). Some years later the same filmmaker's *College Chums* (1907) contains some theatrically conceived scenes, while other sequences involve an ingenious use of animated titles and split screen possibly inspired by comic-strip layout.

Even Méliès, the filmmaker who exemplifies the theatricality of early film for Sadoul and Mitry, does not fit neatly into this category. The frontality of the camera, the prosceniumlike space of the frame, the tableau style of single-shot scenes, and the use of artificial decor all link Méliès's films to theatricality. His dependence on the scenography of the fairy pantomime of the Chatelet and the magical performance of his own Théâtre Robert-Houdin argued a strong relation to the theatricality which Sadoul dubbed the style of "le monsieur de l'orchestra."

However, Méliès's editing procedures also included a number of nontheatrical approaches to space and motion, as André Gaudreault has pointed out: for example, the descent of the rocket in A Trip to the Moon (1902) is covered by four shots in only twenty seconds of film time. The rescue of Princess Asurine in The Kingdom of the Fairies (1903) breaks a single fictive location into six shots that present different aspects or angles within the rescue.[22] The cinematic trick of substitution so important to Méliès films drew on both the enframed image and editing levels of filmic discourse. Examining the actual prints of Méliès's films, Jacques Malthete discovered that the substitution trick almost always involved an act of splicing as well as camera stoppage in order to control the illusion of substitution precisely. Examined from this viewpoint, stop motion becomes, in effect, a form of editing.[23] Likewise, a technique such as superimposition (which also often involved refinement through splicing) presents a nontheatrical manipulation of space through the devices of re-photography. This is particularly clear in such films as L'Homme orchestra (1900) or Le Melomane (1903), which involved the multiplication of a single figure (Méliès himself), or the Man with the Rubber Head (1902), which combines this duplication with an effect of enlargement and conflict of scale. This manipulation of the film image creates an ambiguous space of often-contradictory orientations, quite different from the stable proscenium space of theatricality.[24]

Before 1907 theatricality as a mode of early filmmaking jostled for dominance with several other approaches. It is precisely the multiplicity of modes of representation and types of filmic discourse that characterize this "ambivalent" (to use Noel Burch's term) era of pre-Griffith cinema. Limiting pre-Griffith cinema to a simple reproduction of theatrical practice becomes a dangerous oversimplification.

The second assumption of the traditional view of Griffith's transformation of filmmaking, his rejection of theatricality, demands further historical precision. Around 1906–8, the relation between film and theater changed. The increased demand for fiction films and the longer length of such films gave the legitimate theater a new relevance to filmmaking. Film began to draw on new theatrical models as well, showing a new awareness of classical and contemporary theater, although without abandoning melodrama and vaudeville. Mitry first noted this change, describing a new approach that entered film around 1908, "théâtrialité pure," marked by an increased use of contemporary theatrical practices rather than the already outmoded theatrical styles evident in the work of Méliès or in Porter's *Uncle Tom's Cabin* (1903).[25] This new style of theatricality reached its height in the French *films d'art*, but originates in such earlier films as *Un drame a Venise* (Pathé, 1906) and *Francesca di Rimini* (Vitagraph, 1907).

Many of the qualities of the earlier theatricality persisted in the new style: maintenance of frontality, prosceniumlike space of the frame, and distance between performers and camera. However, decor and costuming became more elaborate, with constructed sets replacing painted flats. Further, as Mitry points out, the discontinuous succession of tableaux that marked the earlier theatricality gave way to a series of more closely linked scenes.[26]

Far from rejecting it, Griffith's filmmaking in 1908 and early 1909 identifies with this new style of theatricality—at least initially. Too rigid a dichotomy has been drawn between Griffith's Biograph films and the *films d'art*. Many of Griffith's early Biograph films are clearly indebted to this French film company, as I will show in chapter 6. Mitry does acknowledge the influence of the *films d'art* on Griffith's early work, but sees this only as an early stage in his career, divorced from his true path of development.[27] Mitry defines Griffith's principal development as a tendency toward narrativity, an approach that he diametrically opposes to theatricality. While theatricality simply adapted its mise-en-scène to cinematic possibilities, narrativity involved "a continuous following of an action freed from the confines of the stage—relying entirely on the dynamic possibilities of editing."[28]

There is no question that the *films d'art*, exemplified by *La mort du duc de Guise*,[29] approached the narrative discourse of film in a very different manner from a film like Griffith's *The Lonely Villa*. Griffith's radical development of film editing establishes this divergence; *The Lonely Villa* contains fifty-two shots compared to *La Mort*'s nine. But this difference should not condemn Griffith's relation to the *films d'art* as a wayward flirtation, soon repented. A new conception of the fiction film underlies both Griffith's narrativity and the theatricality of the *films d'art*. Ignoring this common ground obscures our understanding of Griffith's transformation of film narrative, and the role a new relation to theater played in it.

But the key transformation in film's relation to theater during this period derives less from the new theatrical models on which the films drew (which both Jean Mitry and Noel Burch emphasize) than a new attitude to the act of storytelling.[30] The new style placed an unheard of value on the story itself, on narrative coherence and completeness. Films such as *La mort du duc de Guise* present themselves as dramatic wholes. In the earlier form of theatricality, the presentation of a coherent and complete story was simply not a major concern. Porter's *Uncle Tom's Cabin*, for example, does not include certain important key incidents of the story. Méliès has declared that the narrative line of his films was little more than a pretext, the very last element of a film that he considered, subordinated to concerns about costuming, staging, and the creation of novel "tricks."[31]

A complete and coherent story was of such little interest to the first filmmakers that adaptations of famous plays frequently consisted only of "peak moments" from stage productions such as the five tableaux from the famous temperance play *Ten Nights in a Barroom* that Biograph released in 1903: "Death of Little Mary," "Death of Slade," "The Fatal Blow," "Murder of Willie," and "Vision of Mary." These films do not even attempt a condensation of the play's action and would remain incomprehensible to a viewer unfamiliar with the play. The publicity bulletin for the Biograph production of *Rip Van Winkle* the same year stressed that "We have not attempted to show the play in its complete form, but have chosen instead the various dramatic events."[32] Such "peak moment" films exemplify what I have called "the non-continuous style of film,"[33] which showed a lack of interest in narrative continuity. Filmmakers depended on the audience's previous knowledge of a specific work to make their films comprehensible.[34] Telling a complete and coherent story was either secondary to the effect of film tricks or the thrill of a famous moment, or else narrative coherence came from outside the film through the audience's previous knowledge of the source.

The *films d'art* and other theatrically conceived films of the later period approached film narrative in an entirely different manner. Henri Lavedan wrote *La mort du duc de Guise* as an original and complete work for the screen. It was not an excerpt from an established classic, but a film intended to be comprehensible on its own. That it is based on a famous event in French history, however, indicates that it had not entirely liberated itself from a dependence on the audience's foreknowledge—at least in France. (The film met with some audience incomprehension in the United States.) This may explain the apparently paradoxical fact noted (but not explained) by Mitry that these later theatrical films often show advances in editing, a tendency toward a "certain narrative continuity." In fact, the first stirrings of "narrativity" before Griffith often appeared in films that also strive for an elaborate theatricality in sets, costume, and acting, for example, *Francesca di Rimini*, with its close-ups of the narratively important lockets, or *Un drame a Venise*, with its matched cuts into the actors framed at the waist. Further, the plots of these theatrical films placed a considerable emphasis on character motivation. Earlier films like *The Great Train Robbery* or *A Trip to the Moon* had also presented complete stories, but without the characterization present in these later films.

If a common purpose unites Griffith and the *films d'art*, then why do they eventually diverge? Ultimately the *films d'art* failed to bring the equivalent of the theatrical experience to film because they lacked precisely the essential element of the theater they tried to recreate—the verbal text. The ambitions of *films d'art* in providing a model for a new, narratively coherent film based in character motivation encountered a devastating check. As Burch states, this was "due precisely to the basic incompatibility between the primitive mode of representation [in film] and the codes of the bourgeois theater."[35]

Griffith was presented with a problem which the *films d'art* had raised but could not solve: the creation of a complete and coherent dramatic whole, founded (as was the respectable theater of the period) on characterization and comprehensible to the audience even in a nonverbal presentation. The style of narrativity arose as a solution to the ambitions of theatricality. Rather than a simple liberation from the confines of the theatrical model, the transformation in filmic discourse which Griffith represents can be seen as the fulfillment of the theatrical ideal. Burch puts it quite explicitly: "it is not until the system of narrative editing, with its close-ups, matching devices, etc., was fully developed that it became possible to recover the theater's power of characterization, personalization, etc. Paradoxically it is for the development of this system that Griffith is celebrated as the man who brought cinema out of the theatrical stage!"[36]

Griffith's style of narrativity was the offspring of this later form of theatricality. Only the style of narrativity could convey the essentials of the theatrical experience in a medium deprived of the spoken text. Narrativity provided the "signifieds" of drama at the cost of deviating from theatrical practice, the "signifiers" of theater. Mitry is quite correct that by the end of Griffith's Biograph career his films differed considerably from films such as *Queen Elizabeth* (Mercanton, 1912), which continued (somewhat anachronistically) the approach of the *films d'art*. However the demise of this theatrical style as a unified approach to filmic discourse, although it survives intermittently in sequences of films—including Griffith's features—must be explained by the fact that narrativity itself was a closer equivalent to the theatrical experience.

The elaboration of editing (as well as other elements of filmic discourse as the following chapters will show) provided Griffith with a new set of signifiers to fill the void left by the spoken text. This does not mean that Griffith's filmic devices simply translated theatrical speech. A transformation does occur here by which film establishes itself as a narrative art form with basic differences from the theater.

It is the establishment of a filmic discourse that provides a comprehensible, complete narrative based on characterization that separates Griffith's filmmaking from that of Méliès or Porter. Inspired by the theatrical model, Griffith nonetheless chose not to rely on it exclusively. He drew upon elements of filmic discourse introduced by his predecessors, but redefined them by bending them to the task of storytelling. Metz's discussion of Griffith supplies an extremely subtle understanding of this redefinition. For Metz, the essential event lies in film's encounter with narrativity. Griffith's transformation consists of codifying filmic devices pioneered by others in terms of storytelling.[37]

Griffith's revolutionary role in film history consists precisely of committing filmic discourse to the expression of a story. The coherence between filmic discourse and the telling of a story is so historically entrenched that it now seems natural. Film before Griffith has primarily been investigated for its narrative developments; the lesser importance that storytelling actually played in pre-Griffith cinema has been lost sight of in the rush to find the roots of narrative cinema. Although there was a narrative cinema before Griffith, storytelling became fully defined as film's primary role during the period when he began making films.

André Gaudreault and I have termed the primary motive force of the earliest filmmaking the *cinema of attractions*.[38] This term indicates that film-makers such as Méliès or the British pioneer G. A. Smith were fascinated by other possibilities of cinema than its storytelling potential. Such apparently different approaches as the trick film and actuality filmmaking unite in using cinema to present a series of views to audiences, views fascinating because of their illusory power (from the realistic illusion of motion offered to the first audiences by Lumière, to the magical illusions concocted by Méliès) and exoticism. The cinema of attractions, rather than telling stories, bases itself on film's ability to show something. Contrasted to the voyeuristic aspect of later narrative cinema analyzed by Metz,[39] this is an exhibitionist cinema, a cinema that displays its visibility, willing to rupture a self-enclosed fictional world to solicit the attention of its spectator.

As my previous quote from Méliès indicates, the trick film, perhaps the dominant nonactuality film genre before 1906, works as a series of displays— of magical attractions—rather than a primitive sketch of narrative continuity. Many trick films are, in effect, plotless, a series of transformations strung together with little connection and practically no characterization. But to approach even the plotted trick films, such as *A Trip to the Moon*, simply as precursors of later narrative structures misses the point. Méliès's story merely frames a display of cinema's magical possibilities.

Modes of exhibition in early cinema also reflect this lack of concern with creating a self-sufficient narrative world upon the screen. As Musser has shown, early exhibitors exerted a great deal of control over the shows they presented, actually reediting the films they had purchased and supplying a series of off-screen supplements such as sound effects and spoken commentary.[40] Perhaps the most extreme exhibition strategy was that of Hale's Tours, the largest chain of theaters showing films exclusively before 1906. Not only did the films consist of nonnarrative travel sequences taken from moving vehicles (usually trains), but the theater itself was also arranged as a train car;

a conductor took tickets while sound effects simulated the click clack of wheels and hiss of air brakes.[41] Such viewing experiences relate more to the attractions of the fairground than to the traditions of the legitimate theater.

During the earliest years of exhibition, the cinema itself was an attraction. Early audiences went to exhibitions to see machines demonstrated, as they did for other technological wonders such as the widely exhibited x-rays or the phonograph, rather than to view films. It was the Cinématographe, the Biograph, or the Vitascope that were advertised on the variety bills in which they premiered, not *The Baby's Breakfast* or *The Black Diamond Express*. After the initial novelty period, this display of the possibilities of cinema continued, and not only in magic films. Many of the close-ups in early film differ from later uses of the technique precisely because they do not use enlargement for narrative punctuation, but rather as an attraction in its own right. The close-up cut into Porter's *The Gay Shoe Clerk* may anticipate later continuity techniques, but its principle motive is pure exhibitionism, as the lady lifts her skirt hem, exposing her ankle for all to see. Biograph films such as *Photographing a Female Crook* (1904) and *Hooligan in Jail* (1903) consist of a single shot in which the camera is brought close to the main character until they are in midshot. The enlargement is not a device expressive of narrative significance; it is an attraction in itself and the primary motivation for the film.[42]

The types of narrative films, chases, and sequential farces that succeeded the cinema of attractions prepared the way for the more narrative centered films of Griffith (chapter 3). But the cinema of attractions still exerted a force on American filmmaking at the time of Griffith's first films and provides the clearest contrast to the cinema of narrative integration that Griffith pioneered. The transformation from the cinema of attractions to one that sees its primary task as the telling of stories provides a more accurate picture of the primary change that occurred during Griffith's Biograph career than a dichotomy between theatricality and narrativity.

Despite his claims in the New York *Dramatic Mirror*, Griffith did not invent the devices he claimed, such as the close-up and the fade-in; all had appeared in cinema before him, as film historians such as Sadoul and Mitry have emphasized. To say that Griffith arranged these devices into a language, that he devised from them a rhetoric or grammar, or that he raised them to the function of signs is potentially misleading. If these terms have any meaning, they are applicable to such earlier filmmakers as Porter, Méliès, Williamson, and others who employed within their cinema of attractions an often-complicated visual rhetoric based on a series of signs. What is missing in these earlier filmmakers, although it appears at points in their work, is an unambiguous subordination of filmic discourse to narrative purposes. Under Griffith, the devices of cinema that were generally displayed for their own sake as attractions in the work of earlier filmmakers became channeled toward the expression of characterization and story. The often free-floating filmic attractions of early film became part of a narrative system as film unambiguously defined its primary role as a teller of tales, a constructor of narratives.

The general movement of the cinema of narrative integration toward storytelling—exemplified by Griffith's narrator system—is best described by the concept of narrativization (chapter 1). Here theory lends precision to historical periodization; Griffith narrativized previously introduced figures. With Griffith, the relation between filmic discourse and the story of a film was given an importance unheard of in previous film history, thus narrative film often is assigned a foundation in Griffith's work. This "narrativity" was not the result of film's liberation from the constraints of theater, but of centering filmic discourse on story through the narrativization of the filmic sign.

History also helps clarify theory. Although the process of narrativization makes the bind between story and filmic discourse appear natural, it is a historical process. Méliès and Porter developed filmic discourse (relatively) independent of storytelling. Griffith narrativized the three levels of filmic discourse already considerably developed by his predecessors, channeling them toward the primary task of storytelling. In contrast to the cinema of attractions, which accented film's ability to present a view of an event curious or astounding in itself, the story became the unifying structure of a film, the center that determined the filmic narrator's choice of elements of filmic discourse. And it is in terms of the story that the spectator understood the figures of filmic discourse presented. The bond between filmic narrator and spectator is guaranteed by narrativization.

The move from the cinema of attractions to a cinema of narrative integration forms the basic plot of my account and investigation of Griffith's first Biograph films. The narrator system focuses the frame more narrowly on the individual response of D. W. Griffith within a broader transformation of film history. But what exactly do I mean by D. W. Griffith, if, as I have indicated, my intent is not biographical?

D. W. Griffith was the director of the films that form my principle texts, and he enters my investigation through the ways in which he is entangled in these films. This raises two issues. First Griffith's role as director, his involvement in the production of these films, must be specified. Likewise, the origin of the director, too often taken for granted by film historians, must be investigated. Then one more theoretical beast looms—Does film analysis have anything to say about a director? What problems are involved in approaching Griffith as the author (or auteur) of these films?

Griffith's *Dramatic Mirror* advertisement includes, along with the claimed innovations, a list of nearly 150 films that he directed at Biograph (from some 450 he directed for the company). That he provided such a list reveals

Griffith's need not only to identify himself as director for the Biograph Company, but also to assert his authorship of specific films. Biograph films carried no credits referring to Griffith in contrast to his later features, which not only bore director credits, but also emblazoned Griffith's name or initials on intertitles. Griffith has been identified as director of these films retroactively, with the 1913 advertisement serving as primary evidence. The degree of Griffith's involvement in all Biograph films during his employment is unclear. After 1909, Biograph hired secondary directors who made films under his supervision, and it is not known which of the films made after 1909 they directed.[43]

However, for the years I am investigating, attributing films to Griffith is easier. The date of the introduction of secondary directors is relatively certain. The memoirs of Billy Bitzer,[44] Linda Arvidson,[45] and statements by Frank Powell, the first of these secondary directors, all indicate Powell's first film, All on Account of the Milk, was shot on December 9, 10, and 11, 1909. Therefore, we can assume Griffith directed nearly all Biograph films from June 1908 until nearly the end of 1909. The only uncertainty comes at the very beginning of his career. What films (or parts of films) may Griffith have directed before The Adventures of Dollie (shot on June 18 and 19, 1908), and did he have a hand in the Mutoscopes after Dollie? None of these peep-show films seem to survive, but Arvidson indicates that Griffith directed a few.[46]

But what does it mean to declare Griffith as the director of these films? What was the role of the film director in 1908 and 1909, and did it differ from that in earlier filmmaking? And how does the director relate to the cinema of narrative integration? In uncovering the archaeology of the film director, one must recall that in theater (from which the term comes) the director is a comparatively recent phenomenon. As Helen Kritch Chinoy demonstrates, the concept of the theatrical director emerged gradually at the end of the nineteenth century.[47] Although precursors of the theatrical director can be found, the director as the unifying force of a production appeared in the late 1800s. Previously, a traditional way of presenting plays, embedded in actors' training and the design of performing space, determined elements that later became the director's responsibility.

With the breakdown of this tradition, directors began to supply the cohesiveness that formerly resided in conventions shared by audiences and theater artists. Director served "to impose a point of view that would integrate play, production and spectators."[48] At end of the nineteenth century, directors emerged who unified productions around conceptions of realism—Antoine, Otto Brahm, the early Stanislavsky, and Griffith's personal model, David Belasco. These realists introduced attention to naturalistic environment, verisimilar acting, and, particularly with Belasco, the use of recent innovations and technology in stagecraft and lighting.

Film appeared soon after the emergence of the director in theater. Popular theater in the United States during the period, exemplified by the "Uncle Tom" shows still touring at the beginning of the century and captured on film by Edwin Porter in 1903, still relied on the traditional staging and acting styles, and certain early films adopted this style. Griffith, as well as other directors who entered film around the same time, came to film from theater, bringing an awareness of the revolution that had occurred in theatrical presentation.

In film, the director was an even more recent concept. In *The Classical Hollywood Cinema*, Janet Staiger describes the first mode of production in the American film industry as the "the cameraman system of production," which she dates from 1896 to 1907.[49] Although this describes the actual mode of production which gave much essential control to the man who actually operated the camera, in our context it ignores the important role the production company played in making production decisions and particularly in asserting ownership and authorship of the film. This separation can be elusive, as in Staiger's citing of W. K. L. Dickson, because the first cameramen were often associated with the ownership of the production company and were more than mere employees. The first "Lumière films" such as *The Arrival of the Train at the Station* were actually filmed by Louis Lumière for the production company that bore his family name. Soon however "Lumière films" were being shot by a group of peripatetic cameramen-showmen—such as Promio and Doublier—and a basic split in film authorship emerged. The extraordinary "Brighton School" of British filmmakers, such as G. A. Smith and James Williamson, were also cameramen-producers.

When we refer to "Méliès' films" we are invoking a production company model because, except for some early films, Méliès did not operate the camera. The artisanal conditions of Méliès's productions, in which he exercised close control over all aspects of production—writing the scenario, overseeing the costumes, originating the key "trick" effects, designing the sets, and often performing principal acting roles—make Méliès seem like a film director. But it was as head of a production company that he placed his imprint on his films.

The figure in American film most often cited as a filmmaker before Griffith, Edwin S. Porter, seems to be part of the cameraman mode. It was primarily as camera operator that Porter was employed by the Edison Company, although at points he was also in charge of Edison film production generally. Placing a cameraman in charge of production marks film as primarily a technological product that needed the experience of a machinist, rather than as a dramatic work in need of supervision from someone with theatrical training. In 1904, in a deposition given to the United States circuit court, Porter gave a description of his wide-ranging duties at the Edison Company: the technical tasks of camera work and processing the negative, as well as managing pro-filmic events specified later in Griffith's contract as director at Biograph such as selecting locations, "engaging the pantomimic performers," and "instructing them as to the scenes which I wished to have enacted."[50]

However, research by Charles Musser calls into question a sharp division in the United States between the cameraman mode of production and what Staiger terms the "director system of production," which she claims replaced it around 1907. Investigation of Edison payrolls reveals that Porter was paired with other employees from as early as 1901. These men—George S. Fleming, William Martinetti, J. Searle Dawley, who directed *Rescued from an Eagle's Nest* as well as other Edison films, and Wallace McCutcheon, Sr., who directed *Daniel Boone*[51]—were primarily men of the theater, who worked with actors and staging. Grace Dawley told Barnet Braverman that her husband's work with Porter followed a strict division of labor. Porter "busied himself with the camera while Searle rehearsed the scene and when he said 'All ready to shoot, Ed,' Ed shot and that was all there was to it."[52] Musser feels that similar collaborative pairings of workers with complementary talents were probably the most typical form of production in early American cinema, finding evidence for similar pairs at Vitagraph, Essany, and even Biograph. But the early directors did not assert artistic control over the film. As Musser states, the pairs were noted for their basic equality, with each member sticking to his area of expertise.[53] The concept of the director as a unifying force was not a factor.

In later years after leaving Edison, Porter became a director in the sense that Griffith was, overseeing the whole production and using a cameraman to operate the camera. The cameraman, Arthur Miller, recalled that Porter continued to be obsessed with technical details and constantly became involved with the cameraman's tasks, often ignoring the actors.[54] Porter's late films at Edison, which directly precede the work of Griffith at Biograph, show a technical ingenuity such as the animated titles in *College Chums* (1907) or the split screen in *Cupid's Pranks* (1908) but lack articulation of the dramatic content through filmic means. Although narrative films, they seem more related to the cinema of attractions' display of technological novelties. Porter's technical bent was typical of the earlier era of production and contrasts sharply with the later director's role based on narrativization.

The exact date on which a director, separate from the cameraman, was introduced at Biograph is unknown (if there ever was a record kept of Biograph directors, it no longer exists), but it is likely to have come with Biograph's increased production of fiction films around 1903. Although Bitzer indicates that for his first "staged" (i.e., non-actuality) film he was "director, camera-man, props and writer . . . all rolled up in one," this does not seem to have lasted long if it was ever strictly true. Bitzer refers to Wallace McCutcheon,

Sr., as "the director of our pictures."[55] Although the exact chronology of Bitzer's memoirs tends to be hazy, he seems to indicate that McCutcheon was directing films at Biograph about 1903, which, given evidence that he directed *The Moonshiner* in 1904, seems a likely date.[56] Musser stresses the collaborative team of McCutcheon and Francis Marion during Biograph's early days, with both of the pair working on the directing, rather than photographing, aspects of filmmaking.[57] By the time Griffith was hired as director at Biograph, directors had long been established; he replaced a series of disastrous tryouts in the position. Bitzer indicates that Wallace McCutcheon, Sr., his son Wally McCutcheon, Jr., and Stanner Taylor all briefly directed films at Biograph immediately before Griffith's debut.[58]

If Edison and Biograph employed directors well before Griffith, how important is Griffith in the evolution of the director? It seems that specialists were early hired to collaborate with cameramen on the production of American fiction films. However as the relation between Porter and Dawley shows, these collaborations were based on an esthetic division of labor rather than the dominance of the director. The relation between Bitzer and Griffith became markedly different from that of Dawley and Porter's. Bitzer, with a trace of pique, describes Griffith's growing dominance: "Before his arrival I, as cameraman, was responsible for everything except the immediate hiring and handling of the actor. Soon it was his say whether the lights were bright enough, or if the make-up was right."[59] Bitzer's memoirs are filled with the numerous "suggestions" that Griffith made to Bitzer about the visual presentation of scenes.

With the director's new involvement in the visualization of the film, which Dawley's and Griffith's predecessors at Biograph left entirely to the cameraman, the equivalent of the theatrical director appeared in film: a role that integrates elements of production around a unifying center. With Griffith, and most likely other film directors around the same time, the director was no longer an independent expert working with the actors and then relying on the cameraman's expertise for visualization. Rather, the dramatic purpose within a scene determined its visual presentation as well, creating a filmic discourse which expressed dramatic situations. This constitutes the essence of the cinema of narrative integration and the narrator system. Although this new conception of the film director was inspired by the theater director, it dealt with filmic discourse. Whereas Dawley and McCutcheon seem to have restricted their attention to the pro-filmic level of filmic discourse, Griffith directed his attention to the other levels as well—the enframed image and, particularly, editing. Integrating these three levels through narrativization constitutes the role of the director that Griffith pioneered and which shaped the narrator system.

Although theoretically narrativization of film style need not depend on the actual production role of the director, it is historically significant that they appear at the same time. The integrative and dominant role of the director at Biograph was not the simple result of the force of Griffith's personality, but the product of an industrywide redefinition of the film commodity through a new emphasis on film as a fictional dramatic medium.[60] Nonetheless, Griffith responded to these forces with a new production role for the director, undoubtedly inspired by contemporary theater. Nothing in his contract with the Biograph company hints at this change.

Griffith's original director's contract with the Biograph Company specified his involvement with pro-filmic elements and selecting and arrangement of script material.[61] Besides his responsibility for screen stories, his duties as film director included arranging sets or choosing actual locations, selecting performers and overseeing their costuming and makeup, rehearsing performances, and enforcing company discipline. The contract envisions a man with theatrical experience who could arrange and manage what went on in front of the camera. It by no means redefines the relation between director and cameraman. The only section of the contract that could relate to Griffith's new interpretation of his role is the first paragraph, which refers to the "composing, selecting and modifying subjects, stories and plays." Although this seems to refer to the preparation of shooting scripts, Bitzer indicates that Griffith's "composing and modifying" soon extended to the way things were shot and their breakdown into shots that would guide their final edited form.

This contract is possibly identical to those of Griffith's predecessors, and Janet Staiger has indicated that it was typical of other production companies of the period. Although Griffith's understanding of his role as director in determining filmic discourse seems to have been in the vanguard of film practice in 1908–9, and may have been more intense than that of his peers, it was not an anomaly. The move to the director system was a widespread industrial change, as Staiger has shown, based on economic changes in the industry.

Griffith began his film career at a point of transition which opened new opportunities for the director, and he contributed to this transition through his production practices. But if we have established the importance of Griffith's production role, the implicit claim to authorship contained in the *Dramatic Mirror* advertisement encounters more recent theoretical opposition. In 1913, Griffith retroactively claimed the output of a studio as his corpus, citing it as evidence that he "revolutionized Motion Picture drama." This claim goes beyond production modes and raises theoretical issues.

Film criticism treatment of the director as author (and, for some, treatment of directors at all) has fallen into disrepute. This has been in part a response to the "death of the author" in contemporary literary criticism, as well as a reaction against the often-naive assumptions of certain auteur film critics.[62]

Beginning in the seventies, a number of film critics bracketed a director's name with quotation marks, identifying this rubric with the structure found by the critic in a body of texts rather than an actual biological and historical person.[63] This practice not only short-circuited reference to a real person and the consequent understanding of auteur criticism as biographical and psychological, but it also side-stepped objections that the auteur theory provided an unrealistic account of how films were made, inaccurately privileging the director's contribution in a collaborative art form.

My textual analysis basically operates within these revisions of the notion of director/author. The "D. W. Griffith" referred to herein is rarely a biographical, biological person. Griffith stands as the theoretically posited source of the films I am discussing, even though it is known that the original film stories were usually written by someone else, the film was shot by Bitzer or Marvin, and the splices were not made by Griffith's hand. "D. W. Griffith" basically corresponds to Wayne Booth's "implied author." Defined by Booth as the decisive power behind a text, but different from the actual author as a person, the implied author "chooses, consciously or unconsciously what we read; we infer him as an ideal, literary created version of the real man: he is the sum of his own choices."[64] The implied author exists, not outside the text, but as a function of its discourse.

However, as useful as this concept may be in untangling the problems of auteur analysis, it does not address the issues raised by the "death of the author."[65] From this perspective it is not simply the association with a biological person that makes the concept of an author problematic. Critics such as Roland Barthes find that traditional criticism posits the author as a semi-theological figure, the ultimate point of origin of the work and guarantor of its unity and coherence of meaning.[66]

Separating the author as biographical person from the text may be a methodological necessity, but it can also become an historical blind spot. The revisionist redefinition of the author as a critical construct and function of the text insulates films from contact with historical forces. By introjecting the author into the text, or using the concept of text to entirely displace the author (as Barthes may seem to do), we run the risk of endowing it with the theological attributes formerly reserved for the author.[67] The idea of an author can be valuable insofar as it opens texts to historical forces, and pernicious insofar as it insulates films in an ahistorical cult of personality.

As Robert C. Allen and Douglas Gomery have pointed out, the auteur approach deflected attention away from investigation of actual production practices and other historical issues in pursuit of an author's signature.[68] An analysis of art works seeking to reveal subjective experiences, individual world views, or biographical traumas as the true source and ultimate significance of the work has limited historical or esthetic value. Likewise, an all-powerful author who creates works *ex nihilo* forbids historical understanding. The author as producer is also a product, constrained by the means of production available to him or her and the host of social relations which it is the historian's task to describe. Confining our understanding to Griffith's intentions is not only a critical fallacy but also impoverishes the films' address to us as both spectators and historians. As Hans Georg Gadamer states, the historian's task "is not to understand the subjective intentions, plans and experiences of the men who are involved in history. Rather, it is the great matrix of the meaning of history that must be understood and that requires the interpretive effort of the historian."[69]

It is precisely in this context that David Wark Griffith, the historical and biological person reemerges. As John Caughie has pointed out, "in placing the author as a fictional figure inside the text, we remove the most accessible point at which the text is tied to its own social and historical outside."[70] Griffith, the actual person outside the text, is important to this work not as a personality who expresses himself through these films, but as a force in their production, through whom other forces enter. Vital to a historical understanding of his films is the Griffith who expressed his admiration for Zola's naturalism in 1907, who styled himself on the muckraking journalists of his time, who worked within the romantic performance idiom of Nance O'Neil, and who tried to imitate David Belasco in the orchestration of details in his playwriting. Griffith as director stands as an important relay for these and other forms of discourse as they enter the Biograph films during 1908 and 1909.

But just as the concept of the director has a historical context, the idea of an author of a film, and particularly understanding a director as an author, exceeds theoretical concerns and plays a historical role. Michel Foucault's essay "What Is an Author?" provides a basis for a historical investigation by focusing on what he terms the "author-function." Foucault points out that the author-function exceeds text-immanent concerns and is determined by the social understanding of discourse. Texts do not obtain authors spontaneously. Authors are attributed through a series of complex operations with links to other institutions, legal and cultural. Further, not all discourses are considered as "authored," and the types of discourse that can possess authors change with the social context.[71]

Griffith's *Dramatic Mirror* advertisement claiming authorship of the films he directed exemplifies Foucault's description of how authorship must be asserted outside the works themselves. Although Griffith did not claim legal ownership, he called for recognition of his authorship. In doing so he also announced that films are an authored discourse rather than anonymous studio products. While Biograph could still assert legal ownership of the films listed—

and continued, in fact, to release and rerelease Griffith's films for several years after he had left the company, often invoking his name in publicity—Griffith countered ownership by asserting authorship.

Griffith's advertisement combated the effect of the Biograph Company's policy of anonymity. The lack of credits on a Biograph film, a practice the company maintained long after the rest of the film industry had abandoned it, meant that the host of contributors to its production—actors, scriptwriters, cameramen, technicians, as well as directors—went unacknowledged. However the films were not issued anonymously. The name of the production company was emblazoned not only on opening credits, but also on all intertitles; it even appeared on interior sets as a trademark. The Biograph Company consciously suppressed all other names associated with their films while it publicized the company itself. In pursuing this policy, the company proclaimed the films as products, complete with trademark, rather than an authored discourse. Although shortly before Griffith's departure in 1913 Biograph eventually followed the practice of other American production companies and announced the name of cast and directors of their films, Griffith's self-promotion responds to the previous occulting of his name and redefines film as an authored discourse.

The author-function also depends on structures within the text itself. As Foucault points out, the author-function does not refer to a real person, but to a variety of positions within discourse itself, such as the implied author and the narrator. Authorship depends on the process of narration as well as on the conditions of reception.[72] In 1913, Griffith based his claim of authorship on the development of the narrator system. The advertisement makes this explicit because it claimed not only the authorship of a number of films, but also the development of basic elements in film's narrative discourse. The concepts of the author in film and that of the narrator (or in this specific context, the narrator system), although theoretically separate entities, imply each other. The appearance of an explicit filmic narrator grounds the ideology of the filmic author. As the narrator system highlighted the filmic narrator with new clarity, it also allowed the emergence of the concept of the film director as author.

Concentrating on the films of Griffith avoids a "film history without names." The actual productive forces of film history include individuals as well as production modes. But at the same time, individuals do not receive primacy, and a "great man theory" of film history must also be avoided. My description of the narrative style of Griffith's films—the narrator system—ultimately forms part of a broader history of the transformation of American narrative film that occurred at this time, the move to a cinema of narrative integration. The starting point is a series of specific films from which a particular narrative stance and address can be abstracted: the narrator system that casts the shadow of D. W. Griffith onto the field of American film history.

Notes

1. For treatment of the role of plot in the writing of history, see Paul Ricoeur *Time and Narrative* (especially vols. 1 and 3), trans. Kathleen Blamey and David Pellauer (Chicago: University of Chicago Press, 1984–88); Paul Veyne, *Writing History*, trans. Mina Moore-Rinvolucri (Middletown: Wesleyan University Press, 1984); Hayden White, *MetaHistory: The Historical Imagination in Nineteenth-Century Europe* (Baltimore: Johns Hopkins University Press, 1973).

2. Biographical information relevant to the Biograph period has been assembled in Robert Henderson, *D. W. Griffith: The Years at Biograph* and has been related to broader social history in Russell Merritt, "The Impact of D. W. Griffith's Motion Pictures from 1908 to 1915 on Contemporary American Culture," Ph.D. diss., Harvard University, 1970.

3. See, for instance, my review of Richard Schickel's *D. W. Griffith: An American Life* in *American Film* 10 (June 1984): 57–59, 70, 72.

4. Lewis Jacobs, *The Rise of The American Film: A Critical History, with an Essay, Experimental Cinema in America 1921–1947* (New York: Teachers College Press, 1968), pp. 101–5.

5. Georges Sadoul, *Histoire general du cinéma*, vol. 3: *Le cinéma devient un art 1909–1920, premier volume: L'avant-guerre* (Paris: Denoel, 1951), pp. 84–88.

6. Jean Mitry, *Histoire du cinéma: Art et industrie*, vol. 1: *1895–1914* (Paris: Éditions Universitaires, 1967), 1:402–3.

7. New York *Dramatic Mirror*, Dec. 13, 1913, p. 36.

8. Terry Ramsaye, *A Million and One Nights: A History of the Motion Picture* (1926, repr. London: Frank Cass 1964), p. 508.

9. Jacobs, *Rise of the American Film*, p. 98.

10. Ibid., p. 95.

11. Georges Sadoul, *Histoire général du cinéma*, vol. 2: *Les pionniers du cinéma, 1897–1909* (Paris: Denoel, 1951), p. 523, translation mine.

12. Sadoul, *Les pionners*, p. 524.

13. Jean Mitry, *Esthétique et psychologie du cinéma*, vol. 1: *Les structures* (Paris: Editions Universitaires, 1963), p. 159, translation mine.

14. Mitry, *Les structures*, p. 163.

15. Mitry, *1895–1914*, p. 408, translation mine. Mitry refers to Griffith's films from a slightly later date than those of this book, approximately 1912–15.

16. Christian Metz, *Film Language: A Semiotics of the Cinema*, trans. Michael Taylor (New York: Oxford University Press, 1974), pp. 95–96.

17. Metz, *Film Language*, pp. 226–70.

18. John L. Fell, in *Film and the Narrative Tradition* (Norman: University of Oklahoma Press, 1974), outlines some of these sources, with a particularly good treatment of the comic strip.

19. Fell, *Film and the Narrative Tradition,* and Charles Musser, "The Early Cinema of Edwin S. Porter," pp. 261–86; Martin Sopocy, "James A. Williamson: An American View," pp. 297–320; Tom Gunning, "The Non-Continuous Style of Early Film, 1900–1906," pp. 213–30; all in *Cinema 1900–1906: An Analytical Study by the National Film Archives (London) and the International Federation of Film Archives,* ed. Roger Holman (Brussels: FIAF, 1982).

20. David Levy, "Reconstituted Newsreels, Re-enactments and the American Narrative Film," pp. 243–60, in *Cinema 1900–1906,* ed. Holman.

21. On vaudeville, see Douglas Gilbert, *American Vaudeville: Its Life and Times* (1940, repr. New York: Dover Publications, 1963). On the visual tradition in nineteenth-century theater see, A. Nicholas Vardac, *From Stage to Screen: Theatrical Method from Garrick to Griffith* (1949, repr. New York: Benjamin Blom, 1968).

22. Andre Gaudreault, "'Théatralité' et 'narrativité' dans l'œuvre de Georges Méliès," in *Méliès et la naissance du spectacle cinématographique,* ed. Madeliene Malthete-Méliès (Paris: Klincksieck, 1984), pp. 199–200. A somewhat abridged translation of this essay has been published in English as "Theatricality, Narrativity and 'Trickality': Reevaluating the Cinema of Georges Méliès," *Journal of Popular Film and Television* 15 (Fall 1987): 110–19.

23. Jacques Malthete, "Méliès, technician du collage" in *Méliès et la naissance,* ed. Malthete-Méliès; see also Tom Gunning, " 'Primitive' Cinema—a Frame-up? or the Trick's on Us," *Cinema Journal* 28 (Winter 1988–89): 3–12.

24. Tom Gunning, "An Unseen Energy Swallows Space," in *Film Before Griffith,* ed. John L. Fell (Berkeley: University of California Press, 1983). pp. 355–66.

25. Mitry, *1895–1914,* p. 370.

26. Ibid., p. 371.

27. Ibid., p. 401.

28. Ibid., p. 370, translation mine.

29. This film is consistently referred to as *L'Assassinat du duc de Guise* in film histories. However restoration of the film shows its original title was *La Mort du duc de Guise* ; see Pierre Jenn and Michel Nagard, "L'Assassinat du duc de Guise," *L'Avant scene cinéma,* no. 334 (Nov. 1984): 58.

30. See Noel Burch, in *Cinema 1900–1906,* ed. Holman, vol. 1, p. 105.

31. Georges Méliès "Importance du Scènario," in Georges Sadoul, *Georges Méliès: Présentation et bio-filmography; choix de textes et propos de Méliès* (Paris: Seghers, 1961), p. 118, translation mine.

32. Reproduced in Kemp R. Niver, comp., *The Biograph Bulletins 1896–1908,* ed. Bebe Bergsten (Los Angeles: Locare Research Group, 1971), p. 82.

33. Gunning, "The Non-Continuous Style in Early Film," in *Cinema 1900–1906,* ed. Holman, pp. 355–66.

34. Charles Musser, "The Nickleodeon Era Begins: Establishing the Framework for Hollywood's Mode of Representation," *Framework* 22–23 (Autumn 1983): 4–11.

35. Noel Burch, in *Cinema 1900–1906,* ed. Holman, vol. 1, p. 106.

36. Noel Burch, *To the Distant Observer: Form and Meaning in the Japanese Cinema,* rev. and ed. Annette Michelson (Berkeley: University of California Press, 1979), p. 76.

37. Metz, *Film Language,* pp. 95–96.

38. André Gaudreault and Tom Gunning, "Les cinéma des premiers temps, un défi á l'histoire du cinéma?" in *Histoire du cinéma: Nouvelles approaches*, ed. J. Aumont, A. Gaudreault, and M. Marie (Paris: Publications de la Sorbonne, 1989), pp. 49–63; also see, Tom Gunning, "The Cinema of Attractions: Early Film, Its Spectator and the Avant-Garde," *Wide Angle* 8, nos. 3 and 4 (1986): 63–71.

39. Christian Metz, *The Imaginary Signifier: Psychoanalysis and the Cinema*, trans. Celia Britton et al. (Bloomington: Indiana University Press, 1982), particularly pp. 58–80, 91–97.

40. Charles Musser, "American Vitagraph: 1897–1901," *Cinema Journal* 22 (Spring 1983): 10.

41. Raymond Fielding, "Hale's Tours: Ultra Realism in the Pre–1910 Motion Picture," in *Film Before Griffith*, ed. Fell, pp. 116–30.

42. This was pointed out to me by Ben Brewster at the Ohio University Film Conference in 1985.

43. The traditional means for establishing which films Griffith directed during these later years has been Bitzer's claim that all the films he shot were directed by Griffith. Two other sources exist, and others might appear with a detailed search of trade journals from this later period. First, an announcement in *Moving Picture World* of April 5, 1913, states that "David Griffith, the original Biograph producer, is personally directing all Saturday releases," while midweek comedies were directed by Dell Henderson and other releases by Tony O'Sullivan (p. 34). The other source is the Biograph Author's Book preserved in the D. W. Griffith Papers at the Museum of Modern Art Film Library, which records stories purchased by Biograph from 1901 to April 1913. The entries in the book from 1912–13 often include initials or names next to titles of completed films. These are consistent with the announcement quoted above, so that the initial *H* can be assigned to Henderson, *S* to O'Sullivan, and *G* to Griffith. Some of the films photographed by Bitzer (as indicated in the Biograph Cameraman's Book, also preserved at the Museum of Modern Art), are shown by these other sources to be directed by the secondary directors, although the majority of films Bitzer photographed do seem to have been directed by Griffith. The amount of control Griffith might have asserted over the work of these secondary directors is unknown; the *Dramatic Mirror* advertisement stressed that Griffith "supervised all Biograph productions and directed the more important features" (p. 36).

44. In the *Dramatic Mirror* advertisement, Griffith indicated that he directed all Biograph releases for two years after he began directing. However fairly good evidence exists that secondary directors were working during the first Biograph trip to California in the spring of 1910. Bitzer's comments about these secondary directors is somewhat sketchy and, written decades later, may include some errors. Bitzer lists *All on Account of the Milk* (December 9, 10, 11, 1909) as the first film directed by Frank Powell, the first of the secondary directors. However, an earlier film, *His Duty* (May 10, 12, 1909) also carries Bitzer's notation "Frank Powell," but this may be intended to indicate that Powell acted in the film (which he did). Powell himself later cited *All on Account of the Milk* as the first film he directed. Bitzer indicates that Powell directed at Biograph until 1911 (when Dell Henderson and Mack Sennett took over), turning out "1 long 1 short" film a week (presumably a full-reel film and a split-reel film). He also notes that Powell's films were shot by Arthur Marvin or Percy Higginson, adding, "Powell's comedies of 1000 ft. length are distinguishable by the actors when any doubt arises,

i.e. Walthall, Sweet, Mary Pickford, Lucas would not have been directed by Powell, Henderson or Sennett." But several films Bitzer assigns to Powell do not match this profile. For example, *The Dancing Girl of Butte* is not a comedy and was shot, in fact, by Bitzer himself; *A Gold Necklace*, a split-reel comedy shot by Marvin in a hasty, improvised style little resembling Griffith and stars Mary Pickford. Bitzer Papers, in the D. W. Griffith Papers, Museum of Modern Art Film Library, New York City.

45. Mrs. D. W. Griffith [Linda Arvidson], *When the Movies Were Young* (1925, repr. New York: Dover Publications, 1969), pp. 109, 139.

46. Arvidson, *When the Movies Were Young*, p. 69.

47. Helen Kritch Chinoy, "The Emergence of the Director," in *Directors and Directing: A Source Book of the Modern Theater*, ed. Toby Cole and Helen Kritch Chinoy (Indianapolis: Bobbs-Merrill, 1976), pp. 1–77.

48. Chinoy, *Directors and Directing*, pp. 3–4.

49. David Bordwell, Janet Staiger, and Kristin Thompson, *The Classical Hollywood Cinema: Film Style and Mode of Production to 1960* (New York: Columbia University Press, 1985), p. 116.

50. David Levy, "Edison Sales Policy and the Continuous Action Film, 1904–1906," in *Film Before Griffith*, ed. Fell, p. 216.

51. Charles Musser, "Pre-Classical Hollywood Cinema and Its Modes of Film Production," paper delivered at the 1989 Society for Cinema Studies, Iowa City; see also J. Searle Dawley file in Braverman material, D. W. Griffith Papers, Museum of Modern Art Film Library, New York City, and Florence Lawrence, "Growing up with the Movies," *PhotoPlay* (Nov. 1914): 40.

52. Grace Dawley to Barnet Braverman, March 12, 1947, Braverman material, D. W. Griffith Papers, Museum of Modern Art Film Library, New York City.

53. Musser, "Pre-Classical Hollywood Cinema," p. 7.

54. Fred Balshofer and Arthur Miller, *One Reel a Week* (Berkeley: University of California Press, 1967), pp. 48–51.

55. Billy Bitzer, *His Story: The Autobiography of D. W. Griffith's Master Cameraman* (New York: Farrar Straus and Giroux, 1973), pp. 28, 30, 50.

56. Bitzer, *His Story*, pp. 50–51. McCutcheon is an enigmatic figure and it would be valuable to clarify his role in film history. We know that as a cameraman he shot a number of films for Biograph, both actualities and dramas, in 1903. His last film as cameraman for Biograph was *Wanted a Dog* (1905). He also directed dramatic films during this period. At some point he left Biograph for the Edison Company, where he again directed. A *Variety* notice from January 25, 1908, announced that "Wallace McCutcheon, after several years in the employ of the Edison people has returned to the American Mutoscope and Biograph as producer of their supply of new films. In the same capacity Mr. McCutcheon served the Biograph company when that firm was the first of American film manufacturers" (p. 11). This item contradicts Bitzer's memoirs which do not mention that McCutcheon had left for the Edison Company, nor that he had returned not long before Griffith's debut (perhaps as a ploy in the struggle between Edison and Biograph). More information about McCutcheon's role at both companies is needed for an understanding of the archaeology of the film director.

57. Musser, "Pre-Classical Hollywood Cinema," pp. 13–14.

58. Bitzer, *His Story*, pp. 50–51.

59. Ibid., p. 69.

60. Trade journals are equivocal in their terms for the integrating force responsible for films. Frequently, early reviewers of Griffith's films refer to the anonymous force responsible for them as the "stage manager." But more frequently the term used is the one appearing in *Variety*'s announcement of McCutcheon's return to Biograph—*producer*. Eventually the term *director* does appear. Griffith's own *Dramatic Mirror* advertisement refers to him as both director and producer, although this may be in reference to his double role as actual director of his own films and as supervisor of others.

61. Contract, Lawrence Griffith with the American Mutoscope and Biograph Company, August 7, 1908, D. W. Griffith Papers, Museum of Modern Art Film Library, New York City. The 1909 contract is identical in the passages cited. This contract has also been commented on by John H. Whitney, "The Pragmatic Artist," *Classic Film Collector* (New York, n.d.).

62. Many relevant texts on this issue are assembled in *Theories of Authorship: A Reader*, ed. John Caughie (London: Routledge and Kegan Paul, 1981).

63. Peter Wollen, *Signs and Meanings in the Cinema*, rev. ed., anthologized in *Theories of Authorship*, ed. Caughie, pp. 146–47, as well as Stephen Jenkins, "Introduction," in *Fritz Lang: The Image and the Look*, ed. Stephen Jenkins (London: British Film Institute, 1981), p. 1.

64. Wayne C. Booth, *The Rhetoric of Fiction* (Chicago: University of Chicago Press, 1961), pp. 74–75. It is curious that although Booth's concept is close to some revisions of the auteur theory, there is not one reference to him in the Caughie anthology. Booth is discussed in relation to the auteur theory in John Belton, "Implied Author and Implied Reader in the Cinematographic Image," in *Cinema Stylists* (Metuchen: Scarecrow Press, 1983), pp. 1–8, as well as George M. Wilson *Narration in Light: Studies in Cinematic Point of View* (Baltimore: Johns Hopkins University Press, 1986).

65. Relevant texts would be Roland Barthes, "The Death of the Author," in *Image Music Text*, ed. and trans. Stephen Heath (New York: Hill and Wang, 1977); Michel Foucault, "What Is an Author?," in *Language, Counter-Memory, Practice: Selected Essays and Interviews*, ed. Donald F. Bouchard, trans. Donald F. Bouchard and Sherry Simon (Ithaca: Cornell University Press, 1977), pp. 113–38; Stephen Heath, "Comment on the Idea of Authorship," in *Theories of Authorship*, ed. Caughie, pp. 214–20.

66. Barthes, "The Death of the Author," p. 147.

67. See Foucault, "What Is an Author?," pp. 119–20: "In current usage, however, the notion of writing seems to transpose the empirical characteristics of an author to a transcendental anonymity."

68. Robert C. Allen and Douglas Gomery, *Film History: Theory and Practice* (New York: Alfred A. Knopf, 1985), p. 88.

69. Hans Georg Gadamer, "Semantics and Hermeneutics" in *Philosophical Hermeneutics*, ed. and trans. David E. Linge (Berkeley: University of California Press, 1977), p. 103.

70. Caughie, *Theories of Authorship*, p. 3.

71. Foucault, "What Is an Author?," p. 130.

72. Ibid., p. 129.

3

Mastering New Narrative Forms within an Industry in Conflict

O
N JUNE 18, 1908, David Wark Griffith began to shoot his first completed film for the American Mutoscope and Biograph Company.[1] *The Adventures of Dollie* drew on melodrama situations and cultural stereotypes to construct the story of a young girl kidnapped by a vengeful gypsy. Griffith's very first films show a strong inheritance from the decade of film history that preceded him, as well as the stirrings of an important transformation. But to fully understand the revolution in narrative style these early films embody, one must explore the drama unfolding in the film industry which produced them, which could rival Griffith's one-reel melodrama for intrigue, conflict, and fast-breaking action. This drama, too, was the climax of nearly a decade of development. And the American Mutoscope and Biograph Company stood at its center.

Since the turn of the century Biograph's chief rival, the Edison Manufacturing Company, had tried to control the emerging film industry, largely through patents claims. But in 1908 the crisis went beyond rivalry between production companies; relations among all elements of the film industry—production, distribution, and exhibition—were in a state of flux, as was film's role in American culture. A few years before Griffith's directorial debut the sudden appearance of thousands of cheap film theaters—nickelodeons—increased the demand for films beyond the capacities of the new industry. Hostilities among production companies (powered by Edison's legals threats), combined with a chaotic distribution system, made it difficult to meet demand. In addition, the social impact of the nickelodeon revolution caused grave concern to the guardians of official culture, as well as to progressivist reformers investigating its effects on the poorer urban classes.

The roots of this crisis lay in transformations the film industry had already undergone in the relations among production, exhibition, and distribution. Although research on the decade of American film history before Griffith continues (in particular in the detailed and perceptive work of Charles Musser, whose ideas have had a great influence on the comments that follow), three separate periods—each defined by unique relations among production, distribution, and exhibition—can be outlined. I will describe them with special focus on the position of Biograph.

The Self-Contained Producers, 1896–1901

Initially, film companies marketed a self-contained attraction, an illusion-producing apparatus that included the camera that took films, the films themselves, and—most prominently featured—the projection machine that presented the life-sized realistic images of motion to the public. The industry was a self-contained unit, with all phases firmly in the hands of the production company on whom the theater depended not only for films, but also for the means to show them. When vaudeville theaters (the primary exhibition sites during the period) featured "the Biograph," they rented a complete service from the company, including films, the Biograph projector, and an "operator" who ran the machine. The Biograph was a self-contained attraction, like other acts on a vaudeville bill. Its novelty appeal lay in the lifelike illusion of motion the apparatus produced; storytelling was secondary.

In some respects this period was rather brief, perhaps less than a year, because Edison began offering a Projecting Kinetoscope for sale in early 1897. The Biograph Company, however, offered a complete service (films, machine, and operator) until at least the end of 1901, while extending its places of exhibition beyond vaudeville theaters to summer parks and the church lyceum circuit.[2] But by 1902 even Biograph was offering films in "standard size sprocket film" which could be shown on the standard projectors of the Edison sort. Initially Biograph had used a special large-format film which could only be shown on their own machine and which held an advantage of greater clarity over Edison and Lumière projections.[3] Abandoning it in 1902, Biograph signaled the end of the era of the self-contained producers who offered a complete apparatus as a marketable attraction. The company recognized that the industry's major role had become the selling of films, rather than the leasing of a complete projection service. The decision by film manufacturers to sell both projectors and films (although Biograph abandoned manufacture of projectors entirely and sold only films) allowed the separation of exhibition from production that marked the next period.

The Appearance of the Independent Exhibitor: 1902–4

With the possibility of owning projectors and films, exhibitors entered film history separately from production companies. That films had to be bought outright encouraged a peripatetic form of exhibition because the novelty of an exhibitor's selection of films soon became exhausted in a fixed location. The first exhibitors, therefore, tended to travel, following a circuit of bookings in vaudeville theaters, lyceums, or on fairgrounds, and occasionally providing their own exhibition site with a dark canvas tent known as a "blacktop."[4] As Musser has pointed out, this era was also marked by the exhibitors' control over the actual form of films. Exhibitors "usually purchased one-shot films from the producers and arranged/edited these into sequences and programs— often accompanying them with narration, music and sound effects."[5] This individual creation of programs meant that each exhibitor's show could be a unique event, outside the control of production companies.

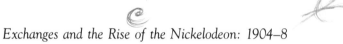

Exchanges and the Rise of the Nickelodeon: 1904–8

Even in the earliest period of film projection, a few theaters showed films as their primary attraction, but the film manufacturers' policy of outright sales had limited the novelty such theaters could offer. The formation of film exchanges—exchangemen operated between producers and exhibitors to buy films from manufacturers and then rent them to exhibitors—soon provided the means for resolving this awkward state of affairs. Simultaneously, improvements in projection machines made them simpler to operate, and projection ceased being a specialized task performed by an expert. The exhibitor Percy Waters trained employees of vaudeville theaters to operate projectors and therefore his film service no longer had to supply operators to theaters along with films. As Musser states, "former exhibitors such as Waters now became renters or film exchangers, while the theaters became the actual exhibitors."[6]

With the exchanges, a new and powerful force entered the film industry, setting up a new balance of power. The impact of the exchanges was initially evident in the form of exhibition. Exhibitors could maintain theaters in one locale because renting made a larger variety of film available at a cheaper price. This new supply allowed a vast increase in film theaters, the "nickelodeon boom." In the period from 1905–8, films continued on vaudeville programs, but the "nickel theater" that made films their main feature made film a new form of mass entertainment. These theaters began primarily as cheap "store shows," converted storefronts with folding chairs and an atmosphere of impermanence, but by 1908 nickelodeons were becoming more permanent and substantial.

The nickelodeon era also saw a sharp rise in the production of story films, which began to replace nonnarrative actualities as the most popular genre. Film chases and other action-based narratives appeared that mediated between the cinema of attractions and the cinema of narrative integration that dominates Griffith's period.

The control of the industry that the production companies had initially enjoyed had slipped through their fingers. By 1908, film manufacturers confronted two powerful and independent factions: film exchanges and nickelodeon exhibitors. Further, the explosion in number of theaters and the exhibitor policy of changing films daily (which began in 1907) created a crisis in film supply. As Musser puts it, "Filmmaking remained a cottage industry while exhibitors had become a form of mass production."[7] G. E. Van Guysling, general manager of the Biograph Company, declared in 1907 that Biograph "is pushed to the limits of its capacity by the demand for new subjects."[8] Manufacturers also claimed that their films were not making a sufficient profit due to the exchanges' control of prices. Production companies felt, according to Robert Anderson, "that they had taken the risks in developing the domestic film business, and now they were being excluded from the majority of the profits."[9] In 1908, production companies found that the industry had expanded not only beyond their expectations, but also beyond their control. New demands exceeded their production capacity in an industry whose fair share of profits, they felt, was going into other pockets.

In addition to conflicts and crisis within, outside social forces threatened the film industry by the end of 1907. The nickelodeon explosion had alarmed government officials and reform groups. The Edison Company in early 1908 lamented that "Two years ago motion pictures were in great public demand, but at the present time they have fallen into disfavor if not actual disrepute."[10] From a scientific novelty on a vaudeville bill, film had become an unprecedented form of mass entertainment, and social attitudes toward it were uncertain and frequently alarmist.

The stage was set for struggle and transformation. Production wanted to reassert control over distribution. Individual production companies fought among themselves for preeminence within the reorganization. Along with this economic struggle, an ideological transformation of the image of film had to take place to turn aside the criticisms of reformers and public officials. For both economic and ideological reasons, film had to be raised from the status of a cheap entertainment and take its place among other socially respectable forms of narrative representation. This transformation would involve not only the way in which films were produced and distributed, but also their narrative construction.

The battle over control of the film industry in 1907–8 took its most visible form in the Edison Company's attempt to assert dominance over all other competitors. Rather than eliminating competition, it was Edison's goal to regulate it and use this control of product to also gain leverage over exchanges. The expanding distribution and consumption of films made the outright elimination of other producers particularly undesirable. Instead, the Edison Manufacturing Company intended to license the other American producers to continue making films while paying Edison a substantial royalty in recognition of his patents. Control of competition through combination had been well established in American industry around the turn of the century, but had also encountered resistance from both state and federal governments, as exemplified by the Sherman Anti-Trust Act of 1890. To avoid these legal restrictions, pooling agreements took a variety of forms; a combination on the basis of the legal control of patents was believed to be the strongest of these and was a frequent strategy.[11]

Edison's attempt to assert control through his patents began as early as 1897, and led to a decade of litigation.[12] Focusing again on Biograph, which Edison regarded as the test case of their patent suits, we can sketch the legal seesawing that left the American film industry demoralized and uncertain up to 1908.

Biograph's patents posed the strongest threat to Edison's. The Biograph camera and its Mutoscope peep-show device were designed by William Kennedy Dickson. As Gordon Hendricks has shown, while employed by Edison, Dickson had been instrumental in the invention of the Edison camera.[13] Knowing Edison's patents in detail, Dickson carefully fashioned the Biograph machines to avoid the specifications of Edison's patents. In 1901 the Edison suit against Biograph was initially decided in Biograph's favor. However, this ruling was reversed by the court of appeals in 1902, a ruling that also found Edison's original patent claims to be too broad and in need of reissue with additional specifications. Edison divided his patent into two parts, and on September 30, 1902, patent no. 12037, covering the motion picture camera, and patent no. 12038, covering the film used for motion pictures, were issued.[14]

With this reissued patent, Edison began to institute lawsuits all over again, starting with a suit against Biograph over the camera patent. In 1906 a preliminary decision was delivered in Biograph's favor by Justice Ray,[15] however, on appeal the judgment was modified; the decision of March of 1907 by Circuit Judge Lacombe defined the final battle in the Edison-Biograph struggle.

Lacombe found that the Dickson-designed Biograph camera did not infringe Edison's camera patents because the Edison camera used a sprocket wheel to move film past the lens "regularly, evenly, and very rapidly without jarring, jerking, or slipping, producing a negative which can be printed from and reproduced as a whole without rearrangement."[16] However, the Biograph camera moved its film past the lens—not with sprocket wheels—but with friction rollers in which, to return to Lacombe's decision, "there is no such interlockings as will hold the film firmly advancing it with mathematical accuracy . . . there is a possibility of slippage." In fact, Biograph negatives did have irregularities in the placement of individual frames that had to be corrected during the printing process. Because of these differences, Lacombe found that "the defendant's Biograph camera is not the type of apparatus described and shown in the original and reissued patent."[17]

This decision also contained a partial victory for Edison. The suit had been brought on the basis of two cameras then in use by the Biograph Company, the original Biograph camera and a camera of British manufacture called the Warwick.[18] Lacombe found that the Warwick camera did infringe Edison's camera patents. Because all other American manufacturers used cameras similar in design to the Warwick, Lacombe's decision could be used as the basis of a judgment against them. This took legal form on October 24, 1907, when Judge Kohlsaat of the U.S. Circuit Court in Chicago delivered a decision in favor of Edison in his suit against the Selig Company. Kohlsaat found that the two cameras used by the company—the "Selig" and the Lumière cameras—were "substantially identical in material respect to the Warwick camera of the New York case."[19] Kohlsaat's decision demonstrated to the other competing manufacturers that Edison's camera patents were valid against their equipment.

Excluding Biograph, the major American film manufacturers approached Edison, as did the French company Pathé, which was building an American plant at the time and wanted to avoid litigation with Edison.[20] They conceded his patent victory and sought an agreement which would allow them to continue making films. This accorded with Edison's desire to control rather than eliminate the other manufacturers and derive profit from their productions.[21] On January 31, 1908, Edison issued licenses to the Kalem, Selig, Essanay, Vitagraph, and Lubin film manufacturing companies—all the major production companies in America except Biograph. Licenses were also issued to two foreign companies, Pathé Frères, the largest film production company in the world at the time, and George Méliès, a company beginning to decline. The licensees acknowledged the validity of Edison's patents and were freed from threats of litigation for past infringement. The licenses allowed them to manufacture films under Edison patents and set a minimum price scale for their sale.[22] Other than a group of marginal manufacturers, Biograph was the only American film company outside the licensees, now known as the "Edison Film Combine." A large number of foreign film companies were also excluded from the Edison scheme.

Acting on its other principal goal, the Edison Film Combine attempted to use its near-monopoly in product (horizontal control) to assert power over the exchanges (vertical control). In 1907 manufacturers had tried to bring some order to distribution through the creation of the United Film Protection

Association, designed to prevent such practices as duping, sub-renting, and the distribution of worn-out prints. However, it had proved impossible for a voluntary organization to enforce such guidelines. At the February 1908 meeting of the United Film Protective Association in Buffalo, the Edison Company blamed "destructive and unbusiness-like competition among the exchanges" for the poor state of the film business.[23]

Its near-monopoly of American films provided the combine with the leverage the Protective Association had lacked. Licenses with the Edison Combine gave the exchanges access to the films produced by combine members, while providing the combine with a means to regulate how distribution was handled. First, the licenses stipulated that exchanges handle *only* films produced by the Edison group, thereby freezing production companies not part of the combine out of the system of distribution. Equally important, submitting to the new regulations was made a condition for obtaining and keeping an exchange license with the combine. The licenses set schedules of minimum rental prices for films and warned that exchanges violating set prices would be dropped. Further, prints had to be returned to manufacturers within a fixed period, removing old, worn prints from circulation. Exchanges licensed by the Edison Combine became known as the Film Service Association.

Although standing nearly alone, Biograph was in a position to defy the Edison Combine, both legally and economically. Besides its legal immunity from Edison's camera patent, Biograph was also a bigger and more firmly established manufacturer than any of the licensees, with the exception of the Vitagraph Company. It found immediate allies in exchanges dissatisfied with the new regulations and importers of foreign films frozen out of the market by Edison, of which George Kleine was the largest and most active. These importers could supply films if Biograph were to mount an all-out offensive.

Economic factors played as important roles as legal ones in Biograph's decision to stay outside the Edison Combine. With the exception of Edison, Biograph was the oldest established domestic film producer. From its inception, the American Mutoscope and Biograph Company had strong links with Wall Street capital. The company had begun with a loan from the New York Security and Trust Company.[24] Terry Ramsaye states that in the early years of the American film industry (circa 1898), Biograph was "the only motion picture enterprise in the world which was directly connected with the great institutions of organized capital and big business."[25]

By 1907 Biograph's major investor appears to have been the Empire Trust.[26] According to Billy Bitzer's memoirs and Ramsaye, the Empire Trust sent J. J. Kennedy to Biograph to oversee its investment in the company, which they felt was on shaky financial grounds.[27] On July 17, 1907, at a meeting of the directors of the Biograph Company, George Van Guysling was removed as general manager, and Kennedy "the president of the [Biograph] company" took over for him.[28] With the advent of Kennedy the investment community exerted a direct influence on Biograph. Although only a decade old, Biograph was no longer a film company controlled primarily by the inventor-mechanics who had founded it. Kennedy demonstrated his managerial ability in orchestrating Biograph's successful resistance of the Edison Combine. With both legal and economic confidence, the Biograph Company prepared to mount a counteroffensive and announced that they would protect exhibitors and exchanges from legal harassment by the Edison Company.

Biograph took the offensive in the patents war. They not only asserted that their camera did not infringe Edison's patents, but also set about acquiring new patents with which to threaten Edison. The key patent of their counteroffensive was known as the "Latham loop," derived from early film devices patented by the Latham family, pioneer film manufacturers and Edison rivals. It consisted of a loop formed by the film as it ran through the apparatus. The loop reduced the strain on the film that was produced by intermittent motion, an irrelevant concern in the period of the very short films from which Edison's patents derived.[29] After their fortunes declined, the Lathams sold the patent claim to the Anthony and Scoville Company.[30] Biograph, and Kennedy in particular, realized the value the patent might have in the conflict with Edison and purchased the patent from Anthony and Scoville (now known as Ansco) on February 9, 1908, five days after refusing to join the Edison licensees.[31]

Biograph also assembled a number of other patents which had important application to projecting machines, to which the Latham loop could also be applied. An agreement with the Armat Company placed on Biograph's side Thomas Armat's patent controlling the use of maltese cross-derived intermittant motion vital to bright and steady projection.[32] The Pross patent for a multibladed shutter which Biograph had obtained in 1903 significantly reduced flicker and gained new significance in this battle of rival patents.[33]

But if Biograph was to offer itself as an alternative to the Edison Combine, the most immediate problem was delivering enough films to the exchanges that would be shut out of the Edison licensees' product. At the beginning of 1908, Biograph was making one film a week, although it soon increased production to two.[34] On February 18, 1908, the Biograph Company entered into an agreement with film importers Williams, Brown, and Earle, Kleine Optical Company, and Charles Dressler and Company, agreeing to buy foreign films through them while licensing the films under its own patents. George Kleine brought with him a host of foreign imports. Biograph also issued licenses to the Great Northern Film Company (the American outlet of the Danish film company, Nordisk) and Society Italian Cines.[35] Counting largely on these foreign films, a Biograph advertisement in February 1908 claimed that the company could supply exhibitors and exchanges with a program of from twelve to twenty reels each week.[36]

In August 1908 *Variety* reported that more theaters were switching to the Biograph service.[37] Exchangemen and exhibitors found the Biograph service attractive for a number of reasons. Many were disturbed by the 60 percent hike Edison had made in rental prices.[38] Edison's change in policy from selling their films to leasing them and demanding their return after a period of time also upset exchangemen, who were concerned about the effect the policy would have on their film reserves. The Biograph Combine still sold their films.[39] In fact, Edison delayed the deadline for return of films until the next year because of objections from exchangemen.[40]

The rival combines maneuvered their claims and counterclaims into court. In 1908 Biograph brought a total of nine suits under the Latham patents and three under the Pross.[41] Edison in turn entered patent suits against Biograph and Kleine under its as-yet untested film patent, including an avalanche of suits against Kleine's exhibitor customers, making a total of forty-six suits.[42] In April 1908, Judge Kohlsaat enforced a halt to Edison's wholesale litigation against independent exhibitors until the suit against Kleine was settled.[43]

The year 1908 saw the first full-scale battle for control and regulation of the American film industry. Film had adopted the methods of American big business of the period, responding to increased demand with a more closely regulated and integrated system. Although Biograph undoubtedly also desired more producer-based regulation, it used exchange and exhibitor dissatisfaction with these innovations as a ploy against Edison. But the positions of Biograph and Edison were compatible. Biograph faced the same problems as the Edison Combine. Victory in the marketplace depended not only on legal processes, but also on producing enough film to match demand, and popular enough to compete with the Edison Combine releases. Newly popular story films had formed the basis of the new demand, and production of such films at an accelerated rate was the company's primary goal. In the middle of trying to put production into high gear, Biograph suddenly encountered a series of problem with directors. Wallace McCutcheon, Sr., who had worked at Biograph some years before, was lured back from Edison but soon became ill. A hasty series of replacements did not work out. The company was probably in near panic when it turned to Griffith, an actor they had employed fairly regularly for the preceding six months, and offered him the position of director.

The Adventures of Dollie (June 18, 19, 1908)[44] immediately reveals Griffith's debt to, and quick mastery of, the visual and narrative forms of films before his debut. The plot was clear and simple. Dollie, a young bourgeois girl, is kidnapped by an evil gypsy. When her father searches the gypsy camp for her, her captor conceals her in a barrel. Later while fording a stream, the barrel providentially falls from the gypsy wagon and floats down stream until it reaches Dollie's home, where she is rescued and returned to her family.

Dollie's story forms a perfect match with Todorov's "minimal complete plot." It provides an archetype for many Griffith Biograph films:the threat to a bourgeois family by an invading alien causes narrative disequilibrium, while narrative closure is achieved by regaining family harmony. Structuring the story through a spatial as well as a narrative circuit, Griffith revealed his debt to genres which appeared with the dawn of the nickelodeon period, the highly spatialized and synthetic forms of the chase and "linked vignettes" that prefigured the move from a cinema of attractions to one of narrative integration. The film creates a coherent geography as it follows Dollie in a circuit away from her home and back. *Dollie's* editing creates a synthetic space by maintaining a line of action progressing continuously through a series of shots; Dollie's odyssey consists of thirteen shots spread over eleven different locations. The narrative logic of the film knits these separate views into a coherent continuous space.

A survey of early cinema's approach to editing and narrative form is needed to understand the structuring spatial role editing plays in Griffith's first film. The cinema of attractions relied primarily on a direct relation to the spectator, rather than on the relation between shots. In fact, a majority of films before 1903 (and a large number until about 1906) consisted of a single shot. Exhibitors could string these short films into thematic groups, but editing played no role in the films themselves.[45] The esthetic of attractions stressed the autonomy of each shot, and even within certain multishot films individual shots still functioned as relatively independent attractions. This is obvious in noncontinuous suites of tableaux such as Biograph's *The Four Seasons* consisting of a series of silhouettes illustrating the seasons of human life, but certain momentary noncontinuous attractions also appear within basically narrativized films, such as the outlaw blasting the audience in *The Great Train Robbery*.

The process of following a continuous action through a series of shots created new relations to the spectator, new approaches to space and time, and a new focus on storytelling. Films based on the physical movement of characters from shot to shot created a synthetic space through freely occurring entrances and exits. Character movement to and from off-screen defines the space appearing on the screen as a metonymic part of a larger whole, a whole so large it can only be presented through several partial views. The edges of the frame therefore are limits easily passed by the characters. When a character exits from a shot, he or she does not disappear into a nebulous "off-stage" space but is likely to reappear immediately in the next shot. Appearing around 1903, this new approach to space formed the basis of the chase-film genre and laid the foundations for the cinema of narrative integration.

The earliest chase films came from England, with Williamson's *Stop Thief* (1900), Mottershaw's *A Daring Daylight Burglary* (1903), and Haggar's *Desperate Poaching Affray* (1903) providing prototypes. The American version of the genre, initially more comic, appeared in 1904 with Biograph's *The Escaped*

Lunatic the first influential example, and *Personal* (1904) the most popular and widely imitated success. From 1904 on, the chase form was one of the staples of international cinema.

Every chase film exploited the permeable barriers of the frame and created, through editing, a synthetic space in which exits from one shot or location were immediately sutured to an entrance in another shot or location. The pattern is consistent: a character is chased by a group of characters from one location to the next. Each shot presents the chased character running at some distance from the pursuing mob. The shot is held until first the pursued, and then the pursuers, exit from the frame. The next shot begins with the entrance of the pursued, and the movement through the frame begins all over again. This action continues through a series of shots until the fleeing character is captured.

Biograph's immensely popular film *Personal* provides a classical example. A French nobleman desiring a wife advertizes in the personal columns for a fianceé, instructing her to meet him at Grant's Tomb. Upon arrival, he encounters nearly a dozen perspective brides desperately seeking a husband. The chase begins, and the nobleman flees over a series of terrains, the women in hot pursuit. Finally the nobleman is seized by the most athletic among them, and the chase ends. This pattern served as a template for scores of films from 1904 to 1908; Griffith, in fact, filmed a comedy chase in 1908, *Balked at the Altar,* that hardly deviated from the established pattern.

Given the simplicity and predictable nature of the story, the chase's enormous popularity is striking. It would seem the form's fascination lay in the spatial continuity it rehearsed, the possibility of stitching together a larger spatial whole from separate shots. This spatial synthesis of separate shots depended on narrative structure. The movement of characters through the frame, exiting, disappearing momentarily, and then reappearing in the next shot, set up a series of well-defined and quickly fulfilled narrative expectations and created a new involvement for the spectator. No longer simply observing the action or directly addressed by an attraction, the spectator now knitted together the space and time of the film following the logic of the narrative. The chase therefore plays a pivotal role in the transition from a cinema of attractions to a cinema organized around storytelling. It provided a model for narrative causality and linearity extending over several shots and established the continuity of space and time that subtended narrative action.[46]

From 1904 to 1908 the chase and related forms were the most commonly encountered narrative genres. After 1907 the simple chase, as found in *Personal,* gave way to a number of related formats which also made use of a synthetic geography linked by continuous action through a series of shots. I have termed one popular variation *linked vignettes.* These films preserve the essential continuity of the chase but substitute a linked series of gags. An

English film, Hepworth's *That Fatal Sneeze* (1907) provides a typical example. The action begins when a man is doused with pepper by a mischievous child. As the victim moves through a series of locales (providing, as in the chase, a trajectory of spatial and temporal continuity), his sneezes trigger a series of disasters. Other films, such as Hepworth's *Rescued by Rover* (1905) used the trajectory of a mobile character to create a synthetic geography within a melodrama, as *Dollie* does, although no actual chase occurs.[47]

Dollie falls into the category of chase-influenced trajectory films. From shot four to shot thirteen (the final shot), we follow Dollie, first being abducted by the gypsy, then floating concealed in a barrel. From shot six on, the barrel and its movement in and out of the frame are the major factors in creating a sense of continuous space. After the barrel falls out of the wagon, the next five shots follow its progress down the stream, with each shot ending as the barrel floats out of the frame. These exits, then reappearances, of the barrel stitch the stream together as a single spatial and narrative entity.[48]

Physical movement in *Dollie* creates a clear narrative spatial-temporal pattern, fairly supplely expressed through the linking of separate shots. But other narratively important sections of the film make no use of editing. The second shot of *Dollie* presents the inciting incident of the story in a single, distantly framed and long-lasting tableau. The shot frames Dollie's estate in a long shot, as Dollie and her mother enter at midground, walk toward the foreground, and sit by the river bank. The gypsy enters from the middle background, moving toward them. He tries to sell them the baskets he carries. The sale is refused, and the gypsy withdraws a bit. Then he rushes toward the mother and tries to steal her purse. At this moment the father enters, rushing from middle background. He fights with, and subdues, the gypsy. Then, gathering his family about him, the father orders him away. The gypsy exits, making threatening gestures.

In the drama of Dollie's abduction and return, the succession of shots seems to follow the unfolding of events, the camera's viewpoint drawn along by the movement of the child. Here, however, the events seem subordinated to a monolithic and unresponsive single viewpoint. Although this narrative sequence contains a series of important incidents, it consists of a single shot. The camera maintains an immobile distance from the action, framing the characters with a great deal of empty space above their heads.

The difference between such a monolithic approach and the synthetic space of the rest of *Dollie* cannot simply be described by Mitry's opposition of theatricality and narrativity. Although the framing of the shot may recall a theatrical treatment of space, its effect does not relate, as Burch points out, to a theatrical experience. The distant tableau, without the actors' voices dramatizing the details or turning points of the story, alienates us from involvement with character or drama. This cinema is truly mute.

The narrative discourse of films before 1908 supplied Griffith with a syn-thetic approach to space and physical movement through editing. However, in scenes such as this which rely on conflict between characters within a single space, this tradition was deficient. Although movement through space could be constructed through editing by a succession of shots, character conflict relied almost entirely on the pro-filmic level of actors' performance. Stock melodramatic gestures (Charles Inslee, the gypsy, makes a gesture indicating a future threat; Arthur Johnson, as the father, stretches out his pointing finger to drive the gypsy off) accent the drama but allow only limited access to characters.

The Adventures of Dollie's narrative discourse is not designed for the psycho-logical development of characters. As in the a-psychological narratives (such as *The Arabian Nights*) analyzed by Tzvetan Todorov, "action is important in itself and not as an indication of this or that character trait."[49] With its stock melodramatic character types and simple moral dualism, *Dollie* deals in action rather than psychology. Camera distance limits access to characters. The small, puppetlike figures are of necessity limited to a series of stock, easily recognizable gestures. Narrative development and closure rely upon a clear pattern of loss and recovery, separation and reunion, abduction and return, easily portrayable in spatial, rather than psychological, terms. The access to characters (Gennette's category of mood) is severely limited. *Dollie*'s editing can follow the course of an action over an extended geography, but Dollie herself is scarcely more of a character than her barrel. Increased access to character separates the cinema of narrative integration from transitional narra-tive genres such as chase films and is one of the cornerstones of the narrator system. In his first film, Griffith showed his ability to supply the easily compre-hensible stories that nickelodeons demanded, but fundamental changes that might have attracted a new audience were lacking.

Years later, Griffith claimed that *The Adventures of Dollie* created a stir among its audiences, with his press agent, Robert Long, intoning in 1920 that "the 'something' contained in the picture *Dollie* was INTELLECT. Naturally the studio rabble did not recognize it; the executives failed to observe it, and how could the exhibitors recognize it? But the public!"[50] Long carefully avoided recounting the story of this "intellectual" film. If *Dollie* did make a stir, no record of it survives. However, Griffith's third film, *The Redman and the Child* (1908) did receive recognition. Significantly this film also shows the first stirrings of the narrator system, as Griffith employed techniques inherited from earlier films to open access to characters. The New York *Dramatic Mirror* called the film "the best Indian film we have yet seen. . . . In many respects it is one of the best handled subjects ever produced by any company," noting that it was held over a second day at the Manhattan Theater, an unusual practice.[51] *Variety* seconded the acclaim, saying the film "compares very favorably with the best material in either the American or European market and makes a decided step forward in the artistic merit and photographic excellence of American films. . . . For solid merit few better motion picture productions have been shown in this city."[52]

Such popularity was essential to Biograph's project to draw exchanges and exhibitors away from the Edison Combine. *The Redman and the Child* owed part of its success to the growing interest in Western and Indian films and the effect its star, Charles Inslee, had on the female audience when he appeared in a loincloth (an appeal on which Inslee managed to found his career after he left Biograph).[53] However, the ability Griffith had already shown in *Dollie* to manage melodramatic action within a continuous geography may also have excited audiences. The New York *Dramatic Mirror* review singled out for praise the fact that "the scenes follow each other consecutively and naturally."[54]

Like *Dollie*, *The Redman and the Child* moves a story based on a pattern of loss and recovery through a continuous geography. Here two objects are recovered—the Indian's gold and his friend, a small white boy, both stolen by evil white men. A climactic canoe chase creates a coherent geography which extends over five shots of the eighteen-shot film. Like the floating barrel sequence of *The Adventures of Dollie,* this sequence creates a synthetic space, linking shots through entrances and exits of the racing canoes. Following the established chase format, in each shot of the chase both Indian and villains appear; no separation of the elements into a parallel edited pattern occurs. However, at points this film pioneers a different approach to character and subjectivity than found in *The Adventures of Dollie.* Although these moments still show Griffith's inheritance from earlier filmmakers, they also show new paths for filmic discourse as they are integrated into a coherent melodramatic narrative.

Redman has a somewhat more complicated structure than *Dollie.* While *Dollie* follows the movement of Dollie herself, *The Redman* divides its narrative focus between the Indian and the child. This allows a less strictly linear editing pattern in which separate actions can occur simultaneously. A cutaway appears in a sequence which also carries a strong indication of character subjectivity. This brief, three-shot sequence is a pivotal point in Griffith's introduction of the narrator system.

While the villains try to force the boy to reveal the hiding place of the Indian's gold, the Indian acts as a guide for some surveyors. Griffith's editing interrelates these actions. We see the surveyors setting up their sighting telescope and encouraging the Indian to look through this white man's wonder (fig. 1). The Indian looks, expresses surprise, then appears alarmed. The next shot is framed by a black circular matte to indicate the Indian's view through the telescope (fig. 2). Within this matte we see the villains force the child to reveal the hiding place of the Indian's gold. They kill an old man who tries

1, 2, and 3: The point-of-view sequence from *The Redman and the Child* (1908), as the Indian (Charles Inslee) sees the old man's murder through the surveyor's telescope.

1

2

3

to help the boy, and then paddle away in their canoe with both gold and child. We then return to the Indian looking through the telescope (fig. 3). He reacts wildly and rushes off.

A *Variety* review described the sequence as follows: "Here a clever bit of trick work is introduced to bring about an intensely dramatic situation . . . immediately the field of the picture contracts to a circle and the scene is brought before the audience as though through the eye of the Indian glued to the telescope."[55] *Variety*'s description of the technique is revealing. Instead of an "invisible" narrative code expressing a character's point of view (as the sequence would probably be understood today), *Variety* describes it as "trick work," relating the technique to the trick-film genre typified by the films of Méliès. As a genre of the cinema of attractions, trick films displayed their devices (magical appearances and disappearance, superimpositions, conflicts of scale, multiple reproduction of images, and primitive traveling mattes) as attractions in their own right, rather than absorbing them as narrative signifiers. The "clever trick work" of such films depended on the fascination technical illusions held for filmmakers and audiences alike, rather than on the creation of a fictional world.

The Indian's look through the telescope captures the process of transition from a cinema of attractions to one of narrative integration. Rather than functioning solely as an attraction, although it still works as such for *Variety*, the "trick" becomes narrativized. The point-of-view shot no longer forms the central attraction of the film but is subordinated to the goals of narrative discourse: it interrelates two lines of narrative action and involves us directly in the Indian's reaction to the child's kidnapping.

The "clever bit of trick work" in the *Redman and the Child* provides a character's point of view. As a device, this, too, is an inheritance rather than an innovation. Griffith drew on another genre of early film, never as widespread or influential as the chase or linked vignettes: the "peeping tom" films, which showed a character looking through some viewing device (telescope, microsope, or simply a keyhole) and then showed, usually framed within an appropriately shaped matte, what he or she saw.[56] Comparison with these earlier point-of-view films reveals a similarity of technique but a difference in narrative form. The point-of-view shots in these films *are* "clever trick work." As Ben Brewster has written of one of the earliest of these films, *Grandma's Reading Glass* produced by G. A. Smith in 1900, "the POV structure is the pleasure point of the film, its attraction" rather than the means to narrative or character development.[57] As examples of the cinema of attractions, these films displayed the subjective view as their raison d'être. Little narrative development was offered other than the act of looking and (sometimes) its consequences. The point-of-view shots provide pure scopic pleasure, often including explicitly erotic material. Griffith, in contrast, harnesses this voyeuristic pleasure to perform a narrative role, providing a reaction to a dramatic incident and motivation for actions to come.

With this three-shot unit which pivots on the point-of-view shot, Griffith moves even further away from the noncontinuous style of a series of loosely linked shots. The narrative interdependence of these three shots goes further than the trajectory-created continuity of the canoe chase in creating a new narrative subordination of shots. Although each shot in the floating barrel sequence of *Dollie* continues an action begun in the previous shot, nonetheless the shots maintain a nearly identical content and emphasis, with almost no hierarchy of importance. In contrast, the point-of-view sequence functions as a multishot unit, with each shot hypotactically subordinated to a significant whole.

The point-of-view sequence in *Redman*, enclosing the spatially and contextually very different point-of-view shot between the shots of the Indian looking and reacting, creates a different sort of narrative unit. The meaning of each shot is dependent on its place within a three-shot editing pattern. The cause of the Indian's alarm in the first shot is revealed by the shot through the telescope. The circular matte in the point-of-view shot is only explained by the look through the telescope. The reason for the Indian rushing off in the last shot is given by what he sees in the shot before. A narrative sandwiching occurs in which none of the shots can be fully understood independently.

This narrative unit is not centered around the physical movement of a character, but around his perception and emotional reaction. The sequence introduces a new spatial freedom to Griffith's narrative discourse. Through an off-screen glance, it fashions a synthetic geography independent of actual character movement from shot to shot (the method used in *Dollie* and the chase sequence of this film). And, in contrast to the second shot of *Dollie*, editing, rather than an actor's gestures alone, gives access to this reaction. Although on the pro-filmic level Inslee's frantic gestures differ only slightly from Johnson's reaction to his daughter's disappearance in *Dollie*, on the level of editing, the reaction is transformed by its division into a series of shots. The spectator discovers the theft of the gold and the abduction of the boy simultaneously with the Indian, viewing it through his eyes. Although the psychology is not complex, the editing conveys the character's motivation. Within Genette's category of mood, Griffith's narrative discourse allows the spectator to share in the character's discovery and reaction. This sequence could be considered the earliest instance of the narrator system in Griffith's work.[58]

The use of point-of-view editing patterns by later filmmakers developed possibilities of characterization only hinted at in this film. But *The Redman and the Child* allows more access to a character than *The Adventures of Dollie*, with its similar narrative. The last shot of the film further develops this. Rather than ending, as *Dollie* does, with the recovery of the child and the completion of the narrative circuit, Griffith supplies a coda. The Indian appears in his canoe, paddling toward the camera with the recovered gold and rescued child. The boy leans back, secure in the Indian's protection, and falls asleep. The Indian smiles and paddles further, moving nearly into close-up. Closer access to character is literalized at the end of *The Redman* by this movement toward the camera, transforming the Indian from the distant figure he has been throughout the film into a character with a recognizable and expressive face.

Shots of calm after narrative resolution reappear in other Griffith Biograph films, as Jay Leyda termed them, "the lyrical postscript." The lyrical postscript performs two principal roles. First, the lack of action contained in the shot emphasizes the closure of the film. Second, the generally closer camera distance to the character(s) in the shots conveys an emotional tone through the character's expression, and later through compositional means. A moment is given over to the spectator's relation to the character, another instance of mood, which the puppetlike figures in *Dollie* were denied.

For audiences in 1908, *The Redman and the Child* may not have appeared radically different from *The Adventures of Dollie*. With their common melodramatic story and coherent spatial discourse, the difference between the two films should not be exaggerated. However the new attention given to access to characters represents more than a single moment of innovation. The new importance of a character's reaction at the turning point of the story shows Griffith's filmmaking responding both to the demands of the nickelodeon audience and to the desire to attract a new middle-class audience which the production companies in 1908 saw as a major goal.

The Greaser's Gauntlet (July 14, 15, 1908), Griffith's seventh film for Biograph, develops the narrator system further, if unevenly, devising a number of ways of providing access to characters through filmic discourse. It also introduces the first extended use of parallel editing in a Griffith film—a syntagma of key importance to the narrator system. Again, the story structure of the film revolves around exchange, then loss and recovery, although less obviously than in *The Adventures of Dollie* or *The Redman and the Child*. The object of loss, a cross embroidered on a Mexican's gauntlet, serves primarily as a symbolic token of his honor and devotion. The film opens with the gift of the gauntlet to Jose (Wilfred Lucas) by his mother.

This is the first shot in a Griffith-directed film that makes strong use of the level of enframed images through pictorial composition. The schema is familiar from landscape painting, two figures posed on a cliff with a vista of a valley beyond them. The composition is not simply visually pleasurable, but is taken up by the symbolic system of the film's story and thoroughly narrativized. The symbolism is clearly readable. The mother sends her son off to make his way in the world; the distant vista represents that possibly dangerous world into which he descends at the end of the shot. The gift of the gauntlet seals his own devotion to the principles his mother has taught him, summarized in the *Biograph Bulletin* for the film as: "to be temperate, honest, and dispassionate; to bear the burden of life's cross with fortitude and patience."[59] The pictorial quality of the shot underscores the allegorical nature of this departure from home.

However, if the opening shot shows a strong use of the enframed image to create narrative meanings, the next shot returns to the more neutral and monolithic space familiar from the second shot of *The Adventures of Dollie*. The shot presents a barroom set framed in long-shot showing the full extent of the set and the bustle of many extras. Here filmic discourse does not articulate narrative events, and pro-filmic elements of performance carry the story. Without dialogue, the dramatic events of the scene remain obscure. The space is broad and expansive; nothing guides attention to the most important events. Such composition, in which a number of events compete for the spectator's attention without filmic discourse establishing a hierarchy of importance, appears frequently in early cinema. It marks one of its strongest deviations from the later classical style of story-based decoupage. As Paul Hammond describes Méliès's composition, "The eye must follow, it does not lead. Since the camera maintains a rigorously discreet distance from events it does not choose for you. In a way the eye is left to make up its own mind."[60] The problem is that the eye could make the wrong choice from the point of view of following the story line. For the less narrativized style of Méliès, this was not necessarily a flaw. However in Griffith's filmmaking, with increased emphasis on characters and their motivations, it posed a serious problem.

Several narratively important actions happen in this barroom shot. The heroine, Mildred (Marion Leonard), is introduced and encounters Jose. They show a mutual interest. However, the distant camera position cannot stress the moment. During this crucial meeting only the gestures of the actors draw our attention, competing with the cowboys playing cards on the left, or the Chinese waiter (George Gebhardt) scurrying about. This lack of a clear dramatic hierarchy within the shot becomes a problem during the key action of the shot: the Chinese waiter picks a cowboy's pocket and plants a bandanna which had contained the money on Jose. Other than the actors' frantic gestures, nothing cues the audience that the Chinese waiter, previously an incidental character, has become the center of the drama. Present-day audiences frequently miss this essential action, which nothing in the filmic discourse (such as a cut to a closer shot isolating the theft) emphasizes. Through the lack of compositional hierarchy the film risks illegibility. Jose exits from the barroom just before the cowboy discovers his loss, and he becomes swallowed by unimaged off-screen space. This disappearance of a major character from the screen is another indication of the nonresponsive, tableaulike nature of the shot. The waiter points an accusing finger off-screen, and Jose is dragged back onto the set. The bandanna is found on him, and the crowd decides to lynch him.

The next shot reveals the area outside the bar and follows the movement of the lynch mob dragging Jose from the bar. With this action we move into the synthetic, linked space of several shots following character movement—familiar from Dollie and the canoe chase of Redman. But instead of simply following the progress of the lynch mob, the next shot switchs to another thread of the story. The waiter, the true villain, lurks in the hotel corridor counting his stolen money. In the following sequence Griffith employs an extended parallel-edited syntagm for the first time in his career.

Although parallel editing plays a key role in the narrator system it was not a Griffith innovation, but another inheritance. However this inheritance is a more recent one, closely tied to the emerging cinema of narrative integration.[61] A survey of existing films up to The Adventures of Dollie shows very few instances of a clear parallel editing structure. The earliest examples date from 1906 (such as Vitagraph's The Hundred to One Shot, which contains a brief parallel-edited rush to the rescue climax), and later examples can be found in Vitagraph and Pathé films from 1907 and 1908, such as Je vais chercher le *pain* (Pathé, 1907) or *Get Me a Step Ladder* (Vitagraph, 1908).[62] In both comedies and melodramas, the early uses of parallel editing showed the movement toward narratively intergrated space and time that Griffith was to develop systematically.

Parallel editing appeared independently of—and, in a sense in opposition to—the chase film. During this period the chase format, which in later years formed a locus classicus of parallel editing, almost never deviated from a strict linearity of action. Pursuers and pursued were shown together, moving through each shot, never separated by the editing pattern. Although the chase format stretched a narrative action over a number of shots, it maintained a strict homology between the continuity of the action portrayed and the linearity of its portrayal. With parallel editing, the narrator system asserts itself through a divergence between action and its portrayal, between story and discourse. By breaking the continuous line of action found in the chase format, parallel editing asserts control over the ordering of the film's signifiers, creating new relations to the spectator in the categories of tense and voice.

The cut from the lynch mob to the Chinese waiter in the corridor not only joins two threads of the story, but also creates a suspenseful effect in the category of tense (meanwhile, the true villain, . . .) by suspending the resolution of the lynching attempt. As the sequence continues, cutting from Mildred as she learns the truth to Jose at the mercy of the lynch mob, the spectator must interrelate the two lines of action, retaining the action of one line (e.g., Mildred's gathering evidence) while anticipating another (the lynch party's progress). This interpolates the spectator into the unfolding of the action in a more complex way than the knitting together of separate spaces found in chase films. Parallel editing represents a dialectical leap in the portrayal of space and time in early film. The physical movement of character is no longer needed to unify space. As Joyce Jesionowski puts it, these first uses of parallel editing brings an end to the "tyranny of physical activity in Griffith's first films."[63] Rather than simply following the course of the action, filmic discourse intervenes, both dividing and uniting space through editing. As it plays with the spectator's expectations by delaying their fulfillment slightly, parallel editing creates a suspenseful relation to the unfolding narrative. The importance of the control of tense will be discussed in chapter 4 in relation to Griffith's *The Fatal Hour*.

At the same time, within the category of voice, this transition functions as what I will term a *contrast edit*, articulating a moral judgment through a thematic opposition between two situations or characters. Griffith contrasts Jose, the persecuted innocent, with the villain savoring his ill-gotten gains. The moral dualism of the melodramatic plot is articulated by the form of the film. Such moral judgments result form Griffith's parallel editing almost as frequently as does suspense. Although only hinted at here, the control of voice allows Griffith to explore narrative forms with a striking degree of abstraction.

The parallel editing sequence continues to develop the lynching attempt suspensefully for the next five shots. The lynch mob drags Jose down the street past some drunken revelers who scorn him. Griffith then cuts to the hotel corridor, where Mildred discovers the Chinese waiter with his loot. With proof of Jose's innocence, she rushes out to save him. The next shot follows Mildred as she rushes from the inn. Griffith then switches to the hanging tree as the mob arrives and tosses a rope over its branch. A noose is placed around Jose's neck. This action is interrupted by a return to Mildred rushing down the street to prevent the lynching.

A spatial articulation of another sort occurs over the next two shots. First we see the hanging tree and lynch mob in long shot. The camera is quite distant from the action, presenting the full height of the tree, leaving space above the heads of the standing figures beneath it. Jose is strung up and dangles from a branch for a moment, as Mildred rushes in with proof of his innocence. Jose is lowered, and the mob breaks up. Freed from the rope, he moves toward Mildred. After this dramatic climax, the filmic discourse takes an unusual turn. We cut in to a shot which frames Jose and Mildred beneath the tree, but from a much closer camera position (fig 4). The full figures of the actors appear in this shot, from head to toe. They are framed slightly above their heads, eliminating the expansive overhead space present in the previous shot and most of the film.

This cut-in creates a spatial relation between shots that had not appeared in any of Griffith's films to this point. Rather than presenting an entirely new space, the closer shot enlarges a part of a space already established. In contrast to the earlier monolithic and neutral presentation of the bar scene, the camera seems to respond to the action within the frame, moving closer to emphasize it.

This editing technique of cutting in to a closer view of a previous shot— a cut-in—is again not a Griffith invention. G. A. Smith pioneered it in *The Little Doctor* (1901) and *Mary Jane's Mishap* (1903). It is found, if not frequently, in American films before Griffith as well, such as Edison's *The Gay Shoe Clerk* (1903) and *The Strenuous Life* (1904) as well as Biograph's *The Lost Child* (1904) and *The Silver Wedding* (1906).[64] However in many of these films the cut-in functions as a scarcely narrativized attraction, an enlargement of a cute kitten (*The Little Doctor*), the grotesque facial expressions of a scullery maid (*Mary Jane's Mishap*), or an erotic glimpse of a lady's ankle (*The Gay Shoe Clerk*) rather than a detail essential to the story.

In almost all cases, Griffith's cut-ins are fully narrativized and essential to the story, again showing his transformation of devices introduced by the

4. The cut-in to a closer view of Mildred (Marion Leonard) and Jose (Wilfred Lucas) before the hanging tree in *The Greaser's Gauntlet* (1908). Frame enlargements from prints made from Paper Print Collection, Library of Congress.

cinema of attractions. In this sequence the cut-in aids narrative clarity by enlarging a detail important in story development but small in the frame. As Jose thanks Mildred, he gives her the embroidered gauntlet he received from his mother in the first shot. The closer camera position helps make this visible. The gauntlet is a small enough object that its exchange might pass unnoticed in the wide-angle view of the preceding shot.

The cut-in also has other effects. The shot marks an important structural moment in the unfolding of the film. The repeated exchanges of the gauntlet chart the key actions of the story. The film opens with the mother giving the gauntlet to Jose, moves to its gift to Mildred (shown in this shot), who toward the end returns it to Jose. The film closes with Jose returning the gauntlet to his mother. More than a series of incidents, these acts of exchange form a narrative armature, with the transfer acting as their center. This exchange between Mildred and Jose also carries emotional overtones of gratitude, unspoken love, and devotion which effect later narrative development. The cut-in brings us closer to the human figures at an emotional moment.[65] Like the lyrical postscript to *The Redman and the Child*, it transforms the actors from distant figures to recognizable characters with visible faces and expressions. Again, access to characters provides a powerful motivation for the introduction of elements of the narrator system.

However the use of the cut-in in *The Greaser's Gauntlet* is far from consistent. The theft of the money in the barroom could have been made the center of our attention by a similar use of a cut-in, rendering a potentially obscure scene clear. The climax of the film likewise takes place in a single distant long shot. Jose has become a barroom drunkard and is hired to help abduct a woman. After the kidnapping Jose discovers his gauntlet, and realizes his victim is Mildred. This recognition is not articulated by a cut-in, but is presented in one theatrically blocked shot. Certainly most of the motivations that lie behind the cut-in at the hanging tree are present here, but the scene is treated monolithically.

These first films represent a transition between approaches to narrative discourse in film. As transitional, they manifest a mixture of styles. Far from a natural evolution to the essential language of narrative cinema, these films formulate an approach to filmic discourse which could express more complex stories based in character psychology as well as action. By 1917, cut-ins formed the basis of the decoupage of scenic space, an essential part of the classical style. Although cut-ins appear in other Biograph films from 1908 and 1909, they were never used as frequently as parallel editing, which became the linch-pin of the narrator system.[66]

The film's last shot continues Griffith's expression of narrative resolution through imagery. The shot basically recreates the composition of the first shot, as though Jose's mother has not moved from the edge of the hill. Her fixed position seems less a naiveté on the part of the filmmaker than a conscious attempt to make her a timeless, nearly allegorical figure of waiting motherhood. Jose mounts the hill he descended years before and is enfolded in his mother's arms. The similarity of the two shots encapsulates the film in a circular structure that Griffith employed in a number of Biograph films. The pair of shots sets up a series of contrasts: Jose's fancy new outfit as he left in the first shot compared to the dirty, ragged clothing he wears on his return; his descent into the world at the opening contrasted to his ascent from it here. The ascent visualizes Jose's moral conversion, marked by regaining the gauntlet his mother had given him. The final shot weaves the themes of the film into the closed circle of a morality tale.

The Greaser's Gauntlet contains the outlines of the narrator system. Working on all levels of filmic discourse, Griffith bent them to narrative tasks within the categories of tense, mood, and voice. The ability to both develop characters and comment on their actions allowed him to fashion narratives that departed from the patterns of previous Biograph nickelodeon fare. *The Greaser's Gauntlet* points towards the sort of films Biograph would offer as evidence that they were uplifting the film industry. Parallel editing to build suspense and contrast, cutting-in to articulate the drama and create empathy with characters, and the allegorical structuring of images became cornerstones of the narrator system.

Notes

1. If the first day of shooting on *Dollie*, June 18, 1908, indicates the date on which Griffith took over directing duties at Biograph, questions could be raised about the status of films such as *The Black Viper*, which began shooting on June 6 but then resumed shooting on June 22. Was this film finished by Griffith but started by another director? Did the work of other directors overlap with Griffith's debut at Biograph? Or did Griffith perhaps actually start directing with some other films before *Dollie* ? Sources that allow us to settle these questions are unavailable. But despite this historical haziness about precisely when Griffith took complete control of directing at Biograph, it is clear that *Dollie* was the first film that he acknowledged.

2. AM&B Co., letter reproduced in Kemp Niver, comp., *The Biograph Bulletins 1890–1908*, ed. Bebe Bergsten (Los Angeles: Locare Research Group, 1971), pp. 55–56.

3. Niver, *Biograph Bulletins*, p. 59.

4. Jacques Deslandes and Jacques Richard have studied in detail this phenomenon in France in *Histoire comparée du cinéma*, vol. 2: *Du cinématographe au cinéma, 1896–1906* (Paris: Casterman, 1968), but research is needed in the United States. Charles Musser's *High Class Motion Pictures: Lyman H. Howe and the Traveling Exhibitor* (Princeton: Princeton University Press, 1990) fills an important gap.

5. Charles Musser, "The Nickelodeon Era Begins: Establishing the Framework for Hollywood's Mode of Representation," *Framework* 22–23 (Autumn 1983): 4.

6. Musser, "Nickelodeon," p. 4.

7. Ibid.

8. *Billboard*, March 16, 1907, p. 32.

9. Robert Jack Anderson, "The Motion Picture Patents Company," Ph.D. diss., University of Wisconsin-Madison, 1983, p. 70.

10. *Moving Picture World*, Feb. 29, 1908, p. 158.

11. Thomas C. Cochrane and William Miller, *The Age of Enterprise: A Social History of Industrial America*, rev. ed. (New York: Harper and Row, 1961), p. 141; Janet Staiger, "Combination and Litigation: Structures of U.S. Film Distribution, 1896–1917," *Cinema Journal* 23 (Winter 1983): 42–43.

12. M. B. Philips and Francis T. Howe, "Memorandum for the MPPC and General Film Co. Concerning the Investigation of Their Business by the Department of Justice," p. 7, Museum of Modern Art Film Library; New York City. A summary of this early decade of litigation can be found in Staiger, "Combination," pp. 45–46, and Anderson, "The Motion Picture Patents Company," pp. 57–66.

13. Gordon Hendricks, *Beginnings of the Biograph* (New York: Beginnings of American Film, 1964), passim.

14. Philips and Howe, "Memorandum," p. 8

15. Ibid.

16. Lacombe decision reproduced in *Moving Picture World*, March 16, 1907, p. 22.

17. Ibid., March 16, 1907, p. 23.

18. Ibid.

19. Decision reprinted in *United States v. Motion Picture Patents Company*, 225 F. 800 (E.D. Pa., 1915), Record, pp. 1617, 1618; hereafter cited as *U.S. v. MPPC*.

20. Philips and Howe, "Memorandum," p. 11.

21. *U.S. v. MPPC*, p. 1561.

22. Volume of legal agreements entitled "Property of Motion Picture Patents Company," pp. 12–28, 64, Museum of Modern Art Film Library, New York City.

23. *Moving Picture World*, Feb. 29, 1908, p. 158.

24. Hendricks, *Beginnings*, p. 30.

25. Terry Ramsaye, *A Million and One Nights: A History of the Motion Picture* (1926, repr. London: Frank Cass, 1964), p. 383.

26. Unfortunately, after the Empire Trust's merger with the Bank of New York, its records were not preserved. Apparently documents from which to write a financial history of the Biograph Company and its investors do not exist.

27. Billy Bitzer, *His Story: The Autobiography of D. W. Griffith's Master Cameraman* (New York: Farrar Straus and Giroux, 1973), pp. 51–52; Ramsaye, *A Million and One Nights*, pp. 468–469.

28. *Moving Picture World*, July 27, 1907, p. 327.

29. *U.S. v. MPPC*, p. 3395.

30. Ibid., p. 2065.

31. Ibid., p. 2066.

32. "Property of Motion Picture Patents Company" file, p. 41.

33. *U.S. v. MPPC*, p. 184, addendum unnumbered in vol. 6.

34. New York *Clipper*, May 30, 1908, p. 400.

35. *Variety*, Aug. 15, 1908, p. 11.

36. *Billboard*, Feb. 29, 1908, p. 21.

37. *Variety*, Aug. 1, 1908, p. 13.

38. Ibid., Feb. 29, 1908, p. 11.

39. *Moving Picture World*, March 14, 1908, p. 211.

40. *Variety*, Oct. 3, 1908 p. 11.

41. *Film Index*, March 21, 1908, p. 3; *New York Dramatic Mirror*, June 6, 1908, p. 6.; *Moving Picture World*, Feb. 29, 1908, p. 155.

42. "Property of Motion Picture Patents Company" file, pp. 12–15.

43. *U.S. v. MPPC*, p. 2546.

44. All dates given after film titles refer to the dates of their filming as indicated in the Cameraman's Book in the D. W. Griffith Papers, Museum of Modern Art Film Library, New York City.

45. An exception to this lack of editing in pre-1903 films would be the "substitution splices" used in combination with stop motion to produce trick effects. However such editing did not involve an articulation of spatial or temporal relations, but rather maintained the appearance of a single shot. See Tom Gunning, " 'Primitive' Cinema— a Frame-up? or The Trick's on Us," *Cinema Journal* 28 (Winter 1988–89): 3–12.

46. See, for example, Noel Burch's discussion of the chase in "Passion, poursuite: La Linearisation," *Communication* 38 (1983): 33–37.

47. With its drama of gypsy kidnapping and rescue of a lost child, *Rescued by Rover* also provides close story parallels to *Dollie*, as do the earlier American chase films, *The Lost Child* (Biograph, 1904) and *Stolen by Gypsies* (Edison, 1905).

48. The late Michel Colin's "Coreferences dans *The Adventures of Dollie,*" in *D. W. Griffith: Etudes sous la direction de Jean Mottet* (Paris: L'Harmattan, 1984), pp. 273–82, deals interestingly with this aspect.

49. Tzvetan Todorov, "Narrative-Men," in *The Poetics of Prose*, trans. Richard Howard (Ithaca: Cornell University Press, 1977), p. 67.

50. Robert Long, *David Wark Griffith: A Brief Sketch of His Career* (New York: D. W. Griffith Services, 1920), p. 47.

51. New York *Dramatic Mirror*, Aug. 8, 1908, p. 7.

52. *Variety*, Aug. 1, 1908, p. 13.

53. Fred Balshofer and Arthur Miller, *One Reel a Week* (Berkeley: University of California Press, 1967), p. 28.

54. New York *Dramatic Mirror*, Aug. 9, 1908, p. 7.

55. *Variety*, Aug. 1, 1908, p. 13.

56. For a wide-ranging consideration of the role of point of view in films before Griffith, see the anthology of essays *Ce Que je vois de mon ciné*, ed. André Gaudreault (Paris: Meridiens Klincksieck, 1988), which also contains a shot-by-shot analysis of fourteen early point-of-view films. In my essay in the volume, "What I Saw from the Rear Window of the Hotel des Folies-Dramatiques or the Story POV Films Told," I try to differentiate early point-of-view films from the classical use of the device.

57. Ben Brewster, "A Scene at the Movies," *Screen* 23 (August 1982): 4–15.

58. Performing an important role in the transition to a cinema of character based narratives, such point-of-view shots appeared within rather complex (even if confused) narrative films shortly before Griffith, such as Porter's *The Trainer's Daughter, or A Race for Life* from November 1907, as well as Vitagraph's *Hundred to One Shot* (1906).

Griffith was a pioneer in the move toward character-based narrative integration but not the only, nor the earliest, one. Earlier films show anticipations of devices Griffith used and even of their narrativization. However neither of the films use the point of view to motivate a major character action as clearly as does The Redman and the Child.

59. Eileen Bowser, ed., Biograph Bulletins, 1908–1912 (New York: Farrar Straus and Giroux, 1973), p. 9.

60. Paul Hammond, "George, This Is Charles," Afterlmage 8/9 (Winter 1980–81): 46. Kristin Thompson makes a similar point in David Bordwell, Janet Staiger, and Kristin Thompson, The Classical Hollywood Cinema: Film Style and Mode of Production to 1960 (New York: Columbia University Press, 1985), p. 175. She states that "Primitive framing and action did not always aid intelligibility," citing Biograph's 1905 film Tom, Tom, the Piper's Son.

61. Georges Sadoul believed that parallel editing could be found as early as 1901 in Williamson's Attack on a Chinese Mission, Histoire general du cinéma, vol. 2: Les pionniers du cinéma 1897–1909 (Paris: Denoel, 1951), pp. 165–66. However, this was based on a catalog description of the film, and Jean Mitry has acknowledged that even in reconstruction Attack on a Chinese Mission could not be considered as truly containing parallel editing. The cut away to rescuing bluecoats does not cut to a distant location, nor to another line of action, Jean Mitry, "Les Mesadventures d'un pompier," Cinématographe, no. 74 (Jan. 1982): 63–64. The other frequently cited early instance of parallel editing, the return to the stationmaster in shot ten of Porter's The Great Train Robbery (1903) is an isolated shot (like the cutaway to the kidnapping in The Redman and the Child), rather than part of a series of parallel edited shots as in The Greaser's Gauntlet.

62. See Barry Salt's discussion of early parallel editing in Film Style and Technology: History and Analysis (London: Starword, 1983), pp. 67, 111.

63. Joyce E. Jesionowski, Thinking in Pictures: Dramatic Structure in D. W. Griffith's Biograph Films (Berkeley: University of California Press, 1987), p. 63.

64. Again, see Salt's discussion of early scene dissection in Film Style, pp. 60–63, 122–24.

65. Jesionowski points out that the emphasis on the characters in this medium long shot expresses "the human content" of the shot rather than the purely "informational detail" that a closeup of the gauntlet might carry. Thinking in Pictures, p. 40.

66. Discussion of this issue and related ones can be found in Noel Burch, "Passion, poursuite: la linearisation," Communication 38 (1983): esp. 36–44.

4

Film Form for a New Audience: Time, the Narrator's Voice, and Character Psychology

T HE NICKELODEON revolution, flooding the United States with thousands of film theaters at an unparalleled cheap price, transformed film into a mass art form in two senses.[1] First, as a means of mechanical reproduction that can be duplicated nearly endlessly, film realized its mass potential through enormous expansion in exhibition outlets and viewing audiences. The number of prints sold of each film increased a great deal from 1904 to 1906, supplemented by the practice, so decried by producers, of duping films.[2] And with an influx of a new class of spectators unable to afford most of the other amusements offered during the period, the nickelodeon became a form of entertainment whose audiences were the masses themselves, the "theater of the working man."

In 1908, according to *Moving Picture World*, there were 8,626 motion picture theaters in the United States. The New York *Dramatic Mirror* placed the number at six thousand.[3] Nickelodeons saw their greatest expansion in urban areas; according to *Variety* there were three hundred bona fide film shows in New York City, six hundred if penny arcades were included.[4]

The large number of theaters must be balanced by the fact that seating capacity in many of them was quite low, including small "store shows," converted storefronts sometimes seating fewer than a hundred. Nonetheless, the number of theaters remains striking, the result of a boom that began in 1904–5 and peaked in 1909. By 1906, it had reached such proportions that one commentator termed it "nickel madness."[5] The masses that flocked to nickelodeons created remarkable profits; as one theater owner said, "if there was ever a get rich scheme, and a legitimate one at that, the 5 cents theater was *the* one."[6]

Moving Picture World provides the following breakdown of the expenses involved in running a nickelodeon:

> Rent: $100–$400 a month
> Decoration and seats: $3,500
> Projector: $175–200
> Minimum rental for daily change of films: $34/wkly
> Projectionist: $9–21/wkly
> Singer: $10–18/wk
> Pianists: $4–12/wk[7]

This accounting can be compared to the weekly expense of $6,000 for a typical "big time" vaudeville house in 1907.[8] The relatively small outlay of capital required for opening a nickel theater allowed immigrants and workers to enter the exhibition field, many directly from working-class jobs.[9] This meant that not only audiences, but also theater managers were frequently working class.

Moving Picture World's budget sketches the typical nickel theater of 1908. The expense for seats and "decorations" indicates something a bit more elaborate than a "store show." Like most film theaters it offered "illustrated songs," tunes sung to the illustration of the lyrics by a series of lantern slides. The "song slide" was an important side attraction to motion picture shows, and few theaters did without them. The price given for film rental reflects the almost universal policy of the "daily change." Films were rented and sold on the basis of their novelty, so it was almost unheard of in 1908 for a film to be shown at a theater for more than one day. This explains the large demand for film and why the Biograph combine had to guarantee exhibitors from twelve to twenty reels a week. The rental price indicates a small number of films in each program, probably not more than two.

A program of two films and an illustrated song was typical, and would last well under an hour. In urban areas film shows were continuous, beginning around noon, so a large number of programs could be squeezed into one day. The nickelodeon program, with several unrelated films and an illustrated song followed the "variety" format, a form of popular scenography institutionalized by the vaudeville program. A modular approach to an evening's entertainment, the variety format presented a "specialized, fragmented format with each performer or act working autonomously."[10] As Brooks MacNamara points out, the structure was not based on transfer of information from one act to the next and had no need of plot or theme.[11] The nickelodeon manager saw his program more as a cheaper mechanically reproduced vaudeville show than as an extended dramatic performance with unified plot and action.

The new nickelodeon audience was part of a broader transformation in American entertainment, the commercialization of the newly won leisure time of the working class. The early twentieth century saw an increase in both the time and money that workers had available to spend on non-necessities. Wages had risen steadily since the Civil War, and working hours had plummeted. By 1910, the average nonagricultural work week had reached 50.3 hours.[12] While time and money certainly remained limited in comparison to the other classes, the efforts of unionization and the demand for "eight hours for what we will" created an new aspect to working-class life, which small-time capitalists were quick to exploit.[13] These entrepreneurs offered turn-of-the-century America a mass of new entertainments: dance halls, roller rinks, competitive sports, chains of vaudeville and burlesque theaters, and amusement parks typified by New York's Coney Island.[14] "Amusing the million" had become big business.

With its comparatively short running time and cheap admission price, film was particularly attractive to the workers whose supply of time and money was limited. Big-time vaudeville tickets were generally beyond the family budget, and most rides at Coney Island were a dime, so an evening's entertainment plus trolley fare there could also be expensive.[15] The nickelodeon's low admission (the price of one beer) was emblazoned in its name. The film program also adapted well to working-class life-styles and values. Its short program and continuous shows meant one could drop in on the movies and stay as long or as briefly as one liked. As the social historian Roy Rosenzweig has pointed out, the nickel bought a seat anywhere in the house, the nickleo-deon's democratic seating plan sharply contrasting with vaudeville's hierarchy of expensive and cheap seats. The variety format allowed socializing between films (as the projectionist changed reels), and the illustrated song fostered communal participation.[16]

The film industry fully realized that its particular audience was comprised of the working class. In an interview in 1908, Edison himself proclaimed film "the entertainment of the working man." The trade paper *Variety* also referred to film as "the amusement of the poor."[17] There is evidence, however, that some middle-class spectators did attend nickelodeons. The continuous show policies of urban nickelodeons and their frequent location in shopping areas indicate an audience that had leisure time during regular working hours. These were the patrons, predominantly women and children, to whom Edison felt the film industry should cater.[18] The convergence of different age groups and both sexes created one of the most heterogeneous audiences of the period.

While many of the new entertainment venues at the turn of the century—such as prizefights and burlesque shows—still related to the male bastions of the "sporting world," film very early formed a relation to female and family audiences. As the social historian Kathy Peiss has noted, everyone went to the movies. Using Peiss's terms, the nickleodeon represented a "hetero-social" environment which mixed genders, in contrast to the "homosocial" world of the saloon, the traditional realm of worker's leisure, which in effect excluded women.[19] Whereas the cinema of attractions had often made use of traditionally male-oriented subject-matter (prizefights and risque comedies), the rise of the story film coincided with a broadening out to a more family-centered audience.

If the audience for motion pictures in 1908 was primarily working class, another potential audience also exerted pressure on the film industry. Behind the economic organization of the Edison Combine stands a phantom audience, the middle class that attended vaudeville and other more expensive amusements. As Russell Merritt puts it, "The blue collar worker and his family may have supported the nickelodeon. The scandal was that no one connected with the movies much wanted his support."[20] These middle-class aspirations shaped the policies of the film industry in 1908, and influenced the narrative form of Griffith's films.

The desire for a higher-class audience also transformed the management of film theaters. Ambitious theater owners paid more attention to the attractiveness of their theaters and to proper ventilation.[21] But the key issue was price. The nickel from which nickelodeons drew their name was still the general price of admission in 1908. However, *Moving Picture World* pleaded for a 10 cent or even 20 cent admission policy, attacking the 5 cent theater as "a cross between Chinese theater and a dime museum."[22] The New York *Dramatic Mirror* reported that the "better houses" were already charging 10 cents. A rise in admission price was seen by many promoters of the "uplift" of motion pictures as a step up in class.[23]

However, the uncertain focus exhibitors had on a middle-class audience is exemplified by *Billboard*'s praise for an exhibitor who promoted a film based on the then-current Gobel trial, with men dressed as prison guards parading in front of the theater. *Billboard* recommended other exhibitors try such "refined ballyhoe."[24] This oxymoron embodies the double vision of the film industry in 1908. Still derived from fairgrounds and cheap urban amusements, the industry was rooted in a tradition of ungenteel showmanship. But from heads of production companies to the exhibitors, the film business also desired the blessing of the middle class—and the social respectability and financial security this would imply. Film exhibitors still felt a need for fairground "ballyhoe," but increasingly desired the refinement of middle-class patronage.

Although trade journals optimistically declared that films were attracting "a higher order of the public than formerly,"[25] it was clearly an uphill fight. In 1908 many of the bourgeois were upset and alarmed by film. Part of this alarm focused on safety. In January 1908, a fire at a projection in Boyerstown, Pennsylvania, killed 169 people.[26] After the disaster, the New York *Herald* attacked motion pictures as a hazard to the public. Concern over safety seemed to mask a more general moral and social uneasiness. As Robert Sklar has pointed out, the movies represented a working-class pasttime that had appeared without the control—or even the knowledge—of the middle-class guardians of culture.[28]

Filmmakers and exhibitors knew they would have to calm such anxieties to win middle-class support. The traditional route taken by purveyors of American popular art to avert middle-class disapproval was to claim that their entertainment was educational and morally uplifting. John F. Kasson claims the appearance of a mass audience discarded this rationalization of entertainment with the popularity of such purely hedonistic phenomena as ragtime, prizefighting, competitive athletics, and amusement parks.[29] Film participates in this movement away from the genteel culture of the Victorian era, but the film industry was as uneasy with this identity as it was with its working-class audience. Industry defenders began to proclaim film as an educational medium, conforming to reformers' views that working-class leisure should consist of informative and uplifting experiences.[30]

The desire for middle-class respectability, which arose soon after the first crest of the nickelodeon explosion, ultimately provoked the narrative discourse of film. Were films actually capable of aspiring to the cultural role of respectable narrative arts? A culturally respected figure like David Belasco was still of the opinion in 1908 that film shows were a passing novelty. According to the great promoter of the star system on the Broadway stage, films lacked the individuality and personal magnetism of the theater. Film did not have the stage's sense of presence and reality, since, Belasco claimed, "the audience would always be conscious that it was witnessing a mechanically produced illusion, and there would be wholly wanting that indescribable bond of sympathy between the actor and his audience. . . ."[31]

For Belasco, film lacked the power of the actor's presence and characterization. *The Adventures of Dollie* certainly exemplifies this criticism, while *The Redman and the Child* struggles to create filmic equivalents for the "bond of sympathy" occurring on the stage. The techniques of the narrator system responded to the industry's desire to attract a new audience through a narrative discourse that could supply the ideological and psychological values the middle class expected.

However, the formulation of a new audience for film was not limited to middle-class aspirations. While on the one hand the narrator system can be understood as an essential move in the American film industry becoming acceptable to the bourgeoisie, Griffith's films expose a web of social transformations that belie any simple dismissal of them as ideological manipulation. The strategy and vocabulary of reform adopted by the American entertainment industry represent a defense against, as much as an alliance with, middle-class reform of working-class pastimes. A new mass audience was being forged, an audience of all classes, acceptable to the middle class but maintaining its hold on the working class. Concern with middle-class taste and a family audience was a widespread phenomenon in popular entertainment at the turn of the century, as evident in the cleaning up of Coney Island and similar amusement centers,[32] but entrepreneurs were also careful not to alienate working-class patrons. The rhetoric of the "uplift" movement was partly designed to reassure reformers that film's affect on its working-class audience was educational, inculcating the audience with middle-class culture. But a movement in another direction also asserted itself.

By overcoming middle-class objections to entertainment, the industry was also transforming certain elements of the Victorian culture whose approval it sought. As the social historians Kasson, Peiss, Rosenzweig, and Lary May have shown, the embrace of the movies by the middle class was part of a new acceptance of leisure pleasure. Catering to the middle class by claiming traditional cultural values, the movies also seduced them with a new sensation of pleasure. The action-based and sentimental narratives of early story films were a very different experience from the less narrativized and more obviously educational actualities that had pleased middle-class audiences on the first vaudeville bills.[33] Griffith's film melodramas show a new control of narrative discourse, but without sacrificing excitement and sensation. The thrills of the cinema of attractions were transmuted into family dramas, and the ballyhoo of the fairground was refined into the suspenseful resolutions of parallel editing. Griffith's films preserved a hedonistic experience, providing thrills that middle-class audiences learned to accept and desire.

But before being seduced by pleasure, middle-class viewers had to be sufficiently reassured to enter a nickelodeon. Film's narrative role had to replace its role as fairground novelty. Objections such as Belasco's had to be addressed, particularly the lack of detailed characterization to which it seemed the absence of sound condemned film, and which Belasco saw as the sign of a passing attraction. Placed alongside the socially respectable forms of narrative which it wished to emulate, the film industry perceived itself as deficient, lacking precisely those qualities which would allow it to tell stories based in characterization as well as physical action.

An anxiety that film needed some sort of supplement may explain the numerous aids exhibitors and production companies used to make the dramatic illusion of their mute spectacles more complete by supplying it with a voice. A variety of possibilities were explored, ranging from exhibitors who employed actors to speak dialogue from behind the screen, to films specially produced for exhibition with sound devices.[34] Sound with film devices had been experimented with since the beginning of film exhibition, but in 1908 their potential to attract a new audience and convey more complex stories was of interest.

George K. Spoor of Essanay announced his production company's intention to film an entire play with a new sound mechanism.[35] Henry Marvin of the

Biograph Company claimed talking pictures would bring in a new clientele, "an intelligent one, capable of supporting a house for which an adequate charge of admission is made in proportion to the cost of production."[36] Spoor's desire to film an entire play also aimed beyond the simple attraction of sound with picture, desiring to bring in the audience which attended the legitimate theater.[37]

But the most strongly recommended and widely employed means of providing the motion pictures with a voice was the film lecturer. This almost forgotten aspect of the early film show exemplified the crisis in narrative form and social acceptance film was undergoing in 1908–9. Growing out of the tradition of the magic lantern lecturer, who survived in some theaters as one element of the variety format, the film lecturer commented on a film while it was running. The lecturer came endowed with didactic connotations which could support claims that film was an educational medium. Throughout Griffith's career at Biograph, trade journals recommended such film commentors.[38]

Like film sound devices, the film lecturer was not a new phenomenon. Oral comments on films began with the first exhibitions. A common exhibition strategy of the cinema of attractions, the first lecturers were showmen who, much like a carnival barker, hyped their films as extraordinary illusions and scientific marvels. Rather than introducing the audience into a fictional world, the first lecturers confronted them directly, as did the films they showed, emphasizing the audience's role as observers and heightening the effects of the attraction.

Although traveling exhibitors may have preserved some of this style, the lecturer recommended by trade journals in 1908 played a different role. An article in *Moving Picture World* emphasized that the lecturer was not simply a return to the fairground barker.[39] The lecturer was needed to solve the crisis in narrative form as filmmakers were caught between new ambitions and older forms. As the *Moving Picture World* article stated, "Why do so many people remain in the moving picture theater and look at the moving picture two and even three times? Simply because they do not understand it the first time; and this is by no means in every case a reflection on their intelligence." The trade journal indicated that the lecturer could make the story clear and enrich a film's reception. "When here and there parts of beauty and power are aptly and eloquently brought out as the picture runs along, the spectator experiences new and pleasing sensations."[40]

A film industry based on the production of story films was still a fairly recent phenomenon in 1908. And in this year, the production of dramas suddenly increased over comedies, up to 66 percent of the total, from 17 percent in 1907.[41] The vein of simple narratives, chases, and acts of mischief had been nearly exhausted, and the industry called for new films with more complex characters and motivations. One response was to adapt films from

well-known novels or plays, drawing directly on respectable narrative traditions. But these new sources caused a crisis in film narrative because audiences
watching silent adaptations of literary works often found them incomprehensible. An editorial in *Moving Picture World* commented on Edison's production
of *Ingomar the Barbarian*, based on Friedrich Halm's then-famous play: "[I]t is
a splendid film, but it was not received by the audiences with anything like the
appreciation it merited. As one intelligent and elderly gentleman remarked in
our hearing—'What is it all about? Very fine but what does it mean?' If the
lecturer of the theater had simply read the synopsis of the play, such as the
Edison Company sends out with all films, the audience would have understood
each scene and left the show with a desire to come again."[42]

The New York *Dramatic Mirror* had similar complaints about Edison's
production of *The Devil*, wondering if the audience would be able to follow
the film if they had not seen Molnar's original play (then playing in New York
City).[43] Productions like this prompted *Variety* to respond, when Kalem
announced it would film Longfellow's *Evangeline*: "it is hoped that whenever
the film is to be shown that the person who is selected to assist the work shall
give an intelligent reading of the book."[44] The lecturer's new role consisted in
aiding spectator comprehension of, and involvement with, the more complex
stories, to *narrate* rather than hype the film as the first lecturers had done.
The film industry in 1908 wanted to make films that would recall the tradition
of bourgeois drama, but found this difficult without exterior aid.

But again the double audience of the nickelodeon—the actual one and the
desired one—asserted itself. Although touted as an element in the uplift of
motion pictures, the lecturer was not simply addressed to the desired middle-
class patron. Films produced for middle-class patrons of vaudeville had drawn
on famous plays but (for the most part) without attempting to provide a
complete adaptation of the story line of the original source. As Musser has
shown, these adaptations relied on audience foreknowledge of the film's
source. In spite of its middle-class aspirations, in 1908 the film industry wanted
to hold on to the audience member who had never heard of *Evangeline*.
Equally important in this era of narratization was the desire to provide even
those who knew Longfellow's work with a complete dramatization, one that
was comprehensible and involving, not just a reference to a previous experience. As Noel Burch indicates, the film lecturer endowed the film image with
narrative order and legibility, a reading at the service of linear storytelling.[45]

But, as Burch also points out, providing added realism and narrative clarity
through an exterior supplement contradicted the traditional diegetic realism
to which American film aspired.[46] The lecturer could supply such values only
as a supplement, an additional aid, rather than as an inherent organic unity.
A lecturer's commentary undermined an experience of the screen as the site
of a coherent imaginary world in which narrative action took place. The

discontinuity between a film unfolding on the screen and a lecturer commenting upon it set up the possibility of unbraiding the various strands of the diegetic effect, creating a fragmented and possibly dialectic effect such as Roland Barthes describes in his discussion of the Japanese doll theater or Brecht intended through alienation effects.[47]

Attempting to reproduce the experience of bourgeois narrative and theater of its time, the narrator system could not afford a discontinuous presentation which might undermine film's illusionism. Such a practice would be totally at odds with the cinema of narrative integration, which maintained the film's illusion through a strong diegetic realism and an empathetic narrative. Within the narrator system, narrative clarity and spectator empathy could not be achieved at the expense of diegetic illusionism.

Furthermore, a lecturer's interpretation of a film was outside the control of the production company, and therefore ran against production companies' policy of asserting control over the film product and allowing less freedom to the exhibitor. Exhibitor control of the films had been one of the hallmarks of the cinema of attractions and included re-editing films and arranging ballyhoo to supplement their projection.[48]

The new era of industry organization demanded a more standardized product, delivered complete by the production company. Films which needed an exhibitor-supplied aid to make them understandable contradicted this orientation. One production company, Kalem, sent synopses of its releases to exhibitors in the form of lectures in an attempt to encourage, and yet exert control over film lectures. The film lecturer could only serve as a short-term solution to narrative comprehensibility. The narrator system offered a more viable solution. It supplied narrative legibility along with diegetic coherence even when tackling adaptations of established literary and theatrical works, and in a form completely controlled by the production company.

The narrator system works as a sort of interiorized film lecturer. It not only involves strategies to make the narrative legible, but it also provides the psychological motivation and more complex characterization that the new, more sophisticated narratives demanded. Furthermore, the narrator system created an intervening narrator who comments on the action of the film through the form of the film itself. Through techniques such as suspense editing and the use of the cut-in, Griffith's filmic style itself emphasized "parts of beauty and power" (as *Moving Picture World* had asked the lecturer to do), while directly involving the spectator in the unfolding of the story. This narrator was not located off-screen, but was absorbed into the arrangement of the images themselves. The narrator system seems to "read" the images to the audience in the very act of presenting them. This narrator is invisible, revealing its presence only by the way images are revealed on the screen.

The adaptation of narratively more complex material for film demanded a stronger contribution from the Genettean functions of narrative discourse. Without the simple linear action of the chase film and related genres, spatial and temporal relations between shots and action needed to be specified. An increased importance given to psychological motivations in the new films (as opposed to the primarily physically motivated action of earlier genres) demanded at least rudimentary means of revealing characters' emotions and thoughts. And the announced cultural and educational ambitions of these adaptations called for ways to convey to the audience particular moments of "power and beauty." Genette's categories of tense, mood, and voice are the locuses of these new narrative tasks.

The narrator system could supply this narrative discourse through signifiers appearing on the screen, under the control of the production company. The decisive quality to the narrator system lay in its ability to "tell" at the same time as it "shows." By narrating through the film images themselves, as opposed to a lecturer *hors cadre,* the narrator system guarantees the narrativization of the film image, as well as its organic unity. In Heathian terms, the narrator system maintains both its sense of realism and the reality of its sense. The historical influence of the narrator system and the demise of the film lecturer marks an important transition in American film history, moving toward narrative clarity, but within an esthetic that also guaranteed the diegetic illusionism of the drama presented.

The narrator system as it had evolved in 1908 did not, of course, immediately supply all of the cultural values of the classical sources of these new films. In fact, the success of Griffith's films (as opposed to the problems encountered by adaptations produced by other companies) rested partly on an awareness of the limited capabilities of film's evolving narrative discourse. Significantly, Biograph in 1908 also produced versions of *The Devil* and *The Barbarian Ingomar,* shortly after the Edison adaptations (which trade journals had found obscure). The *Biograph Bulletin* for *The Barbarian Ingomar* (September 4, 5) stressed that it had avoided the faults of Edison's film: "Our story, though a free adaptation of the play, moves swift and convincingly, eliminating that tediousness unavoidable in a dramatic stage performance."[49] The New York *Dramatic Mirror* found this aspect of Biograph's *Ingomar* laudable: "It is a fine example of what can be done in adapting stage drama for moving picture purposes when there is an intelligent recognition of the limitations of motion photography. Portions of the stage story which could only be interpreted adequately by spoken words are eliminated or rearranged so that the picture reads to the spectator like a printed book."[50]

Biograph's version of *The Devil* departed further from its source, there is no mention of Molnar's play in the *Bulletin* of the film, although this may have been for legal reasons. Again, the *Dramatic Mirror* approved the transformation: "Not hampered by any desire to adhere to the text of a drama not originally written for pantomime interpretation, the Biograph players hav produced a genuine moving picture story of considerable power."[51]

These comments catch the complex nature of Griffith's relation to bourgeois dramatic traditions. It was only by transforming his sources that Griffith could truly relate his filmmaking to them. Straight adaptations of plays were incomprehensible in a silent form, strangely alienated works stripped of the significance the spoken word had given them. Griffith's versions of *The Devil* and *Ingomar* stayed within "the limitations of motion photography." Such an approach grants film a unique narrative discourse while adapting it to such demands of bourgeois representation as characterization, motivation, and narrative coherence. Through filmic discourse, the narrator system constructs films that read "to the spectator like a printed book," rather than faithful but mute adaptation of plays.

Making film comprehensible through filmic discourse involved a compromise between the sorts of stories that might attract the middle class and stories which could be expressed through primarily visual means. This corresponded in many ways to the double address the film industry cultivated in 1908, reassuring the middle class without alienating regular patrons. Griffith and other filmakers handled this transaction by drawing upon a rich but ambiguous heritage—melodrama. A film like *The Fatal Hour* shows the new control and precision the narrator system asserted over filmic discourse. But this more complex narrative form derives more from the melodramatic stage than respectable classics.

Felicitously titled, *The Fatal Hour* (July 21, 27) was made some six weeks after Griffith's directorial debut at Biograph and raises parallel editing to a melodramatic intensity through a new control over the portrayal of time. The discussion of the parallel-edited sequence of *The Greaser's Gauntlet* touched only briefly on its relation to tense. With its parallel-edited climax and invocation of time in its story, *The Fatal Hour* supplies a perfect opportunity to explore the new relations within tense opened by parallel editing.

Parallel editing can be defined by three characteristics. First, it alternates two separable series of shots (and in 1908 was referred to as "alternating scenes"), setting up what is most often described as an *a-b-a-b* pattern.[52] In addition, parallel editing indicates specific temporal and spatial relations. The actions shown alternately are signified as occurring simultaneously in different places, most frequently fairly distant locals.[53] The temporal specificity that parallel editing entails brought enormous changes to the tense of film's narrative discourse.

Some scholars have found the ancestors of parallel editing in noncinematic predecessors such as the melodramatic stage and the nineteenth-century novel.[54] Although such precursors show the debt this device owes to nineteenth-century storytelling, they lack film's unique temporality. The pattern of alternation may have been adopted from noncinematic forms, but simultaneity took on a new quality in film. In defining film's relation to Genette's category of tense, film's unique temporal qualities must be sorted out.

Although the time of the single shot is normally isochronic, editing allows a variety of temporal relations between successive shots. Tense as the divergence between the events of the story and its ordering by the narration enters with editing. Because they consisted of single shots, tense played a fairly neutral role in the earliest films produced. Although multi-shot films appeared before 1900, the single-shot film remained important in production output, actually dominating through 1903, at least in America. Many early multi-shot films function basically as a series of independent shots. This relative autonomy made temporal relations rather simple, with cuts generally marking pronounced elipses.

Once story action extends over cuts, temporal relations become more complex. The chase film and related forms provided one clear temporal relation among shots, that of simple succession with brief elipses. However, before 1908 simple temporal continuity coexists with another editing practice—repeated action edits—whose temporal ambiguity subverts this nascent continuity. This temporal relation occurs when an action is continual over a cut and the shots are in close spatial relation. The action of one shot (filmed from one viewpoint) is repeated either wholly or in part in the shot that follows (filmed from another viewpoint). The time of the film, instead of presenting a continuous linear flow, is staggered, stutters, repeats itself.

Because this practice is basically unfamiliar to contemporary viewers except in the radical experiments of an Eisenstein or a Resnais, it is worth examining an example. The most extensive repeated action edit occurs in the Library of Congress version of Edison's *Life of an American Fireman*, filmed by Edwin S. Porter. The penultimate shot of the film shows the rescue of a woman and her children—shot from a room in flames. The fireman comes through the door and rescues the woman within, slinging her over his back and climbing out the window. After a brief time he climbs back in and rescues a child. The shot ends with other firemen entering and hosing down the room. The following shot shows the same actions as seen from outside the house. The fireman enters the house, emerges from the window, and carries the woman down a ladder. She pleads with him to return for the child. He remounts the ladder and rescues the child. Other firemen enter the building with hoses, as mother and child embrace. This stuttering of action seemed so peculiar to later viewers that the version of this film preserved at the Museum of Modern Art had been "corrected" to accord with later ideas of continuity, intercutting exterior and interior views of the rescue into nine shots.[55]

Similar repetitions of actions over two shots occur in a large number of early American films when characters move over closely situated spaces.[56]

Such repetitions also occur in cut-ins, where the action in the closer shot repeats the action seen in the wider shot. Edison's *The Strenuous Life* (1904), for example, shows a proud father weighing his newborn son in long shot, then cuts in to a closer view of father and child. In the closer shot the father repeats a gesture already shown in long shot, counting out his baby's weight on his fingers.

Such temporal repetitions are examples of the figure of tense that Genette terms "*repeating* narratives" in which "the recurrences of the statement do not correspond to a recurrence of events."[57] In this early period the practice seems to have been employed somewhat at random: films made at the same time by the same companies often include cuts in similar situations that match action and follow temporal continuity.[58]

For contemporary viewers who take the continuity of time in film for granted, such flaunting of our norms may appear as either an avant-garde technique or as a simple carelessness, but continuity was not the natural order of things (or shots) in early cinema.[59] No stabilized approach to temporal relations between shots existed in the era shortly before Griffith. Early cinema employed a variety of treatments of time and tolerated a great deal of ambiguity in temporal relations between shots.

In contrast, parallel editing marks the temporality of shots unambiguously. Griffith's use of parallel editing belongs to a different order of time than a cut from Porter's *The Great Train Robbery*, which has often been described as an early example of parallel editing.[60] The first nine shots of this film follow the progress of the bandits' robbery of a train. Shot ten shifts to another thread of the story, as the telegraph operator tied up by the bandits in shot one is discovered and untied by his daughter. In the following shot, the telegraph operator rushes into a saloon and tells of the robbery. A posse is formed, which in the next shot is shown pursuing the bandits on horseback.

Modern viewers tend to read the cut from shots nine to ten as indicating simultaneity. "The bandits mount their horses; *meanwhile* back at the station office. . . ." But Gaudreault has theorized that the action of untying the operator actually takes place earlier, sometime during the train robbery, and its appearance at this point in the chain of shots is actually a sort of flashback. Although I do not agree with this temporal reading, it does show that the tendency to read the time of the two shots as simultaneous is questionable. The temporal position of the rescue is ambiguous and has not been unequivocally marked temporally. Within Porter's narrative discourse the exact time of this cut remains as ambiguous (or perhaps irrelevant) as the clock painted on the set of the station, which reads 9 o'clock in both shots one and ten, as if the story took place in frozen time.

Such frozen clocks, painted onto the sets of many pre-1908 films, serve as an emblem for the undetermined temporality of the period. In a later Edison film, *Lost in the Alps* (1907), also made by Porter, the mother of children who have lost their way in a blizzard becomes concerned at their absence, and she glances at the clock, which indicates 6:05. Although time plays an important role in the story and the clock even has been pointed out by the actor's gesture, the clock hands never move. When the children are brought home, presumably hours later, the clock still reads 6: 05. Although this is partly explained by the schematic nonrealistic nature of sets during the period, it also reveals a crisis in the portrayal of time. After 1906, film stories rely more and more on temporal deadlines and a clearly determined temporality. However, filmic discourse frequently does not define time with unambiguous clarity.

The climax of *The Fatal Hour*'s melodramatic plot depends directly on parallel editing's ability to specify time. A woman detective (Florence Auer?) trailing white slavers is captured and subjected to an ingenious revenge. She is tied in front of a gun rigged to fire when a large clock strikes 12. Although such machinery of revenge has a long heritage in stage melodrama, this fatal clock inscribes time itself into the narrative and determines the form of the film's parallel-edited climax. A shot-by-shot analysis of the parallel-edited climax reveals the interweaving of temporality and editing:

Shot eight: The interior of the slavers' hideout is shown in a theatrically framed long shot as one of them demonstrates the clock-gun device while the other ties up the detective before it. The time shown on the clock is 11:40. It is demonstrated that the gun will fire at 12. The villains leave their victim (fig.5).

Shot nine: The slavers are arrested in a city street as they get off a street car. With broadly pantomimed gestures, they tell the police of their revenge (fig.6).

Shot ten: The actual parallel edited sequence begins with a carriage rushing down a country road, toward the camera, carrying the police to rescue the detective (fig.7).

Shot eleven: Action returns to the woman's plight, showing both the gun-clock mechanism and the woman, but from a closer camera position than shot 8. In addition to creating suspense, with the parallel edit between shots ten and eleven Griffith shows his understanding of the power of varying camera distance to articulate the drama. With the two slavers gone, the whole room need no longer be shown. The increased concentration on the woman and the fateful machine intensifies the dramatic tension. Emphasizing the movement of the clock hands is another motive for the closer camera position. During the shot we see them move from approximately 11:47 to 11:52 (fig.8). Although not recording real clock time (the hand's movements are speeded up considerably), the passing of time forms the dramatic center of the shot.

Shot twelve: The rescuers are picked up again as their carriage careens down a country road toward the camera (fig.9).

Shot thirteen: Action returns to the woman from the closer camera position of shot eleven, as she anxiously watches the progress of the clock. The clock's hands move from 11:54 to 11:57 (fig.10).

Shot fourteen: Again, we switch to the racing carriage (fig.11).

Shot fifteen: The two lines of action intersect. At the beginning of the shot the clock reads 11:58. The police enter through the window and untie the woman just before the minute hand reaches 12:00 and the pistol fires (fig.12). For this shot, involving more characters and action, the farther-back camera position of shot eight is used.

The temporality of each shot is clearly marked, both by the clock in the shots of the detective and by the position of each shot within the parallel-edited scheme. There is no possibility of rearranging any of these shots and getting a coherent narrative, as was possible with the shot of the release of the telegraph operator in *The Great Train Robbery*. Each shot finds its place in an irreversible linear temporal logic. However, the coherence of that linear

The race to the rescue climax from *The Fatal Hour* (1908), Griffith's first extended sequence of parallel editing. Frame enlargements from prints made from Paper Print Collection, Library of Congress.

5. The woman detective (Florence Auer?) tied up before the gun and clock contraption.

6. The slavers (George Gebhardt, Harry Solter) inform the police of the detective's situation.

7. The police rush to save the detective from her fate.

8. Shot from a closer camera position, the woman watches the clock.

9. The police continue on their race against time.

10. The clock hand approaches the fatal hour of noon.

11. The police near their destination.

12. The police enter the window and free the woman—in the nick of time.

time is, as in *The Greaser's Gauntlet,* founded on a discontinuity on the level of discourse.

Parallel editing, like the continuous movement of the chase format, maintains a linearity of action (the police's ride to the rescue, the clock hand's progression). But by developing two trajectories of action at the same time and intercutting them, it complicates this simple linearity through filmic discourse. The progress of each line of action is interrupted, and therefore delayed, by the progress of the other, manifesting the narrative arrangement of tense. The order of shots no longer indicates a simple succession in time, but the staggered progress of simultaneity.

Equally important, the structure of this sequence intensely involves the spectator through a pattern of delay. A dynamic delaying of action, in fact, defines suspense. As Roland Barthes has shown, suspense maintains a direct and dialectical relation to the spectator. Its pattern of delay and renewal keeps the sequence open, while it also flirts with its own dissolution by seeming to endlessly prolong the sequence, as if it were never going to reach a conclusion. It is this tension, Barthes says, "which is consumed with anxiety and pleasure (all the more so because it is always made right in the end)." Suspense asserts the independence of discourse from the events it describes; it "substitutes meaning for the straight forward copy of the events recounted."[61] By delaying the immediate completion of an action, suspense invokes spectator expectation and plays with it by threatening not to fulfill it. The expectation is, of course, ultimately fulfilled, and the sequence closed. But narration has become foregrounded by flirting with its own dissolution.

Interrupting an action, delaying its resolution, yet creating a structure in which the outcome approaches inevitably, in which the flow of time and narrative is unstoppable (the fatal hour draws near . . .)—these are at the heart of Griffith's temporal and narrative logic.[62] Griffith introduced it in *The Greaser's Gauntlet*, but *The Fatal Hour* features the parallel edited sequence as the film's climax (the *Biograph Bulletin* for the film stressed that the climax of the film was presented in "alternate scenes").[63] The *Dramatic Mirror* found this sequence the saving grace of a film it described as "a wholly impossible story with a series of inconsistent situations, and yet the wild drive to the rescue while the clock slowly approaches the hour of 12 brings a thrill which redeems the picture."[64]

But such articulation of narrative discourse is reserved for the climax of the film. *The Fatal Hour* provides another example of the mixed style of Griffith's first films, with earlier sequences, which contain several actions and much narrative information, appearing as single lengthy shots. Shot seven of the exterior of the slavers' hideout, for example, shows the slavers imprisoning new victims in the hideout; the police raiding the house and freeing the girls; and finally the slavers capturing the woman detective. Whereas the shots in the parallel-edited sequence (shots ten-fourteen) average five feet in length (in a 16mm print), shot seven is forty-seven feet long, while shot six, in which the woman finds out the locale of the hideout and tips off the police by telephone, extends to nearly fifty-four feet. Although the use of parallel editing in the climax of *The Fatal Hour* carries important implications for Griffith's conception of time and narrative, it is restricted to the climax. It forms, in a way, the cinematic equivalent of the melodrama stage's "sensation scene," a climactic scene which employed the full resources of the spectacle stage to create a coup de theatre which would guarantee a production's success.[65] The discourse of the film's climax does not yet represent an approach to narrative as a whole. The narrator system operates sporadically in this film and is mixed with elements of an earlier style.

The unambiguous temporality of the parallel edited climax of *The Fatal Hour* propels the narrative trajectory of the film as it rushes toward closure. The convergent lines of action differ sharply from the potentially endless concatenation of events of the earlier chase and linked-vignette films whose rather arbitrary endings Burch has noted.[66] The resolution of the climax in *The Fatal Hour* is inscribed at the moment the clock is set, and parallel editing marks its relentless unwinding. The film exhibits one of the earliest examples of the temporal deadline which forms a basic element of closure in the later classical Hollywood cinema.[67]

Although deadlines, and even deadly clock mechanisms, appear in stage melodramas, film supplies a manipulation of time which the stage could not easily match.[68] Editing not only allows the temporal layering of tense, but it also creates, as the rush to the rescue shows, an articulation of time, cutting it into discreet and often brief fragments. Parallel editing makes the progression of time palpable through its interruption, imposing a rhythm on the unfolding of events. The climax of *The Fatal Hour* evokes the cutting edge of the instant; time is measured in moments, and the smallest interval spells the difference between life and death.

What did these new games with time and suspense mean to the nickelodeon audience? A urban and industrial working-class audience might find this race against the clock and rhythmic division of time strangely familiar. Social and labor historians such as Herbert Gutman have pointed out that workers unused to the rhythms and temporality of industrial production had to develop new work habits and attitudes toward time to survive in early-twentieth-century factories. A radical worker's Yiddish poem quoted by Gutman expresses the new demands of industrial labor in images recalling the desperate climax of *The Fatal Hour*:

> The maddening pendulum urges me forward
> To labor and still labor on.
> The tick of the clock is the boss in his anger
> The face of the clock has the eyes of the foe.[69]

This new experience of time for industrial laborers had an impact on commercialized leisure. The syncopated rhythms of ragtime and the mechanically produced sensations of speed and force in amusement park rides reproduced the new and often repressive experiences urban workers encountered and transformed them—temporarily—through play. As John Kasson has pointed out, Coney Island's switchback railway (a predecessor of the roller coaster) provided an eccentric version of the mechanical means of transportation in heavy industry, so that "instruments of production and efficiency were transformed into objects of amusement."[70] Likewise, Griffith's parallel editing invokes the split-second timing of industrial production and workers' enslavement to a oppressive temporality. This reproduction of industrial time has opposing functions typical of American popular entertainment in which conservative ideology makes use of anarchic energy, while at the same time tradition is undermined by laying bare social tensions. On the one hand, the film's climax reinforces the experience of temporal enslavement by allying it with narrative pleasure and even offering a lesson in adjustment to industry's quick demands and rhythms. On the other hand, it exposes the unbearable oppression of clock time and acts out a drama of liberation from it. Making the passage of time more palpable, parallel editing offers both a celebration and an overcoming of the new rhythms of modern production in an art form which—like the major attractions of the new amusement parks—was itself the product of industrial production. Griffith's parallel editing, like much of contemporaneous popular culture, clothes a new experience of time and labor in the forms of fantasy and desire.

The temporality explored by *The Fatal Hour* carried a potentially double address. The new precision of tense allowed more sophisticated narrative structure and therefore could be used to attract a middle-class audience by imitating traditional narrative forms. However the film's intensification of time through editing also creates a sensational melodrama.

The *Dramatic Mirror's* criticism of the improbability and inconsistency of *The Fatal Hour* takes for granted a condemnation of melodrama that a new taste for realism and naturalism in the theater had accomplished. In many ways melodrama provides a pivot around which Griffith's transformation in film style turned. On the one hand, melodrama was perceived as outmoded, hardly the model to turn to for either plotting or acting if a filmmaker wished to attract a middle-class audience. On the other hand, melodrama supplied a tradition dedicated to making motivations vividly visual. As a popular form, melodrama had evolved an empathetic approach to both character and action designed to fully involve audience members. Griffith handled this ambiguous inheritance by both drawing on it and transforming it. In *The Fatal Hour* he translated the melodramatic sensation scene into a new elaboration of filmic tense. The experiments in visually conveying characters' thoughts and channeling involvement with their emotions in *The Redman and the Child* and *The Greaser's Gauntlet* also drew upon melodramatic traditions.

Melodrama plays a central role in the transition of early fiction film production from comedy to drama. With its audience-addressing gags or use of broad physical action, comedy was particularly suited to both the cinema of attractions and transitional genres such as the chase. While *The Adventures of Dollie* shows such physical schemas adaptable to melodrama, the form's use of villainy, heroism, and threatened innocence demanded some access to character psychology. And although late-nineteenth-century melodrama made full use of dialogue, its origin as a form of pantomime endowed it with a rich inventory of devices other than words to convey characterization and make dramas comprehensible.

The melodramatic theater employed an elaborate system of conventional visual and aural signs for conveying characters' emotions. Performers in this tradition made use of a firmly coded physical rhetoric, whose function as signs was fully understood by audiences. Gesture, physical postures, and actions conveyed specific emotional states. A melodramatic actor learned how to strike such attitudes as Grief, Despair, or Cowardice. An actor's hand-book from 1882 gives the following instructions for the portrayal of Anger: "All the muscles of the body acquire a convulsive power. The eyes become fiery and roll in their orbits. The hands contract violently, the mouth foams, the teeth grind fiercely. The whole body equally with the soul is in convulsions. The veins of the neck and temples swell, the blood rushes to the face, the movements are violent."[71] Such gestures included a brief pause which stressed their conventional nature by rendering them as a static pose. This pause could be extended to all the characters within a scene and held for a longer period to create a "tableau" or "picture," described by Peter Brooks as "a visual summary of the emotional situation." An acting style encoded as a series of signs interacted with plots whose dynamic, as Brooks has shown, lay in the progressive revelation of the true signs of virtue.[72]

Traditional conventional gestures and poses fill Griffith's 1908 films. Arthur Johnson's outstretched arm and pointed finger as he drives off the gypsy in *The Adventures of Dollie* embody one of the most famous melodramatic gestures, derived from Charles Kemble's "teapot" poses.[73] Tableaux with all the characters holding a pose are seen in *The Vaquero's Vow* (August 31, September 1), and in the presentation of the bride's dowry box and the lovers' final embrace in *The Barbarian, Ingomar*. Griffith also employed a gestural equivalent of the aside, which melodrama preserved long after other theatrical forms had discarded it. Actors in Griffith's Biograph films frequently address the camera directly and pantomime their intentions and feelings in a gestural soliloquy. For example, the evil Mexican woman in *The Red Girl* (August 1, 12) steps toward the camera and mimes her designs on the innocent Indian girl. Jose in *The Greaser's Gauntlet* also mimes his reaction when he discovers the gauntlet and realizes Mildred's identity.

Nowhere is the ambiguous nature of Griffith's debt to melodrama clearer than in his approach to characterization. The first Biograph films show a strong reliance on the conventional broad gestures of melodramatic acting. Although such gestures appear throughout Griffith's Biograph career, they soon give way to another approach to performance, which, following Roberta Pearson, I will term *versimilar* (chapter 7).[74] The discovery of other visual means to express character psychology allowed Griffith to move away from the acting style of melodrama. This work on other levels of film discourse seems inspired by melodramatic devices but transforms its sources fundamentally.

The lyrical postscripts already discussed in *The Greaser's Gauntlet* and *The Redman and the Child* recall the melodramatic tableau's role as visual emotional summaries. Melodrama's use of the stage picture as a narrative and empathetic device inspired Griffith to bend a formal inheritance from the cinema of attractions to the purposes of character access. Closer shots such as the lyrical postscript in *Redman*, far from being a Griffith invention, derive from the "facial expression" genre of the cinema of attractions. Generally lasting for only a single shot, these films showed an actor in medium shot or medium close-up mugging at the audience. The close camera position allows emphasis on the actor's humorous or grotesque facial expressions, which form the film's attraction and purpose.[75]

The earlier transitional narrative films absorbed this one-shot genre without integrating it totally into the world of the film. I have called these "introductory shots."[76] Usually the first shot of a film, they presented a close shot of a main character (as in Biograph's *The Firebug, The Village Cut-up* [1906], or *The Widow and the Only Man* [1904]), frequently shot against a neutral background abstracted from any specific story space. The famous close-up of the outlaw leader in *The Great Train Robbery* remains the most famous and revealing instance of this practice. Following Edison's exhibitor-as-showman-oriented policy, the Edison catalog advised exhibitors that this early close-up could be placed at either the beginning or end of the film.[77] Such introductory shots thus played no role in the temporal development of the story and simply introduced a major character outside of the action of the film. As Noel Burch puts it, *The Great Train Robbery*'s introductory shot seems to "hover on the fringe of a diegesis which cannot assimilate it."[78]

By 1907–8 introductory shots had migrated to the end of films (*Bobby's Kodak* [Biograph, 1908], *The Yawner* [Pathé, 1907], and *Her First Adventure* [Biograph, 1908]) and seemed to sum up the film, often including a narratively important element (e.g., the muzzle used to solve the yawner's problem in the Pathé film). Griffith ends his early comedy chase film, *Balked at the Altar*, in this way, with a waist shot of the romantic old maid against a black background, abstracted from the main narrative development.

While these summing-up shots may anticipate Griffith's endings, his lyrical postscripts are immersed in the films' diegesis. Their use of the story space of the film allows Griffith to employ not only closer shots, but also pictorial landscapes such as the last image of *The Greaser's Gauntlet*. The composition of these long shots carries a strong emotional resonance, with landscape and composition mirroring character's feelings, as can be seen in the melancholy image which ends *The Zulu's Heart* (August 28, 29). In the final shot, the Zulu bids farewell to a Boer mother and child he had rescued, the figures placed on a cliff with a broad vista stretching behind them. After the Boers leave, the Zulu stands alone, a solitary figure in a space more extensive than in any previous shot in the film. The picturesque landscape and isolated figure resonate with his loneliness and grief (as the New York *Dramatic Mirror* noted, describing it as "a pathetic touch of savage simplicity").[79]

A similar mood rules the end of *The Call of the Wild* (September 17, 25).

Indian chief Redfeather (Charles Inslee) has released the white girl (Florence Lawrence) he originally abducted, realizing he could never win her love. In the final shot, Redfeather rides sadly toward the camera, holding the girl's handkerchief. As in the end of *Redman*, he moves toward the camera, ending in a medium close-up. In these films, instead of ending with the victim's release, Griffith lingers on the emotional plight of an isolated character, creating sympathy for these lone figures. By isolating these characters, Griffith also creates a less conventional equivalent to the melodramatic aside. The characters need not step out of the diegesis of the film to express their private feelings. Without dialogue, the composition of these images conveys the characters' grief and loneliness. The spectator is allowed to witness a moment within the world of the story without a diegesis-rupturing direct address.

These approaches to characterization through filmic discourse reach a climax in *After Many Years* (September 22, October 8, 9), a film in which the elements of the narrator system determine the film's structure as a whole, rather than in part. Further, this free adaptation of *Enoch Arden* draws on a source with both a cultural reputation and a long history of melodramatic adaptation. Through Griffith's dynamic use of editing, the film provides the strongest transformation of melodramatic inheritance into film form.

Traditional historians were aware of the importance of the film. However Jacobs, Sadoul, and Mitry derive their comments from Linda Arvidson's memoir, *When the Movies Were Young.* Jacobs repeats Arvidson's claim that the film contained a close-up, which is misleading. Sadoul quotes Arvidson directly, including her equally erroneous claim that *After Many Years* was Griffith's first film to use parallel editing. Although Mitry drops the claim for a close-up in the film, he echoes the assertion that this was Griffith's first use of parallel editing.[80] The importance of the film, however, lies less in introducing innovations than in a new narrative structure. This structure twines around the two centers we have been tracing: the articulation of space and action through editing, and the portrayal of characters' emotions through cinematic means.

The *Biograph Bulletin* for this film describes it as "a subject on the basis of Enoch Arden," the most popular (and widely adapted) of Tennyson's poems, but does not claim the status of a direct adaptation of a literary classic. The film, in fact, transforms Tennyson's work by adding a happy ending. The shipwrecked sailor is finally reunited with his wife and family, a conclusion the *Bulletin* found "more intensely heart-stirring than the original story."[81] The theme of a sailor lost at sea while his wife or sweetheart patiently awaits his return was an extremely popular one in films of the period and appeared not only in a number of later Biographs (*Lines of White on a Sullen Sea* [1909], *The Unchanging Sea* [1910], *Enoch Arden* [1911]), but also in works by other production companies. It is also part of a long tradition in nineteenth-century theater, literature, and painting, finding its classical locus (but neither its origin nor end) in Tennyson's poem.[82]

This motif allowed Griffith to employ the key figure of the narrator system—parallel editing—in a new structural role. The story turns on the geographical separation of the two main characters, the sailor John Davis (Charles Inslee) and his wife (Florence Lawrence). Emotions, rather than character movement, traverse space, as Griffith highlights the couple's love and longing for each other. Parallel editing articulates and interrelates spatial separation and emotional connection. After John's departure from his family cottage, the film interweaves the dispersed characters, alternating back and forth between hopeful wife and shipwrecked husband.

Arvidson claims that Biograph studio heads were disturbed by the film's narrative structure, objecting that the film had no chase and would confuse the audiences because the story "jumped about."[83] Whether or not such a discussion took place, *After Many Years* is the first Griffith film which uses parallel editing extensively without a last-minute rescue. I know of no precedent for the film's narrative structure in the work of any other company. While the suspenseful use of parallel editing found in *The Fatal Hour* primarily related to the category of tense, the spatial articulation of the characters in *After Many Years* is primarily motivated by characters' emotions, allowing the access to characters that mood involves. The cuts frequently come when the characters most earnestly desire contact with each other (particularly the cuts between shots three and four and five and six and, most important, eight and nine).

> Shot three: Interior set of the Davis parlor. The wife is given a newspaper reporting her husband's shipwreck. At the end of the shot she rushes to a portrait on the wall to the right (possibly intended to be a portrait of her husband, one of several token-objects connecting the separated lovers).
> Shot four: The first parallel-edited shot in the film presents John landing a raft on a beach through open surf. He then rushes toward the camera, exhausted.
> Shot five: John on a beach sometime later (this temporal elipsis may well have been bridged by a now-missing intertitle), dressed in skins, seated before a rough hut. He searches the sea which forms the background of the shot.
> Shot six: A garden outside the Davis cottage (the location of the film's opening). Mrs. Davis walks there with Tom Foster (Harry Solter), who is courting her. He offers her a flower which she refuses.
> Shot seven: John's desert island; on the shore he gestures as if signaling a distant boat offscreen.
> Shot eight: John in front of his hut. He takes out a locket (another token object of an absent lover), opens and kisses it. We cut on this action to . . . (fig. 13).
> Shot nine: The porch of the Davis cottage. This was the location of the

13. The cut on the kiss from *After Many Years* (1908), uniting the shipwrecked husband (Charles Inslee) and his wife (Florence Lawrence) at home in England. Frame enlargement from print made from Paper Print Collection, Library of Congress.

second shot of the film (John's leave-taking), but the camera position in this shot is much closer. Whereas all previous shots in this film had framed characters in full figure, or even further back in medium long shots, this shot frames Mrs. Davis in a 3/4 shot. (Presumably it was this closer position that Linda Arvidson referred to as the "first dramatic close-up.")[84] Lawrence spreads her arms as if embracing her missing husband.

Shot ten: Parlor interior (as in shot three). Foster enters and begs Mrs. Davis to marry him, but is again rejected.

Shot eleven: The final parallel cut of the film. John at his hut signals off-screen and rushes to the sea. (The next shot will present his rescue and the succeeding three shots end the film with his return to England and reunion with his wife.)

This alternation does not derive from Tennyson, who avoids interweaving the stories of Annie Lee and the shipwrecked Enoch. After their separation, the poem relates Annie's plight until her marriage to Enoch's rival Philip Ray. Only at this point, with a transition marked by the narrator's question: "And where was Enoch?" (line 523) does the poem pick up Enoch's story, returning to the beginning of his sea voyage, then chronicling his shipwreck, lonely desert life, rescue, return to England, and finally his death after discovering his wife remarried.

The various stage adaptations made of "Enoch Arden" in the late nineteenth century may have provided inspiration for the intercutting of the two characters.[85] Again we are dealing with transformation, and these works of the melodrama stage can only be seen as prototypes of Griffith's structure. Even the 1889 Newton-Beers production which Nicholas Vardac cites as a predecessor of parallel editing primarily interrelates the stories in large, single-act units.[86] Most stage adaptations of the poem did employ a melodramatic device known as a "vision scene" which provides an interesting parallel to the intercutting of John and his wife.

In a vision scene, shutters in the rear of the stage were opened or removed to disclose (usually briefly and without dialogue) a prearranged scene or tableau. This represented either a "pictorial presentation of action proceeding within the mind of one of the characters on stage," a supernatural presence, or action occurring in another location.[87] The incident in Tennyson's poem in which Annie searches the Bible for a sign of Enoch's fate and comes upon the phrase "under a palm tree" was elaborated with a vision scene in both the stage adaptations Vardac cites. The description of the Newton-Beers production is the most elaborate: "the wondrous vision of the Isle of Palms is disclosed; the humble cottage disappears, and a transformation unfolds itself to the audience. Opening with the tropical night, scene follows scene, light gradually growing under a palm tree, upon which beams the blazing light of day."[88]

In Tennyson's poem, Annie misinterprets the biblical phrase as a sign Enoch has died and is in glory, and decides to wed Philip. In contrast to Tennyson's tragedy of misinterpreted signs, *After Many Years* presents a tale of faithful love conquering spatial separation.[89] Although parallel editing produces the ironic effect of an omniscient narrator who knows the location of the shipwrecked sailor, the cuts also affirm the devotion that sustains the characters. The editing creates a nearly supernatural link between the characters, to which the *Biograph Bulletin* seems to refer when it describes the prayers of the separated lovers as "ascending at the same time to the Father Almighty."[90] This theological guarantee of the simultaneity of their fidelity is embodied in the film's cutting pattern.

Nowhere is this supernatural dimension (and the blending of voice and mood) stronger than in the extraordinary cut between shots eight and nine. This cut brings the parallel-edited structure of the film to a climax, as the narrator system asserts its control over discourse more clearly than in any previous Griffith film. In shot eight John Davis takes out the locket (which the *Biograph Bulletin* tells us contains a portrait of his wife, information that may have been conveyed by a now-missing intertitle). He kisses this image and in the middle of this action, we cut to shot nine, in which his wife spreads her arms as if in longing for her husband. These emblematic melodramatic gestures express the emotional motivation for the cut, the couple's transcendent desire. But the precise relation between acting gesture and the cut as a narrative gesture makes this articulation powerful. Griffith transforms the melodramatic tradition of expressive gesture into a discovery in filmic discourse.

John's kiss is directed toward his absent wife and seems to be greeted by the wife's attempt to enfold her distant husband. Through editing, Griffith creates a space of the imagination in which these gestures meet in a phantom embrace. The desert island kiss resounds upon the welcoming wife outside the English cottage, as devotion overcomes geography. The sense of simultaneous prayers united by a transcendent witness is fully realized, in a space knitted together by mutual desire. The narrator system affirms these gestures of devotion, creating an omniscience that allows this paradoxical embrace. In this figure of desire Griffith firmly establishes the omniscient force of the narrator system, which years later in *Intolerance* he christened with Walt Whitman's line "the uniter of here and hereafter."

As is often true of Griffith's approach to mood, the access to characters is not direct. While psychological desires motivate the cuts between the characters in *After Many Years*, the shots are not presented as subjective visions. Rather, they are imaged by an omniscient narrator who unites on the screen what is separate in the space of the story. By foregrounding the narrator's role in interrelating (intercutting) the characters, not only is the mood of Griffith's narration defined, but the omniscient intercutting also displays a close relation to the aspect of voice, the affirmation of the presence of the narrator, what Genette describes as the "directing function" of the narrator.[91] We could describe this cut as a ménage à trois among husband, wife, and uniting narrator, resulting from what Jesionowski describes as "an unexpected blend of physical and mental realities."[92]

The power of the narrator system further reveals itself in the exact placing of the cut. The cut actually interrupts the gesture of kissing the locket. Although this may seem inconsequential, it represents a revolution in the relation between action and editing. The duration of the action (the kiss) no longer determines the length of the shot. Rather, the cut masters the action through interruption, terminating it at a point of intensity. In other words, instead of the shot being a simple container for an action, a means of recording and presenting it, it intervenes and structures it, overriding its natural unfolding. The placement of the cut discloses its own force—its ability to assert itself as a manufacturer of meaning. It forms another step away from the relative autonomy of shots in pre-Griffith cinema, toward a more hypotactic style.

This cutting makes a sharp break with the preservation of continuity found the chase film. In the chase film, cutting followed the unfolding course of action within the shot. The early chase films of Edison, Pathé, Biograph, Gaumont and other companies never cut from a shot until the last member of the chase had filed through the frame. Perhaps the most extreme example of this can be found in Pathé's *The Police Dogs* (1907), which lays bare the device. In this film, a pack of police-trained dogs pursues escaping smugglers. During the chase, one of the dogs has difficulty in clearing the various obstacles in its path, and the shot always lingers until this inept pup finally manages to leave the frame. Although one suspects the Pathé director may have recognized the humor, the film's editing remains dependent on an unambiguous completing of action within each shot before continuing to the next. Only with the last gasp of the unfolding action could the shot end. *After Many Years* not only intercuts action, but also selects a moment of intensity to switch to a thematically related distant location and action. The interrupted kiss resonates with unfulfilled desire, which increases its powerful connection with the responsive wife. The narrator system strongly asserts its presence and fashions events for their appearance on screen.

Griffith had tried out such interrupting cuts before exploring their psychological use in *After Many Years*. In *The Barbarian, Ingomar* he cut from a Germanic barbarian with sword upraised about to strike a Greek girl (Florence Lawrence) to the girl's rescuer, Ingomar (Charles Inslee) rushing toward the barbarian camp. In the following shot, the barbarian's sword is still upraised, as Ingomar arrives and confronts him. Interrupting a character's gesture proceeds logically from suspenseful parallel editing. Because parallel editing derives its effect from switching from one line of action to another, it is a logical next step to make the switch at the highest point of tension, suspending not only the unfolding of action but also a dramatic gesture. This interrupting cut reveals the narrator system; it establishes the power and independence of discourse over story and also displays the tie that binds spectator to the narrator's suspenseful unfolding of the action.

Again Griffith transformed a melodramatic inheritance, inspired not only by the relative spatial mobility of the melodramatic stage (exemplified by the vision scene), but also by the frozen gesture of the tableau. As a device to heighten suspense, the melodrama stage had occasionally combined the two. In *Oliver Twist*, Dickens referred to this stage practice, describing a heroine in a villain's clutches drawing out her dagger, "and just as our expectations are wrought up to the highest pitch, a whistle is heard, [signal of a scene change] and we are straightway transported to the great hall of the castle, where a grey-headed seneschal sings a funny chorus. . . ."[93] Combining the interruption obtained by frozen gesture with the rapid scene shift favored by melodrama, such moments must have provided Griffith's inspiration. The tableau also asserts control over unfolding events as actors' gestures are frozen for a "resolution in meaning," a heightening of significance.[94] But Griffith goes beyond his theatrical legacy. The gesture is interrupted not simply by the actor, but by editing, able to shift the narrative viewpoint through space more precisely than a scene change. Griffith shifts not simply to an irrelevant and suspense building interpolation, but to an answering gesture, responding to the force of his cut. Thus interruption leaps into a new quality, firmly revealing a narrator's presence, the power of the storyteller in the story being told.

Griffith's cutting-on action plays a double role in the history of film continuity. In the later classical style of "invisible editing," cutting-on a gesture guaranteed continuity over cuts. A typical example would be a gesture that begins in medium shot and continues in close-up. This distracts spectators from the cut, masking the discontinuity of shot change with continuity of action. Griffith's cutting-on action serves the opposite purpose. Instead of obscuring the cut, it accents it. It is precisely at the point that two shots join that the narrator system "speaks." This indicates the complex relation Griffith and the narrator system bear to the classical codes of editing Griffith is often credited with founding.[95]

Almost two decades later Sergei Eisenstein explored the disjunctive possibilities of editing interrupting action in a systematic and radical fashion. Eisenstein's radical use of interruption shattered the coherent diegesis which Griffith created, just as in theater (as Walter Benjamin has shown) Brecht radically developed the melodramatic tableau through a conscious exploitation of the political possibilities of interruption. Eisenstein's montage owes a debt not only to the spatial mobility and tempo of Griffith's parallel editing, but also to the narrator system's ability to interrupt action and transform meaning. Benjamin described the effect of Brecht's epic technique in terms of the almost physical impact of its interruption: "The damming of the stream of real life, the moment when its flow comes to a standstill, makes itself felt as a reflux: this reflux is astonishment."[96] Griffith's new mastery of action through editing produced a similar sensational effect, but with effects of involvement rather than distantiation. Drawing on and transforming the tradition of melodramatic astonishment, Griffith exploited a new vein of filmic discourse for the purpose of narrativization, editing's ability to interrupt and master action. But the path he opened ultimately extends beyond this.

While the control editing asserts over action in *After Many Years* reveals the narrator's intervention and relates to voice, access to characters (and the function of mood) played an equally important role in the film's narrative structure. The work that Griffith undertook on all levels of filmic discourse to develop character was tied to the new narrative forms in which character motivations and psychology were essential. Film stories which relied increasingly on a character's decisions and emotions made a portrayal of psychological states a narrative necessity. Communicating these psychological states was a basic impetus for the development of the narrator system and of the cinema of narrative integration generally. As Kristin Thompson has put it, in the films that move toward the classical style, psychology "serves both to structure the causal chain in a new fashion and to make the narration integral to that chain."[97] *After Many Years* does involve physical action (the shipwreck, the rescue), but characters' emotions form its center and knit it together. The importance of character motivation differentiates Griffith's work in the category of mood from earlier cinema which explored numerous devices for conveying characters' subjectivity but rarely used them to drive the logic of the story.

Dreams materialize frequently in pre-1908 cinema. The discontinuity between real life and dreams forms a favorite subject of early cinema, attracting filmmakers between 1900–1906 more than at any other point in film history. The trick work in many early films was often narrativized as dream visions.[98] Dreams also appeared in otherwise realistic narratives. Both *Life of an American Fireman* and Ferdinand Zecca's *Histoire du crime* (Pathé, 1901) portray dreams, placing the dreamer and his dream within the same frame. The criminal's jailhouse nightmare in *Histoire du crime* appears behind him upon the prison wall. A family framed in a circular matte appears next to the fireman as he dozes in Porter's film. Dreamer and dream (or dream and reality) had also been cut into separate shots very early, as in the Lubin Company's *The Tramp's Dream* (1899).

Flashbacks and representations of characters' memories also appear before Griffith, although less frequently than dreams (the dream in *Histoire du crime* in fact consists of memories of earlier events, but presented as a dream of conscience). James Williamson's *The Old Chorister* (1904) uses a superimposition to portray an old man's memory of his youth. However, with a few exceptions which anticipate the narrator system—such as Crick and Sharp's precocious *Drink and Repentance* (1905) in which a vision of his wife—in superimposition—motivates a drunkard's repentance—such mental images do not motivate basic story action.

Following the non-narrativized mode of the cinema of attractions, these films present subjective images as self-contained attractions, of interest in themselves, rather than giving psychological dimensions to an extended narrative. Even the mental images in the non-trick *Histoire du crime* and *Life of an American Fireman* display this lack of narrativization. Although the dream of the past in Zecca's film seems to reveal the prisoner's tortured conscience, no action is motivated by the vision. The narrative role of the dream insert in Porter's film remains even more problematic. Whether the family seen in the "dream balloon" is the same family rescued later in the film, or even whether the dreaming fireman appears as one of the later rescuers, are ambiguities which limit the appropriation of this subjective imagery by the film's narrative logic. Like the early use of point-of-view shots, subjectivity remains an attraction in these early films, rather than a narrative strategy.

Around 1908, films based on memory images became more frequent. Unfortunately, few of these films survive, and we know them primarily from catalogue descriptions (such as Biograph's *The Music Master*, from April 1908 in which Griffith acted). Porter's *Fireside Reminiscences* (Edison, 1908) provides a curious surviving example. Memories appear superimposed over the background of a fireplace, before which the protagonist sits musing. The superimposed images recall the happy stages of his marriage to a woman he has since abandoned. Prefiguring the style of the narrator system, these memories apparently provoke his reunion with his wife, which ends the film. However, this sequence displays the temporal ambiguities frequent in Porter's work. The final superimposed image of the woman waiting in the snow does not represent a memory, but apparently a simultaneous image of the wife, who has collapsed outside as the man sits before his fire. These temporal ambiguities makes the reading of the film's imagery through a character's psychology problematic.

Griffith's psychological cutting such as that used in *After Many Years* was always at the service of narrativization, with access to characters advancing story lines. However, the access to character Griffith creates is also more indirect than the dreams and memories of earlier cinema. None of the available Biograph films portray a dream, although both trick films and dream films continued to be made by other companies during this period, for example *The Dream* (IMP, 1911) and *Princess Nicotine* (Vitagraph, 1909). No flashbacks appear in the available Griffith Biograph films until very late, with *The House of Darkness* (1913), in which the flashback is not indicated as a character's memory. A subjective image, apparently an anticipation of later events, appears in *The Christmas Burglars* (November 28, 30, 1908), but it is not until *The Perfidy of Mary* (1913) that another imagined scene appears.[100] Griffith's access to characters was another sort. Only after creating a different psychological style and leaving Biograph did he return to a cinema of dreams and visions in *The Avenging Conscience* (1914).

After Many Years contains the essence of Griffith's psychological editing: an interruption of a line of action reveals a character's thoughts or emotions. However such cutting need not be part of an extended parallel-edited sequence and is often limited to a single, motivation-revealing cutaway.[101] Such cutting always manifests the indirectness found in *After Many Years*: the cutaways do not function simply as subjective images, but serve as omniscient revelations of actual events occurring simultaneously. The narrator never completely abdicates the authority of these images to the characters. They are not unequivocally marked as mental images, as is the dissolved-in image of *The Christmas Burglars*.

This ambiguity can be explored in a film Griffith made before *After Many Years, Behind the Scenes* (August 10, 13). An actress (Florence Lawrence) must leave her sick child (Gladys Eagan) at home in order to perform at a theater. The film cuts twice from the mother at the theater back to the child's sickbed. One cut particularly reveals this ambiguity. We see the mother dancing on the stage. She falters for a second, probably due to anxiety. She recovers and exits from the stage. Griffith then cuts to her home, where her daughter dies in the doctor's arms. The next shot picks up the action of the mother as she dances into the wings of the stage.

Although omniscient irony is essential to the effect of this cut (revealing the outcome of the event which so concerns the mother), it also allows access to the mother's thoughts. Missing intertitles might make clearer a question which the film's *Biograph Bulletin* description of this scene raises when it describes the dancer's "mother's intuition" as "in her mind's eye she sees her little one—but only for a moment. . . ."[102] Although film publicity can be unreliable, this passage seems to indicate that the parallel cut to the sick child should be read as indicating the mother's vision of her child. In this case the cut supplies access to character psychology, as well as omniscient irony.[103] Certainly, the content of the interpolated shot remains independent of the mother's consciousness; she does not know her child has died. But the cut also articulates her concern, revealing that her mind is "elsewhere." Likewise in *After Many Years*, although the shots of husband and wife are not exclusively presented as mental images of the characters, the parallel editing articulates their desire for each other.

Two three-shot sequences from *A Salvation Army Lass* (December 26, 28) provide further examples of this double role of character-centered cutaways. In this film, Florence Lawrence plays Mary Wilson, a woman who becomes a member of the Salvation Army and tries to convert her gangster boyfriend Bob Walton (Harry Solter). Mary Wilson enters a bar and finds Walton plotting a crime with his cronies. She prays for him, (fig. 14). The toughs leave, but Walton lingers for a moment. We cut briefly to the toughs waiting outside for Walton (fig. 15). When we return to Walton in the bar in the next shot (fig. 16), he is still in the same position he took before the cut. Now he laughs and goes out to join the gang. The interpolation of the shot of the gang articulates Solter's hesitation and his decision to join his buddies. The shot contains little information, but through its interruption of Solter's thoughtful pause in the bar it splits his reaction in two, creating a gap between

Psychological editing in *The Salvation Army Lass* (1908). Frame enlargements from prints made from Paper Print Collection, Library of Congress.

14

14, 15, 16: As Mary (Florence Lawrence) prays, Bob (Harry Solter) hesitates about joining his gang in a burglary. Griffith cuts to the gang waiting outside, then back to Bob, cueing the viewer to his decision to join them.

15

16

hesitation and final decision. It also presages the outcome of the decision (to join his cronies).

This interpretation of these three shots is affirmed by a similar three-shot unit later in the film. Here, Mary has physically tried to stop Walton from committing a burglary with his gang. In anger, Walton knocks her down. Walton and the burglars are then shown creeping along a building wall. Walton is handed a gun. He looks off-screen (fig. 17). Griffith cuts to a very brief shot (one foot in 16mm, but the shot may be truncated) of Mary lying on the ground, stunned from the blow (fig. 18). We then cut back to Walton in the same position as before (fig. 19). He turns to the gangsters, hands back his gun, and leaves. The rest of the film follows his conversion to Mary's Christianity. Again, a decision is articulated by a cutaway. Whether we read the shot of Mary on the ground as something Walton actually sees in his glance off-screen, as a mental image, or as a simple parallel cut back to her, it is clear that it intervenes at the moment of Walton's decision not to go through with the crime. In both sequences, Griffith interrupts a mental process at a crucial point, just as he suspended the downsweep of the barbarian's sword in *Ingomar*.

17, 18, 19: Griffith cuts from Bob as he hesitates in following the gang to a shot of Mary crumpled on the sidewalk where Bob left her after striking her. He then cuts back to Bob, articulating Bob's awakening conscience and his decision to leave the gang.

17

18

19

This interruption does not create suspense, but rather conveys a character's decision and provides a motive for it. In the first sequence the motivation for Walton to continue his life of crime is given by the shot of his cronies waiting for him, indicating the pull the gang exerts on him. In the second sequence the shot of Mary, indicating his concern and love for her, motivates his decision not to go through with the burglary. This pattern of interrupting a decision by a shot which anticipates the final outcome persists throughout Griffith's later Biograph films. Neither of these interpolated shots functions exclusively as mental images, as do dream or memory sequences. They remain cutaways that articulate and indicate a mental process. This is typical of the narrator system's approach to mood. The narrator system reveals characters' motivations to the spectator, but does not indicate the character as the "source" of the shot.

A sequence in *The Reckoning* (November 9, 10, 1908) picks up the parallel editing of *After Many Years* and makes explicit the supernatural overtone of the kiss in that film.[104] In this grim melodrama, a wife (Florence Lawrence) invites her lover in (Mack Sennett) after her husband (Harry Solter) leaves for work. The husband finds the factory shut down and steps into a saloon to have a drink before going home. The following three shots articulate a moment of apparent clairvoyance. In the bar the husband starts to take a drink and then suddenly freezes as if intensely disturbed. The next shot shows the illicit couple at home (also drinking). We return to the husband as he looks very disturbed, puts down his drink, and leaves the bar. He returns home, finds the lovers, and shoots them.

The interpolation of the shot of the couple drinking into Solter's reaction at the bar seems to define it as the husband's premonition of his wife's infidelity—a sort of mental telepathy. However, even if the editing pattern indicates the shot as Solter's mental image, it is not so exclusively. The shot of the couple also is part of a parallel editing pattern that had already cut between the husband and the couple several times. Only with this cut is there any indication that the motivation for the editing is psychological. Once again, the aspects of mood found in the narrator system at Biograph convey subjectivity without detracting from the narrator's voice. Such editing patterns gave Griffith a much-needed tool in creating a character-based narrative form. Although the psychology revealed by such editing remains elementary, it plays a key role in narrative structure and allows changes to come from characters' thoughts rather than from their physical actions.

Notes

1. For revisionary accounts of the nickelodeon era, see Charles S. Musser, "The Nickelodeon Era Begins: Establishing the Framework for Hollywood's Mode of Repre-

sentation," *Framework* 22–23 (Autumn 1983): 4–11; Russell Merritt, "Nickelodeon Theaters 1905–1914: Building an Audience for the Movies," in *The American Film Industry*, ed. Tino Balio (Madison: University of Wisconsin Press, 1976); and Robert C. Allen, "Motion Picture Exhibition in Manhattan 1906–1912: Beyond the Nickelodeon," in *Film Before Griffith*, ed. John L. Fell (Berkeley: University of California Press, 1983), pp. 2

2. Musser, "Nickelodeon," p. 4.

3. *Moving Picture World*, April 18, 1908, p. 344; New York *Dramatic Mirror*, Sept. 26, 1908, p. 9.

4. *Variety*, March 14, 1908, p. 12.

5. Barton W. Currie, "Nickel Madness," *Harper's Weekly*, Aug. 24, 1907.

6. *Billboard*, Feb. 1, 1908, p. 43.

7. *Moving Picture World*, July 25, 1908, p. 61.

8. Robert C. Allen, *Vaudeville and Film, 1895–1915: A Study in Media Interaction* (New York: Arno Press, 1980), p. 228.

9. Roy Rosenzweig, *Eight Hours for What We Will: Workers and Leisure in an Industrial City, 1870–1920* (New York: Cambridge University Press, 1983), p. 211.

10. Allen, *Vaudeville and Film*, p. 47.

11. Brooks MacNamara, "The Scenography of Popular Entertainment," *The Drama Review*, March 1974, p. 19.

12. Rosenzweig, *Eight Hours*, p. 179.

13. Surveys of working-class standards of living in New York City in 1907 found that 10 percent spent nothing on entertainment, whereas a prosperous working-class family's weekly outlay was limited to 35 cents a week; ibid., p. 181, and Kathy Peiss, *Cheap Entertainments: Working Women and Leisure in Turn-of-the-Century New York* (Philadelphia, Temple University Press, 1986), p. 13. Garth Jowett cites a 1910 survey of working-class budgets in a mill town which gives the weekly family allowance for "sundries" as $1.23, "The First Motion Picture Audiences," in *Film Before Griffith*, ed. Fell, p. 206.

14. John F. Kasson, *Amusing the Million: Coney Island at the Turn of the Century* (New York: Hill and Wang, 1978), pp. 6–7 and passim.

15. Kasson, *Amusing the Million*, p. 38.

16. Rosenzweig, *Eight Hours*, pp. 192, 195, 201–2.

17. *Variety*, June 20, 1908, p. 12; Feb. 1, 1908, p. 11.

18. *Variety*, June 20, 1908, p. 12.

19. Peiss, *Cheap Entertainments*, pp. 6–7, 28, 140.

20. Merritt, "Nickelodeon Theaters," p. 65.

21. *Show World*, June 27, 1908, p. 24.

22. *Moving Picture World*, Aug. 29, 1908, p. 152.

23. New York *Dramatic Mirror*, Aug. 22, 1908, p. 7.

24. *Billboard*, March 21, 1908, p. 30.

25. New York *Dramatic Mirror*, Aug. 22, 1908, p. 7.

26. *Moving Picture World*, Feb. 8, 1908, p. 96.

27. *Variety*, Jan. 25, 1908, p. 11.

28. Robert Sklar, *Movie-made America: A Cultural History of American Movies* (New York: Vintage Books, 1975), p. 18.

29. Kasson, *Amusing the Million*, pp. 6–7.

30. Peiss, *Cheap Entertainments*, pp. 164–65.

31. *Film Index*, Sept. 5, 1908, p. 2.

32. Peiss, *Cheap Entertainments*, p. 129; Rosenzweig, *Eight Hours*, p. 175.

33. Eileen Bowser, *History of American Cinema*, vol. 2: *1907–1915* (New York: Charles Scribner's Sons, 1990), p. 2.

34. Trade journals advised exhibitors to hire actors to speak dialogue for the films, New York *Clipper*, Sept. 19, 1908, p. 790. Short of this, a variety of "talking picture" devices were available: Carl Laemmle, an important exchangeman, marketed the Synchroscope (*Show World*, July 4, 1908, p. 11); Gaumont announced it had improved its "chronophone" and offered new films specially made for it (New York *Dramatic Mirror*, Sept. 5, 1908, p. 8); and Cameraphone, a production company specializing in making synchronized films of vaudeville stars, opened their own theater in Brooklyn (*Variety* Nov. 28, 1908, p. 12).

35. *Variety*, June 6, 1908, p. 11.

36. Ibid., Aug. 8, 1908, p. 10.

37. New York *Dramatic Mirror*, March 28, 1908, p. 4.

38. The role of the film lecturer, both historically and theoretically, has been examined by André Gaudreault in his article "Bruitage, musique et commentaires aux débuts du cinéma," *Protée* 12 (Summer 1985): 12–20, and in *Du Litteraire au filmique: System du récit* (Paris: Meridiens Klincksieck, 1988), chap. 12.

39. *Moving Picture World*, Aug. 22, 1908, p. 137.

40. Ibid.

41. Figures quoted in Allen, *Vaudeville and Film*, pp. 159, 212–13. Citing the number of films released in different genres, Allen has pointed out that actuality films outnumbered fiction films until 1906. However Charles Musser has pointed out the danger in dealing with raw percentage of total releases. Story films were longer than actualities as a rule and therefore took up a greater part of a film program. Further, they outsold most actualities and therefore were shown more frequently. Musser therefore argues for an earlier dominance of the market by the story film, around 1904. See "Another Look at the 'Chaser Theory,' " *Studies in Visual Communications* 10, no. 4 (1984): 24–44. By 1904 Biograph had clearly shifted emphasis to fiction production.

42. *Moving Picture World*, 1908, p. 231. The synopsis was the advance bulletin sent to exhibitors by film production companies, as advance publicity from which exhibitors and exchanges would order their films. They were also used as an aid in understanding the films. Some theaters in Boston and Chicago distributed them before showing of the film, *Variety*, April 4, 1908, p. 12.

43. New York *Dramatic Mirror*, Sept. 19, 1908, p. 9.

44. *Variety*, Feb. 1, 1908, p. 11.

45. Noel Burch, "Passion, poursuite: La linearisation," *Communication* 38 (1983): 38.

46. Burch, "Passion," pp. 38–39.

47. Roland Barthes, *Empire of Signs*, trans. Richard Howard (New York: Hill and Wang, 1982), pp. 48–51.

48. See also David Levy, "Edison Sales Policy and the Continuous Action Film 1904–1906," in *Film Before Griffith*, ed. Fell, pp. 207–22.

49. Bowser, *Biograph Bulletins*, p. 27.

50. New York *Dramatic Mirror*, Oct. 24, 1908, p. 8.

51. Ibid., Oct. 10, 1908, p. 8.

52. In my terminology, a cut to a single shot of another location or line of action which does not form part of a series of alternated shots (such as the point-of-view shot in *The Redman and the Child*) would be called a cutaway.

53. David Bordwell uses the term *crosscutting* to cover what I am describing, reserving the term *parallel editing* to refer to alternation in which temporal relations are not pertinent (e.g., ideological contrasts or comparisons). See *The Classical Hollywood Cinema: Film Style and Mode of Production to 1960*, David Bordwell, Janet Staiger, and Kristin Thompson (New York: Columbia University Press, 1985). However this introduces new definitions for old terms, and I agree with Eileen Bowser that this practice can only lead to confusion (*History of American Cinema* p. 87).

54. A. Nicholas Vardac, *From Stage to Screen: Theatrical Method from Garrick to Griffith* (1949, repr. New York: Benjamin Blom, 1968), pp. 235–57; and Sergei Eisenstein, "Dickens, Griffith, and the Film Today," in *Film Form*, ed. and trans. Jay Leyda (New York: Harcourt Brace Jovanovich, 1942).

55. Charles Musser, "Early Cinema of Edwin S. Porter," in *Cinema 1900–1906: An Analytical Study by the National Film Archives (London) and the International Federation of Film Archives*, ed. Roger Holman (Brussels: FIAF, 1982), vol. 2, p. 278.

56. For instance, Biograph's *Next!*, *A Discordant Note* (both 1903), *A Friend in Need Is a Friend Indeed* (1906), *The Firebug* (1905), and Edison's *How They Do Things on the Bowery* (1902).

57. Gérard Genette, *Narrative Discourse: An Essay in Method*, trans. Jane E. Lewin (Ithaca: Cornell University Press, 1980), p. 116.

58. See Biograph's *Off His Beat* (1903), or Edison's *The Maniac Chase* (1904).

59. Robert Gessner, "Porter and the Creation of Cinematic Motion: An Analysis of *The Life of an American Fireman*," *Journal of the Society of Cinematologists* 2 (1962): 1–13; Barry Salt, "What We Can Learn from the First Twenty Years of Cinema," IRIS 2, no. 1 (1985): 85.

60. A discussion of the temporality of this sequence can be found in Andfe Gaudreault, "Detours in Film Narrative: The Development of Cross Cutting," in *Cinema 1900–1906*, ed. Holman, vol. 1, pp. 187–90.

61. Roland Barthes, "Introduction to the Structural Analysis of Narratives," in *Image Music Text*, ed. and trans. Stephen Heath (New York: Hill and Waug, 1977), p. 119.

62. The anticipation of this suspenseful use of parallel editing in Pathé's *A Narrow Escape* will be discussed in chapter 7, in the context of Griffith's remake of this earlier film, *The Lonely Villa*.

63. Eileen Bowser, ed., *Biograph Bulletins, 1908–1912* (New York: Farrar, Straus and Giroux), p. 11.

64. New York *Dramatic Mirror*, Aug. 29, 1909, p. 7.

65. Frank Rahill, *The World of Melodrama* (University Park: Pennsylvania State University Press, 1967), p. 189.

66. Noel Burch, "Un mode de representation primitif," IRIS 2, no. 1 (1984): 116–17.

67. See the discussion of deadlines in Bordwell, Staiger, and Thompson, *Classical Hollywood*, pp. 44–46. Deadlines had appeared in films before Griffith. An earlier pre-Griffith Biograph film, *The Tired Tailor's Dream* (1908), also used a deadline, although without parallel editing.

68. See, for example, Russell Merritt's description of Edward McWade's play *Wincester* in which Griffith acted in 1904. The production actually used a projected film to show a race to the rescue as the hero on stage faced a firing squad. Russell Merritt, "Rescued from a Perilous Nest: D. W. Griffith's Escape from Theater into Film," *Cinema Journal* 2 (Fall 1981): 25.

69. Herbert G. Gutman, *Work, Culture and Society in Industrializing America: Essays in American Working Class and Social History* (New York: Vintage Books, 1966), pp. 19–32; Piess, *Cheap Entertainments*, p. 4.

70. Kasson, *Amusing the Million*, pp. 73–74.

71. Quoted in Michael Booth, *English Melodrama* (London: Herbert Jenkins, 1965), p. 206.

72. Peter Brooks, *The Melodramatic Imagination: Balzac, Henry James, Melodrama and the Mode of Excess* (New Haven: Yale University Press, 1976), pp. 47–48.

73. For a discussion of melodramatic acting as a system of visual and aural signs see Gilbert Cross, *Next Week—East Lynn: Domestic Drama in Performance 1820–1874* (Lewisburg: Bucknell University Press, 1977), pp. 106–67. Kemble is discussed on p. 121, with "teapot" poses illustrated on p. 122. See also Roberta Pearson's treatment of the histrionic acting code as a series of arbitrary signs in " 'The Modesty of Nature': Performance Style in the Griffith Biographs," Ph. D. Diss., New York University, 1987, particularly pp. 48–60.

74. Pearson defines the verisimilar style on pp. 48, 61–81.

75. See such films as *May Irwin Kiss* (Edison, 1896), *Masques and Grimaces* (Smith?, 1901?), *Burlesque Suicide* (Edison, 1902), and *Une bonne histoire* (Pathé, 1903).

76. Tom Gunning, "The Non-Continuous Style of Early Film," in *Cinema 1900–1906*, ed. Holman, vol. 1, p. 227.

77. Edison publicity bulletin quoted in George Pratt, ed., *Spellbound in Darkness: A History of the Silent Film*, rev. ed. (Greenwich: New York Graphic Society, 1973), p. 36.

78. Noel Burch, "Film's Institutional Mode of Representation and the Soviet Response," *October* 11 (Winter 1979): 74.

79. New York *Dramatic Mirror*, Oct. 17, 1908, p. 16.

80. Lewis Jacobs, *The Rise of the American Film: A Critical History, with an Essay, Experimental Cinema in America 1921–1947* (New York: Teachers College Press, 1968), pp. 102–3; Linda Arvidson, *When the Movies Were Young* (1925, repr. New York: Dover Publications, 1969), p. 66; Georges Sadoul, *Histoire général du cinéma*, vol. 3: *Le cinéma devient un art 1909–1920, premiere volume: L'avant guerre* (Paris: Denoel, 1951), p. 90; Jean Mitry, *Histoire du cinéma: Art et industrie*, vol. 1: *1895–1914* (Paris: Editions Universitaires, 1967), p. 402.

81. Bowser, *Biograph Bulletins*, p. 33.

82. I thank Maureen Turim for letting me read her unpublished paper "Layers of Meaning: 'Enoch Arden' and an Historically Wrought Semiotics," which discusses the Enoch Arden motif in several historical periods in differing media.

83. Arvidson, *When the Movies Were Young*, p. 66.

84. Ibid.

85. Vardac, *From Stage to Screen*, pp. 64–73.

86. Although Arvidson's novelistic dialogue in which Griffith claims Dickens as model and justification for the narrative form of this film does not inspire confidence in her memoirs at this point, it seems likely that Dickens may have been a formal

influence on Griffith's narrative form. The role of alternation in Dickens and other nineteenth-century novelists (so beautifully explicated in Eisenstein's "Dickens, Griffith, and the Film Today") may have been as important to Griffith as the "cross-cutting" Vardac describes in nineteenth-century theater. Griffith's film, cutting between brief shots, recalls the freedom of spatial and temporal alternation available to the novel.

87. Vardac, *From Stage to Screen*, p. 171.

88. Ibid., p. 72.

89. Turim, "Layers of Meaning," pp. 7–8.

90. Bowser, *Biograph Bulletins*, p. 33.

91. Genette, *Narrative Discourse*, p. 255.

92. Joyce E. Jesionowski, *Thinking in Pictures: Dramatic Structure in D. W. Griffith's Biograph Films* (Berkeley: University of California Press, 1987), p. 42; see also her treatment of this sequence on pp. 41–42.

93. Charles Dickens, *Oliver Twist* (New York: New American Library, 1961) p. 157.

94. Brooks, *Melodramatic Imagination*, p. 48.

95. Tom Gunning, "Presence du narrateur: L'Heritage des films Biograph de Griffith," in *D. W. Griffith: Études sous la direction de Jean Mottet*, ed. Jean Mottet (Paris: L'Harmattan, 1984), pp. 117–25, and Jacques Aumont, "Griffith la cadre, la figure," in *Le cinéma Amercain: Analyses des films*, vol. 1, ed. Raymond Bellour (Paris: Flammarion, 1980), 57–67.

96. Walter Benjamin, *Understanding Brecht*, trans. Ana Bostock (London: NLB, 1977), p. 13. My understanding of the role interruption plays in film editing was shaped by the lectures of Annette Michelson in a seminar on Soviet Cinema in 1972 at New York University which related this essay of Benjamin to Eisenstein. Michelson has developed this idea in "Camera Lucida/Camera Obscura," *Art Forum* 9 (January 1973): 30–37.

97. *Classical Hollywood Cinema*, ed. Bordwell, Staiger, and Thompson, p. 177.

98. For example, Biograph's *The Artist's Dream* (1903), Méliès's *The Clockmaker's Dream* (1904), Edison's *Dream of a Rarebit Fiend* (1906), and Pathé's *Reve à la lune* (1904)—the list is enormous.

99. Niver, *Biograph Bulletins*, p. 349.

100. In *The Christmas Burglars*, a pawnbroker (Charles Inslee) accidentally discovers a letter to Santa Claus written by the daughter (Adele De Garde) of a poor widow (Florence Lawrence). While the mother and daughter sleep on Christmas eve, the pawnbroker breaks into their tenement flat with the aid of local burglars, leaving a Christmas tree and presents. A three-shot unit in the film is intended to show the pawnbroker's decision to surprise the widow and child. The first shot shows the pawnbroker and a crony reading the little girl's letter. This shot dissolves to a shot of the mother and daughter and a group of children dancing around a Christmas tree. This image then dissolves, returning to the pawnbroker and friend nodding happily as they look at the letter. Unfortunately, a textual problem occurs. The only extant print of the film was made from a paper print at the Library of Congress. The shots of the print are not assembled in order, nor are they numbered to indicate their proper sequence. Because of the dissolves, the three-shot sequence has been preserved as a unit, but the exact placement of the unit is unclear. There seem to be only two places in the film where it could fit. One is just after the pawnbroker has found the letter,

in which case the dissolved-in shot is his mental anticipation of the surprise he has planned. The other possible position comes at the end of the film. In this case the unit would show the pawnbroker musing over the letter and recalling the surprises he gave the family. If the image is a "flash-forward," we must read it as the characters' anticipation. If it is a "flash-back" it must be read as a memory. In either case, the dissolve in and out unambiguously signals that the interpolated shot is a mental image.

101. A one-shot cutaway occurs in a pre-Griffith Biograph film, *Old Isaacs the Pawnbroker*, in which the cut is from a girl waiting in the office of a charity organization to her sick mother at home. The story for this film was written by Griffith. Eileen Bowser has discussed this editing strategy in "Griffith's Film Career Before *The Adventures of Dollie*," in *Film Before Griffith*, ed. Fell, pp 369–70.

102. Bowser, *Biograph Bulletins*, p. 18.

103. Jesionowski reads this cut as primarily psychological; see *Thinking in Pictures*, p. 170.

104. Unfortunately, we are once again faced with textual problems because the only extant print was made from an unassembled paper print at the Library of Congress. However, Jay Leyda has proposed an assembly of the film that seems to be the only one possible. The following discussion is based on that reconstruction.

5

Complete and Coherent Films, Self-Contained Commodities

B Y THE end of 1908, the narrator system came into focus. Although further developments awaited, a firm foundation had been laid. The transformation of filmic discourse reworked devices that Griffith inherited from filmmaking of the previous decade but subordinated them more specifically to the tasks of storytelling and character development. A basic rethinking of the role of film as both a narrative form and as an economic commodity underlies this reorientation of film, which I have called the cinema of narrative integration, and Griffith responded to these changes creatively, formulating the narrator system. By the end of 1908, economic reorganization of the film industry would also take a new configuration: the Motion Picture Patents Company. The MPPC would regularize the American film industry under the aegis of a production monopoly, setting up new relations among production, distribution, and exhibition. The new organization produced a more standardized commodity, primarily based on single-reel narrative films. Internally the new commodity gained a greater coherence and completeness, in part as a response to the new economic environment.

Two films from the latter part of 1908 show Griffith's pivotal position in this transformation of narrative form in film. *The Curtain Pole* (October 16, 22) exemplifies his debt to—and mastery of—the traditional chase format. *The Guerrilla* (October 12, 14), on the other hand, exploits the newfound possibilities of parallel editing. The films also diverge in genre: *The Curtain Pole* is a comic chase, while *The Guerrilla* involves a melodramatic rescue. The two films reveal Griffith's reworking of the transitional narrative forms, from the mastery of the linear schemas of continuity to explorations of tense and suspense by restructuring action into alternating vectors.

The chase format cuts across genres, propelling both comedies and melodramas. Is the chase, then, a genre? Perhaps Mikhail Bakhtin's literary critical term, the *chronotope*, suits it best. For Bahktin, the chronotope is an artistic element in which "spatial and temporal indicators are fused into one carefully thought-out concrete whole."[1] The particular fusion of spatial and temporal relations created by the continuous action of pursuit defines the chase and determines its importance for early film editing.

By 1906–7, the chase had generated a number of related chronotopes, such as linked vignettes and early experiments with parallel editing (in such films as *The Hundred to One Shot*). Griffith elaborated parallel editing into a new but fundamentally related chronotope—the race to the rescue intercutting victims in peril (often struggling with a menacing villain) and rescuers. However, as *The Curtain Pole* shows, the traditional chase format continued to exist alongside the more recent chronotope.

Griffith's 1908 chase films bring innovations to the old form but do not include extended parallel editing. Griffith followed the traditional format, with both pursuers and pursuer tracing a path through the same shot. *Balked at the Altar*, although made after the *The Greaser's Gauntlet*, employs the linear succession of shots following character movement which had formed the pattern of chase films since *The Escaped Lunatic* (1903). This is also true of the chase on horseback in the melodrama *The Girl and the Outlaw* (July 31, August 2, 4). Only in *The Red Girl* does Griffith present a brief canoe chase which cuts once from a pursuing posse to escaping thieves. But when presenting a victim at the mercy of a villain and a rescuer rushing to save them, Griffith always uses parallel editing. Occasionally the mobility of the villain with his victim, such as the lynch mob in *The Greaser's Gauntlet* or the fleeing adulterous couple in *The Planter's Wife* (September 8, 10) may blur the distinction between the two types. Yet these mobile rescues never cut between victims and pursuing villains, only between the abduction and the rescuer.

Within the traditional chase chronotope Griffith innovates by sharpening the cut's dominance over action. Although the chase sequence from *The Call of the Wild* contains no intercutting, the nine-shot sequence diverges sharply from earlier chase films. As a band of mounted Indians pursues a white girl, the film no longer waits for every character to leave the frame before cutting, but edits much more boldly, cutting while riders remain in the frame. The editing in this chase sequence further asserts its power over action by endowing the sequence with a basic accelerating tempo. As the chase moves to its climax, the shots become progressively shorter. In 16mm, the length of the first shot of the chase (shot eleven) is 15½ feet. The shots then become shorter, almost systematically, as the Indians draw closer to the fleeing girl: shot twelve, 10¼ feet; shot thirteen, 6 feet; shot fourteen, 6½ feet; shot fifteen, 5½ feet; shot sixteen, 4 feet; shot seventeen, 3 feet. I have found no earlier example of this creation of rhythm through the lengths of shots. This rhythmic pulse combined with the interrupting cut involves the spectator almost physically.

The Curtain Pole's fourteen-shot chase sequence contains no parallel editing and hardly deviates from the classic form. Returning to a form that Biograph had pioneered with such films as *Personal,* Griffith must have been aware that the French firms of Pathé and Gaumont had recently outstripped the American company in imagination and ingenuity. *The Curtain Pole* seems to acknowledge the chase's detour through France by making the film's protagonist (Mack Sennett) a French dandy. The dandy's costume and mannerisms were modeled (as Sennett admitted) on Pathé's rising comedian of genius Max Linder. Griffith also lifted the film's use of reverse motion from an enormously popular Pathé film, *The Runaway Horse,* released in the United States early in 1908.[2] *The Curtain Pole* seems to predict the future of American film comedy by situating Sennett at the center of the film's mayhem, prophetically announcing the blend of Griffith's editing tempo with comic anarchy that Sennett concocted later at Keystone.

Like *Dollie,* the film traces a narrative circuit. Sennett's dandy sets out from a party to bring back a curtain pole to his hosts, only to cause a series of disasters en route with his unwieldy burden. His evergrowing group of unintended victims becomes an angry pursuing mob as the dandy makes his way back. With one exception (shot eight, which shows Sennett ducking into a bar only to be found by his pursuers in the following shot), both elements of the chase—the dandy and his mob of pursuers—appear in each shot of the chase sequence. Most shots begin with Sennett running into the shot, moving from background to foreground. After he collides with some object in the foreground (a baby carriage, a vegetable pushcart, some rubes examining a sign, a man fixing a street lamp, or a whole marketful of stalls), he rushes from the frame. Then the mob enters, similarly wreaking havoc and gathering irate new pursuers.

The film carefully escalates its devices, beginning with the dandy carrying the curtain pole and knocking down passersby as he stops to speak to a beautiful lady. As the pursuing mob gains members, he commandeers a carriage complete with drunken driver, and the destruction accelerates. The reverse motion appears seamlessly at this point. After the carriage seems to shake off its pursuers for a moment, a strange man in the foreground steps forward, seizes one of its wheels, and thrusts it backward. Following a skillful substitution splice, the action goes into reverse, which continues in the next two shots. The film returns to forward motion with another trick splice, as the hero maneuvers the curtain pole to reverse the carriage's direction as it goes around a tree.

Although his debt to *The Runaway Horse* stands out, Griffith's reverse motion shows signs of narrative integration. In the Pathé film, no diegetic action motivates the reverse motion; it simply occurs as a playful escalation of the film's anarchic energy. In Griffith's film the trick is "caused" (even if absurdly) by a force within the diegesis—the mysterious man who reverses the carriage's direction. Again Griffith's narrator system contrasts with the earlier cinema of attractions, still influential in a transitional film like *The Runaway Horse*. When trick work appears in Griffith's films (which is rarely), some attempt is made to rationalize it, to absorb it into a narrative logic, however fanciful.

The Moving Picture World found *The Curtain Pole* old fashioned, wondering what made Biograph follow "the worn-out scheme of foreign producers and introduce these long chases and destruction of property as a part of their amusement films."[3] The New York *Dramatic Mirror*, however, welcomed the classic formula: "It has been so long since we have seen a 'chase' picture from the Biograph people that we had commenced thinking they had forgotten how to make one. Generally speaking this would not be a matter for regret, for the chase has been done so much and often so badly that it has grown into disrepute, except when produced with exceptional originality."[4]

If *The Curtain Pole* showed a mastery of the invention and pace of earlier chase films, *The Guerrilla* sets the chronotope for many of Griffith's later parallel-edited, last-minute-rescue films. This one-reel film, 898 feet long in 35mm, contains forty-five shots, more than any other Griffith film of 1908. Three months earlier *The Greaser's Gauntlet* contained only sixteen shots in a longer film (1,027 feet in 35mm). In fact, the film that Griffith shot just before *The Guerilla, Pirate's Gold* (October 8, 10), had only fourteen shots in its 966-foot length (35mm).

Griffith's first film with a Civil War setting, *The Guerrilla,* deals with a Union officer's wife besieged in her own home by a brutal Confederate guerrilla while her husband rides to the rescue. Alternate editing patterns become quite complex, interrelating several lines of convergent action in different locations. The film not only cuts between the Union troops led by the officer rushing to the rescue while the wife struggles with the guerrilla, but also intercuts the cowering wife barricaded in her parlor and the guerrilla battering the other side of the door. For the first time Griffith uses a three-pronged editing pattern found in his later last-minute-rescue films such as *The Lonely Villa* (1909), *The Lonedale Operator* (1911), and *An Unseen Enemy* (1912). At one point even a fourth element is added briefly to the editing pattern, with a cut to the guerrilla's troops preparing to ambush the rescuers.

Although it makes little use of the new access to characters the narrator system allowed, *The Guerrilla* displays a complexity of narrative discourse that contrasts strikingly with *The Adventures of Dollie*. Developing the forms introduced in *The Fatal Hour*, *The Guerrilla* initiates a series of action-based melodramas structured around a suspenseful manipulation of tense. With its free manipulation of space and time, *The Guerrilla* exemplifies Griffith's transformations of the action-based narrative, freed from a simple linearity of movement.

While *The Guerilla* sets the pattern for later last-minute-rescue melodramas, *The Song of the Shirt* (October 19, 20) sketched the schema used in Griffith's later films of social criticism such as *A Corner in Wheat* (1909), *The Usurer* (1910), *Gold Is Not All* (1910), and *For His Son* (1911). All these films use parallel editing to contrast the fortunes of the upper and lower classes, morally condemning the heartlessness of greedy capitalists. This dual basis of contrast, economic and moral, defines these film's ideology. Griffith's attacks on capitalism for the most part present moral judgments, contrasts between good and evil, rather than economic analysis and class conflict.

This moral dualism finds perfect expression in parallel editing, which can contrast directly two forms of behavior or ways of life. However moral dualism limits social analysis. As Sergei Eisenstein showed in his famous critique of Griffith's editing, parallel editing also expresses the limits of this social conception, in which "society perceived *only as a contrast between the haves and the have-nots,* is reflected in the consciousness of Griffith no deeper than the image of an intricate race between two parallel lines."[5] Griffith's social rhetoric basically adopts the moral dualism of nineteenth-century melodrama, expressed cinematically through parallel editing.

The social rhetoric of *The Song of the Shirt* exemplifies Griffith's work in Genette's category of voice, expressing the filmic narrator's judgments about characters or actions through contrast edits. For Genette, voice refers to the act of narrating the story and to the elements in the text which refer to this act.[6] However, not many of the instances of voice that Genette discusses in his treatment of Proust are applicable to Griffith's Biograph films. Such issues as the time of narrating, the narrative levels of embedded stories, or the blending of diegetic events with the extradiegetic act of narration simply do not apply to these one-reel films.[7] But one function of voice discussed by Genette clearly corresponds to Griffith's moral judgments through contrast edits, "the ideological function," moments of authorial commentary on narrative action.[8]

The contrast edit does more than simply present events; it intervenes to comment on them and expresses that comment by an ideological reference. A contrast edit differs from the suspenseful use of parallel editing which concerns itself primarily with temporal relations, although a sequence of two shots may certainly function in both categories, as do the opening shots of the parallel-edited sequence of *The Greaser's Gauntlet* and several cuts in *The Song of the Shirt*. The contrast edit primarily compares the content of shots ideologically, expressing a paradigmatic relation, a comparison of types.

The story of *The Song of the Shirt* implies social criticism; some nickelodeon-era films, regardless of comments by some historians, did deal with the lives of working-class patrons.[9] A sewing machine girl (Florence Lawrence) labors for food and medicine for her sick sister (Linda Arvidson). She is refused payment because of an imperfection in one of the shirts she has sewed. Although she begs the factory owner (Harry Solter) and his foreman (Mack Sennett) to reconsider, they refuse. She returns home to find her sister dead.

Filmic discourse elaborates this story into social commentary. Through its use of parallel editing the moral discourse of *The Song of the Shirt* reads "like a book."[10] The film's first two shots set up the contrast to be developed later. The first shows the seamstress leaning over her sister's sickbed, while the second cuts to the owner of the shirt-making company surrounded by his underlings. No relation has yet been established between the two in the story; the seamstress applies for work at the factory only in the following shots. The cut anticipates their actual interraction.

After the seamstress receives work from the factory the cuts between management and labor continue. We cut directly from the factory-owner entertaining a showgirl at a restaurant to the seamstress's cramped apartment, her sister writhing in pain while the seamstress works furiously. The contrast and implied moral indictment is clear. It is further underlined in the final three shots of the film, after Lawrence's payment has been refused and her plead unheeded. The factory owner dances, drinks champagne, and kisses showgirls in a restaurant (fig. 20). In the following shot, the foremen of the sweatshop are also shown eating in an ornate dining room (fig. 21). Then, in the final shot of the film, Lawrence returns to her apartment. Her sister twists in pain on her bed and dies in the arms of the seamstress, who collapses in grief over the body. This grim image ends the film (fig. 22). The paradigmatic aspect of these contrast edits is obvious. Although the cuts also function as parallel editing, their temporal dimension is much less important here than in rush-to-the-rescue suspense films. The cutting is not motivated by temporal deadlines but by a juxtaposition of the life-styles of the rich and the exploited. Although simultaneity sharpens the edge of the irony, its sticking point is moral judgment.

While these contrasts primarily express a moral dualism, the editing does approach a social analysis. Parallel editing can indicate certain "invisible" causes, in this case economic ones, that link characters. The first cut from the owner to the seamstress working shows this most clearly. At this point in the story the seamstress and the factory-owner have not met and have never been seen in the same shot. The seamstress had received her work from the

The concluding images of *The Song of the Shirt* (1908). Frame enlargements from prints made from Paper Print Collection, Library of Congress.

20. While the factory boss (Harry Solter) cavorts with a show girl. . . .

21. . . . . and his foremen (George Gebhardt, Mack Sennett) enjoy a fine meal. . . .

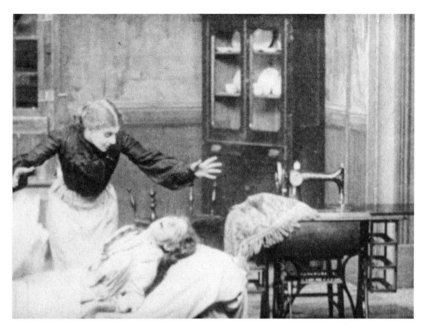

22. . . . . the seamstress returns to find her sister (Linda Arvidson) dead.

sweatshop foreman, and only confronts the boss later when she begs for her payment. This cut, therefore, joins two characters who have never seen each other, articulating the seamstress's economic dependence on the factory-owner. That Griffith's editing can articulate such abstract relations between characters shows its transformation from the editing based on physical movement found in *The Adventures of Dollie*. Editing pushes against the edge of abstraction, a project which *A Corner in Wheat* would bring to a climax.

But if this film opens toward the possibilities of editing explored by the later Soviet filmmakers, it still very much belongs to its particular historical horizon. Although social rhetoric pushes editing toward abstraction, it does not do so at the expense of the film's diegesis. The voice of the narrator system is an indirect one, soliciting the viewer through the way the world of the film is presented, rather than addressing him or her directly as the cinema of attractions did. A comparison with *The Kleptomaniac* (1905), Porter's famous film of social criticism, shows how Griffith integrated voice into the narrator system's project of creating a coherent, diegetic world.

Contrary to its description by Lewis Jacobs, who summarizes the story of the film, rather than its actual filmic discourse, Porter's film does not use contrast editing.[11] Only the story line contrasts the treatment of a rich woman who is a "kleptomaniac" with a poor woman caught stealing bread. At no point does Porter intercut the women's plights to create a contrast. Shots one through five follow the story of the rich thief. Shots six and seven present the poor woman and her theft. Their contrasting treatment in court (the rich woman is let go, the poor woman taken to jail) occur in a single shot. Only shots eight and nine present something of a contrast, showing first the rich woman arriving at the police station in a carriage, the poor woman in a patrol wagon.

Rather than using editing to express social criticism, Porter presents in the final shot a symbolic tableau of a figure of justice against a black background, her scale tilted toward the side loaded with money. Porter relies on an image abstracted from the diegesis of the film to comment on the action. The black background of the tableau marks it as an illustrated intertitle. Certainly the shot in Porter's film acts as an instance of voice, showing that this aspect of narrative discourse was not absent in pre-Griffith cinema, but simply constructed differently. Its extradiegetic nature (it is even introduced by a intertitle reading "Tableau"), puncturing the world of the narrative, defines its deviance from Griffith's concern with a coherent fictional world.[12] In the narrator system such comments are absorbed into narrative discourse, occurring simultaneously with it. Instances of an intrusive, commenting voice occur without deviating from the presentation of the story.

This concern for the integrity of the film's fictional world, a desire to interweave the element of voice with the presentation of a diegesis, relates Griffith's filmmaking to the seamless esthetic of the classical film as surely as it differentiates him from the noncontinuous approach of Porter. The cinema of narrative integration introduces not only characters whose desires and fears motivate plots, but also a new wholeness and integrity to the fictional world in which action takes place. In contrast to The Kleptomaniac's sharp transitions in modes of discourse (from theatrical scene to editorial cartoon), films of this later period show an increased homogeneity and present the film as a complete and self-contained entity. For Griffith and other filmmakers of the period, this translated into a new attention to the dramatic milieu and narrative closure. Although its achievement was uneven in 1908, situating stories within a realistic environment became an important element as the narrator system developed. Detailed realistic settings provided a varied spontaneous world beyond the demands of significance and naturalized the narrator's interventions, guaranteeing the diegetic unity of a film. In Griffith's films this realistic diegesis balanced the "sense" of the narrator system, presenting story within a believable world. His meanings appear immanent to the narrated world, not abstracted in the manner of Porter's cartoonlike tableau.

It would be misleading to see Griffith's interest in placing film stories within a realistic environment as simply another step in the discovery of film's essential differences from theater. Here again, although a strong difference between the two forms ultimately appeared, Griffith's initial inspiration in this direction came, in fact, from theater. The stimulus came less from melodrama than the emerging naturalist theater. However, as Nicholas Vardac has shown, these theatrical styles shared a concern with theater's visual impact. David Belasco exemplifies naturalistic stagecraft's rechanneling of the visual energy of melodrama. In contrast to the conventional staging of classical theater or early melodrama, Belasco attempted to create on stage a nearly photographic simulcrum of reality, declaring, "Beyond the margins of a miniature, the whole world can be seen, if the miniature is faithful."[13]

War and *A Fool and a Girl,* the plays Griffith wrote shortly before he entered film, show his fascination with the detailed environment of the naturalist theater. Whether or not he had read Zola's essay "Naturalism in the Theater," Griffith had certainly absorbed its lesson, that in the new stagecraft "a climate, a region, a horizon, a room often have decisive importance."[14] *A Fool and a Girl* (the only Griffith play that was produced, premiering in Washington in 1907) opens with a prologue in the Bull Pup Cafe, a low-life dive that swirls with the action of minor characters—prostitutes, roughnecks, homosexuals, drunks—before the leads appear. This attention to a disreputable environment prompted the reviewer Hector Fuller to complain in the Washington *Herald:* "If one wanted to tell the old, old and beautiful story of redemption of man or woman through love, it is not necessary to portray the gutter from which they are redeemed." Fuller pronounced Griffith's play "as inartistic as a Zola novel," whereupon Griffith fired off a response declaring that he was proud to be classed with Zola.[15]

Environment also precedes dramatic action in *War,* Griffith's never-produced spectacular play of the American Revolution. The first act presents a typical day in a New England village, the passage from dawn to night conveyed by elaborate lighting effects. The action is episodic, a host of characters enacting everyday events of village life rather than building dramatic situations. Only at the end of the act does this typical day become raised from the ordinary, as messengers arrive with news of the battles of Lexington and Concord.

Detailed environments as well as elaborate lighting effects formed the center of the innovations Belasco and others brought to the American stage in the early 1900s, and Griffith clearly identified with this new form of theater.[16] But applying these ambitions to film (which Belasco dismissed as a mere mechanical illusion) initially eluded Griffith. A stylistic influence from Belasco may be at work in *The Helping Hand* (November 23, 27, 1908), as Griffith arranged a hurly-burly of extras in a deliberate attempt to create a milieu—from the stream of people passing in the background corridor of an office, to the twenty-six guests at Daisy's (Linda Arvidson) wedding. But little is achieved beyond a sense of confusion. The author of *War* must have felt hemmed in by the film's fifteen-minute length and the cramped dimensions of Biograph's 14th Street studio. Griffith was not proclaimed "the Belasco of motion pictures" until 1910.[17] The inadequate mimicry of stage realism in *The Helping Hand* was a dead-end; Griffith would once again have to transform a theatrical inspiration to achieve his desired effect.

At its very origin film had been recognized as fulfilling the "photographic ideal" of the naturalist theater. At the premier of the Vitascope in New York in 1896, the impresario Charles Frohman had declared, "That settles scenery. Painted trees that don't move, waves that get up a few feet and stay there, everything we simulate on our stages will have to go."[18] However, as the films of Méliès and Porter's *Uncle Tom's Cabin* show, fiction films before 1908 were more often indebted to pre-naturalistic conventional staging and sets. Griffith's desire to imitate the environments of the naturalist stage led him and others to return to film's realistic illusion which Frohman had admired. This "documentary" quality had, of course, been used in narrative films very early. As David Levy has pointed out, the popularity of "faked" or reenacted news events—"actuality films"—such as the Boer or Russo-Japanese War battles refought in New Jersey, or the execution of famous criminals influenced the shooting style of certain fictional films.[19] A number of fictional films, such as Biograph's *The Skyscrapers of New York* and *The Tunnel Workers* (both from 1906), added a realist touch by intercutting actuality footage into their dramas.

Actuality films had formed an important aspect of Biograph's first early productions, and Billy Bitzer was well trained in capturing reality with a camera.[20] With his aid, Griffith began to achieve the photographic ambitions of the naturalist stage through location shooting. *The Stolen Jewels* (August 25, September 15) includes a shot of the curb market on Broad Street, and Griffith himself can be seen bouncing about in the crowd causing a disturbance, probably to distract attention from the camera. The shot was singled out by the film's publicity bulletin, as well as the New York *Dramatic Mirror* and the *Moving Picture World.*[21] Likewise, *The Romance of a Jewess* (September 15, 1908) contains shots of Lower East Side street life—sidewalks crammed with peddlars' carts and shoppers, stoops filled with women and children. The spontaneous life of the street provides a background for Biograph actors as they move about; the lack of attention paid to the camera seems to indicate that it was concealed, possibly in a wagon parked at the curb. Similar street shots occur in *The Christmas Burglars,* with Florence Lawrence mingling with crowds of people doing their Christmas shopping.

Griffith's integration of actors into actual locations contrasts with the use of actuality material in earlier films such as *The Skyscrapers of New York* and *The Tunnel Workers.* Staging dramatic action within actual locations exemplifies the homogeneity and continuity the cinema of narrative integration introduced. In the earlier films actuality sequences served as semi-detached prologues to the scenes staged with actors.[22] In Griffith's film the documentary aspects literally create a realistic background for the story, providing an expansive and realistic environment, as Belasco's staging had done in theater.

Attention to naturalistic environment endowed Griffith's films with a coherence and completeness by grounding them in a fictional world whose familiarity naturalized the process of narration. But the cinema of narrative integration also achieved unity through a new emphasis on narrative closure. Endings take on a new importance in the narrator system, creating a stronger sense of completion and guaranteeing that audiences left the theater with a sense of narrative satiety. This was more than simply a matter of narrative structure. Closure intersects and becomes enclosed in the family, as domestic ideology naturalizes narrative form. The loss and recovery of the child in *The Adventures of Dollie* sets the pattern. Again and again Biograph films center on families threatened either by social embarrassment (which led to comedies) or physical harm (which led to melodramas). The disruption and regaining of equilibrium that Todorov describes is achieved by threatening and then restoring family order. Saving the family brought a definitive resolution to narrative complications and a clear closure to the film.

Griffith's melodramas generally placed wife or child in harm's way, often threatened by a villain outside the family. The villain's alien nature was occasionally intensified by making him (or her) a different race or nationality, such as the vengeful gypsy woman who threatens the judge's wife in *An Awful Moment* (November 19, 21), or the black burglar who assaults the young daughters in *The Girls and Daddy* (January 1, 14, 1909). But outsiders do not pose the only threat to family harmony. A major source of conflict comes from characters who violate their proper family roles. In 1908 this usually meant adultery (or its suspicion), or a conflict between parents and children (usually over a daughter's choice of a husband).

Comedies as well as melodramas centered increasingly on the bourgeois home. In 1908 Griffith began a series of comedies with Florence Lawrence and John Cumpson as the middle-class "Jones" family.[23] The series continued into 1909 with considerable popularity. The comic structure of the Jones films revolves around the proper domesticity of a bourgeois household, with Mr. Jones's infraction of propriety providing the narrative disequilibrium. The middle-class setting differentiated the series from Griffith's broad farces such as *Monday Morning at the Coney Island Police Court* (August 7), *Balked at the Altar*, or *The Deceived Slumming Party* (May 27, July 14), which drew on earlier film chases and farces. It also signaled Biograph's wooing of middle-class family audiences with a form of comedy unlikely to offend their sensibilities with slapstick rowdiness.

The ideology of domestic contentment led to new forms of narrative containment. Noel Burch has pointed out that many pre-1908 films are resolved through what he calls a "catastrophe ending"—the sudden interruption of a potentially endless sequence of events, as in chase and linked vignettes films. These transitional narratives employ an additive structure—one thing after another—that often calls on some repressive outside force to halt it. Frequently the law itself intervenes, usually a policeman who seizes the chief culprit, arresting both criminal and narrative flow. Griffith's 1908 films, on the other hand, present a problem to be resolved: a threat to family harmony, the overcoming of which ends the film. Thus these films achieve the classical closure Burch describes as the "true" ending "with its impression of natural completion rather than brutal arbitrary interruption, which allows the spectator to *withdraw satisfied.* . . ."[24]

The economics of family harmony provided Griffith with both motive force for his stories and a satisfying means for their conclusion. It is important to keep in mind both these narrative forces. On the one hand, there is the valorization of family unity through its final restoration. On the other, many threats to that unity allow the story to unfold and express a subterranean fascination with the forces of chaos. In fact, a number of films from 1908 have grim endings that mark the destruction of family unity rather than its restoration, for example, *The Song of the Shirt* and *The Reckoning.*

Most often, however, family harmony prevails and places the seal of closure on the story. Griffith ends a large number of 1908 films with a shot of the reunited and secure family embracing. The family embrace becomes a ritual gesture signaling the closure of comedies in which social embarrassments have been resolved and melodramas in which threats to life and security have been withstood.[25] Filmic discourse occasionally also marked the final containment of narrative energy with a cut in to a closer shot. The gypsy woman's plot foiled, *An Awful Moment* ends with a three-quarter short shot of the family standing beside a Christmas tree after a long shot of them all embracing, the closeness of the final shot expressing intimacy and unity.

These shots of order regained, like the lyrical postscripts discussed previously, announce to the audience that they have seen a coherent and completed story. In 1908, this rounded-off completion was expressed by a number of devices of filmic discourse: the circular structure of *The Greaser's Gauntlet,* the lyrical postscript, and the shots of an embracing family. Such completion also defined the film as a commercial unit, a unique commodity under the control of the production company and devised to provide a unified experience for its audience. Family ideology regulated this consumer satisfaction in many films, indicating the cultural values with which the film industry wished to be identified. Combined with the placement of the story within a continuous, all-embracing diegesis, narrative closure marked films as self-regulated narrative experiences possessing their own unifying forces rather than a noncontinuous suite of attractions held together by an off-screen lecturer. The new film stories absorbed spectators into a diegetic illusion and held them until a narrative closure, defined both formally and ideologically, released them.

The narrative form of this new film commodity, while not simply determined by struggles in the economic arena, nonetheless responded to the forces reshaping the film industry. Story films were the staple of the nickelodeon, and their underproduction was the major crisis facing the beleaguered industry. The popularity of story films had allowed a more predictable production process. In contrast to actuality films, the success of story films, as Robert Allen points out, "did not depend on exigencies external to the production situation."[26]

As Charles Musser has shown, an industry based on story films signals an increased control over the product by production companies. The story film could provide a coherent unified commodity, complete in itself, without need of the explanatory context provided by exhibitors (which actuality film often demanded). Editorial strategies such as parallel editing took narrative control out of the hands of the exhibitor and lodged it firmly in the film itself: "as a result, the reel of film came much closer to being a 'pure' commodity. . . ."[27]

The narrator system functions within this scheme by creating complete, coherent narratives that can be turned out by the production company on a regular basis, satisfying the audience's hunger for stories. The narrator system therefore plays an essential role within the economic stabilization of the film industry, represented by the formation of the Motion Picture Patents Company.

At the end of 1908 the enmity between Edison and Biograph in the struggle to control the American film industry gave way to accommodation. Unable to defeat each other, the two companies decided to merge and perhaps assert control over the entire industry through their combined production capability, patent strength, and economic unity. The Edison Combine and the Biograph Combine were replaced by a new entity which formed the center of American film for the next few years, the Motion Picture Patents Company. The domination which had previously eluded Edison now seemed within with his grasp. Not only would competition be controlled in film production, but exchanges and even exhibitors also became subject to new regulations under the MPPC.

In spite of their legal and economic enmity, Biograph and Edison had envisioned some form of combination almost from the start. Documents outline the nature of such a combination as early as February 1, 1908. Behind the lawsuits and public denunciations which marked most of 1908, a series of friendlier negotiations were underway. Defining the exact nature of the new combination and the role Biograph would play within it delayed an immediate alliance. Biograph felt the power of its patents entitled it to a higher status than the other production licensees, as well as a share of the royalties Edison was collecting. The trade papers of late 1908 were filled with rumors of the imminent announcement of the combination.[28]

The Motion Picture Patents Company was incorporated on September 9, 1908 in New Jersey, superseding and integrating the Edison and Biograph combines.[29] In his admirable early study of the MPPC, Ralph Cassady described the new company as "a patent-pooling and licensing organization."[30] The various manufacturers transferred their patents to the holding company, which then licensed them to manufacture films under the patents it now held. Control of patents formed the basis for a series of interlocking agreements which allowed the MPPC to organize and regulate all the areas of the motion picture industry, from the manufacture of raw stock and projection machines, through distribution, down to exhibition.

The MPPC was officially launched on December 18, 1908, when all of the previous Edison licensees—Vitagraph, Kalem, Essanay, Selig, Lubin, and Pathé—signed licenses. A license was drawn up for the Méliès Company, but problems with the newly formed American branch delayed the granting of its license until July 20, 1909.[31] From the opposite camp, the Biograph Company and George Kleine were licensed. Production licenses stipulated that producers would pay Edison a royalty based on his patents, lease their films to exchanges rather than sell them, and deal only with exchanges licensed by the MPPC. The MPPC agreed to grant no further production licenses, unless a majority of present licensees agreed.

With the proclamation of peace among production companies, the MPPC geared up to tackle the pressing problem of meeting the demands of the burgeoning nickelodeon market. New production schedules established an increased and stable rate of production with regular release dates. With the addition of Biograph and the films imported by Kleine, five reels of films a week were added to the program of the Edison licensees. At the beginning of 1909 the MPPC production companies offered exchanges and exhibitors eighteen new reels of films each week, which increased to twenty-one reels a week by the end of the year.[32] Production companies also felt secure enough to invest more money in their films. Florence Lawrence said that after joining the MPPC, Griffith was allowed to raise his production budget to $500–$600 per film, compared to $300–$400 in 1908.[33]

MPPC licenses extended beyond the film manufacturers to interrelate practically all areas of the industry. The MPPC licensed the Eastman-Kodak Company to manufacture "licensed film" stock for the production companies; manufacturers of projection machines to produce machines under the MPPC patents; exchanges to handle the films of the production licensees; and exhibitors to show licensed films on licensed projectors. These licenses gave MPPC leverage over all branches of the industry.

Licensed exhibitors and exchanges encountered constraints on their business which ended the days of freewheeling, individualistic dealings. They had to adhere strictly to the conditions of their licenses or risk being dropped by the MPPC, which would shut them out of the only reliable and plentiful source of films. Renting only to licensed exhibitors, dealing exclusively with licensed films, returning films leased from manufacturers after a set time, and observing release dates were all conditions specified by the MPPC exchange licenses, effectively reforming distribution according to production's desires.

Although exhibitors were restricted to licensed films, this initially caused little problem. The license stipulation that most upset exhibitors was a weekly royalty of $2 due to the MPPC for the use of projection machines. Every exhibitor was subject to this fee, no matter the type of projector, or how long he or she had owned it. Projector royalties became the MPPC's largest source of revenue, double that of film royalties.[34] Biograph's patents controlling film projectors inspired this new source of income, and Edison and Biograph split the proceeds equally. As middlemen dealing directly with exhibitors, exchanges were delegated the task of collecting this unpopular royalty from their customers.

Room was cleared for the new influx created by the MPPC's increased production schedules by requiring exchanges to return films to producers after a set period of exploitation. In later testimony Frank Dyer of the Edison Company and MPPC president described the logic of this system in images that came close to characterizing old films as excrement: "there is a definite track over which the films pass. They start out at one end, and when they come out at the rear end of the track, they have served their usefulness and further uses would only be to injure the public and injure the art."[35]

The new rental schedule of the MPPC was based entirely on the age of the film. A film got its highest rental on the day of its release and declined sharply as time went on (one exchangeman estimated the commercial life of a film as four months). Dyer compared the film business in this respect to the ice business, with some of its value melting away every day.[36] Making the ultimate owners of the films the production companies (who only leased them to exchanges) and dictating the limited commercial life of films made the exchanges even more dependent on the producers because exchanges could no longer rely on a library of previously accumulated films. These policies regularized the film commodity, defining each individual film as a unit in a continuous series coming from the production company, and whose value depended on its novelty.

The economic organization introduced by the MPPC institutionalized the industry's middle-class aspirations. The MPPC announced its goal as "the general betterment of the entire business, from the manufacturers to the exhibitors."[37] While the new trust primarily intended to "better" profits for its production companies, the MPPC clearly identified its new system with the ideals of middle-class reform. The motto the MPPC placed on advertisements for films early in 1909 proclaims their sterling bourgeois virtues: "Moral, Educational, and Cleanly Amusing."[38]

The earliest publicity announcements of the MPPC heralded its "uplift" of the film industry, which it portrayed as dependent on their economic reordering. An MPPC announcement soon after the trust's formation declared it would "insure to the manufacturer a fair and reasonable price for his films so as to enable him to maintain and improve the quality of his pictures." Economic gains for the manufacturers, who had felt shut out of the profits of the nickelodeon explosion, the MPPC claimed would result in "the improvement of the tone and quality" of the films produced.[39]

In setting a minimum price schedule for film rentals, the manufacturers felt they would guarantee their share of income. Throughout 1909, the MPPC was besieged with requests from exchanges begging that they be allowed to cut prices as they had before. But the MPPC wanted film to be a more expensive commodity, removing the opprobrium of "cheap entertainment."[40] It encouraged exhibitors to raise the standard admission price from a nickel to a dime, claiming the price increase would create a more "respectable" class of patrons, as well as allow exhibitors to pay higher film rentals.[41]

In return, manufacturers pledged to raise the quality and tone of their product. This ideological linking of a higher rental price with an increase in quality shows how intertwined the MPPC's economic policies were with a new attitude toward the social status of its product. The increased ambition in the Biograph films during 1909 (particularly such tangible qualities as more elaborate sets and costumes, increased number of extras, and longer film lengths) shows the effect of this policy.

The MPPC's restriction of foreign competition from the American domestic market was also couched in terms of "educating the public taste." The MPPC publicity soon claimed that the new combination would "eliminate the cheap and inferior foreign films" by producing homegrown products which would establish "that only high class and attractive films will be accepted as reaching the American Standard."[42] The exclusion of the bulk of foreign producers other than Pathé, Méliès, Gaumont, and Urban-Eclipse from the MPPC was an achievement that members of the trust later pointed to with pride. Dyer stated that foreign films had represented 60 percent of the films shown in the United States before the formation of the MPPC. By 1914 he claimed that the number had been reduced to 10 percent.[43] This commercial victory was painted as a triumph of taste and morality. Witnesses at the antitrust suit testified that foreign films were not as moral as American films, a claim repeated in trade journals as well, although often aimed at Pathé. The "American Standard" was that of genteel, middle-class taste.

The MPPC's first publicity announcement ended by proclaiming its purpose, "to encourage in all possible ways the commendation and support of the moving picture business by the better class of the community."[44] Wooing a middle-class audience was an acknowledged goal of the new corporation. The "better class" would be drawn by the MPPC's reform of both films and their place of exhibition. Cleanliness, morality, and education had not been universally apparent in either films or film theaters in 1908. First, the MPPC addressed the films themselves, announcing in April 1909 that all material that did not possess either educational or "cleanly amusing" value would be eliminated from licensed films. The means of overseeing this would be the National Board of Censorship (chapter 6). Dyer later claimed the MPPC had radically transformed film theaters:

> At the time the Edison licenses were made, almost the only theaters in existence were the small store shows. It was generally one room with some battered chairs in it, and a screen at one end, and the projecting machine at the other. The exhibition was given in absolute darkness. The place was badly ventilated, extremely dangerous in case of fire, and being in absolute darkness, terrible complaints of all kinds of immoral practices were made; in fact the ordinary motion picture place was looked upon almost as a house of assignation.[45]

One of the primary means the MPPC devised of redeeming the film theater's reputation was by overcoming the literal darkness of the nickelodeon. For anti-film reformers, the darkness of movie theaters summoned up visions of moral turpitude. In their minds nickelodeons swarmed with mashers and "disorderly women" performing acts of darkness in the film's dim flicker. Respectable audiences would not enter such a "house of assignation." The MPPC declared the "light theater" "one of the most desirable changes that can be made toward the elevation of the motion picture business."[46] The company outlined for theater managers a lighting arrangement that allowed the theater to remain lit without interfering with the screen image.

The Motion Picture Patents Company was, first and foremost, an attempt to assert monopolistic control over all areas of the film industry in order to limit competition and increase profits—creating an industry secure enough to attract large investment. An important part of this stabilization was the "uplift" of the business, designed to raise film from "a side show proposition to a high class theatrical proposition," as Dyer testified.[47] This meant removing the stigma of lower-class popular entertainment from film and associating it with the traditions of respectable, "moral, educational, and cleanly amusing" means of expression. However, filmmakers like Griffith had to respond to the challenge of balancing new cultural pretensions with the need to make films which were narratively comprehensible to the broadly based nickelodeon audience. Attaining social respectability while maintaining the new discoveries in filmic discourse involved an often-delicate transaction.

Notes

1. M. M. Bakhtin, *The Dialogic Imagination: Four Essays by M. M. Bakhtin*, ed. Michael Holquist, trans. Caryl Emerson and Michael Holquist (Austin: University of Texas Press, 1981), p. 84.

2. *Film Index* [known in 1908 as *Views and Film Index*], Feb. 8, 1908, p. 5.

3. *Moving Picture World*, Feb. 20, 1909, p. 202.

4. New York *Dramatic Mirror*, Feb. 27, 1909, p. 13.

5. Sergei Eisenstein, *Film Form*, ed. and trans. Jay Leyda (San Diego: Harcourt Brace Jovanovich, 1942), p. 234.

6. Gérard Genette, *Narrative Discourse: An Essay in Method*, trans. Jane E. Lewin (Ithaca: Cornell University Press, 1980), pp. 213–14.

7. Genette, *Narrative Discourse*, pp. 215–37.

8. Ibid., p. 256.

9. Although he is right about general tendencies, I feel Russell Merritt overstates his case in "Nickeleodeon Theaters 1905–1914: Building an Audience for the Movies," in *The American Film Industry*, ed. Terio Balio (Madison: University of Wisconsin Press, 1976), p. 72. One could more than double his number of 1908 films concerning immigrants or the poor from 1908 Biograph films alone, including such titles as *Over the Hills to the Poorhouse, Romance of a Jewess, The Song of the Shirt, The Christmas Burglars*, and *One Touch of Nature*. If one includes working-class characters (such as mill workers), the number is even higher.

10. The intertitles to *The Song of the Shirt* no longer exist, so the extent to which Griffith used them to comment on the action is not known, although we do know they contained several lines from the eponymous poem by Thomas Hood.

11. Lewis Jacobs, *The Rise of the American Film: A Critical History with an Essay, Experimental Cinema in America 1921–1947* (New York: Teachers College Press, 1968), p. 47.

12. Tom Gunning, "The Non-Continuous Style of Early Film," in *Cinema 1900–1906: An Analytical Study by the National Film Archives (London) and the International Federation of Film Archives*, ed. Roger Holman (Brussels: FIAF, 1982), vol. 1, pp. 226–27.

13. Lise-Lone Marker, *David Belasco: Naturalism in the American Theater* (Princeton: Princeton University Press, 1975), p. 46.

14. George Becker, *Documents of Modern Literary Realism* (Princeton: Princeton University Press, 1963), p. 225.

15. In clipping file for *A Fool and a Girl*, Theater Collection, Library for the Performing Arts, Lincoln Center, New York City; clipping of published letter dated Oct. 3, 1907, in D. W. Griffith Papers, Museum of Modern Art Library.

16. Marker, *David Belasco*, pp. 87, 108; A. Nicholas Vardac, *From Stage to Screen:*

Theatrical Method from Garrick to Griffith (1949, repr. New York: Benjamin Blom, 1968), p. 124.

17. New York *Dramatic Mirror,* Dec. 28, 1910, p. 29.

18. Quoted from New York *Dramatic Mirror* in "The Vitascope Press Comments" [May 1896] included in *Motion Picture Catalogs by American Producers and Distributors 1894–1908: A Microfilm Edition,* ed. Charles Musser, Thomas A. Edison Papers (Frederick, Md., 1985), reel 1, frame A-025.

19. See, David Levy, "The Fake Train Robbery: Re-constituted Newsreels, Re-enactments and the American Narrative Film" particularly his discussion of the style in Edison's Boer War re-enactments, in *Cinema 1900–1906,* ed. Holman, vol. 1, p. 250.

20. See his description of filming the Spanish-American War in Billy Bitzer, *His Story: The Autobiography of D. W. Griffith's Master Camerman* (New York: Farrar Straus and Giroux, 1973), pp. 33–42.

21. Eileen Bowser, ed., *Biograph Bulletins, 1908–1912* (New York: Farrar Straus and Giroux, 1973), p. 23; New York *Dramatic Mirror,* Oct. 10, 1908, p. 9; *Moving Picture World,* Oct. 30, 1908, p. 338.

22. Gunning, "The Non-Continuous Style," pp. 225–26.

23. In 1908 this series includes *Mr. Jones at the Ball* (September 23, 24), *Mrs. Jones Entertains* (Oct. 3, Nov. 2), and *Mr. Jones Has a Card Party* (Dec. 17, 23). The earlier *A Smoked Husband* (Aug. 26, 27) should probably be included since it is a domestic comedy starring Lawrence and Cumpson as man and wife, although the Biograph *Bulletin* gives their family name as Bibbs.

24. Noel Burch, "How We Got into Pictures," *AfterImage,* no. 8–9 (Winter 1980–81): 36.

25. Films from 1908 which end with this image include *The Barbarian Ingomar, The Honor of Thieves, The Guerrilla, The Ingrate, The Sacrifice, The Welcome Burglar, The Clubman and the Tramp, A Rural Elopement, A Wreathe in Time, The Planter's Wife, Mrs. Jones Entertains, One Touch of Nature, The Maniac Cook, After Many Years, The Greaser's Gauntlet, The Helping Hand, The Taming of the Shrew,* and *Pirate's Gold.*

26. Robert C. Allen, *Vaudeville and Film, 1895–1915: A Study in Media Interaction* (New York: Arno Press, 1980), p. 218.

27. Charles Musser, "Another Look at the 'Chaser Theory,' " *Studies in Visual Communications* 10 (1984): 40; Charles Musser, "The Nickelodeon Era Begins: Establishing a Framework for Hollywood's Mode of Representation," *Framework* 22–23 (Autumn 1983): 10.

28. See *Show World,* Aug. 29, 1908, p. 3; Oct. 3, 1908, p. 3; *Variety,* Aug. 15, 1908, p. 11; Sept. 19, 1909, p. 11; Sept. 26, 1908, p. 12; Oct. 17, 1908, p. 11; Oct. 31, 1908, p. 11.

29. For some reason, a number of sources, including Cassady and Anderson, indicate that the MPPC was incorporated in Maine on this date. However, the film scholar Martin Sopocy has found the papers of incorporation in New Jersey, while no such papers exist in Maine. These original articles of incorporation are intentionally vague on the purposes of the corporation and do not mention any of the principals. They are signed by Hugh Harris, George Murray, and William Lave, who play no important role in the later combination. I thank Mr. Sopocy for sharing this discovery with me.

30. Ralph Cassady, "Monopoly in Motion Picture Production and Distribution, 1908–1915," *Southern California Law Review*, no. 32 (Summer 1959): 329. Cassady's pioneering work has been well supplemented by Janet Staiger in "Combination and Litigation: Structures of U.S. Film Distribution, 1896–1917," *Cinema Journal* 23 (Winter 1983); and Robert Jack Anderson, "The Motion Picture Patents Company," Ph.D. diss., University of Wisconsin, Madison, 1983.

31. Cassady, "Monopoly," p. 335.

32. *Show World*, Dec. 18, 1909, p. 18.

33. Florence Lawrence, "Growing up with the Movies," *PhotoPlay* (Jan. 1915): 104.

34. Ibid., p. 350.

35. *U.S. v. MPPC*, p. 1588.

36. Ibid., pp. 2021, 1627.

37. *Film Index*, Jan. 2, 1909, p. 4.

38. New York *Clipper*, 5:233.

39. MPPC, "Announcement to Exhibitors," Feb. 1, 1909, Edison National Historic Site Archives, West Orange, N.J.

40. See the editorial in the trust organ, *Film Index*, May 22, 1909, p. 3.

41. Ibid., July 24, 1909, p. 12; Aug. 7, 1909, p. 3.

42. MPPC, "Announcement to Exhibitors."

43. *U.S. v. MPPC*, p. 1585; Anderson stresses this as well, see "The Motion Picture Patents Company," pp. 121–22. The most complete treatment of American wresting of control of their domestic market from foreign producers is found in Kristin Thompson, *Exporting Entertainment: America in the World Film Market 1907–1934* (London: British Film Institute, 1985), particularly pp. 1–27.

44. MPPC, "Announcement to Exhibitors."

45. *U.S. v. MPPC*, p. 1589.

46. *Moving Picture World*, May 15, 1909, p. 631.

47. *U.S. v. MPPC*, p. 1589.

6

From Obscene Films
to High-Class Drama

O N Christmas Eve of 1908, Mayor McClellan of New York City
delivered a surprise gift to more than five hundred motion picture
exhibitors in the metropolitan area when he ordered their nickelodeons closed.[1] The action stunned New York exhibitors and attracted
nationwide attention as the strongest action taken by anti-film reformers reacting to the nickelodeon explosion. The motives for the shut-
down are entangled in big city politics and turn-of-the-century blue laws. The
mayor was legally able to close the nickelodeons because most of them operated
under a "common-show" license. A license for merry-go-rounds and other
cheap amusements including theaters which limited their programs to motion
pictures, songs, and "recitation not rendered on stage," the common-show
license cost only $25 a year and was controlled by the mayor's office.[2]

The common-show license permitted operation seven days a week, and
nickelodeons often had their biggest audience on Sundays. Objections to
this violation of the Sabbath by members of the clergy had prompted an
investigation of picture shows in New York City. On December 23, 1908,
the mayor called a hearing on the Sunday shows specifically and into "the
condition of motion picture shows generally in regard to the safety of their
patrons."[3] Most of the witnesses who opposed motion pictures were members
of the clergy. The mayor testified that on his personal inspection he had found
numerous theaters whose exits were blocked, ran into cul-de-sacs, ended in
forty-foot drops, and, in one case, led into a turkish bath.[4] The clergy testified
that motion picture theaters were breeding places of vice. Film theaters,
they claimed, were particularly a danger for children. The Reverend Evers,
chaplain of City Prison, testified that "I was amazed by the exhibitions I saw

for the benefit of the little boys and girls of our city. The most suggestive, the most enticing actions which appeal only to the lowest and most evil passions in men and women were thrown upon the screen for small boys and girls to look upon. I was indeed saddened by this open exhibition of depravity."[5]

Few specific objections to films are given in the accounts of the hearing. Films of prizefights alarmed some witnesses.[6] Canon William Sheafe Chase of Brooklyn, who for the next few years would be a tireless campaigner against the immorality of the picture show and an advocate of Sunday closing and government censorship, found that some films "exalted horse racing and gambling."[7] Other witnesses testified that films depicted "kissing, etc." as well as "lovemaking, etc."[8] Films dealing with burglaries and train robberies also disturbed the clergy.[9] The *Film Index* delighted in providing a few of the more absurd objections: a circus film showing ladies in tights, a trick film which was condemned as "impossible," and a film that featured Julius Caesar in a very short skirt.[10]

The clergy pronounced the film theaters themselves dens of iniquity and particularly unsafe for children. The Reverend Fellow Jenkins of the Society for the Prevention of Cruelty to Children testified that "the darkened rooms combined with the influence of pictures projected on the screen, have given opportunities for a new form of degeneracy."[11] Mayor McClellan claimed evidence of "a class of disorderly women who confine their activities to the motion picture shows, which, operating with the darkened rooms afford unusual facilities for a traffic of scandalous proportion."[12]

While this testimony shows a puritanical and narrow-minded clergy, its attitudes were not confined to the lunatic fringe. A New York *Post* editorial greeted the mayor's action with applause, stating that "Most of them [motion picture theaters] have little but their disgusting vulgarity to attract. At any rate, the city will gain immensely if the closing of most of the existing shows is permanent."[13] An article in Joseph Pulitzer's New York *World* by Vincent Pissaro, chief investigator for the Society for the Prevention of Cruelty to Children, saw motion picture theaters as centers for the corruption of children, with boys turning to pickpocket and girls selling their innocence. He noted that the Society for the Prevention of Cruelty to Children had found a decrease in actual physical brutality to children but an increase in their "seduction." The motion picture theater, Pissaro claimed, encouraged this premature sensuality in young people, citing "the darkness of the auditorium during the exhibitions, with its opportunities for 'puppy love' affairs."[14] Moving pictures were therefore rife with anxieties for the genteel representatives of American culture, including the issues of a working-class audience and the sexual awareness of children.

But the newly organized film industry desperately wanted to allay the fears of genteel society. Gustavus Rogers, the lawyer who represented the film interests at the mayor's hearing, invoked the values of education and temperance, defending film shows as the poor man's theater and claiming that on Sundays "many a former drunkard now spent that day in such shows with his family."[15] He proposed elimination of immoral films through appointing a police censor, such as existed in Chicago.[16] The newly formed MPPC saw the attack upon motion pictures not as an irrationality to be denied, but as an a concern to be addressed and allayed. J. Stuart Blackton of the Vitagraph Company represented the manufacturers and announced that when the MPPC was formed manufacturers had agreed to end production of "indecent or suggestive" films.[17]

Immediately following the hearing the mayor announced his decision to revoke all common-show licenses for moving picture shows, citing concern for public safety and declaring that no future licenses would allow Sunday shows. He added that in the future he would revoke licenses "on evidence that pictures have been exhibited by the licensees which tend to degrade or injure the morals of the community." The motion picture representatives organized a swift and unified response. A meeting of exhibitors held at 8 P.M. on Christmas Day created a new organization, the Moving Picture Association, to fight the mayor's action. The association wished to represent only "respectable" motion picture exhibitors; managers of theaters that were unsafe or unsanitary were warned not to join.[18]

However, film's opponents had other social axes to grind. The Sunday closing issue contained a strong element of anti-Semitism, with some of the anti-film clergy claiming the film industry was "a Jewish syndicate furnishing indecencies for the city."[19] An anti-Semitic and xenophobic attitude is discernible, for example, in the New York *Daily Tribune*'s coverage of the founding meeting of the association: "Chubby faced Irishmen with clay pipes between their teeth were there, as were Hungarians, Italians, Greeks and just a handful of Germans, but the greater portion of the assembly were Jewish-American who practically control the enterprise. An Irishman demanded more light. Some wag of a Hungarian remarked that a Celt couldn't see through the smoke of a Turkish cigarette."[20]

The organization was effective. The next day, four temporary injunctions had been granted against the mayor's action, ruling that a blanket revocation was an arbitrary action and that licenses could only be revoked individually and for cause.[21] The nickelodeons hastened to open for Saturday night, but the mayor had not given up and decided to push the Sunday closing issue with a vengence. Extending his attack to vaudeville theaters, he warned managers that their usual fare would no longer be tolerated on Sunday. Only orchestral music or song performed without costume would be allowed, as would educational lectures or recitations and "motion pictures illustrating lectures of an instructional or educational character."[22] These Sunday performances were attended by police charged with enforcing the mayor's ruling; the New York *Herald* carried a cartoon of a cop looming over a youngster in a vaudeville show and warning, "If I see you smile again, I'll arrest you, young fellow."[23] Motion picture theaters played it safe with this Sunday closing for the most part, reverting to the actuality dominated program of the years before the rise of the nickelodeons and story films. One exhibitor was arrested for showing films the police did not find educational, melodramas with a robbery on a public street and the kidnapping of a child.[24]

Suddenly every theater in town needed a lecturer, who under the mayor's edict could endow a film with educational value. Most were improvised, as ushers with good lungs were pressed into service. The New York *Herald* recorded the attempts of one such draftee at the Hammerstein, a vaudeville theater, accompanying an actuality film of travels in Northern Europe:

> "A railroad track," said the lecturer, the motion picture having been taken evidently from the front of a train.
> "Some men," continued the educationalist presently, when a group of men on skis were shown. The next scene revealed them speeding downhill.
> "Men skiing," announced the man.
> The picture again switched to the railroad tracks.
> "Another railroad track."
> The track led across a low trestle.
> "The Brooklyn Bridge," bellowed the announcer.
> Pictures showing reindeers tramping about in the snow were explained as "Animals eating snowballs."[25]

Justice Blackmar of the Supreme Court of New York in Brooklyn made the injunctions against the mayor permanent. Although elated by this legal victory, motion picture exhibitors were still concerned with improving their public image and eliminating those elements they felt had given the business a bad name. When the mayor's attorney at the hearing before Justice Blackmar cited a theater whose exits were blocked and whose Sunday audience was made up of "white women and Chinese men," Rogers, representing the exhibitors, objected that he himself had drawn the mayor's attention to this theater and helped to close it.[26]

Mayor McClellan's Sunday show edict demonstrated that along with dark-ened theaters and immigrant exhibitors, the emergence of the story film caused anxiety among would-be film reformers. While the actuality program with educational lecture recalled the middle-class experience of the first vaudeville exhibitions and the "high-class" picture shows of entrepreneurs like Lyman Howe, story films seemed stocked with thrills and titillations.[27] Social reformers were not only confronting a new medium of expression, but also a new form of narration. Story films formed the basis of film production in 1909; the MPPC's campaign of "uplift" needed to establish that they could also be moral and educational. This called both for new forms of filmic discourse and a way of certifying the moral value of these new forms of narration. The moral discourse of Griffith's Biograph film was a response to the first need, and the formation of the National Board of Censorship partially supplied the second. Mayor McClellan's attack on motion pictures had supplied the MPPC with a specific program for the uplift of motion pictures: the campaign for lighted theaters addressed reformers' fears of the dark; the MPPC pledged to produce films that would not be harmful to children;[28] and the formation of a Board of Censorship would guarantee that no immoral or indecent films were released.

At the mayor's hearing on motion pictures one witness had testified that films could be a positive force in city life, and that films needed only supervision, not eradication. When he declared that there were many things in New York City more rotten than motion pictures, he drew sustained applause from the exhibitors, which caused a rebuke from the mayor.[29] This witness was Charles Sprague Smith, director of the People's Institute. The People's Institute was an important reform organization and settlement house of a liberal rather than a clerical bent. John Collier, a member of the institute, described it as "an organization supported by voluntary contributions doing educational work, civic educational work, among the immigrants of the Lower East Side and wage earners generally."[30] The People's Institute had undertaken an investigation of cheap amusements in Manhattan in early 1908. Reporting their findings, Collier had found that the nickelodeon presented inoffensive and often educational entertainment. "A visit to more than 200 nickelodeons has not detected one immoral picture or one indecent feature of any sort."[31]

Shortly after their victory over Mayor McClellan, the New York Exhibitors Association approached the People's Institute to set up a censorship board to review all the films to be shown in New York City and eliminate anything immoral or indecent. Inaugurated in March of 1909, the Board of Censorship was a form of industry self-censorship. Manufacturers submitted their films to it voluntarily, and its suggestions were followed on a voluntary basis. The board emphasized its nonantagonistic relation to the film industry. Collier, named to head the board, characterized it as "anxious to avoid unnecessarily 'jarring' the trade."[32] Rather than an outsider to the film industry, the Board of Censorship saw itself as a form of "internal trade regulation."[33]

The MPPC soon realized that the Censorship Board could certify that it had eliminated all vulgar and immoral subjects from films. The manufacturers of the MPPC not only announced they would submit all their films to the board for approval, but also supplied it with a screening room for their work and a stipend for expenses. This recognition by the MPPC allowed the Board of Censorship to view itself as something more than a local organization and its name was changed to the National Board of Censorship.[34] The board's membership consisted of "persons connected with public and private educational institutions in New York" and two moving picture exhibitors, one MPPC-licensed and one independent.[35] Although officially embraced by the MPPC, the board remained neutral in the conflict emerging between the trust and the independent factions.

With the National Board's official relation to the MPPC, censorship became a factor in film's narrative form as well. Submitting his films to the Censorship Board certainly encouraged Griffith's use of moral discourse. However, the National Board of Censorship did not "cause" Griffith's development of parallel editing for moral contrast, which had appeared in films like *The Song of the Shirt* months before the board was proposed. Both Griffith's filmic discourse and the establishment of the board were responses to the film industry's desire for social respectability.

Were films before 1908–9 morally depraved? A great deal of the alarm over immoral film seems to have been imaginary, or the product of *very* genteel sensibilities. But the cinema of attractions did occasionally disregard conventional morality and disrespect the bastions of genteel culture, as is common in popular entertainments. In describing this earlier esthetic as "exhibitionistic," I alluded to its direct address to spectators, but the erotic connotation of the term is not out of place. Films of erotic display made up an important genre of the cinema of attractions. Pathé produced films with frontal female nudity early in the century, such as *Five Ladies* (1900?) *Student Prank* (1902?), *The Baron and the Maid* (1902?), and *In Flagranti* (1902?), and bits of a Biograph mutoscope containing nudity are preserved at the Museum of Modern Art. Although explicit pornography was not common, films of erotic exhibition—women in their underwear or wearing body stockings, couples kissing, girls kicking up their legs or dancing in pajamas, and women wrestling—appeared frequently until at least 1906.[36]

Eroticism certainly played a part in Griffith's 1909 films—consider, for example, the appeal of Florence Lawrence, Marion Leonard, or Mary Pickford. But in place of direct display, eroticism became routed through elaborate scenarios of desire and repression. Films no longer centered on simple erotic revelation—women getting undressed as in *From Show Girl to Burlesque Queen* (Biograph, 1903), or a close-up of a lady's ankle as in Edison's 1903 *The Gay Shoe Clerk*. The contrast between these earlier films of erotic display in which story plays little or no role and the narrativization of eroticism in a melodrama like *The Lonely Villa* is ideologically significant. Presenting both a moral transgression and its restraint, Griffith can invoke forbidden erotic desires only to have them repressed and punished within the story line. This underground life of transgressive moments is typical of melodrama and basic to the logic of later Hollywood genres. *The Lonely Villa* was passed without objection by the National Board of Censorship but encountered police censorship in Chicago.

The comic exploitation of female sexuality found in earlier erotic films does not appear in existing Griffith Biograph films, but the primary outlet for erotic films at Biograph had been the mutoscopes, the short films the company made to be shown in peep show devices rather than on the screen. Apparently Griffith directed a number of these in 1908. Linda Arvidson claims he directed only about six of these short films—although she also indicates he selected the actresses' underwear![37] Mutoscopes directed in 1908, around the time Griffith took over directing, include such intriguing titles as *The Girl's Dormitory, The Girl's Boxing Match, Too Many in Bed, Fluffy's New Corset,* and *The Soul Kiss,* none of which have been preserved.[38] Toward the end of 1908 Biograph dropped mutoscope production, possibly influenced by the formation of the MPPC, and ceased producing openly erotic films.

Biograph's *Heathen Chinee and the Sunday School Teachers* (1904) typifies the irreverent and risque films of the earlier period. After a Sunday meeting singing hymns together, white female missionaries and Chinese men go to an opium den. There they lie on beds together and smoke opium until the place is raided by the police. Later the Sunday school teachers visit the Chinese in jail, bringing presents of flowers and candy which are confiscated by the guards. The film implies miscegenation and shows drug-taking, presenting them as subjects for an ungenteel laugh rather than moral condemnation. Nor does the film seem to condemn the jailing of the Chinese while the Sunday school teachers apparently go free, or the corruption of the guards. It simply avoids, as does much of early film, specific moral judgments. While some of Griffith's Biograph comedies such as *Balked at the Altar* or *Mrs. Jones Entertains* contain satiric digs at official genteel culture, the mood is decidedly muted compared to these earlier films. Of course, there are films from this earlier period that revere conventional morality or piety, but these films hold no privileged place in the output of production companies. The same Pathé catalogue contains "Scenes grivoises d'un caractere piquant" and "Scenes religieuses et bibliques."[39]

Reformers also objected to gruesome and violent subjects in early films. W. Stephen Bush particularly condemned such subjects in a call for industry self-censorship in *Moving Picture World,* attacking films which lingered over the morbid details of murders and executions.[40] Griffith did not eliminate gruesome moments from his Biograph films entirely; however, a vein of Grand Guignol-esque horror evident in certain 1908 films did disappear in 1909. Scenes such as a man caught in a bear trap (*The Ingrate,* October 2, 28, November 2), a baby nearly baked in an oven (*The Maniac Cook,* November 25, 27), or even Jose dangling from the lynch rope in *The Greaser's Gauntlet,* disappeared after the formation of the MPPC. In Griffith's Biograph films from 1909 on, scenes of violence or brutality always carried moral condemnation, with gruesome scenes absorbed or given an alibi by moral discourse.

What were the principles of the National Board of Censorship? First, it refused to draw up a list of forbidden topics. The board maintained that films were a dramatic art and each must be viewed as a dramatic whole, rather than seized upon for a single suggestive incident or violent act. As a representative of the board stated:

> barring indecency, barring ghoulishness, there is hardly any incident in life or drama that may not be *so treated*—presented with such a purpose, shown in such a connection—as to be acceptable to a board of censorship which recognizes this as a fundamental fact:
> *That motion pictures are a legitimate form of the drama, and that the motion picture is entitled to draw with discretion on any field of human interest for its theme.*[41]

Some years later the board officially amplified this remark, stating that it occasionally found it necessary to pass films showing certain objectionable scenes that were essential to the plot of a film in order "to avoid arbitrarily and irrationally limiting the possibilities of photoplay development."[42]

However, around 1911 the board did publish a list of subjects that filmmakers should handle with care. Because this list perhaps reflects unspoken standards of 1909, it is worth examining. The comments show that the board encouraged filmmaking based on a moral discourse, not simply the elimination of taboo subjects.

> *Barrooms, Drinking, Drunkenness*
> such scenes must be used with discretion and made significant in the drama.
> . . .
> *Vulgarity*
> *Prolonged Passionate Love Scenes*
> *Costuming—Tights and Insufficient Clothing*
> *Infidelity and Sex Problem Plays*
> The Board has never denied that this is a legitimate subject for the motion pictures, but it has insisted that it be treated with seriousness and artistic reserve.
> *Women Smoking and Drinking*
> *Underworld Scenes—Opium Joints, Gambling, Dance Halls, and Objectionable Dancing, Vulgar Flirtations, Questionable Resorts*
> When scenes of this general type listed above are produced it must be in such a manner that no spectator is stimulated to attempt to duplicate them . . . rather their true character as being inately low, vulgar and indecent should be brought out . . . the scenes themselves must have dramatic usefulness in the play and may not be introduced as so much padding or vaudeville entertainment.
> *Deeds of Violence*
> The National Board requires that such violence be not degrading but rather

have educational and social value . . . the spirit of struggle at the present stage of human development is a phase of growth, both spiritual and physical, necessary to continue and advance the race.
The Senseless Use of Weapons
Treatment of Officers of the Law and Respect for the Law
Advisability of Punishment Following Crime
The Board's Attitude Towards Crime
The Board should not attempt to eliminate evil from the picture since, broadly speaking, that would be to destroy the drama.
The Motives and the Results of Crime as Shown in Motion Pictures
an adequate motive for committing a crime is always desirable in a picture and in some cases is a *sine qua non.* . . it is desirable that the criminal be punished in some way, but the Board does not always insist upon this.
Crimes of Violence Against Property or Persons
[The board recommended "distant views of darkness to conceal methods" in portraying crimes. It specifically cited train-wrecking, arson, and suicide as crimes that should not be portrayed.][43]

The board also felt the need of a new middle-class audience. The pamphlet quoted previously predicted a gradual raising of the standards of the film "through the constructive reports of the Board and the influence of the better class of audiences who are filling many of the theaters."[44]

A few of the Censorship Board's reports on the first films they viewed have survived and offer a vivid picture of the arguments surrounding film's moral discourse. The comments on films shown on May 10, 1909, are typical:

One picture was condemned *in toto* as follows:
Pathe: Le Parapluie d'Anatole. This picture, while a farce, deals throughout with corrupt people in corrupt relations and finally closes with a sign (the two horns) familiar to the vulgar as a sign of adultery.
One picture was passed provided changes be made as follows:
Le Boucher de Moudon, Pathe. This picture is the height of the gruesome throughout and many of those who support the Censorship among the public would expect that it is to be condemned *in toto*. The Committee, however, after discussing the picture on two separate days is willing to approve it with these changes:
1–Cut out letter from son to mother, "I am condemned, etc." Either substitute a title such as "remorse" or leave no title here. That is, a certain moral lesson is given to the picture if we believe that remorse for the deed, works upon the mother; this interpretation is negatived [sic] by the epistle in question.
2–There are two visions—the first wherein the woman sees the recollection of the scene of murder, the second where she remembers the secreting of the victim's body under the hay. Cut out the first of these, representing the murder.
3–In the prison scene immediately before the mother's confession is brought in, a morbid scene is shown depicting the cutting of the man's shirt prepatory to the guillotine. Eliminate this; it is not generic to the plot and is gratuitously

gruesome in a tale too gruesome already. That is, cut out a few feet where the jailers are slicing the man's clothing. The Committee would be glad if this were submitted again after the cuts have been made. But its decision in favor of the film as amended is final.

One picture on which report had been previously rendered but on which there had later developed a difference of opinion in the Committee was reconsidered. To Wit: "Two Memories," Biograph. The Committee recognized at once that the revelling, the champagne bottles etc. were not presented for their own sake but to heighten dramatic effect through contrast. The picture takes itself seriously and will be so taken by most of the public. The Committee still believes that a dramatic contrast fully as satisfactory might have been obtained without employing a device as shocking to many, but this is a matter of debate, and there was divergence of opinion in the Committee. The severe intent of the picture and the fact that it is an earnest effort at dramatic method proper to the moving picture carried it with the Committee in spite of the doubtful point. This picture is approved.

Yours very truly,
John Collier, Secretary[45]

In essence, the Censorship Board "remade" the films they passed with "changes," as in *Le Boucher de Moudon,* reedited to create a "moral lesson." This concern with the moral discourse of the films as well as the "dramatic method proper to motion pictures" demonstrates how central filmic discourse was to the issue of censorship in 1909. The issue was no longer a glimpse of Dolorita's ankles in a peep show as it had been with the earliest recorded film censorship.[46] Although disturbed by the revels in *Two Memories,* the board acknowledged their place within a larger figure, officially recognizing the moral force of the element of voice in Griffith's narrator system.

However, relations between Biograph and the board were occasionally stormy. One of Griffith's 1909 films, *The Heart of an Outlaw* (July 14, 16, 20, 28), so offended the censors that it was never released in the United States. The film is typical of a sort of grim melodrama Griffith made in late 1909, revolving around isolated and alienated protagonists. A westerner (James Kirkwood) ambushes and kills his wife (Marion Leonard) and her Mexican lover (Henry Walthall). He also accidentally wounds his young daughter (Gladys Eagan) and believes he has killed her. Years later, as the leader of a notorious band of outlaws, he kidnaps the daughter of a sheriff responsible for the killing of several members of his band. He holds her prisoner in his cabin, arranging that she will be shot by the outlaws as she leaves. As he attempts to rape her, he discovers she is his own daughter, adopted by the sheriff after he disappeared. Helping her escape through a secret door, the outlaw dies in her place, shot by his own men as he exits.

Misnaming the film *The Honour of an Outlaw,* the board admitted it was a "very well acted and a well-staged play," but found its "suggested seduction and the rather blood thirsty adventures of an outlaw" beyond the pale. The report concluded, "An outlaw type of this kind is sure to arouse adverse criticism and when coupled with what is morally worse, this picture would undoubtedly work more or less harm to the Moving Picture interests."[47] Apparently reacting to Biograph alarm, a later report proposed extensive cuts to render the film inoffensive:

> Cut out all that portion of the picture introducing the Mexican, save where he enters the automobile with the wife. Also all of the scene entitled "A Jealous Husband's Vengeance for a Fancied Wrong" where the husband shoots the wife, child and Mexican. In the scene entitled "Shoot when you see this cloak emerge from the shack," cut out the part where the girl is forced to look on the dead outlaw's face and also cut the choking scene so as to make it appear that the girl has fainted. To be consistent with this rearrangement the titles, "The Temptation" and "The Husband Becomes a Social Outcast, thinking he has killed his child, whom the sheriff adopts," should be changed.[48]

These changes show the board was disturbed as much by the film's assaults on family order as its violence. The themes of miscegenation, adultery, and incest are most likely the "what is morally worse" whose corrupting influence the board feared. However, the outlaw's final moment of noble conversion and sacrifice do not place film outside the moral context of Griffith's melodramas, even if it is somewhat excessive in its portrayal of transgression. Apparently, Biograph objected to the demand for extensive cuts. Collier in a letter to the MPPC stated the board's decision was final and denounced the film as "an exhibition of gross immorality, presented in such a form that it would tend to corrupt the morals of the young."[49] Biograph finally gave in and did not release the film.

Even if *The Heart of an Outlaw* was condemned by the Board of Censorship, the moral ambition of Griffith's films, particularly in 1909, was widely recognized. Moral discourse formed an essential element of the narrator system. A letter to *Moving Picture World* from an enthusiastic film viewer, Carl Anderson, provides a contemporaneous reaction to Griffith's narrative discourse. Declaring, "none of the producers put out the quality of goods that the Biograph Co. does," Anderson praised the Biograph style:

> In nearly every case the pictures show the plot so clearly that no trouble is experienced in understanding the theme of the story; the photography is above the average, probably due to the fact that they place the machine nearer the subject, thereby insuring sharper detail. One noticeable point in Biograph goods is the clearness of features of the actors, every little change of expression is noticeable, and every delicate shadow that marks expression or helps to accent expression is plainly marked. And the Biograph actors act. There is no apparent make-believe about it, they do the things they are supposed to do . . . .

> But what appeals to me more than all other things about the Biograph subjects
> is the finish, the roundness, the completeness of the story. . . .

For Anderson, narrative coherence and closure was linked to the moral quality
of the films:

> The melodramatics of the cheaper sort find no place in Biograph goods. "The
> Drunkard's Reformation" is a story of exceptional cleverness. The little girl at
> the play—hesitating between fear of and love for her father—tells the story of
> her thoughts through her wonderful eyes. And this story is a sermon; a masterful
> powerful sermon on the evils of the drink habit. "The Salvation Army Lass" is
> another of those splendid preachments. I heard a minister say, as he left the
> theater after seeing this picture, "That's a better sermon than I could ever
> preach."
>
> The Biograph subjects all mean something and they help those who see
> them.[50]

Films that "mean something," picture-sermons that "help those who see
them," these phrases encapsulate the narrative ambitions of Griffith in 1909.
The narrator system delivered understandable stories and moral lessons. Psychological editing (as in A Drunkard's Reformation) and "dramatic contrast"
through parallel editing were narrative techniques interwoven with moral
evaluations. And both morality and narrative clarity were necessary to the
MPPC if they were to attract audiences of the "better class" to motion pictures.

Among the films passed at the Board of Censorship's first meeting was
Biograph's A Drunkard's Reformation.[51] This temperance drama exemplifies
the methods of the narrator system, as well as the MPPC's desire to establish
film as a respectable part of social discourse. The film pushs Griffith's development of character psychology to its farthest point thus far, making the aspect
of mood central to its story. Although shot some weeks before the establishment of the Board of Censorship, but not long after the McClellan hearing,
the film responds to the anti-film agitation with a carefully framed argument
for film as a force in social reform. And by adopting the rhetoric of the
temperance movement, A Drunkard's Reformation launches a sally into a
political controversy, one which had a peculiar relevance to film's place in
society. Promoting nickelodeons as replacements for saloons in the social life
of the working class had been a counterargument to the anti-film reformists,
and one freighted with a tangle of class and gender implications.

In 1909 the anti-drink movement, represented most powerfully by the
Anti-Saloon League, solidified its progress of the previous three years. Tennes-
see became the ninth state to approve a statewide prohibition law. The league
estimated that with hundreds of counties and localities across the country
"dry," forty-one million Americans lived in areas where it was illegal to sell
liquor.[52] Reporting on a visit to the Biograph studio, Variety found A Drunkard's Reformation in the middle of this prohibitionist campaign:

"There is hardly a mail that does not bring us a letter extolling our pictures in some way or another. Here's an odd one," said the Biograph man picking up a letter from an exhibitor in an Iowa town stating that "The Drunkard's Reformation," a recent Biograph subject, had caused the town to "go dry" at the election which occurred the week after the film was shown.

"I was visited by a delegation of 'The Wets,' " wrote the exhibitor, "asking if I would take the picture off for the week. Of course I did not and the town went prohibition by a big majority."[53]

From the very beginning of the temperance movement, popular entertainments had hawked the gospel of abstinence.[54] A *Drunkard's Reformation* belongs to a long tradition of nineteenth-century songs and plays—such as "Father Dear Father, Come Home with Me Now" and *Ten Nights in a Barroom*—which were still powerful propaganda tools in 1909. The first model of what Frank Rahill calls "the *delirium tremens* drama" was provided by Douglas Jerrold's *Fifteen Years of a Drunkard's Life* in 1828.[55] The play followed the drunkard's fateful path from happy home to his first fateful drink, then progressively downhill to insanity and death, a pattern closely followed by Zecca's 1902 film, *Les victims de alcoolisme*. W. H. Smith's *The Drunkard, or The Fallen Saved* (1844) added a new element, ending with the drunkard's reformation. The very title of Griffith's film announces its optimistic reformist intentions. The film contrasts sharply with the earlier Zecca film by centering on the drunkard's emotions rather than simply his misfortune, an emphasis congruent with the increased importance of characterization in the narrator system.

The promotion of the nickelodeon as the "substitute for the saloon" (to use the phrase of Vachel Lindsay, poet, early American film theorist, and one-time Anti-Saloon League field worker) reveals that the anti-saloon movement was concerned not only about alcoholism, but also about how the working class spent its newly won leisure time.[56] As Herbert Gutman and Roy Rosenzweig have shown, the rationalization of industrial labor brought an end to the time-honored custom of drinking on the job, once an accepted part of the work day. Banishing such leisure activities from the workplace led to the creation of the saloon, which became a realm of male relaxation, ultimately divorced from home as well. For the working man of the turn of the century, adjusting to the new disciplines and time constraints of industrial labor, saloons provided a haven of relaxation and communal interaction as much as a dispensary of alcohol.[57]

To attack saloons (the place and institution as much as alcohol) became, as Rosenzweig says, an action with "direct class implications."[58] Saloons challenged middle-class ideals of work efficiency (hung-over workers were cited as reasons why employers should support anti-saloon legislation) and home-centered family life. However, as Kathy Peiss has pointed out, saloons

also formed a male bastion which not only excluded women but also threatened their families' livelihoods.[59] As Griffith's film shows, saloons tore at the
fabric of family unity, as men caroused and women and children suffered.
This threat to family unity may have been a middle-class concern, but it also
formed a very real issue for the female half of the working class.

Some working-class movements, including those with a politically radical
agenda, addressed the problems of alcoholism.[60] However, as Rosenzweig has
pointed out, ethnic working-class temperance movements, such as the Irish-
based Father Mathew's Society, stressed individual pledge-taking and the
provision of alternate recreation activity rather than closing saloons. Such a
program appealed to a temperance radical like Lindsay, who pronounced the
nickelodeon the ideal alternative. "Why do men prefer the photoplay to the
drinking place?" he asked rhetorically. "For no pious reason surely. Now they
have fire pouring into their eyes instead of into their bellies."[61]

That the nickelodeon drew customers away from the saloon was more than
a reformer's project, it was an economic fact. *Variety* in 1909 quoted Edward
P. Kelly, the chief inspector of amusement places in Chicago as saying that
"No one realizes this better than do the saloonkeepers and they are almost
invariably opposed to the locating of a nickel theater in their neighborhood.
In some instances a single nickel theater is said to have cut the business of
several nearby saloons practically in half. . . . The man who after his day's
work and supper would wander to the neighborhood saloon . . . now takes
the family to the nickel theater."[62] The working-class family audience for the
nickelodeon provides another motivation for the overdetermined centrality of
family harmony in Griffith's Biograph films. Like the temperance movement,
family harmony and the idealization of domesticity were certainly middle-
class values but could be used to appeal to the working class as well. A
Drunkard's Reformation centers on the saving of the family as much as on the
reformation of a drunkard. Again, the double address of the film industry
asserts itself, catering to middle-class approval but without alienating its
working-class patrons.

The *Biograph Bulletin* for *A Drunkard's Reformation* described it as "the most
powerful temperance lesson ever depicted."[63] Blending this didactic vision
with new explorations of character psychology makes the film central to the
development of the narrator system. From the beginning, film inherited
moralistic themes from other forms of popular culture. Biograph's *The Downward Path* (1900), for example, depicted the grim fate of a girl seduced away
from her parents by a "fresh book agent." But in pre-Griffith cinema the
devices of filmic discourse are rarely used to convey moral judgments. Moral
positions are simply implied in the presentation of stereotyped situations such
as the girl's seduction in *The Downward Path* and the conventional responses
filmmakers could expect from audiences. The films, in effect, use no rhetoric

to persuade or convince through their filmic discourse; they cannot "depict a powerful lesson." The lesson of *The Downward Path* would have had to be conveyed by a lecturer accompanying the film, or in a printed bulletin.

The Great Train Robbery exemplifies this nonmoralizing aspect of pre-Griffith cinema. At no point does the narrative discourse of the film create empathy for the characters or moral judgments about their actions. Porter filmed the violence of bandits and posse with equal detachment. A British film chronicling the career of a real-life criminal, *The Life of Charles Peace* (1905), shows the same ambiguity. There is no indication of whether we are to react to Peace's murders, burglaries, and daring escapes with admiration or horror. The unyielding discourse of the film refuses to pronounce Peace either hero or villain. Its moral voice is silent.

With Griffith and the narrator system, this voice began to be heard. Filmic discourse created character motivations as well as moral judgments as part of the "dramatic method proper to the motion picture" which the Board of Censorship commended. The principal form of filmic discourse that expresses these aspects is once again editing, particularly the contrast edit. The beginning of *A Drunkard's Reformation* contrasts the family waiting patiently at home with a shot of the drunkard father loitering in a saloon with his drinking buddies. This spatial separation of the family unit also poses the initial disequilibrium that the film's story works to correct, grouping the family together in harmony for the final shot. The contrast between the separated family of the opening and the reunited one at the close parallels the roles of the two nondomestic locales of the film: the saloon which tears the family apart and the theater which becomes the means for its restoration.

When John Wharton, the film's young husband and father (Arthur Johnson), finally returns home from the saloon, he creates a drunken scene. Later, somewhat recovered, he takes his young daughter (Adele De Garde) to the theater, where they see a dramatization of Zola's *L'Assommoir*.[64] The scenes at the theater form the center of the film and give it a unique narrative structure which inspired the *Biograph Bulletin* editor to a curious bit of structural analysis: "the whole construction of the play is most novel, showing, as it does, a play within a play. It is a sort [sic] of triangular in motive, that is to say, the play depicts to the leading actor in the picture the calamitous result of drink, while the whole presents to the spectator the most powerful temperance lesson ever propounded."[65]

The "play within a play" format allowed Griffith to create the most extended, twenty-shot sequence of psychological editing thus far in his career.

Shot eight: Interior of a theater, showing the stage midground with the curtain drawn. Several rows of seats occupy the foreground, filled with spectators with their backs to the camera. Wharton and daughter enter and take seats near the stage.

Shot nine: The stage, with the shot's frame slightly below the proscenium arch, the bottom of the stage and footlights visible, as well as music stands from the orchestra. The curtain opens. The character Coupeau (Herbert Yost) enters a set of a town square, with the exterior of a tavern on the right. He is greeted by friends.

Shot ten: The audience. Wharton and daughter are in the foreground with other spectators visible behind them. Wharton looks a bit distracted, then smiles.

Shot eleven: On stage, Coupeau greets Gervais (Florence Lawrence) and her companion. He takes Gervais' hand. In response she pantomimes drinking, points at the tavern, and shakes her head "no." A temperance lecturer enters, followed by a crowd. They carry a poster proclaiming "Beware of the Demon Rum." The lecturer opens a book. A man signs the pledge. A bumpkin (Mack Sennett) starts to sign, then thumbs his nose. Coupeau signs with a flourish and then embraces Gervais.

Shot twelve: The audience. Wharton smiles, speaks to his daughter, then points at the stage. This pointing gesture will repeatedly serve to unite Wharton and the drama on stage.

Shot thirteen: Coupeau is approached by another woman (Marion Leonard). He spurns her and she exits. Gervais rushes on and gives Coupeau a flower. The spurned lady reenters and watches from the side as Coupeau and Gervais kiss.

Shot fourteen: Audience. Most applaud. Wharton crosses his arms in apparent boredom.

Shot fifteen: Stage. Coupeau sits with Gervais and a young daughter. He takes the child on his lap and embraces her.

Shot sixteen: Audience. Wharton nudges his daughter and points at the stage. He repeats the gesture twice, drawing a comparison between the stage drama and his own life. (This is the first time a cut to the audience has interrupted the action of a scene on stage, rather than coming between stage scenes.)

Shot seventeen: Stage. Coupeau playfully spanks his daughter, and then kisses her as well as Gervais, who then exits with their daughter. Coupeau's cronies (Sennett and Harry Solter) enter. In pantomime they ask him to go for a drink. He replies with a pantomime of signing the pledge. He starts to leave, but they hold him back.

Shot eighteen: Audience. Wharton looks disturbed, stares at the stage intently and takes his daughter's arm. (Again this reaction interrupts action on stage and here articulates the turning point of the stage drama, Coupeau's decision to take a drink.)

Shot nineteen: The cronies have been raising their index fingers ("Just one"). At last Coupeau raises his, too, and exits into the tavern.

Shot twenty: Stage. The curtain opens on the interior of a bar, where Coupeau drinks with his friends. He starts to leave, but they restrain him. He agrees to another drink. He starts to leave again, but they grab his lunch bucket and clown around with it.

Shot twenty-one: Audience. Holding his daughter's hand, Wharton looks away from the stage, upset, then looks back again (fig. 23).

Shot twenty-two: In the bar, Coupeau is now thoroughly drunk. Gervais enters with their daughter. She tries to keep him from drinking. He struggles with her and knocks her to the floor (fig. 24).

Shot twenty-three: Audience. Wharton grabs the arm of his chair and draws his daughter closer to him, intently watching the stage (fig. 25). (Again, this cut interrupts action on stage.)

Shot twenty-four: Stage. The daughter helps her mother off the barroom floor. Gervais exits, shaken. Coupeau stands drunkenly. The curtain closes.

Shot twenty-five: Stage. The curtain opens on a set of a cottage interior. Gervais sits in sorrow at a table, her daughter trying to comfort her. Coupeau is brought in by a doctor and nurse, a trembling invalid. He is placed in a chair. The doctor and nurse leave. Gervais and her daughter go out shopping.

Shot twenty-six: Audience. Wharton looks quite disturbed and grasps his daughter even closer.

Shot twenty-seven: Stage. Coupeau sits alone in the cottage. The woman he rejected early in the play sneaks in and places a bottle of wine next to him, then steals out. She watches him through the window. Coupeau turns and sees the bottle. He reacts wildly, takes a drink, and walks off exultantly.

Shot twenty-eight: Audience. Wharton, still embracing his daughter, nods his head slowly as he watches.

23, 24, and 25: In *A Drunkard's Reformation* (1909), the young husband (Arthur Johnson) reacts to the scene of domestic violence on the stage which seems to predict his own fate. Frame enlargements from 35mm prints, courtesy of the Museum of Modern Art.

24

25

Shot twenty-nine: Stage, cottage interior. Gervais and daughter enter. Coupeau comes on stage in the throes of delerium tremens. He grabs his daughter and bounces her madly on his knee, then throws her off.

Shot thirty: (a title bearing this number interrupts the stage action, and may well indicate an intertitle here in the original print). On stage, Coupeau chases Gervais around the room and then collapses. Gervais and the child bend over his dead body.

Shot thirty-one: Audience. Wharton leans forward on the edge of his seat. He looks up, taps his chest, making a gesture of analogy with the stage action. He bows his head and embraces his daughter. The audience applauds. With bowed head, Wharton holds his daughter. As the audience rises to leave, he touches his chest again.

For the first time in Griffith's filmmaking, and probably in the history of film, the psychological development of a character, primarily conveyed by editing, forms the basis of a film. Never before had Griffith so probed a character, taken him so slowly through so many reactions: from bored restlessness to increasing concern, to his final realization of the play's relevance to his life. By intercutting the play and Johnson's reaction, Griffith allows the film to take place—so to speak—in the character's mind. We have an extended sequence within the aspect of mood allowing access to a character's thoughts and motivations.

This psychological portrayal rests on intercutting spectator and stageplay, forming a proto-point-of-view/reaction shot pattern. However, the access the narrator system offers to Wharton differs a bit from later point-of-view shots which indicate a character's view through an exact matching of position and angle. The shots of the stage are not marked as Johnson's subjective view in the way the iris in *The Redman and the Child* marked the shot as the Indian's view through the telescope. Likewise, the "reaction" shots of the audience are not restricted to Wharton alone because they include his daughter and a dozen other spectators. Griffith uses a sight link, in which what a character sees and reacts to is made clear by the editing pattern, but without the camera assuming the exact position of the character, or the shot being understood as the character's literal point of view. As in earlier Griffith films, psychological meanings are developed from the articulation of shots rather than the creation of unambiguously subjective mental images. The narrator system seems to mediate point of view, allowing the spectator access to the character's vision, but not absolutely identifying a particular shot with the character's point of view.

However, composition and Johnson's acting center our attention on his reaction; the camera placement in these shots is among the closest to the actors in any Griffith film to date, allowing clear view of facial expressions. Likewise, editing pattern and narrative development leave no doubt about the play's most important witness. The scene is organized around, and made meaningful by, Johnson's gaze and reactions. The sequence forms a climax to Griffith's exploration of character psychology to this point. Further, this gradual unfolding of the psychology of a character is the means for the resolution of the drama. In this film the family is saved—not by a last-minute rescue from a perilous situation—but by a character's reformation. And this is accomplished through the laying out of an emotional conversion through editing. Griffith constructs Wharton through what he thinks and feels, rather than any physical action he undertakes. Wharton's role as witness gives the film meaning, his reaction to what he sees determines the film's narrative logic.

Although earlier films had intercut theatrical audiences and stage performances, such as Griffith's A Wreathe in Time (1908),[66] I know of no sequence as extended as the one in A Drunkard's Reformation or as central to the psychological exploration of a character.[67] Further the role of theater in Wharton's reformation creates a nearly self-reflexive structure, as the aspect of voice is highlighted almost self-consciously. The film's "triangular" structure not only proposes theater as a moral and didactic medium, but it also draws attention to film itself as the vehicle of the "most powerful temperance lesson" to the audience. Griffith would draw on this didactic possibility repeatedly throughout his career, as "sermons in film" became almost a cliche in reviews of Biograph films. Within the narrator system the aspect of voice intervenes in the unfolding of a film narrative to judge and evaluate the behavior of characters; to propose some as models, condemn others, and offer the possibility of reformation to both characters and spectators.

A Drunkard's Reformation follows the story pattern of many 1908 films: family security threatened and then restored. The concluding image of family harmony found in so many 1908 films here receives even more rhetorical emphasis. The last shot of the film closely groups the reunited family before the parlor hearth (fig. 26). To emphasis the glow of the fireplace, Griffith elaborates the directional light he had used earlier in Edgar Allen Poe. An arc light placed in the fireplace casts a strong glow on the little family while the lighting from above used in other shots has been dimmed, creating a sense of warmth and security. Thus, for the first time in Griffith's career, lighting plays a key role in the narrator system. The glowing hearth reflects the resolution of the family conflict, indicates the rewards of reform, and helps create the closure of the drama through connotations of warmth and intimacy. Further, the lighting contrasts with the overall illumination of earlier shots of the parlor, as do the close family grouping and unusually low camera height. The family forms a figure of close interaction and repose: the husband domestically clothed in robe and slippers, his wife embracing him, and their daughter sitting on the floor below them and reading a book in the fire's glow. This

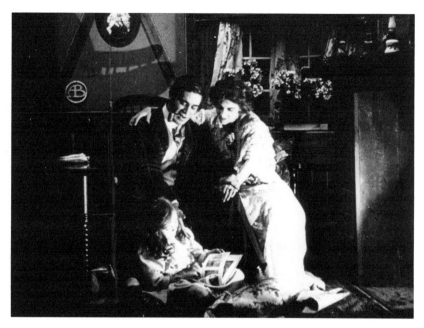

26. The concluding shot of *A Drunkard's Reformation*. The husband now reformed and restored to his family (Linda Arvidson, Adele De Garde), basks in the light of the hearth. Frame enlargement from 35mm print, courtesy of the Museum of Modern Art.

central composition was lacking in shots in which the father was absent or in which family conflict dispersed action across the frame. Through formal elements of filmic discourse (here, pro-filmic and compositional), the narrator system is endowed with a rhetoric to argue the moral lesson implied in its resolution.

Neither Griffith nor Bitzer "invented" directional film lighting. The significance of its use in this scene derives from its narrativization, rhetorically shaping the spectator's reception of the drama. In 1905, Edwin Porter had used a similar lighting set-up in the Edison film *The Seven Ages* to indicate a fireplace's glow, with pictorially striking profile and back lighting. Porter's firelit shot is a gem from pre-Griffith cinema and certainly creates connotations of warmth and security in this tableau of love in old age. But because the film does not consist of a continuous story or involve character development (showing a series of tableaux of life and love at Shakespeare's "seven ages of man"), the lighting cannot relate to character motivation or narrative resolution as it does in *A Drunkard's Reformation*.[68]

Although the scene at the theater in *A Drunkard's Reformation* can be read as a reference to the uplifting effects of morally didactic films as well, the reference to the older and more "legitimate" form was part of a strategy pursued by MPPC companies. Adapting legitimate drama and classics from literature provided filmakers with a badge of cultural respectability vital in their campaign to attract middle-class audiences. Isolated attempts to bring "high art" to the screen occurred earlier as well, for example, the various versions of the *Passion Play*, Méliès's *Faust* films, Biograph's *Duel Scene from Macbeth*, and Edison's *Parsifal*. But these films tended to be either fragments of the original work or experiments for synchronization with phonographs. From 1907 on, literary adaptations accelerated. In 1908 Griffith drew on Shakespeare, Tennyson, O. Henry, Thomas Hood, and Ferenc Molnár for film stories. In 1909 the adaptations of classics became epidemic at Biograph and other American and French production companies, with the classic sources of these films widely publicized, which had not been the rule in 1908.

France gave the movement its rubric and model—the *film d'art*. The first public showing of the films made by the production company Films D'Art premiered in Paris in November of 1908.[69] The key film of this first evening's presentation, *La mort du duc de Guise*, was released in the United States by Pathé on February 17, 1909. However, news of the undertaking had already been announced in American trade papers in May 1908.[70] The January 9, 1909, issue of the *Film Index* had carried a long feature on the movement, translated from an article by Gustave Babin in *L'Illustration*.[71] Babin describes the *film d'art* as a "special dramaturgy" adapted to film, but making use of "eminent writers and artists," "skilled stage managers," and "the very kings and queens of the stage who would play their parts before sumptuous scenery, or in the august settings of some historic castle or within a sunlit landscape, or beside the sea or some lordly river." The *films d'art* assembled an impressive group of actors, directors, composers, and writers, including Le Bargy of the Comedie-Francaise as director; writers Henri Lavedan, Victorien Sardou, Anatole France, and Jules Lemaitre; composers Saint-Saens, George Hue, and Fernand Le Borne; actors Sarah Bernhardt, Paul Mounet, Albert Lambert, Delauney, and Max Dearly; as well as established scenic designers.[72]

The American reception of *La mort du duc de Guise* was mixed. The *Moving Picture World* reviewer noted that the audience did not seem to follow the picture, but added, "I have never seen a better motion picture drama." A review a week later in the same periodical declared "while technically a good film . . . few understand to what it alludes."[73] *Nickelodeon* praised the *films d'art* series but made a plea for the "more powerful" if less well-made American films.[74] But the concept of "art films" harmonized with the cultural ambitions and middle-class aspirations of American production companies.

In 1908–9, *film d'art*, with its pedigree from established art forms, carried the mark of social respectability and therefore provoked imitation on the part of American producers. The Edison Company in their new publicity periodical, the *Edison Kinetogram,* announced in August 1909 a new policy inspired by "the movement begun in France to employ famous writers and actors."[75] Once again, employing artists from established media guaranteed artistic worth. In the following months, the *Kinetogram* trumpeted Edison films starring established actors such as Miss Cecil Spooner and written by (or authorized adaptations from) such authors as Mark Twain, Richard Harding Davis, and Rex Beach. The *film d'art* rubric was imitated by the Vitagraph Company, which called its more pretentious releases "high art films," and later "films de luxe." Somewhat later Carl Laemmle gave the rubric a characteristic twist and advertised his films for the new Independent Production Company (IMP) as "films d'knockout."[76]

Biograph associated itself with the French movement less overtly, but it definitely inflected Griffith's filmmaking in 1909. In the early months of 1909, *Biograph Bulletins* highlighted the status gained by classic reputations: *Edgar Allen Poe* ("this subject is one of the most artistic films ever produced"); *A Fool's Revenge* ("A Free Adaptation of Rigoletto"); and *Resurrection* ("Free Adaptation of Leo Tolstoy's Powerful Novel").[77] These films display a theatricality that somewhat sets them apart from other Biograph films, particularly more elaborate and detailed sets and costumes. Poe's garret is a unique set never before seen in a Biograph film, with slanting mansard windows that provide the first directional lighting in a Griffith film. *A Fool's Revenge* has a variety of sets, ranging from the king's court to the gypsy's cabin in the forest, all created within the 14th Street studio. And if *Resurrection*'s indoor Siberia looks rather pasteboard now, it won commendation from the New York *Dramatic Mirror* in 1909: "Not the least to be commended in the picture are the studio scenes representing the frozen way through Siberia. These are marvels of realistic stage craft for picture purposes."[78]

Much of the praise given to the *films d'art* rested on the style of acting in them, which demonstrated a new restraint and precision.[79] This group of adaptations by Griffith seems to show a French influence on its acting as well. The "Spectator," writing in the New York *Dramatic Mirror,* observed about *The Fool's Revenge:* "This is the first American film that we have felt justified in pronouncing the equal in smoothness of construction and power of dramatic action of any of the Pathé 'films d'art.' . . . The manner in which the court fool is acted reminds us strongly of Severin. The clear facial expressions as well as the natural but intensely suggestive gestures and poses of the character approach perfection in pantomimic art."[80]

The *Biograph Bulletins* for both *A Fool's Revenge* and *Resurrection* stressed the fact that these are "free adaptations." As with *Ingomar* and *The Devil,* Biograph maintained that special care must be taken in filming literary works. The *Bulletin* for *Resurrection* in particular stressed that "Restricted as we were as to length, we have successfully portrayed a story which comprises the most stirring incidents with an absolute continuity that is wonderful in motion pictures."[81] In contrast to earlier "peak moment" adaptations of famous plays, Biograph publicity stressed both its condensation and its "absolute continuity." The cachet of literary adaptation was balanced with narrative coherence and comprehensibility.

Griffith and Biograph realized that bringing dramatic and theatrical values to motion pictures must involve a transformation in style to balance the loss of the spoken text. The *films d'art*, with their emphasis on pro-filmic elements and devotion to the theatrical model, are somewhat at odds with the approach of the narrator system, which developed all levels of filmic discourse in the service of the story. Certainly Griffith's principal development leads away from the approach of the *film d'art* and particularly toward the exploitation of the resources of editing. However, the *films d'art* were influential upon Griffith's development in a number of ways. Seeing films aspire to an equal status with the legitimate theater and attracting eminent artists as the *films d'art* did must have raised Griffith's ambitions as a filmmaker. The movement showed a clearly defined way to present films as something more pretentious than simply nickelodeon fare for the masses.

In 1908 and 1909, the *films d'art* did not represent a reactionary return to an earlier style of discontinuous tableaux. *La mort du duc de Guise*, for example, although strongly theatrical in composition and basic decoupage, also includes some awareness of the continuity of action and space that film made possible. The action leading up to and including the actual assassination contains a continuous movement of the duke over five separate shots, through three separate rooms and back, with some cuts on movement.[82] As Barry Salt has pointed out, this movement through a number of rooms may well have influenced Griffith's later staging of action.[83] Finally, the *films d'art* stimulated the transition to more complicated narratives based on character motivations, one of the major innovations underpinning the narrator system. While the development of filmic discourse is still elementary within the *films d'art* system of pro-filmic elaboration, narrativization is an announced goal of the movement.

In 1910, an exhibitor writing to a trade journal identified Griffith's achievements at Biograph with the ambitions of the *films d'art*, while at the same time emphasizing their unique development of filmic discourse:

> While the French pictures were very fine they did not compare in originality and beauty to those unnamed films d'art produced by the American Biograph, the films d'art players contenting themselves with turning out beautiful imitations of plays, photographed, while the Biograph originated an entirely new art in such pictures as *The Unchanging Sea*, *The Way of the World* and a picture the name of which I forget but which we call the "wheat" picture—a new art in which poetry, the stage and painting were all called upon to make one exquisite form of expression.[84]

If Griffith betrayed, or went beyond, the theatrical ideal in order to fulfill its ambitions of coherent narrative based on character motivation, A *Drunkard's Reformation* could be seen as a response of the narrator system to the challenge raised by the *films d'art*. Clearly a "high class" drama, this temperance film set a model for characterization and use of filmic discourse that later Biograph films followed.

In the first half of 1909 many Biograph films showed an increased narrative scope, inspired as much by the challenge of literary adaptation as the resources of the legitimate theater. The majority of films Griffith had made previously showed a strong unity of place, time, and action typical of the short plays that formed part of a vaudeville program and the O. Henry-esque short stories which were often sources for the films.[85] (Of course, certain films from 1908, notably *The Greaser's Gauntlet* and *After Many Years*, had already departed from this tendency.) Parallel editing allowed Griffith to depart from unity of place, but often reenforced unity of time and action. Although many Biograph films continued to work within a restricted period of time and with one strand of plot development, Griffith dealt increasingly with longer periods. At the same time he devoted an increased number of shots to character development and details of environment. Focusing on characters and supplying motivations for their actions became more central to Griffith's filmmaking, and expanding the time of film stories allowed him to trace actions back to motivating causes.

An adaptation from Dickens, *The Cricket on the Hearth* (April 8, 18, 24), shows the inspiration literary sources could provide for environmental detail and characterization, benefiting from a successful integration of the methods of the *films d'art* as well as the expanded narrative scope Griffith was exploring. Dickens's story, as well as its authorized theatrical adaptation by Albert Smith, covers only a few days. Griffith's film untangles the expository information scattered through the original sources, stretching it out in an extensive chronological line. The Biograph adaptation begins with Edward (Owen Moore) leaving for sea, three years before the main action of the plot. We see Edward's return from sea, and his discovery of his sweetheart's betrothal to Tackleton (Harry Solter). We watch him don the disguise of an old man in order to enter the town incognito. Dickens's text (and Smith's play, which followed it faithfully) withheld this information for a climactic revelation. The narrative form of Griffith's film presents events in strict chronology, ignoring the unities of space and time, and withholds nothing from the spectator.

But if Griffith reworked the temporal order of Dickens's story, the textural richness of the original source shines through in a new complexity of story line, characterization, and even mise-en-scène. The opening shot presents the clutter of Caleb Plummer's toy workshop as described by Dickens—dolls, blocks, wooden houses, toy horses, and drums suspended from the ceiling, even Caleb's burlap greatcoat stenciled with the words "Glass Handle with

Care." The richness of Dickens's descriptive detail inspired Griffith throughout the film, even in sequences not directly taken from the source. When Dot (Linda Arvidson) and John Peerybingle (Herbert Prior) come to tell Caleb of their marriage, he happily taps them with the doll he is making. Returning from the sea, Edward pauses outside a tavern while carefully placed extras smoke and talk on the porch. Before he enters, Edward turns and pats a dog. As Edward is disguised as an old man by a traveling mountebank (Mack Sennett), we see in the background not only bustling customers and bar maids, but also a white-faced Merry Andrew who pirouettes and dances for bystanders. Griffith develops here the fascination with environmental detail already hinted at in the 1908 films. Extended narrative scope encouraged the picturesque details that could create a lifelike environment.

Dickens's story provided Griffith with a more complex plot than any of his previous films. Whereas *The Devil* and *Ingomar* had been pared down to one basic line of action, here Griffith makes use of two dramatic focuses: the love story of Edward and May (Violet Mesereau) and the suspicion which arises between John and Dot Peerybingle, with bachelor Tackleton circulating between both stories. The increased number of major characters makes full use of the Biograph stock company, equal importance given to the performances of Solter, Moore, Messereau, Prior, and Arvidson, creating a true ensemble performance.

John Peerybingle's suspicion (planted by Tackleton) about his wife's relation to the stranger (her brother Edward in disguise) provides another climax based on character psychology rather than physical action. Prior's performance in this scene is exemplary of the increasing restraint in Biograph acting. Shot seventeen takes place in the parlor of the Peerybingle cottage as all the guests are leaving. Solter leaves last, pausing to ask Prior about his wife's attention to the stranger. Prior remains standing by the door while Arvidson tidies up in the background. When she approaches Prior, he is short with her and she leaves disturbed. Prior is left alone in the frame. He picks up a pistol hanging over the mantelpiece and moves to the door of the room in which the stranger is sleeping. But he then puts the pistol down and shakes his head. He moves over to the table and snuffs out the candle.

To express John's brooding suspicion, Griffith reworks the directional light premiered in *A Drunkard's Reformation*. The Peerybingle parlor has been lit by two lighting systems: an overall illumination coming from Cooper-Hewitt lamps mounted above the set and to the front, and a directional (probably arc lamp) light coming from the fireplace. In addition to serving as a realistic and picturesque detail, this arc light has a thematic purpose. It accents the hearth of the film's title, the metonymy Dickens provides for the warmth and security of home and family. As Prior snuffs out the candle, the bank of lights illuminating the set from the front are switched off. Prior stands in the now much darker parlor before the glowing hearth, then slumps into a chair. The light from the fireplace casts his shadow on the wall behind him. The lighting change and the directional light from the hearth provide a realistic means for creating a thoughtful mood, as John Peerybingle broods over the possible collapse of his household. The restraint in Prior's performance is made possible because other visual elements convey his somber state of mind. The lighting functions as both realistic detail and psychological sign.

Here Griffith avoids entering into the nonrealistic portrayal of subjectivity provided by the vision scenes of the nineteenth-century theater and early film. At this point in Dickens's text, the hearth becomes the locus of a series of images of Peerybingle's previously happy marriage, revealed by the "Cricket Fairy." Smith's play easily adapted this sequence to the stagecraft of the contemporary fairy pantomime: "the chimney above the mantelpiece opens slowly and discovers a tableau vivant—a fac-simile view of the interior of the cottage with a miniature figure of DOT sitting by the fireside, as in Act 1st. TILLY SLOWBOY, BABY, etc. At the same time troops of small fairies appear from every available position; some forming a sort of border to the tableau, others run to JOHN and pull him by the skirts to call attention to the picture."[86]

Such Méliès-like fancy does not appear in Griffith's film. Vision scenes of this sort were not infrequent in narrative films before 1908. In fact, Porter's *Fireside Reminiscences* (1908) had treated a series of memories in precisely this way, as images superimposed within a fireplace. Vitagraph's *Napoleon, Man of Destiny* (1909) used vision scenes to recount Napoleon's military career as he recalls it in exile, and Feuillade's *La mort de Mozart* (Gaumont, 1909) used them in a similar manner to present flashbacks of Mozart's life recalled on his deathbed. But Griffith avoids this type of subjective imagery and its *feerique* trappings, eliminating the Cricket Fairy and his minions. Griffith's portrayal of character psychology avoids dreamlike subjective imagery, and he tailors the inspiration provided by classic works of literature to the already solidifying practices of the narrator system.

The influence of the *films d'art* specifically—and the related impulse to raise film's status through adaptation of classic works of literature and drama—continued to be an important factor throughout 1909, with Biograph producing nearly a dozen acknowledged adaptations from such authors as Hugo, George Eliot, James Fenimore Cooper, Dickens, and Tolstoy, as well as unacknowledged "borrowings" from O. Henry, Maupassant, Balzac, and Frank Norris. This rush to the classics reached a climax in the late summer of 1909 with the publicized adaptations of George Eliot's *Silas Marner*, titled *A Fair Exchange* (August 14, 23), Robert Browning's *Pippa Passes* (August 17, 21), and Cooper's *The Last of the Mohicans*, titled *Leatherstocking* (August 24, 25,

26, 27), as well as the borrowing of certain motifs from Balzac's *La grande Breteche* (and not, as some sources indicate, Poe's *The Cask of Amontillado*) in *The Sealed Room* (July 22, 23).

In October 1909, the New York *Times*, which did not pay much attention to films, noted with some surprise this new nickelodeon fare and related it to the film reform movement: "Since popular opinion has been expressing itself through the Board of Censor of the People's Institute, such material as 'The Odyssey,' The Old Testament, Tolstoy, George Eliot, De Maupassant and Hugo has been drawn upon to furnish the films, in place of the sensational blood-and-thunder variety which brought down public indignation upon the manufacturers six months ago. Browning, however, seems to be the most rarified dramatic stuff up to date."[87] The *Times* reporter was particularly taken by Biograph's adaptation of *Pippa Passes* and drew a contrast between the "tired businessman at a roof garden and the sweat shop worker applauding Pippa."

Browning's poetic drama offered challenges in adaptation that surpassed those of Griffith's other literary sources. Although originally written as a stage piece, *Pippa Passes* had never succeeded in the theater. There had been a New York production of it in 1906 by Henry Miller, the impressario who Griffith had hoped would produce his play *War*. The cast of this series of matinee performances of Browning included two regular members of the Biograph stock company in 1909, Henry B. Walthall and William J. Butler, in minor roles. However, the production was not particularly well received. Although praising the staging and performances, the *Evening Post* had found, "it only offered additional confirmation to the old belief that studies of this kind are for the library, not the stage."[88] The principal reason for most critics' discomfort with the work—the extended monologues—were not a problem for a silent version. But finding a dramatic center that would hold the attention of a nickelodeon audience in this poetic work must have taxed Griffith (or any unknown adapter who assisted him). Linda Arvidson indicates that Griffith had wanted to adapt Browning's work for some time, but had encountered skepticism from Biograph executives.[89] Permission could only have been granted in hope of garnering the cultural prestige that the company so strongly desired in 1909.

Biograph's adaptation considerably simplifies its original source. Two of Browning's subplots—the scenes with Luigi and his mother, and the Monsignor and Muffeo—have been eliminated. Further, although Browning's text has a clear moral and didactic purpose, its tone has been considerably brightened and its moral lesson simplified in the Biograph version. The subtitle Biograph provided for the film, *The Song of Conscience*, defines an easily understood allegorical role for Pippa (Gertrude Robinson), and the results of her song are uniformly benevolent and transforming. For example, in the

Biograph film, Pippa's song interrupts and prevents the attempted murder of Luca (Arthur Johnson) by his wife Ottima (Marion Leonard) and her lover Sebald (Owen Moore), whereas in Browning's poem the murder has already taken place and Pippa can only awaken remorse in the perpetrators.

For Griffith then, Pippa's song embodied the voice of morality, much like the temperance drama in *A Drunkard's Reformation*. As if to mark the homology between these two films, the first dramatic episode of *Pippa Passes* became a mini-temperance drama, an episode invented for the Biograph version. In this sequence George Nichols plays a worker who neglects his family for evenings at the local tavern. Like Wharton's night at the theater, hearing Pippa's song causes the worker to reform and return home. Pippa's effect on the two other episodes is much the same: transforming the sculptor Jules's (James Kirkwood) anger at Phene, his wife (Linda Arvidson), into kindness and preventing the adulterous lovers from committing their intended murder. The effect of Pippa's artistry is consistently moral, combining Griffith's artistic ambition (the adaptation of Browning) with his creation of a moral role for the narrator system. Pippa operates in this film as the personification of the moral force of voice.

This call to conscience makes use of already established devices of the narrator system. In the first episode, Pippa's effect is conveyed within a single shot through set construction. We see the drunken worker at the tavern, within a split set showing both tavern interior and an area outside. Griffith then uses the parallel-edited contrast from drunkard to neglected family (familiar from *A Drunkard's Reformation*), cutting to the family at home, his wife slumped over a table in despair. The next shot returns to the split set as Pippa passes by playing her guitar and singing. Both worker and Pippa are visible in this shot: Pippa as she moves through the area outside the tavern, and the worker within as he starts to take a drink. He stops drinking and listens to Pippa's song. Seized with emotion, he puts his tankard down and leaves the tavern. The following shot shows him entering his cottage. Pippa passes by, visible through the window and still in song, as he stands before his despairing wife. The worker then embraces his wife and child, forming the frequent Biograph tableau of narrative resolution.

Pippa's call to conscience was conveyed in this sequence by placing both characters within the same shot, separated by walls within the sets. Narrative articulation and relation are accomplished on a pro-filmic level. Such split sets were often used in stage melodrama to portray simultaneous events and were not infrequent in early cinema. Griffith had used them several times before this film.[90] But editing presents Pippa's transforming effect more forcefully and is used in the next two sequences. Interrupting characters' actions and articulating their decisions, editing highlights the intervening force of voice.

In the following sequence, Jules moves angrily toward Phene, his fists raised as if to strike her as he learns that their love affair began as a practical joke. Griffith cuts to Pippa as she strolls along singing her song of faith. The next shot returns to Jules, his fists still raised. He slowly lowers them and backs away from Phene, transformed by Pippa's song. The shot ends with Jules and Phene embracing. Using interruption, Griffith both suspensefully delays an action and creates a space for a psychological conversion.

The same device climaxes the third and final sequence of the film, the attempted murder of Luca by Ottima and Sebald. As Sebald moves toward the sleeping Luca, dagger upraised, Griffith cuts to Pippa passing by outside with her guitar. Although Sebald's position has changed a bit in the shot that follows, he still holds the dagger in his upraised hand. Both he and Ottima suddenly look astounded, conscience-struck. He casts the dagger away. Compared to the more cumbersome pro-filmic staging of the first sequence, these last two episodes show the narrator system at full steam.

It was undoubtedly the success of psychological cutting in previous films that led Griffith to tackle Browning's poem. But the overall structure of *Pippa Passes* brings new challenges to Griffith: three brief episodes, each with its own set of characters, embedded in the framing story of Pippa's day. No previous Biograph film had used such a complex structure, and this indicates again the opportunities for innovation that literary adaptation brought Griffith.

However, this innovative structure posed some temporal problems which Griffith's strictly chronological approach to exposition could not solve. Shot eight crowds the whole of Jules and Phene's courtship and marriage into the space of about a minute, without any cuts that could express an elision of time. At the beginning of the shot, the sculptor is introduced to Phene by his prankster friends. The couple exits, then reenters as the friends hide. Jules proposes to Phene, and they exit again, the students emerging from hiding. Then Jules and Phene return, Phene now wearing a bridal veil, and the students reveal their role in the arranged romance. Many Biograph films have sequences in which the pro-filmic action is extremely compressed, a few symbolic gestures standing in for important narrative processes, but none so schematic as this. The unique framing story must bear the blame. The progression of Pippa's single day overrides the time scheme of the individual stories. Lacking devices for introducing past events, such as flashbacks or, as in Browning's play, dialogue, the duration of this episode pops out of joint with the single day of the frame. The result is one of the most temporally ambiguous shots in a Biograph film, a lack of precision in tense.[91]

Pippa, as she moves from locale to locale weaves the diverse episodes together. Griffith further unified the film by giving it a circular structure, from Pippa rising in the morning to her return home at night to sleep. Circular structure had already appeared in *The Greaser's Gauntlet* and *The Country Doctor* (May 29, 31, June 7), and Griffith's mastery of the form may have attracted him to Browning's poem, which also contained a circular pattern. *Pippa Passes* adds an experiment in lighting to the circularity of the earlier films, creating the most elaborate of his many lighting effects in 1909. Browning's poem is demarcated according to the stages of the day, moving from morning through noon and evening to night, and begins with Pippa's lyrical invocation of the coming dawn.

This extraordinary word picture of the world of newborn light has often inspired theatrical producers to create lighting effects to accompany this opening speech. For example, the *Evening Post* review of the 1906 Broadway production of *Pippa Passes* had noted that "the reflection of the dancing sunbeam was very prettily managed."[92] Griffith was no exception. In the lighting effects that he devised for the opening and closing of his film, he again asserted the director's control over the visualization of the image. Whereas the hearth lighting effect in *A Drunkard's Reformation* had been technically pioneered by Bitzer and Porter, there seems no precedent for the complicated lighting effect Griffith demanded for this film. Linda Arvidson indicates that Billy Bitzer resisted Griffith's ideas (Bitzer's memoirs pass over the film) and that it was Arthur Marvin who was responsive to the experiment. Arvidson's claim that the whole Biograph technical staff became involved in the film seems plausible; it is the first film in the Biograph Cameraman's Book for which all three Biograph cameramen—Bitzer, Marvin, and Percy Higginson—are listed as working.

Arvidson has described Griffith's lighting effect:

> He figured on cutting a little rectangular place in the back wall of Pippa's room, about three feet by one, and arranging a sliding board to fit the aperture much like the cover of a box sliding in and out of grooves. The board was to be gradually lowered and beams of light from a powerful Kleig shining through would thus appear as the first rays of the rising sun striking the wall of the room. Other lights stationed outside Pippa's window would give the effect of soft morning light. Then the lights full up, the mercury tubes a-sizzling, the room fully lighted, the back wall would have become a regular back wall again, with no little hole in it.[93]

It is hard to identify the rectangular slot Arvidson describes when looking at the film. There is a long strip of light in the wall above Pippa's head as she sleeps in bed. This appears to be lit from the back and may be formed by a slit in the wall, but gives no evidence of a sliding board, nor does it totally disappear when the room becomes fully lit. But the lighting scheme of the opening shot is certainly complex, involving more light sources than any previous Biograph shot. The shot begins in near darkness, with only the strip of light above Pippa's head visible. Then a spotlight with a clearly defined circular border illuminates Pippa's head as she begins to awake, a strongly directional kleig arc lamp that must have been placed in front of the set and to the right. Then other arc lamps, positioned outside the windows of the set to the right, are turned on, sending directional light through the window and forming a bright rectangle of light on the wall perpendicular to it. Perhaps unintentionally, the light seems to blink a bit, rippling through the room. This light from the window increases in intensity as Pippa gets out of bed. Then the overall lighting system of mercury vapor lamps comes on and washes out the shadows in the room although the arc lamps continue to supply highlighted areas next to the windows and above Pippa's bed.

When Pippa returns home at night, Griffith runs his opening lighting effects in reverse, stressing the film's circular structure. First he shuts off the overall lighting; then the light from the window is removed; finally, the strip of light over Pippa's bed disappears, leaving only the spotlight on Pippa as she settles down to sleep. These two shots with lighting effects bracket the film with highly esthetic images, unifying a widely dispersed narrative within a daily cycle.

The lighting effects in *Pippa Passes* are restricted to the first and last shot of the film. Lighting effects occur generally in final shots of Biograph films following Griffith's tendency to end films with esthetic images such as the lyrical postscripts. The majority of Biograph interiors from 1906–9 employ lighting from above, the side, and the front which effectively washes out all shadows and bathes all areas of the set with a uniform bright light. Any shot that departs from this scheme takes on stylistic and narrative significance.

Lighting effects in the 1909 films generally play clearly defined roles within the narrator system. Their frequent appearance in final shots underscores narrative resolutions and carries clear thematic meaning. A directional light illuminating figures in an otherwise darkened area usually accompanies scenes of spiritual devotion or conversion, for example, the reunited family bathed by hearth light in *A Drunkard's Reformation;* the boy's decision to enter the priesthood in *The Baby's Shoe* (April 5, 6, 12); the cripple's self-sacrifice in *The Violin Maker of Cremona* (April 21, 22, 23), the restoration of the husband's sanity in the Roman drama *The Slave* (June 22, 23); or the repentant woman at the altar in *A Strange Meeting* (June 11, 17).[94] Less frequently Griffith stresses the enshrouding shadows of a highlighted scene and creates a sinister mood, such as the scene illuminated by a single lantern in *Fools of Fate* (August 27), as an errant wife discovers her husband's suicide. In all these instances the lighting creates a mood, generally reflecting that of the characters within the shot. Occasionally it also creates an authorial intervention, as an illuminating beam pronounces benediction on a scene of self-sacrifice or religious conversion. Lighting therefore becomes an expressive pro-filmic device of the narrator system within both mood and voice.

As narrative discourse, the devices of the narrator system are specifically filmic. Even those pro-filmic elements of performance and lighting which it shares with theater are transformed in varying degrees by the act of filming. However, in defining the change in filmic discourse in which Griffith participates, recourse to arguments about the essential nature of film are not very helpful. Although the narrator system did develop an approach to narrative without exact equivalent in any other medium, the influence of theater and literature played an important role. And over Biograph's rush to the classics loom a series of social pressures: the economic policies of the MPPC designed to attract a larger and higher paying audience and the assaults of genteel reformers. The desire to imitate respectable forms of art and to counter allegations of obscenity provided a spur for the creation of a filmic rhetoric that could convey the mental life of characters and preach a sermon of morality. The narrator system took shape from this interweave of factors, rather than a single-handed discovery of the essential language of film.

Notes

1. Although this discussion of the closing of New York's nickelodeons is based on primary material, the subject has also been treated in less detail in Garth Jowett, *Film: The Democratic Art* (Boston: Little, Brown, 1976), pp. 111–13, and by Lary May, *Screening Out the Past: The Birth of Mass Culture and the Motion Picture Industry* (Chicago: University of Chicago Press, 1980), pp. 43–44, who places it in the context of progressive reform.

2. Apparently limiting nickelodeons' capacities to fewer than three hundred was not a provision of the common-show license, but an aspect of a separate building code. Contemporaneous accounts seem erroneous in this respect. See "Report on the Condition of Moving Picture Shows in New York City," Office of the Commissioner of Accounts, City of New York, March 27, 1911, pp. 2–3, which gives the authoritive information, and *Variety*, Jan. 2, 1909, p. 10.

3. *Film Index*, Jan. 2, 1909, p. 5.

4. New York *Post*, Dec. 28, 1908, p. 1.

5. New York *American*, Dec. 24, 1908, p. 2.

6. New York *Times*, Dec. 24, 1908, p. 4.

7. *Brooklyn Eagle*, Dec. 26, 1908, p. 4.

8. New York *American*, Dec. 24, 1908, p. 2.

9. *Brooklyn Eagle*, Dec. 26, 1908, p. 4.

10. *Film Index*, Jan. 2, 1909, p. 5.

11. New York *Daily Tribune*, Dec. 24, 1908, p. 4.

12. Ibid., Dec. 29, 1908, p. 2.

13. New York *Post*, Dec. 26, 1908, p. 4.

14. New York *World*, Dec. 27, 1908.

15. New York *Times*, Dec. 24, 1909, p. 4.

16. New York *Herald*, Dec. 24, 1908, p. 7.

17. New York *Daily Tribune*.

18. *Film Index*, Jan. 2, 1909, p. 5.

19. Ibid., Jan. 30, 1909, p. 3.

20. New York *Daily Tribune*, Dec. 26, 1908, p. 1.

21. *Film Index*, Jan. 9, 1909, p. 4; New York *World*, Dec. 27, 1908, p. 1.

22. Ibid., Dec. 27, 1908, p. 1.

23. New York *Herald*, Dec. 28, 1908, p. 4.

24. New York *Sun*, Dec. 27, 1908, p. 1.

25. New York *Herald*, Dec. 28, 1908, p. 7.

26. New York *Evening Mail*, Dec. 29, 1908, p. 7.

27. Charles Musser, *Lyman Howe and the Forgotten Era of Traveling Exhibitions, 1880–1920* (Princeton: Princeton University Press, 1991).

28. *Moving Picture World*, 4: 117.

29. *Film Index*, Jan. 2, 1909, p. 5; New York *Times*, Dec. 24, 1908, p. 4. The formation of the National Board of Censorship and Griffith's early films are also treated, in less detail, in May, *Screening Out the Past*. The basic thesis of May's early section—the desire by reformist politicians to control the new mass culture that the movies represented—is congruent with my view of the uplift of the film industry by the MPPC. Although May does not intend to offer film analysis, his lack of attention to the evolution of film language during this period undercuts his discussion. Further, many of his comments on plot summary are erroneous. A pioneering treatment of the National Board of Censorship can be found in Robert Fischer, "The National Board of Censorship of Motion Pictures, 1909–1927," *Journal of Popular Film* 4, no. 2 (1975): 143–56, with an excellent treatment of the board's relation to its parent organization, the People's Institute. I thank Janet Staiger for directing my attention to this article.

30. *U.S. v. MPPC*, pp. 2894–95.

31. John Collier, "Cheap Amusements," *Charities and the Commons*, April 11, 1908, pp. 73–74.

32. New York *Dramatic Mirror* April 3, 1909, p. 13.

33. "The Standards of the National Board of Censorship of Motion Pictures," (New York, n.d., ca. 1911), p. 3. Pamphlet filed under "Nation Board of Review" at the Library of the Performing Arts at Lincoln Center, New York City.

34. *Film Index*, March 6, 1909, p. 3.

35. *Moving Picture World*, Oct. 16, 1909, p. 524; *Film Index*, April 24, 1909, p. 4.

36. See John Hagan, "Erotic Tendencies in Film, 1900–1906," in *Cinema 1900–1906: An Analytical Study by the National Film Archives (London) and the International Federation of Film Archives*, ed. Roger Holman (Brussels: FIAF, 1982), pp. 231–33. The eroticism of early cinema has also been treated from a feminist perspective by Judith Mayne in "Uncovering the Female Body," *Before Hollywood: Turn of the Century Films from American Archives*, ed. Jay Leyda and Charles Musser (New York: American Federation of Arts, 1986).

37. Linda Arvidson, *When the Movies Were Young* (1925, repr. New York: Dover Publications, 1969), p. 69.

38. Biograph Cameraman Book, D. W. Griffith Papers, Museum of Modern Art Film Library, New York City.

39. Jacques Deslandes and Jacques Richard, *Histoire comparee du cinéma*, vol. 2: *Du cinematographe au cinéma, 1896–1906* (Paris: Casterman, 1968), vol. 2, pp. 313–14.

40. *Moving Picture World,* Jan. 9, 1909.

41. Ibid., June 12, 1909.

42. "Standards," pp. 9–10.

43. Ibid., pp. 13–27.

44. Ibid., p. 14.

45. "Report of the Board of Censorship on Film Shown May 10th, 1909" (spelling and punctuation corrected in some instances), Edison National Historic Site Archives, West Orange, N.J.

46. For the traditional account of early film censorship, see Terry Ramsaye, *A Million and One Nights: A History of the Motion Picture* (1926, repr. London: Frank Cass, 1964), pp. 256–61; for a documentary account of early kinetoscope censorship see Gordon Hendricks, "History of the Kinetoscope" in *The American Film Industry,* ed. Tino Balio (Madison: University of Wisconsin Press, 1976), p. 40.

47. "Report of the Board of Censorship on Film Shown August 6th, 1909," Edison National Historic Site Archives, West Orange, N.J.

48. Collier to MPPC, Aug. 13, 1909, Edison National Historic Site Archives, West Orange, N.J.

49. Ibid., Aug. 16, 1909.

50. *Moving Picture World,* July 31, 1909, p. 165.

51. Eileen Bowser, *History of American Cinema,* vol. 2: *1907–1915* (New York: Scribners, 1990), p. 71.

52. *Anti-Saloon League Yearbook 1910* (Columbus: Anti-Saloon League of America, 1910), p. 59.

53. *Variety,* June 12, 1909, p. 13.

54. See Alice Felt Tyler, *Freedom's Ferment: Phases of American Social History from the Colonial Period to the Outbreak of the Civil War* (New York: Harper and Row, 1944), pp. 308–50.

55. Frank Rahill, *The World of Melodrama* (University Park: Pennsylvania State University Press, 1967), p. 240.

56. Vachel Lindsay, *The Art of the Motion Picture* (1915, repr. New York: Liveright, 1970), p. 235.

57. Herbert Gutman, *Work Culture and Society in Industrializing America: Essays in American Working Class and Social History* (New York: Vintage Books, 1966), pp. 33–38; Roy Rosenzweig, *Eight Hours for What We Will: Workers and Leisure in an Industrial City, 1870–1920* (New York: Cambridge University Press, 1983), pp. 44–49, 53.

58. Rosenzweig, *Eight Hours for What We Will,* p. 101.

59. Kathy Peiss, *Cheap Amusements: Working Women and Leisure in Turn-of-the-Century New York* (Philadelphia: Temple University Press, 1983), pp. 27–28.

60. Rosenzweig, *Eight Hours for What We Will,* p. 104.

61. Lindsay, *Art of the Motion Picture,* p. 236.

62. *Variety,* Aug. 28, 1909, p. 12; see also "Picture Shows and Saloons," *Nickelodeon,* 2:72.

63. Eileen Bowser, *Biograph Bulletins, 1908–1912* (New York: Farrar Straus and Giroux, 1973), p. 77.

64. According to the *Biograph Bulletin;* Zola's novel had great success on American stages in *Drink,* a melodramatic adaptation by Charles Reade. In 1909, Pathé released a version of the novel in America with this title. Sadoul also assumes that *L'Assomoir*

is the source of Zecca's *Les victimes des alcoolisme, Histoire général du cinéma*, vol. 2: *Les pionniers du cinéma, 1897–1909* (Paris: Denoel, 1951), p. 188.

65. Bowser, *Biograph Bulletins*, p. 77.

66. A review of Edison's *The Saleslady's Matinee Idol* in the New York *Dramatic Mirror* criticized a scene showing a stage production: "If short scenes had alternated back and forth between the stage and the balcony showing the progress and the effect on the balcony audience concurrently, the effect would have been greatly increased" (Feb. 20, 1909, p. 16). This review by Frank Woods "The Spectator," later a close associate of Griffith's and the author of a number of Biograph film stories, appeared a week before Griffith began filming *A Drunkard's Reformation*. Linda Arvidson testifies to the close attention Griffith paid to "The Spectator's" reviews (*When the Movies Were Young*, p. 65).

67. The example of such stage-spectator cutting that is reproduced in Noel Burch's film *Correction Please* as *Twins at the Theater* and dated 1905 has been identified by Emmanuelle Tourlet as *Rosalie et Leonce à Théatre* and dates from approximately 1910. Further, the cutting within this delightful burlesque comedy serves no psychological purpose.

68. In early 1908, Biograph had released *Music Master* in which Griffith acted. The still which adorns the *Biograph Bulletin* for this film also shows a use of directional light coming from a fireplace, Kemp R. Niver, comp., *The Biograph Bulletins 1896–1908*, ed. Bebe Bergsten (Los Angeles: Locare Research Group, 1971), p. 349. This fact, as well as the curious flashback structure indicated by the synopsis, makes one regret that no print of this film is available for viewing.

69. For a discussion of this showing, see Sadoul, *Histoire général du cinéma*, vol. 2, pp. 504–7.

70. New York *Dramatic Mirror*, May 30, 1908, p. 4.

71. The French text for most of this article can be found in Sadoul, *Histoire général du cinéma*, vol. 2, pp. 5–502, where the date of original publication is given as Oct. 31, 1908.

72. *Film Index*, Jan. 9, 1909, p. 5.

73. *Moving Picture World*, Feb. 20, 1909, p. 200; Feb. 27, 1909, p. 236.

74. *Nickelodeon*, 2:37.

75. *Edison Kinetogram*, Aug. 1, 1909, p. 14.

76. New York *Dramatic Mirror*, June 26, 1909, p. 12; Sept. 18, 1909, p. 14; *Moving Picture World*, April 2, 1910, p. 497.

77. Bowser, *Biograph Bulletins*, pp. 69, 91.

78. New York *Dramatic Mirror*, May 29, 1909, p. 15.

79. Sadoul, *Histoire général du cinéma*, vol. 2, pp. 508–10.

80. New York *Dramatic Mirror*, March 13, 1909, p. 16.

81. Bowser, *Biograph Bulletins*, p. 91.

82. See Pierre Jenn and Michel Nagard, "L'assasinat du duc de Guise," *L'Avant Scene Cinéma* (Nov. 1984): 57, 70–71.

83. Barry Salt, "L'Espace d'à Cote," *Les premiers ans du cinéma francais* (Paris: Collections des Cahiers de la Cinématheque, 1985). A similar point was made by Ben Brewster in his article "Les mise en scène en profondeur dans les films francais de 1900 à 1914" in the same book.

84. New York *Dramatic Mirror*, Dec. 28, 1910, p. 28. The "wheat" film is undoubt-

edly *A Corner in Wheat.* This letter is striking for its anticipation of later approaches to Griffith's career, as well as an early example of the view of film as a *gesamkunstwerk.*

85. For a detailed and insightful discussion of the evolving literary sources of early film and their narrative implications, see David Bordwell, Janet Staiger, and Kristin Thompson, *The Classical Hollywood Cinema: Film Style and Mode of Production to 1960* (New York: Columbia University Press, 1985), pp. 160, 163–73, a section written by Kristin Thompson.

86. Albert Smith, *Cricket on the Hearth; or, A Fairy Tale of Home* (New York: Samuel French, n.d.), p. 22 (first performed in 1859).

87. New York *Times*, Oct. 10, 1909, quoted in Arvidson, *When the Movies Were Young*, pp. 130–31.

88. Clipping, *Evening Post*, Nov. 13, 1906, in Robinson Locke Scrapbooks, Library of the Performing Arts, Lincoln Center, New York City.

89. Arvidson, *When the Movies Were Young*, p. 97.

90. For example, split sets were used in the 1908 melodramas *An Awful Moment* and *The Honor of Thieves* (December 4, 10); in the latter film the set is further emphasized by a repeated pan from one side to the other.

91. This multipart structure revolving around the "song of conscience" was a form Griffith would return to twice in his later filmmaking. In 1913 he filmed a near re-make of *Pippa Passes, The Wanderer.* In this later film a wandering flute player (Henry Walthall) has a beneficent influence on a number of characters through the pure tones of his music as he passes by. He reconciles lovers, prevents a peevish young girl from throwing away a crucifix, and, in the clearest parallel to *Pippa Passes*, stops a pair of adulterous lovers from murdering the woman's husband. However, the extended time period of *The Wanderer* (covering nearly a decade), the flutist's interaction with the other characters (he marries the young girl when she grows up) and its ninety-six shots compared to the seventeen in *Pippa Passes*, mark the transformation in style that occurred between 1909 and 1913. After Griffith left Biograph, one of his first feature films, *Home Sweet Home*, had a similar structure, containing three separate narrative sequences. In each, the overhearing of the song "Home Sweet Home" causes a transformation in a character. However, the singer is a different character in each episode, and the three sequences had only a thematic link.

92. Clipping, Robinson Locke Scrapbooks, Library of the Performing Arts, Lincoln Center, New York City.

93. Arvidson, *When the Movies Were Young*, p. 128.

94. This identification of a shaft of light with spiritual forces brings to cinema an association basic to Western ideology and used in other visual arts for centuries. Griffith's immediate inspiration is likely to be the work of Belasco, who created otherworldy effects with light in *The Darling of the Gods* and *The Return of Peter Grim*, in addition to his realistic evocation of sunsets, twilights, and sunrises, Lise-Lone Marker, *David Belasco: Naturalism in the American Theater* (Princeton: Princeton University Press, 1975), pp. 83, 92–94.

7

The Narrator System Establishes Itself

Wᴴɪʟᴇ ᴛʜᴇ influence of culturally prestigious films either adapted from literary classics or modeled on ideals of reform and moral uplift exerted a vital influence on the narrator system, action-based melodrama never failed to inspire Griffith's filmmaking. Of course, drawing the line between these two sources is not simple. Many of the classic authors on whom Griffith drew—Dickens, Hugo, and even Tennyson—had long been adapted to the melodrama stage, and the genre of temperance melodrama shows how intertwined melodrama and morality are.

Editing: From "Dramatic Trick Work" to Narrative Armature

Griffith's exploration of both suspense and psychology generally involved some form of intercutting. In fact, cutting between spaces, whether distant or nearly adjacent, provided almost the only articulation available to Griffith in 1909. At this point in his career, editing was primarily a spatial and temporal articulation. The psychological, suspenseful, or moral effects of this articulation remained dependent on a movement between separate locations. If the plot called for a single location or strand of action, Griffith rarely cut to make a narrative detail clear or create empathy with a character. Without a temporal or spatial articulation, the effect of the narrator appeared fitfully in Griffith's early films. Mood and voice remained by-products of tense. Particularly in the first months of 1909, static, long-lasting, unarticulated shots with numerous narrative events still appeared.

Within a single location, without the possibility of interpolating another line of action, Griffith seems restricted to a monolithic approach to narrative.

The Prussian Spy (February 1) is a good example of this uneven development in articulation. The first shot of the film lasts an agonizing ninety-nine feet (16mm), more than half the length of the entire film. An enormous amount of information is contained in this shot, with characters entering, exiting, and reentering. A spy (Owen Moore) is concealed in a closet by his lover (Marion Leonard); the concealment is discovered by a French officer (Harry Solter). To torment the woman and destroy his enemy, the officer tacks a target onto the closet door, claiming he must practice his aim with his pistol. All of this takes place in a single shot. Only the gestures and expressions of the actors convey narrative information; no attempt is made to create suspense or empathy through cinematic techniques. There is a near neutrality of narrative discourse, as though the narrator system did not exist.

However, as soon as a parallel editing schema can be introduced, the film alters radically. The second half of the film fragments into ten shots. The woman has sent her maid (Florence Lawrence) to open a trap door above the closet and help the spy escape. The sequence alternates dramatically between the trap door and the parlor containing the closet. Griffith repeatedly interrupts action with a cut on gesture (the French officer aiming his pistol at the targeted door), switching to the progress of the maid as she pries the trap door open and attempts to get the spy out of danger.

Compared to the frequent multipurpose use of parallel editing, overlapping cuts were relatively rare in 1909 and limited in their expressivity. The psychological use of a cut-in introduced in *The Greaser's Gauntlet* appears again in muted form in the last shot of *Resurrection,* with a cut-in to a full shot of Katucha and Dimitri in Siberia, framed with a large cross alongside them. But cut-ins in 1909 primarily enlarged a narratively important but small object. A hypodermic to inject candy with deadly poison, diamonds being sewed into a valise's handle, Katucha's finger tracing out a Bible verse—these and other details are enlarged by close-ups, but not the faces of actors. In spite of the legendary importance of the close-up to Griffith's style, and his supposed role in inventing it, it became an important device only rather late in his Biograph career, in 1912 and after, and played a determinate psychological role only in 1914 in *The Avenging Conscience.* Parallel editing ruled the narrator system.

In early 1909, parallel editing was still an element remarked upon by trade papers. *Variety* reveled in its novelty in a review of a suspense melodrama, *The Medicine Bottle* (February 3, 4, 10, 16), which was reviewed under the title *The Wrong Bottle:*

> The Biograph studios have a producer who is a wonder at dramatic trick work. In this subject a situation is worked up to a tremendous pitch of suspense by alternately switching the spectator to either end of a telephone wire while life and death hang on the outcome of a telephone call. No better handling of a dramatic subject comes to mind. . . . The tension of suspense tightens almost

painfully until just in the nick of time the telephone connection is established and the sick woman's life is saved. The production is a remarkable one. As a bit of strong dramatic work it stands unique.[1]

The reviewer's term "dramatic trick work" is revealing, relating the technique of parallel editing to the devices of the trick films of Porter, Méliès, Gaston Velle, and others. But the term is something of an oxymoron, yoking the methods of the trick films of the cinema of attractions with the narrative devices of the narrator system. In parallel editing, the "magical" switches from one line of action to another are not the product of a Méliès-like prestidigator, nor indications of a marvelous overturning of the laws of space and time. Rather, they embody the operation of the filmic narrator, coordinating a realistic diegesis within a coherent space and time through the functions of tense and suspense. By referring to parallel editing as "dramatic trick work" this contemporaneous reviewer is unconsciously marking a change in film's approach to narrative. In contrast to Méliès and others, Griffith's "trick work" is in the service of the drama, a narrativizing of the possibilities of filmic discourse.

Griffith continued to refine the suspenseful possibilites of parallel editing in the first months of 1909. Placing the cut so that it interrupts a dramatic gesture and suspends its outcome became a common device. In *The Fatal Hour,* the ticking of the clock as it moved toward the moment of detonation measured out the suspenseful progression of the narrative. In later films Griffith more frequently derived suspense from a chance triggering of a deadly device by an unaware human agent. This provided a potentially fatal gesture to cut on, and the ingenuity of Biograph's writers supplied a paranoid's nightmare of unsuspected dangers. Boys target practice with their father's pistol in *Those Boys* (January 5), unaware that their sisters sit in the line of fire on the other side of an attic partition. In *The Cord of Life* (January 6, 8, 13), a vengeful Sicilian (George Gebhardt) has suspended an Italian family's baby from a rope which will be released if the window is opened. *The Medicine Bottle* presents a young child told to give medicine to her ailing grandmother, unaware that her mother has mistakenly left her a bottle of poisonous lotion. A gun concealed beneath the altar and ready to fire when the priest steps forward is featured in *At the Altar* (January 30, February 8), while candies poisoned by a woman scorned and sent to her former lover's new fiancee provide the danger in *The Drive for Life* (January 15, March 23, 30). The Italian mother about to open the window, the priest ready to make the fatal step, the spoon of poison poised in the little girl's hand all provide gestures of heightened dramatic intensity that are interrupted by a cut to the alternate strand of the parallel-edited sequence—the husband, lover, or policeman rushing to warn the innocent of the danger.

As Meir Sternberg has pointed out in his treatment of the retardatory structures of suspense, the effects of delay can be caused by both events within the diegesis and the narrator's structuring devices.[2] While the suspenseful delays of *The Fatal Hour* derived from parallel editing alone, Griffith soon developed a number of delaying devices within the story, both in the carrying out of the fatal action and the rescue. The little girl spills the poisonous medicine spoon just as she is about to give her grandmother a fatal dose in *The Medicine Bottle* and has to re-fill it, while the anxious mother, telephoning to warn her, encounters gossiping switchboard operators who ignore their signals. Nearly all the melodramas of 1909 include such suspenseful delays.

The climax of *The Drive for Life* is typical of this sort of pattern:

Shot eighteen: Exterior of widow Lebrun's house. The former lover (Arthur Johnson) rushes out into his waiting auto, having just learned of the poisoned chocolates. He orders the chauffeur to drive off. The car exits from the frame.

Shot nineteen: A country road, recessive from the camera at a slight diagonal. The car rushes toward the camera and exits.

Shot twenty: Another location on the road. Car drives toward the camera and exits.

Shot twenty-one: The porch of the fiancee's house. A messenger boy arrives with the package of chocolates and goes in the door.

Shot twenty-two: The country road. Car rushes toward camera and exits.

Shot twenty-three: Interior set of the parlor of Mignon, the fiancee (Florence Lawrence). She sits reading with her mother and sisters. A butler brings in the messenger boy, who gives Mignon the package. She opens the card (a section of leader saying "letter" intervenes) and kisses it. She starts to open the package. Cut on this action to:

Shot twenty-four: Road with suburban houses on right. The car exits toward camera.

Shot twenty-five: Country road. Car comes toward camera and stops. The lover and the chauffeur get out and make an adjustment to the engine. The car starts up again and exits.

Shot twenty-six: Mignon opens the box, takes out a candy, and puts it to her lips (fig. 27). Cut on this action to:

Shot twenty-seven: Country road, shot at a diagonal. Car passes, moving from left to right (fig. 28).

Shot twenty-eight: Toll gate. A carriage passes through, and the toll-taker closes the gate and exits. The lover's car appears in the background; it smashes through the gate and exits. The toll-taker reenters the shot, yells after the car, shaking his fist.

Shot twenty-nine: Parlor. Mignon takes out the candy again, merely kisses it, and then replaces it in the box. She sits down again. One of the sisters takes a candy and holds it before Mignon, who opens her mouth (fig. 29). Cut on this action to:

Shot thirty: A dirt road. A carriage crosses the road and stops, with its wheel still on the shoulder. The lover's car barrels toward the camera, hitting the carriage as it passes (fig. 30).

Shot thirty-one: The side of the road. Men yell off at the car from the carriage wreckage.

Shot thirty-two: Road. The lover's car turns a corner.

Shot thirty-three: The sister's hand is still poised above Mignon's mouth. One of the other sisters tickles her, and she drops the candy. They bend down to pick it up.

Shot thirty-four: Long-shot of the wall of Mignon's estate. The lover's car enters and goes through the gate; some men run after it.

Shot thirty-five: The parlor. Mignon gives out candies to her sisters and mother (fig. 31). They are about to eat them when the lover rushes in and tells them of the widow's revenge. The chocolates are dropped. The lover and Mignon embrace.

The apparent repetition in shot twenty-nine of an action already shown in shot twenty-six, and the freezing of the sister's gesture from shot twenty-nine to shot thirty-three show some indecision in working out the exact

27, 28, 29, 30, and 31: Parallel editing and the "fatal gesture" in *The Drive for Life* (1909). Griffith cuts continually between the fiancee (Florence Lawrence) about to eat the poisoned chocolate and the hero in his automobile racing to warn her. Frame enlargements from prints made from Paper Print Collection, Library of Congress.

27

28

29

30

31

temporal relations within this sequence. It is a temporal ambiguity that the most perspicacious of contemporary film reviewers, the New York *Dramatic Mirror*'s Spectator, caught and criticized in his review of *The Drive for Life*:

> The thrilling suspense at the finish of this picture is too long drawn out to be fully effective. . . . In alternate scenes we see him racing through the streets and we see the fiancee and her friends about to eat the candy. They have the sweets at their lips for an interminable length of time, so long that we are sure their arms will be paralyzed, while the young man in the automobile is crashing through toll gates knocking over wagons, and whirling around corners. Of course, he arrives in time, as we knew he would, but either the chase is too long or the act of eating the candy is commenced too early in the picture.[3]

The constant strategy of interruption of dramatic action, both by plot contrivances such as toll gates and engine trouble and the editing pattern, shows the increased complexity of Griffith's races to the rescue in early 1909. From stage and literature Griffith adapted the narrative device which the Russian formalists called "retardation," the need to brake the action and structure the narrative through postponing resolutions.[4] Delays accomplished through the structuring devices of parallel editing form the cornerstone of Griffith's suspense melodramas.

A series of films from both 1908 and early 1909, such as *The Guerilla, The Medicine Bottle*, and *The Drive for Life*, laid the foundation for the most famous of Griffith's early suspense melodramas, *The Lonely Villa* (April 29, 30, May 4, 6, 14). *The Lonely Villa* perfects the melodramatic formula Griffith had rehearsed in numerous films: the shattering of bourgeois domestic order by an outside intruder. The basic action recalls *The Guerrilla*, with an invader trying to force his way into the room containing the lady of the house, intercut with her husband rushing to the rescue. This threat and rescue are crossbred with a device from *The Medicine Bottle*: the major sequence of cross-cutting occurs as the husband learns of the burglary over the telephone. The film does not simply grow out of elements found in previous Griffith films, but draws on a rich melodramatic tradition in both theater and earlier films.

The telephone call and the basic plot and suspenseful situation of the film derive from Andre de Lorde's play *Au telephone*, as Kemp Niver has pointed out.[5] In this 1901 one-act play by the most famous dramatist of the Grand Guignol, a businessman named Andfe Marex leaves his wife and children at their suburban chateau in the care of elderly servants. He calls from Paris, and as he speaks to his wife, burglars invade the house and the husband must listen to, first, the terror and, then, the murder of his wife and child.[6] De Lorde's play provided a field day for the actor playing Marex (who, in the original production, was the famous naturalist actor and director Antoine), conveying the effect of distant unseen events through his reactions alone and driven mad by his inability to respond.

Early filmmakers found the melodrama irresistible, and Griffith's film was only one in a long line of film adaptations. In 1906 Pathé produced a fairly faithful adaptation under the title *Terrible angoisse*,[7] and Edwin S. Porter photographed a film for the Edison Company in August 1908 entitled *Heard over the Phone* that borrows its climax from de Lorde's play (or the Pathé film), with a father hearing over the telephone the murder of his family by a hostler he had fired earlier for mistreating horses.[8]

Unfortunately neither of these films seem to have survived. Was the suspenseful interrelating of the two locations through the telephone accomplished through parallel editing as it is in Griffith's film? The written descriptions, all that seems to remain of the films, are open to interpretation. The Pathé film certainly covers incidents in two locations, but how they are filmically portrayed is not clear. The more detailed synopsis of the Edison film seems to indicate the telephone conversation may have been handled by a filmic equivalent of the melodramatic vision scene, perhaps through superimposition: "AS IN A VISION—Husband wrought to a pitch of madness—In dreadful agony—Powerless to move—Hears every word—Witnesses as in a vision every scene enacted."[9] Porter had used a superimposed vision in *Fireside Reminiscences* that same year and had used a matted-in split screen to convey a telephone call in *College Chums* a few months earlier. But how he treated this scene remains conjectoral.

The plot of *The Lonely Villa* has a fundamental difference from de Lorde's play and from both film versions detailed herein. Griffith's film exchanges the Grand Guignol-esque ending of death and insanity for the restoration of family security through the defeat of the invaders. Marex's helplessness plays no role in *The Lonely Villa*. The father returns, accompanied by the law, and routs the invaders. In contrast to Marex's immobility and impotence, Griffith's film moves effortlessly, cross-cutting from one end of the telephone line to the other. The spatial-temporal fluidity of the narrator system overcomes the gruesome affect of the original play.

But these changes are not attributable simply to Griffith, or to Mack Sennett, whom Linda Arvidson claims "gleaned it [the film story] from a newspaper."[10] Pathé, which was given to remaking its own films with slight variations, released in the United States in March 1908 a film with the American release title *A Narrow Escape*, which reworked the basic material of *Terrible angoisse*.[11] The basic transformations of *Au téléphone* found in *The Lonely Villa* are present in this film released more than a year before: the false message that draws the father away, the desperate ride home, and the last-minute rescue. The father is a doctor drawn to an aristocratic patient by a false telegram sent by tramps planning to rob his house. Alone in the house his wife hears the entrance of the thieves and barricades herself and her son in a room for protection. She calls her husband on the telephone; in his car, he rushes from his patient's chateau, picking up two policemen en route. He reaches home just as the burglars force the barricades. Wife and child are rescued, and the thieves arrested.

But if this film served as Griffith's model, he took more than the plot from Pathé. The film contains a sequence of parallel editing which, while certainly more elementary than the climax of *The Lonely Villa*, lays down the basic schema of alternation found in Griffith's film. Like Griffith's melodramas of 1908, *A Narrow Escape* creates suspense through parallel editing, using the pattern to create an agonizing delay. The sequences in several Pathé films from this period that contain parallel editing are all fairly brief, and none involve the suspenseful effects found in *The Narrow Escape*, which is a direct pre-figuration of the narrator system. It is unfortunate that more Pathé films from 1907–8 are not available for study to determine their role in this transitional period in the history of narrative style. However, based on the available films, Barry Salt's conclusion seems reasonable: "American directors developed the stylistic traits which were present in an embryonic state in the french films of 1908, while the French directors found themselves incapable of developing these traits themselves."[12]

The Lonely Villa's three-pronged editing pattern—from threatened wife and children to intruding burglars and absent husband—appears, albeit briefly, in the Pathé film. The central sequence of *A Narrow Escape* runs as follows:

Shot thirteen: The dining room of the doctor's house. The wife and child rush in and secure the door, barricading it with chairs and tables. They then run out of the room through another door.

Title: ARRIVING AT THE CASTLE

Shot fourteen: The gate to the castle. An attendant opens it and lets in the doctor's automobile.

Shot fifteen: Interior set of the parlor of the castle. The nobleman and his wife sit with their children, two daughters and an infant. The doctor enters and examines the baby. He shows his telegram to the nobleman, and they all talk excitedly.

Shot sixteen: Parallel edit to the doctor's study in his home. The doctor's wife and child rush in through the door, which they shut and barricade with furniture.

Shot seventeen: The dining room in shot twelve. The tramps push through the door and enter the room. They then exit through the other door, through which the woman and child had run.

Shot eighteen: Return to the study. The wife goes to the table, where she finds a copy of the telegram. She lifts the receiver of the telephone.

In the Biograph film, the same three elements are set up in a similar manner:

Shot sixteen: A sitting-room in the family's house. The mother and her three daughters seem to hear something off-screen. The mother (Marion Leonard) and her eldest daughter (Mary Pickford) exit left to investigate.

Shot seventeen: The foyer of the house, with the front door on the left. Mother and daughter enter from right and creep over to the door. Mother kneels before it, as if looking through a keyhole.

Shot eighteen: A shot of the front of the house filmed from the front yard. We see the veranda and the stairs leading up to the house. The burglars are visible, somewhat dimly, in the shadow of the porch, prying open the front door. (This cut is partly motivated as the mother's view through the keyhole. However, it definitely does not match as a point of view, given the camera position outside the house.)

Shot nineteen: Return to foyer. A sort of reaction shot, as mother, alarmed, rises from her knees. She stops her daughter from screaming. The front door falls in, and mother and daughter rush back into the room on the right as the thieves enter.

Shot twenty: The sitting-room shown in shot sixteen. Mother and daughter enter and slam the door; the other girls gather around them in terror.

Shot twenty-one: Foyer. The burglars begin to work on the door to the sitting-room with a crowbar. (A brief shot, 1.5 feet in 16mm.)

Shot twenty-two: The sitting-room. Mother and daughter begin to barricade the door with tables and chairs; the younger girls huddle fearfully.

Shot twenty-three: A country inn beside a dirt road. The husband's car drives up (slight pan to the left). The husband (David Miles) gets out. His chauffeur and another man examine the car's engine. The husband goes into the inn.

Shot twenty-four: The interior of the inn, an elaborate set with a bar in the far background and a reception desk in the foreground right. A number of extras involved in various tasks (nine actors in the shot besides the husband). The husband telephones from the desk.

Indebted although it may be, Griffith's film elaborates on the Pathé pattern through further articulation. Griffith takes nine shots to accomplish what the Pathé film established in six. Further, in Griffith's film the shots are interrelated from one shot to the next through characters' reactions, creating less autonomous shots and more hypotactic interrelations. The movement out into the hall is motivated by the off-screen sound heard. The burglars are introduced through a sort of "sight link," which is followed by a reaction shot.

Griffith's cross-cutting is more extensive than the Pathé film's, as is particularly clear in the sequence of the telephone call. In the Pathé film, the call is limited to four shots:

Shot nineteen: The parlor of the castle. A servant enters to indicate there is a call; the doctor goes to the telephone and picks up the receiver.

Shot twenty: The doctor's study. The wife is framed at the bust as she speaks into the telephone (fig. 32). This shot is much closer than most shots of a character in Biograph films of 1909 or 1910.

Shot twenty-one: Parallel edit to the doctor in the parlor as he speaks on the telephone (fig. 33). He, too, is framed at the chest.

Shot twenty-two: A cut-out to a long shot of the parlor (leaving plenty of space above the characters' heads). The doctor hangs up and explains the situation to the nobleman. They rush out the door together.

The corresponding sequence in *The Lonely Villa* extends to seventeen shots, interpolating shots of the burglars, the husband's trip outside to check on the car, and the added diegetic delay of the telephone line being cut:

Shot twenty-five: The sitting-room. Mother reacts to the sound of the telephone, which is mounted on the wall to the right. She rushes over to answer it.

Shot twenty-six: The inn interior (a further bustle of extras, as a group of women walks through). Husband speaks into the telephone, listens, looks concerned. He points to the left.

Shot twenty-seven: The sitting-room, but now the camera distance is somewhat closer to the mother, framing her at mid-calf. Speaking into the receiver, she also points off left. The three daughters cower together in the background, in slightly softer focus than their mother.

Shot twenty-eight: Inn interior. The husband puts down receiver, rushes out.

Shot twenty-nine: The exterior of the inn. He rushes over to the car; the mechanic gestures that it will take time to fix it.

Shot thirty: The foyer. The burglars continue to work on the door to the sitting room. One rushes off to the left.

Shot thirty-one: Inn interior. Husband picks up the receiver again.

Shot thirty-two: The sitting-room as in shot twenty-seven. Mother listening to the telephone.

Shot thirty-three: Inn interior. Husband speaks passionately; bystanders begin to listen.

Shot thirty-four: The sitting room, from the farther back camera position. Mother leaves the telephone and crosses to the desk. She picks up the revolver and returns to the telephone (fig. 34).

Shot thirty-five: Inn interior. Husband speaks into the telephone, mimes firing a pistol (fig. 35).

Shot thirty-six: Sitting-room. Mother at the telephone, fires the gun but nothing happens. She opens the revolver and finds it is unloaded.

Shot thirty-seven: Inn interior. Husband frantic as he hears the news.

Shot thirty-eight: Exterior of the family house. A low angle of a burglar mounted on a pillar of the veranda, cutting the telephone wire (fig. 36).

Shot thirty-nine: Inn interior. Husband jiggles the bar of the telephone and discovers he is cut off (fig. 37).

Shot forty: The sitting-room, from the closer camera position of shot twenty-seven. Mother realizes the telephone is dead (fig. 38).

32

32 and 33: The telephone call from Pathé's version of De Lorde's *Au téléphone* (the source for Griffith's *The Lonely Villa*), *A Narrow Escape*, or *The Physician of the Castle* (1907). Frame enlargements from 16mm prints.

33

Shot forty-one: Inn interior. Desperate, husband puts the receiver down and rushes out of the inn.

Given the almost baroque variation that Griffith plays on the elementary Pathé theme, it is surprising that he did not use the effective medium close-ups found in the telephone conversation in *A Narrow Escape*. Shot twenty-seven of *A Lonely Villa* was taken from a closer camera position than previous shots in the same set, but only advanced as far as Leonard's calf. Of course, it is possible that Griffith had not actually seen the Pathé film. Facially dominated close shots in Griffith's films had only appeared thus far in the penultimate shot of *The Curtain Pole*, which basically functions as humorous "facial expression" gag.

The penultimate six shots of the Pathé film (shots twenty-three–twenty-nine) follow the doctor's mad rush home, where he arrives just as the thieves are laying hands on his wife and child. The car's trajectory is followed without parallel editing until it reaches the doctor's home in shot twenty-eight. Griffith's film, providing complications which extend the action, adds the twist that the husband's car is still not repaired. He finds it necessary to

34, 35, 36, 37, and 38: In *The Lonely Villa* (1909), Griffith complicates the editing of the telephone call by interpolating a shot of the burglars as they cut the wires. (Husband, David Miles; wife, Marion Leonard; elder daughter, Mary Pickford.) Frame enlargements from 35mm print, courtesy of the Museum of Modern Art.

34

35

36

37

38

commandeer a wagon from a nearby gypsy camp. All of this is intercut with both the progress of the burglars and the plight of the threatened women. Once the wagon is on the road, parallel editing switches action between the family peril and the husband careening down country roads.

Whereas parallel editing makes a dramatic appearance in the early Pathé film, it is limited to a sequence of ten shots. In Griffith's film, parallel editing functions throughout the film, involving more articulation within sequences. *The Lonely Villa* contains fifty-two shots compared to thirty for *A Narrow Escape*; the French film is about two-thirds the length of *The Lonely Villa*, 416 feet compared to 750, in the original 35mm length. Fifty-two shots is the largest number in any Biograph film made to this date and would not be equalled again for some time.

Trade papers were enthusiastic about Griffith's most extended use of parallel-edited suspense; a review in *Moving Picture World* commented on the audience's tremendous absorption in the film:

> "THE LONELY VILLA" (Biograph)
> "Thank God, they're saved!" said a woman behind us at the conclusion of the Biograph film bearing the above title. Just like this woman, the entire audience were in a state of intense excitement as this picture was being shown. And no wonder, for it is one of the most adroitly managed bits of bloodless film drama that we have seen . . . [a summary of the action of the film follows]. . . . Indeed, when we saw the picture at Fourteenth St. the house literally "rose" at the story, it is so closely, effectively, and convincingly told. As good a piece of sharp, rapid, decisive dramatic work as we have seen.[13]

The film's impact alarmed the Chicago police in charge of film censorship, who promptly banned it.[14]

Parallel editing and Griffith's archetypal drama of a threatened bourgeois household derive from a tradition of both stage and film melodrama which preceded him. But this defines rather than eliminates the zone of Griffith's originality. The parallel-edited sequence from *A Narrow Escape* remains a brilliant, isolated coup de theatre. With Griffith, not only is the device elaborated, but parallel editing also becomes a narrative structure, a way of shaping the relations of space and time that can be used in a variety of situations and with a range of effects.

In addition to creating contrasts, articulating characters' decisions, and presenting a moral viewpoint, parallel editing provides the basic armature for many of Griffith's narratives. Divorced from the many dramatic effects that parallel editing could make available, it could also provide an elegant way to tell a story with a maximum of variety and interest. In *Her First Biscuits* (April 20), filmed about a week before *The Lonely Villa*, parallel editing structures the gags, creating one of the more enjoyable Jones family comedies. The device reveals the pervasive ill effects of a batch of Mrs. Jones's (Florence Lawrence) biscuits on unwary consumers. The film intercuts Mr. Jones (John Cumpson) at his office, a group of actors in his waiting room, the iceman at the Jones's home, and a burglar who invades the Jones kitchen, all of whom are trying to keep down the indigestible fare. For some twenty shots, the pattern of alternation juggles four locations and as many groups of sufferers, orchestrating a farcical image of simultaneous nausea that continues to gather more victims.

Parallel editing is a narrative armature, interlacing the narrative progress of characters separated in space, in a variety of genres other than suspense films throughout 1909. The technique becomes both ubiquitous and varied. In *The Indian Runner's Romance* (June 29, 30, July 2, 3), parallel editing is finally introduced into an extended chase sequence, the chronotope that previously showed a strict linearity of action and editing. Griffith clearly assumed that the technique was immediately understood by the audience, had become fully encoded, and no longer had to be approached as an exceptional bit of "dramatic trick work." In *With Her Card* (July 7), for example, a telephone call is conveyed through three parallel-edited shots, without the call playing the suspenseful and central role it had in *The Medicine Bottle* or in *The Lonely Villa*. The scene operates simply to transmit important information among characters. This film continually crosscuts among main characters, as an actress (Marion Leonard) plots, with the help of a stockbroker (Frank Powell), the downfall of the suitor who has jilted her (Owen Moore).

The lesson *Her First Biscuits* provided on the comic uses of parallel editing was also put to use. *His Wife's Visitor* (July 13) intercuts a young wife (Mary Pickford) preparing "evidence" that she has had a male visitor while her husband was away, with her husband (Billy Quirk) having a night out with the boys at his club. *Pranks* (July 19, 20, 28) intercuts the plights and trajectories of Marion Leonard and Arthur Johnson after mischievous boys have switched their clothes in a bath house and they have to make their way home dressed in clothing of the opposite sex. Perhaps a simply linear presentation of a story without cross-cutting made Griffith uncomfortable, and he valued the technique as much for the variety it offered in construction as for its possibilities of irony, contrast, or suspense.

Extended uses of parallel editing in already-established melodramatic contexts remained a Biograph mainstay, however. In *The Children's Friend* (July 30, August 12), a group of young girls caught in a sand pit are intercut with their parents' search for them. *1776, or, The Hessian Renegades* (July 23, August 2, 3) intercuts James Kirkwood as an American yeoman during the revolutionary period gathering his neighbors to defend their homes, while Hessians mistreat his daughter (Gertrude Robinson) in his commandeered farmhouse. *The Sealed Room* intercuts a queen (Marion Leonard) and a troubador (Henry Walthall) making love while her husband (Arthur Johnson) discovers them and has the only exit from their room bricked over. The final sequence of the film crosscuts the lovers' panic as they discover their fate and then suffocate, while the king exults in his revenge on the other side of the wall.

Effects of irony and psychology, the combining of mood and voice which *After Many Years* first developed, form the center of the parallel editing in *The Broken Locket* (August 10, 11, 19). Parallel editing is a logical outcome of the film's geographic structure. George Peabody (Frank Powell), an occasional drunkard, promises his faithful sweetheart Ruth King (Mary Pickford) that he will reform and sets out for the West to make his fortune. As it progresses, the film continually cuts back and forth from Powell in the West to Pickford's vigil at home as she waits for his return.

A lover's token, the broken locket of the title divided between George and Ruth, supplies a diegetic reflection of the theme of geographic separation and emotional connection. Parallel editing expresses the situation on the level of discourse, but with a harsh ironic effect that contrasts with the faithful lovers of *After Many Years.* As in the earlier film, the most powerful cut unites separated lovers and interrupts a kiss. In a western bar, George has begun drinking again and become involved with a Mexican girl (Marion Leonard). She sits on Peabody's table and toys with his half of the locket; he grabs her hand and kisses it passionately. In the middle of this gesture, Griffith cuts to Ruth back East, kneeling in prayer in her parlor. The next shot returns to the bar, as the girl writes a letter to Ruth with George's consent and tells her that he is dead. While George is kissing another woman, Ruth remains faithful, presumably offering up a prayer for his well-being.

The final shots of *The Broken Locket* continue the irony of this cross-cutting, as it moves from George, a drunken vagrant, to Ruth, who has gone blind. George wanders back East and passes Ruth's house. He encounters Ruth with her mother (Kate Bruce) at the gate to her house and learns of her blindness. Thanks to her condition, George and her mother are able to conceal his destitution from her. Ruth goes back inside, believing George has made good and will soon come again. The last three shots of the film intercut George as he stands in the road, reeling with self-disgust, with a shot of Ruth in her parlor, still awaiting his return. In the last shot, George bends down and picks up a cigar butt from the ground, lights it, shrugs his shoulders, and walks off.

Parallel editing creates the filmic equivalent of an omniscient and omni-present narrator who selects and shapes the information conveyed to the spectator, playing with expectations through effects of irony and suspense. In *The Broken Locket,* or suspense melodramas such as *The Lonely Villa,* these authorial interventions pummel viewers through a highly forceful rhetoric.

However, the same basic structure underlies most of the films Griffith made in the latter part of 1909, even if such strong effects of voice are not always derived from it. Parallel editing had become a system that could serve Griffith as a basic narrative armature, as well as a means of strong authorial comment.

Enframed Image: Layering, Camera Movement, and Thematic Spaces

If editing, and specifically parallel editing, seems to rule the narrator system, important transformation did occur on the level of the enframed image during 1908. In 1909, composition and camera movement, while certainly secondary to editing, nonetheless formed an important aspect of the narrator system, creating some of the strongest moments in Griffith's filmmaking. The composition of certain shots, such as lyrical postscripts, already carried strong elements of mood in 1908. In 1909, Griffith organized the space within the frame more commandingly, making it a powerful aspect of narrative discourse.

The composition in Griffith's earliest Biograph films such as *The Greaser's Gauntlet* tended to be restricted to one plane of action placed at considerable distance from the camera. The shallow space of the 14th Street studio made depth difficult in interiors, although distant backgrounds occasionally appeared in location shooting, as in the opening shot of *The Adventures of Dollie*. But even in exteriors, the distance the camera maintained from the actors in the early films (other than exits toward camera) placed most action in one rather shallow plane.

The basic camera distance for most shots in 1909 crept closer than the distant tableau found in some of Griffith's first films. The full shot of the character from head to toe predominates over shots with plenty of space above the head of the actor and "six feet of boards" below. Increasingly, characters stepped into the foreground, where they were framed between ankle and knee. The frame became an actor's space rather than a proscenium arch, determined by the actor's height and position rather than the extent of the set. This anthropocentric frame size, which seems to have been pioneered and popularized in Vitagraph films, clearly differentiates Griffith's style from the extensive frames of Mélîes or Porter, which seem to dwarf their actors.

As the camera was moved closer to the actors, the possibility of a foreground playing area, juxtaposed to a midground and background, appeared. In 1909, actors were never shot closer than a medium shot which framed them somewhere between ankle and thigh, except, again, for exits toward the camera. But this allowed Griffith to use a deeper playing space within the frame in exteriors, ranging from this new "medium shot" foreground to a far distant background.

The opening shot of *The Renunciation* (June 2, 14, 18) shows the expansive space Griffith created through the use of several planes of action in exterior shooting. The shot begins as two miners, Joe Fielding (James Kirkwood) and Sam Walters (Harry Solter) enter the frame from behind the camera. They sit down in the foreground together, facing the camera. The viewer's eye is led into the background of the shot by the compositional elements of a large cliff and rock quarry, as well as by the movement of miners picking their way through the rocks far into the background. Sometime into the shot Kitty Ryan (Mary Pickford) accompanied by her uncle (Tony O'Sullivan) enter the frame from the right, far in the background. The pair cross to the middle of the frame and then turn toward the foreground. The two miners turn and notice them; they approach and are introduced.

The use of several planes of action in this shot shows Griffith's and Bitzer's appreciation of layered compositions. Kitty and her father could have entered in the foreground, but the visual articulation of deep space would be lacking. Likewise, Kitty's movement toward the foreground defines her as a narratively important character, as opposed to the nameless and faceless miner-extras restricted to the background, creating a sense of distance and environment.

In 1909 Griffith still arranged space differently in exteriors than on studio sets. Stage blocking and conventions were more frequent in interior sets than in natural landscapes. Although use of the foreground does occur now and then in interiors, this foreground playing occasionally recalls stage traditions, as a shot in *The Renunciation* shows. Joe practices target shooting in preparation for a duel with Sam over Kitty's affections. Being a crack shot, he hits the bulls-eye. To convey this to the spectator, Joe detaches the target from the wall and brings it to the foreground, toward the camera.

Although his movement is somewhat realistically motivated (he crosses to the table in the foreground to put down his pistol), the display of the target becomes a form of direct address aimed out of the diegetic world toward the spectator. As in a theatrical aside, this action uses the foreground for access to the audience. This theatrical convention is at odds with the style of the narrator system, which labors to preserve diegetic coherence. Griffith's style generally conveys narrative information through filmic discourse, and one would expect a cut-in to a close-up. However, again Griffith is hesitant to use cut-ins, even when narrative clarity demands them; the address to the spectator retains something of the cinema of attractions.

But for the most part, the use of foreground and background in the films of 1909 created a self-contained fictional whole within an expansive space, with layers of characters building up an encompassing environment. *The Convict's Sacrifice* (June 10, 16) introduces a line of prisoners, hands on each other's shoulders, entering the prison work yard and setting to work in the right background. Another line of convicts enters from the right, moving at a diagonal toward the foreground, where they begin hammering rocks under the watch of the guards. The prisoners in the foreground include the main character of the story (James Kirkwood). Once again, the position of this group in the foreground signals its narrative importance, but the background group plays an important role in giving the image depth and a naturalist sense of milieu.

The creation of compositional depth aided Griffith's emulation of the detail-laden stage settings of Belasco. The former playwright's obsession with authentic environments finally began to pay off in films like the Indian drama *The Mended Lute* (June 28, 29, 30, July 2). Griffith's Indian dramas of 1909 were praised by trade journals for their accurate details and use of landscapes. The Indian characters in the film move and live in an environment and culture of their own. The first shot establishes the Indian village and is filled with details of everyday life: Indian hunters enter and move into the background, game hanging from wooden slings; Indian women in the mid-ground cook, care for their children, or do beadwork. Some time into the shot, Rising Moon (Florence Lawrence) enters from the background, carrying a water jar. She moves into the foreground and pauses, framed above the knee. This movement into foreground, to an area of greater visibility where her face can be seen clearly, signals Rising Moon's importance in the story. Character and context are evoked in the areas of foreground and background respectively.

The Mended Lute was the first film Griffith shot in Cuddebackville, New York, a rural area in the Orange Mountains. He had convinced Biograph executives to allow his cast and crew to make the summer outing because of the area's scenic possibilities, its rivers and mountains.[15] Griffith was no longer satisfied with exteriors shot in Fort Lee, New Jersey, across the river from Upper Manhattan. He and Bitzer were developing a heightened pictorial sense of landscape which they could indulge in Cuddebackville. The meeting of Rising Moon with her secret lover Little Bear (Owen Moore) takes place before the white threads of a mountain cascade, a picturesque background that endows the scene with lyrical emotional resonance appropriate to the clandestine tryst. After introducing the pair, Griffith cuts out to a more distant shot of the location, presenting the Indian lovers as rather small figures against three levels of the cascade of white water. The cut increases the impact of the landscape as the falling water expresses the power of the pair's forbidden love. This distant view recalls the lyrical postscripts, a mood-endowed image which conveys the emotions of the characters. The emotional role of the landscape contrasts with the preceding shot in which Rising Moon encounters Standing Rock (the older and richer suitor her father favors), which lacks any landscape pictorialism.

The Mended Lute ends with a lyrical postscript which directly recalls the last shot of *The Redman and the Child.* As Little Bear paddles and Rising Moon leans back against her lover, the couple comes toward the camera in their canoe, moving almost into close-up. As in the earlier film, we draw near to the characters in a moment of repose and intimacy after the tension of the story has been resolved. Whereas in 1908, such lyricism only appeared in the finale of the film, signaling the film's closure, in 1909 Griffith began to thread pictorial compositions throughout the film, building a greater emotional expressiveness through imagery. Composition often functions in these instances as an element of mood, shaping audience responses to the characters within the shots.

Camera movement could potentially play an important role in the narrator system, but, like the cut-in, it remains underdeveloped in Griffith's early Biograph films. The only type of camera movement found in Griffith's 1908 films are pans, which were frequent and often elaborate—as in Porter's *Stolen by Gypsies* (Edison, 1905)—in European and American narrative films before Griffith.[16] Pans in films in 1908 were generally brief and often followed the movement of characters, usually as they arrive at or leave an important location. A pan follows the Union soldier as he rides away from his home in *The Guerrilla* and the guerrilla as he arrives at the same location. An unusual tilt up follows the gypsy woman (Marion Leonard) as she climbs up the wall of the judge's home in *An Awful Moment.* These pans are purely functional and play no important role in the narrator system.

A few pans in 1908 are either more extensive, such as one in *The Call of the Wild,* or seem to take on more ambitious narrative roles. The opening pans of *The Ingrate* (October 2, 28, November 2) and *Ingomar* seem designed to mark these opening shots esthetically with brief panoramas of landscapes. One film seems to use pans to set up contrasts that are more frequently handled by editing. *The Salvation Army Lass* follows Mary Wilson with a pan to the left as she is hustled away from a Salvation Army street meeting by a woman shoplifter (Florence Lawrence). When Mary realizes the nature of her supposed friend two shots later, she rushes out of the thieves' den and rejoins the Salvation Army meeting, the camera now paning to the right. This pair of complementary pans underlines the girl's moral decision, with the contrast in direction reflecting her deviation from righteousness and return to the true path. A thematic reading of these opposing pans may seem too farfetched, but, Griffith often used spatial oppositions to express thematic contrasts, as the analysis of *In Old Kentucky* (July 29, August 3, 5, 6, 1909) will show. But given the rather slight development of camera movement in 1908, this cannot be read as confidently as contrast edits expressing moral dichotomies.

Griffith's first extended tracking shot occurs in the first months of 1909, in *The Drive for a Life.* Tracking shots, or cameras mounted on moving vehicles, began with the Lumìere cameramen and were particularly exploited in 1904–5 by Hale's Tours.[17] A film like Biograph's *Hold Up of the Rocky Mountain Express,* photographed by Bitzer in 1906, placed the technique in a fictional context, the camera on the front of a locomotive filming a train robbery and the bandits' escape by handcar. Edison's comedy *The Boarding School Girls* (1905) more directly recalls *The Drive for a Life,* with a camera mounted on an automobile tracking in front of girls out for a spin.

The Drive for a Life combines a moving camera (presumably mounted on an automobile) and movement within the frame to create an extensive and complex shot. It begins as a stationary view of a deserted country road. As a car containing the hero, Harry Walker (Arthur Johnson), and his fiancee, Mignon (Florence Lawrence), appears, the camera begins to withdraw slowly, allowing the car to come quite near it as Walker and Mignon move into medium close-up. The camera tracks in front of them, maintaining a consistent distance. Then the carriage of the villainess, the Widow Lebrun (Marion Leonard) appears in the background trailing the car. After these two dramatic focuses are established, Walker's car picks up speed and exits toward the camera right. Widow Lebrun's carriage nears the camera and then pivots as it reverses direction, her face glaring from the side window as the vehicle turns. The carriage then withdraws down the road into the distance as the camera remains stationary. Curiously, Griffith did not mount a camera in a car again until October 1910 in *When a Man Loves.* And one could argue that none of the later uses of a moving camera in Griffith's Biograph films are as complicated as this one, with its switch in dramatic focus from one vehicle to the next.

Some months later, in *In Old Kentucky,* Griffith experimented boldly with camera movement, using pans to interrelate actions usually brought together by editing. This film of brothers divided by their loyalties during the Civil War uses composition to establish spatial oppositions that function throughout the film. *In Old Kentucky* was shot in Cuddebackville, and, like the Indian films shot there, made full use of the area's picturesque landscapes. The pursuit of Robert Wilkinson, a Confederate courier behind Union lines (Henry Walthall) moves through mountainsides, flower-covered meadows, and rocky streams, with Griffith and Bitzer keenly aware of compositional possibilities. A Union sentry takes his post on a mountainside against a broad landscape vista where brighter light creates a near silhouette, one of Bitzer's first uses of natural backlighting. The pastoral beauty of a field of daisies sets up a pictorial counterpoint to the tense chase of Wilkinson as he rushes toward the camera. The hilly geography also provides a variety of angles, with Wilkinson often shot from a high angle. One shot begins with a high-angle view of a hillside and field below. Robert appears about midway down, scrambling over a fence, apparently having left his pursuers far behind. However, soon after he clears the barrier, Union troops appear, climbing over the fence and in close pursuit, having been hidden by the fence at the beginning of the shot.

The shot containing extended camera movement begins by framing the mountain vista and sentry post introduced earlier, as Robert tries to sneak past the Union picket. The camera pans to the right, away from the sentry, moving across the vista of the river valley below. When the pan has reached its full extent to the right, Robert creeps up from the bottom of the frame. He moves cautiously to the left, still only visible in the lower part of the frame; the camera reverses its direction and follows him. When he reaches a small rise, Robert pauses, and the camera stops with him. He looks off-screen to the left, and then ducks down low, apparently having glimpsed the sentry. The camera continues its pan to the left, leaving Robert, coming to rest on the Union sentry, and remaining stationary as he is relieved by Robert's Union brother, George, who takes up the watch. George seems to respond to an off-screen noise and moves right. Following him, the camera pans to the right, pausing as he stops, rifle in hand, at the edge of the rise; his Confederate brother is visible crouching at the bottom right of the frame. George sees him and shoulders his rifle as Robert makes off to the right. George fires and rushes out of the frame in pursuit, accompanied by several other Union soldiers.

Most of the pans and reverse pans of the shot are motivated by the movement of the characters. However, at several points the camera moves independently from the characters, revealing suspenseful narrative relations among them. The first of these is the opening pan to the right that links the Union sentry to the Confederate courier in a suspenseful camera movement that performs the omniscient function usually achieved by parallel editing. The next independent camera movement is motivated in part by Robert's off-screen look, as he seems to see the sentry off to the left. This pan functions much like a sight-link pattern, as it moves to reveal the sentry on watch. In both these pans Griffith achieves effects he usually accomplished through editing. A further tension is created by including all these actions within a single shot, with the Bazinian unity of space and time well exploited. In this lengthy shot (forty-one feet in 16mm), Griffith seems to work out a mise-en-scène approach to narrative style, in contrast to his usual dependence on montage. The clear and suspenseful articulation of the action shows its distance from earlier lengthy unarticulated shots in such films as *The Prussian Spy*. Camera distance and framing mark the dramatic turning points of the shot precisely, creating the dramatic analysis on which Griffith's usual decoupage rested. Although restricted to the enframed image level of filmic discourse, this shot fulfills the narrator system purposes of narrativization and suspense.

But this shot represents a path not taken by Griffith. No later example exists in available Biograph films of an extended pan which interrelates a number of narrative actions and characters. Why Griffith tried it in *In Old Kentucky* (and why he then abandoned it) is a fascinating but unanswerable question. The mountain vista that forms the background of the shot may have summoned up the scenic possibilities of a panorama shot, which he then bent to narrative tasks. Or perhaps time constraints during location shooting made a division of the action into separate camera set-ups impracticle. In any case, the shot reminds us that editing is not the only filmic discourse capable of narrating a story. The primacy of editing during the Biograph period undoubtedly came from a number of factors. Editing offered one form of production efficiency. A small number of actual camera set-ups could, when intercut, generate a large number of shots. In addition, with the director rather than cameraman asserting control over storytelling, editing could provide a strong element of control within a minimum of production time. Because this control could be asserted after shooting, it gave Griffith greater independence.

In Old Kentucky also creates a recurring spatial opposition through its positioning of actors within the frame. The film's composition develops a consistent thematic opposition between left and right in portraying the conflict between the two Kentucky brothers who choose opposite sides in Civil War. The opening shot establishes this opposition, visualizing it with a schematic blocking. In the family parlor, the sons sit at opposite sides of a table in the foreground. George (the brother sympathetic to the Union) sits on the left, while Robert (who will join the Confederacy) is on the right. Their father (Verner Clarges) enters, bringing news of the declaration of war. As the sons rise from the table, this left to right opposition is maintained. Even when George crosses to the right to get an American flag, he returns immediately to the left of the frame to display it. Likewise, the parents, whose sympathies are also divided, stand near their children, the Union father on the left, the mother whose sympathies are Southern (Kate Bruce) on the right.

Such blocking is hardly surprising, nor startlingly original, for anyone with a modicum of stage experience. What is surprising is that Griffith maintains this left to right opposition in every succeeding shot in which both brothers are present. In the sequence of camera movement, George is at the left extent of the pan, Robert at the right. In the scene of Robert's capture, George enters from the left and stands to the left of Robert where he is taken. At the film's climax, Robert takes refuge in his family's house, hiding in his mother's bed from the Union patrol led by his brother. When George enters, his mother refuses to let him search her bed. Even in this scene in which Robert is hidden behind his mother and not visible, George stands on the left of the frame (after entering from right), and the mother and the hidden Robert are on the right. This pattern is brought to a resolution in the final shot of the film after the war is over. Robert returns home defeated and encounters a victory celebration hosted by George. The two brothers again take up their usual left to right opposed positions. Maintaining distance from each other, each holds the flag of their respective causes. Then, moving from their opposed positions, the brothers join hands in the center of the screen. The family, and implicitly the nation, are reunited; left and right positions move into the center and the narrative is resolved, marked by a tableau that freezes the action.

It may seem unlikely that this consistent opposition is anything other than coincidental, particularly since in this period Griffith, like most other filmmakers, had not even established consistent screen direction. But given Griffith's stage experience, working out thematically based spatial oppositions within shots might well precede a directional matching among shots. A number of Griffith's later Biograph films continue this thematic use of spatial oppositions, often in complex relation to parallel-edited sequences.[18]

The decorative opening pans in the 1908 films *The Ingrate* and *The Barbarian, Ingomar* anticipate Griffith's strongest use of camera movement in his first years of filmmaking in *The Country Doctor* (May 29, 30, June 7, 1909). The strong imagery of *The Country Doctor* makes it one of Griffith's most powerful films.

After the first shot, a series of shots portray the felicity of the doctor's family and place it in the bosom of nature. The second shot does this rather humorously. The doctor (Frank Powell), his wife (Florence Lawrence), and their young daughter (Gladys Eagan) are literally swallowed by nature as they navigate through a field of wheat or tall reeds, with only the doctor's tall top hat showing above the stalks to trace the family's route. At the end of the shot, they emerge from the field and walk toward the camera, all holding hands. The next shot sets their springtime walk on a daisy-covered hillside as they walk from the background toward the camera into full shot. The daughter bends to pick a flower and hands it to her mother. The mother kneels beside her and embraces her as the doctor watches, standing on the right. Mother and daughter then rise, and the family exits from the frame. The bourgeois family is placed in the lap of nature, and the order and beauty of a springtime landscape expresses family bliss.

Although these images seem to endow the family with rather trite connotations, Griffith's use of setting and composition to create such a family image represents an innovation seldom seen in earlier narrative cinema. These opening images of beauty and contentment play an ironic role in the dynamics of the film's story, however. In the very next shot, the little girl who sat happily among the flowers is stretched out on her sickbed, seriously ill. The doctor's sense of duty draws him away to treat a poor neighbor girl while his own daughter becomes worse. Griffith suspensefully employs parallel editing, cutting between the two young victims as the doctor rushes back and forth, torn between duty to his poor patient and the needs of his daughter. At last the doctor returns home after a successful operation on his patient, only to find his own child dead. As happens more often in Biograph films than cliched views of Griffith would indicate, the rush to the rescue fails, and we are confronted with the grim image of a child's death and a family's despair. Parallel editing does not always announce a victory over time. Family order does not always defeat the forces that threaten it.

This grim family drama does not end with the image of parents grieving over the dead body of their child. Griffith cuts to the exterior of the doctor's house, seen from some distance. The camera then pans to the left, moving away from the house, past a grove of trees, and continuing until it frames the lush springtime foliage of the river valley. The compositional resonance of the shot comes in part from the fact that it echoes and reverses the opening shot of the film. The film began with the image of "the peaceful valley of Stillwater" that now closes it.[19] In the opening shot the camera panned to the right from this vista, crossing the grove of trees and ending on the exterior of the doctor's house, from which the doctor, wife, and child emerged to begin their springtime stroll. This pair of complementary pans brackets the film, giving it (like *The Greaser's Gauntlet*) a circular structure. These opening and closing shots make *The Country Doctor* an exciting film. They embody the unique power of the narrator system, this time using camera movement to structure the film as a whole.

Like many of the devices of the narrator system, this particular use of the pan reinvests and redefines some of the energy of the cinema of attractions. What is immediately striking about this pair of pans is their difference from all of Griffith's previous pans and from how pans were used in early narrative cinema. These pans do not follow the action of any of the film's characters, although in most early narrative films that was the case. In the opening shot of *The Country Doctor*, however, the camera itself initiates a movement through a landscape to introduce the film's characters and begin the narrative action. A few early films, such as Biograph's *The Lost Child* (1904) and Edison's *Stolen by Gypsies* (1905), feature pans which move from one set of characters to another, rather than simply following a moving character. None, however, introduces a film or explores a landscape.

A few interesting exceptions both prefigure *The Country Doctor* and— ultimately—contrast with it, such as Porter's film for Edison, *The Execution of Czolgosz with Panorama of Auburn Prison* (1901), title of which is revealing and joins two autonomous phrases. The film begins with a panning shot of the exterior, and then the interior, of the state prison at Auburn, New York.

These actuality shots are a prologue to a staged reproduction of the death of President McKinley's assassin in the electric chair. The difference in style between the two sections of the film immediately strikes the modern viewer. The staging of the execution, the bareness and artificiality of the set, the theatrical performance of the actors, all contrast sharply with the documentary quality of the film's opening. Actuality footage has been juxtaposed with fictional shots, subverting any sense of a continuous "world," either fictional or documentary. Similar effects also appear in Biograph's *Skyscraper of New York* (1906), which opens with actuality footage, including two panning shots, of work on New York skyscrapers. Often the actuality footage that served as prologue to these films could be purchased separately from the film story, marking again its relatively autonomous and detachable nature.

The panoramas in these early "non-continuous" films come from the other side of early cinema, the neglected methods of actuality filmmaking. They were the mainstay of a very common genre of actuality films known as "scenics." Panoramic shots of natural or man-made wonders were popular subjects for early filmmakers. Painted panoramas, canvases on rollers por-traying landscapes, had also been used in staging melodramas. Usually func-tioning as backgrounds to suggest motion for stationary sets of locomotives, chariots, or race cars, they sometimes took on a more powerful role. For example, Belasco's production of *The Girl of the Golden West* (1905) began with a moving panorama which took the spectator through the western landscape that surrounded the play's action, ending on the exterior of the saloon in which the first scene took place.[20] Possibly the direct inspiration for *The Country Doctor*, this prologue vividly set Belasco's drama within a specific environment.

However, *The Country Doctor* integration of landscape and story differs from these predecessors. In Griffith's film, the panorama not only situates the narrative in a specific environment, but it also introduces the main characters. The earlier panoramas stayed within the realm of actualities; none of the fictional characters appeared in these sequences. Griffith's pan leads directly into the fiction, bringing the audience to the characters. The opening pan is an establishing shot, situating the family drama of the doctor in a greater spatial whole. It also prepares us for the story, guides us into it, the trajectory of the camera introducing the spectator to the world of the film. The opening pan transforms landscape into diegesis.

This camera movement brings the audience into the story with a strong stylistic flourish, stressing the storytelling role of the narrator system, like the particularly charged opening of a literary narrator. As such, it falls into Genette's "directing function" of voice in which the act of narrating overtly organizes the text. The shot visualizes the narrator system's ability to begin a story and guide the spectator into it, as if the moving camera conjures the entrance of the characters.

This opening pan sets off greater resonances when placed alongside the pan which closes the film; the shots are mirror reflections, reversing natures and roles. The closing pan moves left, reversing the direction of the opening pan. Instead of introducing a group of cheerful characters as they leave the doctor's house, the shot begins before the closed door of the same house, only no characters appear. Instead of opening the film, it closes it.

The very emptiness of this closing shot reveals the power Griffith has given the enframed image in his narrative style. The pan across an empty landscape recalls the actuality panoramas formally; it contains no characters and presents no narrative actions. It is as empty as the ending of an Ozu film, but it by no means returns the audience to a denarrativized actuality style. The structure of the film has embedded this image into the very web of the narrative. Thus within the narrator system, a shot that seems to carry no narrative information can signify the process of narrativization itself. This image carries an emotional load. The empty landscape vibrates with the tragic tone of the film's denouement. The absence of the characters becomes a signifier of the destruction of the happy family. And, most firmly, it stresses the closure of the film. As the opening pan introduced the fiction, this final pan draws away from a completed story. The narrative sum of the film, the loss of family balance, is imaged in this reversal of the opening shot. The the formal repetition of the pans demonstrates the mediating role of the filmic narrator, its position as storyteller between the events of the story and the spectator who receives them.

And what of the movement itself of this final shot, which creates one of the most powerful images in any Biograph film? The camera movement takes on a gestural expressiveness, like a response on the narrator's part to the loss portrayed as it turns from human grief back into the realm of nature. I find this pan so overdetermined that it is not easily translatable. Is it possible that this movement, out to the world at large, is one of consolation for the grief within the house, setting it in context of the rhythms of nature? Given the Christian ideology inherent in many Biograph films, one might see this movement as expressing transcendence. The *Biograph Bulletin* seems to read it this way: "The Valley of Stillwater is shrouded with darkness. Such are the temporal deeds that will find reward eternal."[21] But another resonance of the image leads in the opposite direction, to Griffith's fascination with literary naturalism. Nineteenth-century scientists, as well as such American writers as Stephen Crane, Jack London, and Frank Norris, had discovered the small place of human joy and tragedy in the natural order of things. This landscape, unchanged after the child's death and reflecting none of the family's loss, operates in naturalistic counterpoint to the grief behind the closed door.

The closing shot of the film becomes an image with a series of implications and resonances created by its place in the narrative structure. In its ambiguity, the etheticised image solicits interpretation without limiting its meaning. Resolving the film with this camera movement rather than the customary embrace of the reunited family emphasizes its grim ending and the increased power Griffith invests in filmic discourse.

The Pro-filmic: Acting Styles and Movies Stars

By the summer of 1909 a strong transformation in acting style was underway at Biograph. Something of this change in acting styles is captured in a literal changing of the guard, as the first "Biograph girl," Florence Lawrence, left the company and another, Mary Pickford, was groomed to take her place. This change in acting personnel also brought into focus a phenomenon that had great consequences for motion picture acting and the film commodity—the appearance of the "picture personality" and eventually the institution of the star. This phenomenon went beyond acting style and laid the groundwork for a new relation between films and viewers.

Because there were no credits on Biograph films until 1913, all the performers were anonymous. The rubric "Biographic girl," like the contemporary "Vitagraph girl" which described Florence Turner, was created first by audiences to describe the leading ladies they recognized from film to film. For want of anything better, the term was named after the production company. The first Biograph girl, Florence Lawrence, had come to the studio soon after Griffith began directing in 1908, and was immediately cast in the leading role in *The Girl and the Outlaw*. Before that, she had appeared in a number of films for other production companies such as Edison's *Daniel Boone* and Vitagraph's *The Despatch Bearer*. Before her film career, Lawrence had been a stage actress in repertory theater. Her mother, Lotte Lawrence, had headed a traveling stock troupe, and Florence had begun as a child performer. Between work with Edison and Biograph, she returned to the stage, touring with a show called *The Seminary Girls*.[22] Lawrence's background was typical of most Biograph actors, nearly all of whom were stage performers before coming to films. This pattern seems to be the case for other production companies as well; by 1909 most film actors had been professional stage experience.[23]

During 1908, Lawrence took the female lead in the majority of Biograph films, appearing much more frequently than Linda Arvidson or Marion Leonard, the other regular leading ladies at Biograph that year. She appeared in both comedies and melodramas in an amazing variety of roles: society kleptomaniac, Japanese court lady, Boer pioneer woman, Grecian patrician, Lower East Side Jewess, Canadian trapper's wife, Katherine in *The Taming of the Shrew*, and, of course, her recurring comedy role as Mrs. Jones. With such constant exposure, Lawrence's face soon became familiar to nickelodeon audiences. However, company policy enforced Lawrence's anonymity; letters to the studio asking her identity went unanswered, and the "Biograph girl" rubric appeared and stuck. The anonymity of film performers was a general policy with American film production companies in 1908. The motives for anonymity seem to be various and may have initially included the actors' desire to remain unknown, concealing from theatrical agents the fact they had stooped to "posing for pictures." But it also reflects manufacturers' desire to have a single name associated with their films, that of the production company. The audience was to see a *Biograph* film, not a Florence Lawrence film.

The apparently new phenomenon of audiences identifying and becoming curious about actors rested on several of the changes in filmic discourse. The progressive closeness of Griffith's camera made actors literally more recognizable. A shot such as the lyrical postscript which ends *The Ingrate,* which shows Florence Lawrence nearly in close-up for some time, was bound to contribute to the phenomenon of a recognizable "picture personality."[24] Likewise, film's desire to imitate the legitimate theater was bound to carry over the concept of a "star" performance, as the *films d'art* showed. Although the Biograph Company repressed Lawrence's name, the narrator system, with its increased characterization and techniques for creating empathy, made her an individual and created the paradox of an unknown star.

The archaeology of the film star is not easy to uncover, with earliest account written rather late.[25] But it seems that Lawrence's star reputation was not the result of publicity, studio or otherwise, but the outcome of audience preference. Trade papers commented on it only after it was already established. Lawrence—without being named, of course—*was* singled out for praise by the Spectator in his review of *The Song of the Shirt,* while *Moving Picture World* praised her for *The Taming of the Shrew.*[26] However, it is not until April 1909, in a review of *Lady Helen's Escapade* (February 10, 11) that a trade journal calls Lawrence the "Biograph girl." The reviewer praises Lawrence as well as expressing a high opinion of Biograph films generally and linking new styles of characterization with the "uplift" of the motion pictures:

Each character stands out individually and distinctively. During the few minutes the film is being run, one gets in touch, as it were, with the personalities of each of the people shown in this moving picture. Now we look upon this as a very great triumph for the Biograph Company, who, in the last few weeks, have by common consent placed themselves at the very head of American film manufacturers, alike for the technical and dramatic qualities of their pictures. This film is, indeed, what we have recently very emphatically asked for, a well-written, carefully rehearsed play, well-produced and photographically good. . . . Of course, the chief honors of the picture are borne by the now famous

Biograph girl, who must be gratified by the silent celebrity she has achieved. This lady combines with very great personal attractions very fine dramatic abilities indeed. Some of the scenes of this film, if acted on the talking stage, would make the fortune of the play . . . we do suggest that in cultivating the representation of finished comedy, and above all of the delineation of character in the moving picture, the Biograph Company can contribute much towards the "uplift" about which the self-constituted oracles of the daily press are talking and writing so much.[27]

The phrase "the now famous Biograph girl" seems to confirm that Lawrence was already a recognized figure. However, this popularity and public recognition did not lead to a "star building" reaction on the part of Griffith or Biograph. In fact, in 1909 Lawrence's position as leading lady at Biograph is less secure than it was in 1908. The return of Marion Leonard to the studio led to a sharing of starring roles. Although the Spectator singled out Lawrence's performance in his review of A Note in the Shoe, saying, "One actress in particular, a favorite in Biograph subjects, shines to an exceptional degree,"[28] the most frequent praise of Biograph acting in the trade journals went to the company as a whole. Moving Picture World, reviewing the same film, referred to "the clever acting of the now popular Biograph stock company."[29] It is clear that Griffith preferred the concept of the ensemble to the development of a star. Lawrence was cast in minor parts in films long after her widespread recognition, appearing in A Sound Sleeper and A Troublesome Satchel as little more than a featured extra.

While a stock company approach was common to many American production companies in 1909, the appearance of the films d'art caused American companies to rush to employ theatrical stars. With established artists of the French stage lending their names and prestige to films, an American response could not be far behind. The Edison Company led the way, publicizing not only its hiring of theatrical actors such as Miss Cecil Spooner and the French pantomimist Pilar Morin, but also members of their stock company William J. Sorrelle and Herbert Bostwick.[30] That Edison was one of the first American film companies to give publicity to its actors shows that the traditional view, that the MPPC refused to publicize its stars and the Independents were the first to do so, is untrue. In 1909 other Trust companies also publicized the players in their films. Kalem published pictures of their stock company, and Vitagraph publicized the appearance of Elita Proctor Otis in their film Oliver Twist.[31]

Traditional historians frequently cite Carl Laemmle's publicity for Florence Lawrence after she joined his Independent Motion Picture Company (IMP) as the beginning of the star system in American film. However research shows that this event is usually chronicled inaccurately. The actual (and not fully explained) events are worth detailing not only because they deal with Biograph's first star, but also because they reveal how complex the construction of a film star was. *The Mended Lute* in June of 1909 was Lawrence's last film for Biograph. The traditional account claims that she was fired along with her husband, Harry Solter, when it was discovered that they were negotiating with Laemmle for acting jobs with his Independent Production Company.[32]

But it may not have been that simple. Linda Arvidson seems to indicate that Lawrence and Solter were fired for negotiating with another Trust company.[33] One of the more reliable secondary sources, Edward Wagenknecht's *The Movies in the Age of Innocence,* claims that negotiations with Essanay led to the firing, but unfortunately gives no source for this claim.[34] Lawrence's own account of her career, "Growing up with the Movies," skips over why she left Biograph but does not indicate that she left in order to join Laemmle's new company. According to Lawrence, she went on stage after leaving Biograph for a road engagement with Ezra Kendall. It was while on the road that she received a telegram from William Ranous, a former Vitagraph director working for Laemmle, asking her to come for an interview.[35]

Although IMP was formed in June of 1909, the company did not release a film until October. *Variety* publicized Laemmle's signing of Lawrence who was a member of the company from the beginning, with a small article, "Has Star Actress," stating, "Miss Lawrence, the former star actress of the Biograph's stock company has been with the Laemmle firm for the past six weeks. She will appear in the first Laemmle release of Oct. 25."[36] In Lawrence's memoir, the first IMP film she mentions appearing in is *Love's Stratagem,* released on November 1, 1909.[37] It may be presumed that she appeared regularly in IMP films during the last months of 1909 and the beginning of 1910. An advertisement for the IMP film *Coquette's Suitor* in the January 22, 1910 issue of *Show World* described it as "a picture that gives Miss Lawrence the best opportunity she has had for months to work up some hilarious comedy."[38] Not until March 5 of 1910 did IMP advertisements capitalize on her previous Biograph fame by announcing *Mother Love* and identifying its star as "Miss Lawrence, known to 1000's as Mrs. Jones."[39]

But these months of employment were eclipsed by a sudden flurry of publicity in March of 1910, the famous "We Nail a Lie" advertisement which trumpeted, "The Biograph Girl Is Now an IMP" and refuted a rumor that Lawrence had been killed in a traffic accident. A report of her death had appeared in *Billboard* on March 5, 1910, including an "In Memoriam" poem. Laemmle denied the rumor in the St. Louis *Times* of March 21, 1910, and scheduled a public appearance in St. Louis, as well as the "We Nail a Lie" advertisement. Most historians of American film have cited the incident as marking the dawn of the era of the publicity agent.[40] Even at the time there was such speculation; *Moving Picture World* noted that Robert Cochrane, IMP's publicist, was taking a film to St. Louis that showed "how the reading of Miss Lawrence's obituary notice affected the other members of the IMP Co." The journal commented "If anyone can see the hand of the press agent in this, that person must at least be credited with a clever and original idea."[41]

If this was the first big publicity stunt designed to create recognition for a star, unanswered questions linger. The traditional account of the story indicates that it was Laemmle's way of introducing Lawrence.[42] However she had been appearing in IMP's films for months, and her name had appeared in IMP advertising. This was clearly acknowledged in the advertisement which denounced the rumor of her death: "Miss Lawrence was not even in a street car accident, is in the best of health, *will continue* to appear in IMP films. . . ."[43] If the whole story was a Laemmle stunt, why did he wait so long to pull it? Could it be that contrary to traditional accounts, he was inspired by the publicity the Trust was giving their actors? Or did the launching of a film star in 1910 require such elaborate high jinks?

Although the Laemmle advertisement referred to Lawrence as "The IMP girl, formerly known as the Biograph Girl," it also publicized her name and included a photograph of her face, the one sign of her identity upon which fans relied. The shift from "the Biograph girl" to "Florence Lawrence" was significant and an important factor in the formation of the star system. A term such as "the Biograph girl" was an uncertain signifier and could be applied to any leading lady of the Biograph Company.

Controversy surrounding a *Moving Picture World* review of the Biograph film *Through the Breakers* (October 29, 30, November 1, 10, 1909) shows that the emergence of the star system was by no means simple. The reviewer began by stating that a rumor had spread that the "famous Biograph Girl—our girl, our only girl, whom we have silently worshipped in effigy these many months . . . just as much a personality in the Biograph Stock Company as any well-known actress would be at a Broadway house" had left the company. However readers were reassured that the "Biograph Girl" played the lead in this film and hoped she would continue to appear in "the well-dressed, well-mounted, well-finished Biograph pictures."[44]

These phrases seem to describe Florence Lawrence, whom the *Moving Picture World* had called the "Biograph girl" some months earlier. However, by the time of this review Lawrence was long gone from Biograph, and the leading lady in *Through the Breakers* was Marion Leonard. Did the reviewer mistake Leonard for Lawrence? Or was the term so shifting that it could be applied to Leonard as current leading lady? In any case, the reviewer was taken to task for his error by a film viewer—it was, after all, the fans who had introduced the term "Biograph girl"—in a January 30, 1910 letter to *Moving Picture World:*

Dear Sir—I have the honour to announce that your man who writes "Comments on the Films" is as crazy as a bedbug. Through the courtesy of manager Keller of the Orpheum here, I have just seen what you say in your issue of December

18 about "Through the Breakers" and "The Biograph Girl." That picture was shown here during the past week, and—that isn't the Biograph Girl at all. She is all right; she is the handsomest girl (or lady) on the moving picture stage; she is a superb and charming actress; she is in every way adorable; we are all glad to see her appearing again regularly, for we thought, a while back, that we had lost her—but she is not "the Biograph Girl" not THE Biograph Girl.

The Biograph Girl who won all the hearts, male and female, in this neck of the woods was the one who used to play Mrs. Jones in the Jones comedies. I could mention a lot more of her parts, but that one is the easiest to clearly and briefly designate. She has been gone from "the bunch" for months and the Biograph people ought to be lynched for letting her get away. She is, or was, with the IMP and appeared in "The Forest Ranger's Daughter" which dropped in here on a special occasion. Look in the IMP ad in your issues of above date and you will see a horribly poor picture of her. Now that is, or was, the Biograph Girl—and I am confident that you could find about 8,000,000 people in the United States who would agree with me. You could find a lot of them in this town, and only one who would agree with you in liking the Beauty better.

But that girl was simply out of sight—unapproachable. She was in a class by herself. In every part she played she was an exquisite delight. Whether comic, pathetic, dramatic, tragic or any other old thing, she simply took the rag right off. The power of expression that lay in her features was nothing less than marvelous, and the lightning changes were a wonder. In fact, she was a wonder altogether, and her versatility would be unbelievable, if a fellow hadn't seen it. To see her play Mrs. Jones in a tantrum and then see her as the Russian nihilist girl, for instance, in a drama of which I have forgotten the name; as a young girl; as a mother; to see her as a highly polished society lady, one time, and at another time see her straddle a cayuse as a Western girl and ride like a wild Indian—to see her take these widely varying parts and play each as though she were in her native elements, with every pose and motion and expression in perfect harmony with the character—all this was a revelation. And to see her in a love scene was enough to draw a fellow right across the continent, if he were not fifty years old, and married—and broke.

And now you think someone else is the Biograph Girl! If you think I am off my base, you go and see that girl in some IMP Picture where she has some chance—if they make any such. And that is the deuce of it. She doesn't belong anywhere else but with the Biograph people. They are the only ones who seem to have regularly plays that call for and bring out her grade of talent. But look it up, anyway, and see if I am not right.

Yours very truly,
P. C. Levar
Marshfield, Coos Bay, Ore.[45]

Mr. Levar's passionate panegyric describes Lawrence's irreplaceable, even if anonymous, appeal to her fans and the emotional investment they had in her identity. Such devotion laid the foundation for the star phenomenon. An article which appeared in *Show World* further shows the slippery identity of an actress without credits, claiming that the Biograph Company, smarting from Lawrence's defection to the Independents, had hired "an actress who resembles her to a marked degree."[46] It is unclear to whom *Show World* refers; the full-figured Leonard hardly resembles the rather tomboyish Lawrence. Could it be Pickford, who took over many of Lawrence's gamin roles?

The identity of a film star depends on more than simply the physical identity of a particular actress. The establishment of an actual name rather than a generic company rubric, studio publicity, and audience recognition from film to film are all fundamental to the star effect and would become solidified by such later practices as screen credits, fan magazines, and the circulation of photographs, not to mention key close-ups in films. Confusion over the "Biograph girl" and Lawrence's identity may have set Laemmle's publicity campaign into motion, determined to imprint Lawrence's name and face in the minds of the audience and identify her with IMP.

Although the star phenomenon in film was in many ways based upon, and analogous to, the star system in legitimate theater and vaudeville, introducing it to film signaled another redefinition of the film commodity, one which the Biograph Company resisted. While hardly the first to publicize actors in his productions, Laemmle should be credited as one of the first to invest in the popularity of film players rather than established stage stars, in contrast to the *films d'art* approach. By channeling and controlling the nascent fascination with the figures on the screen, he defined and capitalized on a new and powerful film attraction. In the public appearances that Florence Lawrence made in St. Louis the newly resurrected star was greeted by crowds that equaled those that had rushed to see Commodore Perry or President Taft. Her appearance at two local theaters "nearly caused a riot . . . when she was mobbed by an army of enthusiastic admirers."[47]

While the phenomenon of the star depends in part on the character-centered narrative style that the narrator system typifies, nonetheless the role Griffith and Biograph played in developing stars was ambiguous. Biograph's policy of keeping its actors anonymous was common among film producing companies in early 1909, but by the end of 1909 it was becoming anomalous. In 1910, it continually frustrated film fans, who besieged trade journals with requests for the names of Biograph players. By 1911, the policy was a scandal, and the column responding to letters in the newly formed "fan" magazine, *The Motion Picture Story Magazine,* lamented Biograph's intransigence in every issue. Robert Grau in *The Theater of Science* (1913) speculated that the policy may have originated with Griffith himself.[48] The Spectator summarized Biograph's policy in the New York *Dramatic Mirror,* saying "it is not the personality of particular players that makes for success in picture production." Biograph ranked the contributions to filmmaking as "first the story, second the direction, and third competent people as a class and not as individuals." The Spectator supported these principles in his comments, noting that the

Biograph stock company had constantly changed without the quality of their films declining.[49]

Biograph's policy accords with the intention of the MPPC to consolidate control of films in the production company, suppressing the independence of actors, as its economic policy had limited the independence of exhibitors and exchanges. However, other licensed producers felt cultivating public interest in actors was more in line with the new image of film they were promoting, stressing its close relation to legitimate theater and "high class" vaudeville. Biograph's, and possibly Griffith's, insistence on actors and remaining anonymous marks a transitional period in the gradual institutionalization of the film star that would come with feature films. As the Florence Lawrence episode shows, the Biograph policy of anonymity was at odds with Griffith's narrative development. The narrator system provided means for dramatizing characters and providing psychological motivations, and therefore encouraged the perception of actors as living and vivid personalities. The style of Griffith's films was conducive to the development of stars, even if studio policy repressed the publication of their names.

Laemmle's publicizing of Lawrence's name was a creative act. It allowed audiences to fix upon a new phenomenon, the star with an identity separate from the production company, and ultimately separate from the roles she played. But this creation had its ironies for Laemmle. Less than a year later, Lawrence changed companies again, this time returning to the fold of the Trust and signing with the Lubin Company. In 1910 Laemmle repeated the cycle with a new "Biograph girl," luring Mary Pickford. Pickford's popularity at Biograph had possibly even exceeded that of Lawrence's, although she never dominated the leading female roles as had Lawrence in 1908. When Laemmle announced Pickford's switch to IMP, his advertisement identified her as the "Biograph Comedy Girl."

The arrival of Pickford at Biograph in the spring of 1909 marks one stage in the gradual change in Biograph acting. This change in performance style was already sporadically evident in the 1908 films. Terming the Biograph acting style "restraint in expression," in his 1913 advertisement in the New York *Dramatic Mirror*, Griffith claimed it as the innovation through which he raised "motion picture acting to the higher plane which has won it recognition as a genuine art."[50] Roberta Pearson, who has studied Biograph acting with a great deal of precision and insight, in her dissertation, " 'The Modesty of Nature': Performance Style in the Griffith Biographs," defines this ongoing transformation as a move from a "histrionic" performance style to one of the "verisimilar."[51]

Pearson finds that the "histrionic" style relates to performances styles found in theatrical forms such as melodrama and pantomime and was common in early cinema. Pearson sees the histrionic style as reflexive, consciously theatrical, and aware of its spectators. Histrionic performers use stylized conventional gestures with a limited lexicon of preestablished meanings. These gestures are performed quickly, are heavily stressed, and the actors tend to extend their arms fully in making them. This performance style depended on preestablished character types and nonpsychological storylines. In contrast, the verisimilar style appeared in response to storylines that were increasingly psychological. The verisimilar actor used small gestures and developed unique individual performances, rather than employing a conventional gestural lexicon. By-play with properties and facial expression were prized for their ability to reveal a character's thoughts and feelings.[52]

More than any other transformation in Griffith's Biograph films, this change in acting derives from a large number of factors and cannot be attributed simply to Griffith. The adoption of more psychological film stories forced rethinking of acting and characterization. But the change in acting models was also inflected by contemporary theatrical styles such as the acting innovations of Eleanora Duse and Minnie Maddern Fiske, the acting styles of other companies (e.g., *films d'art* and Vitagraph, which preceded Griffith in this area in some respects), and trade journal criticism, most of which, as Pearson shows, attacked melodramatic acting and encouraged the new verisimilar style.[53]

Pickford surpasses any other Biograph actress in mastery of the new verisimilar style, particularly when contrasted with Florence Lawrence's predominantly histrionic performances. Pickford generally employs a slower pace, and her gestures appear intended to reveal psychological traits through behavior, whereas Lawrence tended to use a pantomime of conventional significations. However a number of factors undoubtedly determine this. Acting styles changed quickly, and Griffith may not have always been in the vanguard. Some years later Lawrence claimed that she and other Biograph actors pleaded with Griffith to allow them to use the slower style of acting they had seen in the *films d'art,* but Griffith had continued to demand a faster, more histrionic pace. Lawrence claimed that Griffith only allowed the stock company to act at a slower pace shortly before she left.[54] This indicates "restraint in expression" was an idea Griffith accepted gradually, and the difference between Pickford's and Lawrence's performance styles may partly reflect the periods during which they worked under Griffith.

Another factor, at least in 1909, is the acting requirements of different genres. For most of 1909, Pickford appeared primarily in comedy roles, and even when she took more dramatic roles later in the year—such as *The Restoration* (September 22, October 1), *The Mountaineer's Honor* (October 14, 19, 20), or *To Save Her Soul* (November 22, 27)—she still played ingenues. The more purple roles of ladies of grand passion were taken by Marion

Leonard, whose acting shows the broad romantic gestures Griffith probably absorbed during his tour with Nance O'Neil. Only in 1910 did Pickford frequently take over leading dramatic roles in such films as *In the Season of Buds, An Arcadian Maid, The Sorrows of the Unfaithful,* and *Simple Charity.* By that time the acting style of the stock company as a whole had undergone a strong movement toward the verisimilar, but undoubtedly the skills and backgrounds of the two "Biograph girls" tended in different directions. Both Pickford and Lawrence had been child actresses. Whereas Lawrence's early career had been with her mother's touring company, however, Pickford came to Biograph direct from acting under Belasco in *The Warrens of Virginia.*

Along with a slower pace, the verisimilar style valued facial expression over the extended bodily gestures of histrionic acting. Although trade journals tended to single out Biograph (and sometimes Pathé) for this virtue, it became a general concern in American film production in 1909. As a letter from Frank Dyer, head of the Edison Company, to Horace Plimpton, head of negative production at Edison, states: "We mean to depend more and more upon facial expressions and small movements instead of extravagant gestures. We must find a better class of actors who are able to intelligently convey such actions."[55]

In *The Edison Kinetogram,* the company announced this new style of film acting, declaring "the day of extravagant gestures has passed, that of quiet tense action and meaning conveyed by facial expression has come."[56] This new emphasis on the face as the ultimate signifier in performance evolved symbiotically with closer camera positions. John Collier, head of the National Board of Censorship, advised Plimpton of the importance of placing characters in the foreground so they were "satisfactorily visible; you can watch their facial play."[57]

Individual contributions to this change in acting style are hard to establish, however, there is some truth to Robert B. Cushman's claim that Mary Pickford exerted pressure on Griffith to change the acting style at Biograph. Cushman points out that "Mary often gave a restrained and wholly individualized performance while Griffith allowed the actors surrounding her to use the conventional, exaggerated mannerisms of the day."[58] The contrast between Pickford and Billy Quirk in *Oh, Uncle* (July 21, 22, 1909), for example, is extraordinary. But in 1909, Pickford's own acting varied widely. She had her share of conventional gestures: burying her head in the crook of her arm as she falls on her knees to express despair in *The Broken Locket*; extended gestural soliloquies to the audience in *His Wife's Visitor*; stamping up and down the room and flailing her arms in *The Test*; and scenes of hysteria in the grand romantic style, as when Arthur Johnson threatens to shoot her in *To Save Her Soul* (November 22–27). Pickford crawls on the floor, bites her

own hand, tears her hair, and finally, dramatically, bares her breast to Johnson's pistol.

But if Pickford's performances in 1909 still show elements of the histrionic
style, there are also moments when the verisimilar takes over. While Pickford's
miming of despair in *The Broken Locket* remains extreme and conventional,
her performance later in the film when she meets her fiance after going blind
belongs, with its nuanced and slow gestures, to another style. Likewise, in
The Awakening (August 16, 17, 20), Pickford's reaction to the departure of
her young husband mixes the two styles. Using conventional, fully extended
gestures, she stretches out her arms toward him and holds the position beseech-
ingly after he has gone. But instead of turning then to the camera and miming
out her grief as Lawrence frequently did, Pickford remains with her back to
the camera, drops her arms, and bows her head in despair. Playing a scene
with one's back to the audience had been used as a special effect by actors
throughout the history of the theater, but it took on a new significance and
frequency in naturalist theater. Mrs. Fiske was famous for the technique, and
even a romantic actress like Nance O'Neil employed it. *The Awakening*
marks one of the earliest uses Griffith made of this acting technique, which
reappeared in such later Biograph films as *His Trust* (1910) and *Swords and
Hearts* (1911) and became one of the most powerful examples of restraint in
Biograph acting.

Pickford's ability to create fully rounded and entirely individualized charac-
terizations stands out in 1909, and was perhaps her strongest personal contribution to acting style at Biograph. Her portrayal of a harum-scarum mountain
girl in *The Mountaineer's Honor* (October 14, 19, 20) could hardly be called
restrained. But unlike earlier frenetic and fast-paced performances, such as
whomever plays the French Canadian girl in *The Woman's Way* (1908),
Pickford's thoughtful characterization includes mannerisms calculated to portray a specific culture and situation. The way she stands with her hand on her
hip, jumps up and sits on the supper table to prepare a plate of food for the
stranger, or leaps from behind a tree with tom-boy zeal, makes her performance
unique in a way that Lawrence, despite the great variety of her roles, rarely
achieved. Pickford's ability to alter her acting style enormously from role to
role is more evident in her later performances, climaxing in her portrayal of
the simple-minded, unattractive country maid-of-all-work in *An Arcadian
Maid* (1910), perhaps the single finest performance in a Biograph film.

The move toward verisimilar acting formed an essential part of the narrator
system. The cinema of narrative integration was fashioning a dramaturgy
centered on characterization, and Griffith in 1909 bent all three levels of
filmic discourse, editing, enframed images, and the pro-filmic to this task.
The new style of performance interacted with other levels, the closer camera
positions allowing greater use of facial play; as well as editing patterns which

revealed motives and intentions eliminating the need for gestural soliloquies. By the end of 1909, the narrator system provided devices on all levels of filmic discourse to convey narrative information, access to character psychology, the dynamization and continuity of film time, and the creation of a coherent diegetic environment. Griffith had created a filmic narrator to comment on overtly, and to guide spectators' reception of, film stories.

Notes

1. *Variety*, April 3, 1909, p. 13.

2. Meir Sternberg, *Expositional Modes and Temporal Ordering in Fiction* (Baltimore: Johns Hopkins University Press, 1978), pp. 161, 175.

3. New York *Dramatic Mirror*, May 1, 1909, p. 42.

4. Victor Erlich, *Russian Formalism: History-Doctrine*, 3d ed. (New Haven: Yale University Press, 1981), pp. 245–46.

5. Kemp R. Niver, *D. W. Griffith: His Biograph Films in Perspective*, ed. Bebe Bergsten (Los Angeles: John D. Roche, 1974), p. 91.

6. *London Times* clipping in file *Au Telephone*, LPALC.

7. See *Pathé Freres Catalogue 1907*, pp. 195–96. I know of no surviving print of this film; my comments are based on the catalogue description.

8. I am indebted to Charles Musser for this information. Four stills submitted for copyright survive at the Edison National Historical Site in West Orange, N.J. (1) A long shot of the lawn of the estate. The father stands next to wife and daughter, ordering the hostler off the property. (2) A richly appointed interior, as the husband bids wife and child farewell. (3) The same set from a slightly closer camera position as the wife telephones on the left, her daughter clinging to her in terror. (4) The same camera position with the wife apparently dead on the floor, her daughter crouching over her and the hostler standing over them holding a gun.

9. *Film Index*, Sept 5, 1908, p. 14.

10. Linda Arvidson, *When the Movies Were Young* (1925, repr. New York: Dover Publications, 1969), p. 100.

11. *Moving Picture World*, March 28, 1908, p. 270. I am indebted to Jay Leyda for calling my attention to this film and to Cooper Graham, who originally located this synopsis. Barry Salt has also discussed A *Narrow Escape* in "The Physician of the Castle," *Sight and Sound* 54 (Winter 1985–86). Salt reconstructed the film based on collations of a British print (*The Physician of the Castle*), a German print (*Der Arzt des Schloss*), and a Spanish print (*El Medico del Castillo*). The German print adds three shots at the beginning and one at the end. I follow this reconstructed version. However the shot numbers vary a bit between my version and Salt's. In order to have a consistent basis for comparison, I do not count the intertitles as shots, the titles for Griffith's film not having been preserved.

12. Barry Salt, "L'Espace`a Cote" in *Les Premiers ans du cinema francais*, ed. Pierre Guiert (Paris: Collections des Caliers de la Cinematheque, 1985), pp. 198–205 (my translation).

13. *Moving Picture World,* June 19, 1909, p. 834. "Bloodless" means the film showed no bloodshed.

14. Ibid., p. 825.

15. Arvidson, *When the Movies Were Young,* p. 117.

16. See Jon Gartenberg, "Camera Movement in the Films of Edison and Biograph," in *Cinema 1900–1906: An Analytical Study by the National Film Archives (London) and the International Federation of Film Archives,* ed. Roger Holman (Brussels: FIAF, 1982), pp. 169–80.

17. See Raymond Fielding, "Hale's Tours: Ultrarealism in the Pre-1910 Motion Picture," in *Film Before Griffith,* ed. John Fell (Berkeley: University of California Press, 1983).

18. See, for example, my discussion of *A Woman Scorned* (1911) and *Sunshine Sue* (1910) in "Weaving a Narrative: Style and Economic Background in Griffith's Biograph Films," *Quarterly Review of Film Studies* 6 (Winter 1981): 19–21.

19. Eileen Bowser, ed., *Biograph Bulletins, 1908–1912* (New York: Farrar Straus and Giroux, 1973), p. 105.

20. This opening is described in A. Nicholas Vardac, *From Stage to Screen: Theatrical Method from Garrick to Griffith* (1949, repr. New York: Benjamin Blom, 1968), pp. 126–27 and Lise-Lone Marker, *David Belasco: Naturalism in the American Theater* (Princeton: Princeton University Press, 1975), pp. 141–44.

21. Bowser, *Biograph Bulletins,* p. 105.

22. Lawrence's memoirs, "Growing up with the Movies," were serialized in *PhotoPlay* during 1914–15.

23. Janet Staiger, "Seeing Stars," *Velvet Light Trap,* no. 20 (Summer 1983): 10–14, and "The Eyes Are Really the Focus: Photoplay Acting and Film Form and Style," *Cinema Journal* 23 (Winter 1983): 14–23 for accounts of the early star system and acting styles. Staiger carefully relates the new restraint in film acting to evolving styles in stage acting, including emphasis on facial expression.

24. For the role of the close-up in the star phenomenon see Richard Dyer, *Stars* (London: British Film Institute, 1979), p. 16. The earliest fan letter preserved for Florence Lawrence, from Dec. 17, 1908, asks specifically for the identity of the female lead in *The Ingrate,* as well as *After Many Years,* which also features a close shot of Lawrence. The letter is preserved in the Florence Lawrence Collection at the Museum of Natural History, Los Angeles. My thanks to Roberta Pearson for telling me of its existence and special thanks to John Belton for photocopying it. Richard deCordova, in "The Emergence of the Star System in America," *Wide Angle* 6, no. 4 (1985): 4–13, introduces a useful distinction between *picture personalities* and *stars,* reserving the latter term for the exploitation of the private lives of motion picture actors, something not typical in the period under discussion. However, because the term *star* was applied to film actors during this period, I have not maintained this methodologically useful distinction.

25. See, for example, Lawrence "Growing up," Nov. 1914, and "Why Is a Star?", *PhotoPlay,* Oct. 1919.

26. New York *Dramatic Mirror,* Nov. 28, 1908, p. 8; *Moving Picture World,* Nov. 28, 1909, p. 423.

27. Ibid, April 24, 1909, p. 515.

28. New York *Dramatic Mirror*, May 15, 1909, p. 15.

29. *Moving Picture World*, May 8, 1909, p. 595.

30. *Edison Kinetogram*, Oct. 1, 1909, p. 13; Oct. 15, 1909, p. 13; Nov. 1, 1909, pp. 2, 12–13.

31. New York *Dramatic Mirror*, May 1, 1909, p. 43.

32. Robert Henderson, *D. W. Griffith: The Years at Biograph* (New York: Farrer, Straus and Giroux, 1910), pp. 86–87.

33. Arvidson, *When the Movies Were Young*, pp. 190–91.

34. Edward Wagenknecht, *The Movies in the Age of Innocence* (New York: Ballantine Books, 1971), p. 44.

35. Lawrence, "Growing up," Jan. 1915, p. 142.

36. *Variety*, Oct. 16, 1909, p. 13.

37. The Florence Lawrence Collection, Museum of Natural History, Los Angeles, preserves two fan letters in response to this IMP film: one from Nov. 6, 1909 and one from Dec. 27, 1909. Both mention Lawrence's previous roles at Biograph; neither address her as Florence Lawrence. The earlier seems to read "Miss Flo," while the later one is addressed "Dear Stranger." These letters are from a thirteen-year-old girl and a sixteen-year-old boy, respectively. The boy writes "Your acting is realistic in many way [sic] mostly the way you make love." Again, my appreciation to Roberta Pearson and John Belton.

38. *Show World*, Jan. 22, 1910, p. 27.

39. *Moving Picture World*, March 5, 1909, p. 323.

40. Lewis Jacobs, *The Rise of the American Film: A Critical History, with an Essay, Experimental Cinema in America 1921–1947* (New York: Teachers College Press, 1968), pp. 86–87.

41. *Moving Picture World*, April 2, 1910, p. 517.

42. From Jacobs, *The Rise of the American Film*, although the groundwork was laid by Terry Ramsaye, *A Million and One Nights: A History of the Motion Picture* (1926, repr. London: Frank Cass, 1964), pp. 523–24.

43. *Moving Picture World*, March 12, 1910, p. 365, emphasis added.

44. Ibid., Dec. 18, 1909, p. 881.

45. Ibid., Feb. 19, 1910, p. 262.

46. *Show World*, Feb. 26, 1910, p. 16.

47. Ibid., April 2, 1910, p. 12.

48. Robert Grau, *The Theater of Science* (1914, repr. New York: Benjamin Blom, 1966), p. 321.

49. New York *Dramatic Mirror*, July 16, 1910, p. 18.

50. Ibid., Dec. 3, 1913, p. 36.

51. Roberta Pearson, " 'The Modesty of Nature': Performance Style in the Griffith Biographs," Ph.D. diss., New York University, 1987, p. 48.

52. Pearson, "The Modesty of Nature," pp. 52, 49, 54, 60, 150, 156, 74, 76, 81, 103, and 127.

53. Ibid., pp. 96, 1056; Pearson also points out some early attacks on the new style in motion picture acting, for example, p. 92.

54. Lawrence, "Growing up," Jan. 1915, p. 104.

55. Frank Dyer to Horace Plimpton, June 10, 1909, Edison National Historic Archives, West Orange, N.J.

56. *Edison Kinetogram*, Aug. 1, 1909, p. 14.

57. John Collier to Horace Plimpton, May 26, 1909, Edison National Historic Archives, West Orange, N.J.

58. Richard B. Cushman, "A Tribute to Mary Pickford," n.p., n.d., Mary Pickford file, Film Study Center, Museum of Modern Art.

8

The Structure of Imagery and the Film Editorial

W HILE THE devices of the narrator system accomplish the storytelling and character-developing purposes of the cinema of narrative integra-tion, there is a recurrent feeling of a surplus in Griffith's Biograph films, of something excessive which gives these films their uniqueness and flavor. This is in part attributable to the extreme development of parallel editing, its overdetermination in all narrative functions. But, particularly after 1908, Biograph films take on a power of imagery that cannot be attributed to any one level of filmic discourse. The resonating overtones of the opening and closing pans in *The Country Doctor* do not come simply from their use of camera movement. The structure and emotional effect of the film as a whole pivots on these overdetermined images. Creating images which act as emotional conductors throughout his films became a narrative strategy which began in 1909 and which Griffith used throughout his later Biograph career. Combined with parallel editing, it would yield a style of extraordinary abstraction.

A film with a remarkable title, *Lines of White on a Sullen Sea* (September 11, 18), plays a key role in the development of this imagistic style. Like many of the devices of the narrator system, highly estheticized images in Biograph films function simultaneously on the levels of voice and mood, with the task of expressing of a character's emotional situation usually predominating. Such images as the many lyrical postscripts which end Biograph films from *The Greaser's Gauntlet* on; the hearthlight finale of *A Drunkard's Reformation*; and the cascading waterfall for the lovers' tryst in *The Mended Lute* all visualize the mood of a character within the shot. At the same time, images like the opening and closing lighting effects of *Pippa Passes* or the pans in *The Country*

Doctor reflect a structuring narrator whose imagistic power encloses the film and marks it as an esthetic object. The images in *Lines of White* straddle these roles, expressing not only a character's longing, but also creating a larger pattern beyond her consciousness, a pattern which becomes the dominant structure of the film itself. Griffith develops for the first time a pattern of recurrent imagery which structures the film as a whole.

In *Lines of White on a Sullen Sea* Griffith gives the situation of his earliest masterpiece, *After Many Years*, an ironic twist, portraying again the anguish of a woman waiting for a sea-faring lover's return.[1] But in place of a parable of faithful love fulfilled, the characters of *Lines of White* are faithless or self-deluding. Emily Brockett (Marion Leonard) accepts a bracelet from Bill, a fisherman (James Kirkwood), as a pledge of his intention to marry her on his return from a voyage. However, on his voyage Bill falls in love with a girl in another fishing port and marries her, delaying his return home for years. Emily remains true to her vow, stationed by the seashore waiting for some sign of Bill's ship. After years of this vigil, she becomes ill and lies dying. Bill happens to return to the village and is forced by Emily's loving but rejected suitor Joe (George Nichols) to pretend that he has returned to wed her. On her death-bed, Emily embraces her counterfeit fiance and dies, solaced by this deception.

An image composed of seashore and sky structures the film and gives it emotional resonance and unity. In thirteen shots of the nineteen-shot film the elemental zones of sea and sky form a backdrop against which human drama is enacted. Griffith's naturalist concern for environment, in which dramas take place and characters dwell, in part motivates the constant presence of the sea, an essential element of the milieu of a fishing village. The backgrounds of the first two shots of the film are filled with details of fishermen's work and characters who play no direct role in the narrative action: men pull carts filled with netting, fishermen prepare their oars, women repair nets, and boats are loaded.

But the sea is a culturally overdetermined image whose meanings quickly exceed the role of providing a realist environment. Griffith invokes these symbolic associations in a number of key shots. In shot four, Emily and Bill withdraw to an isolated area of strand, where he gives her a bracelet to pledge his troth. The withdrawal from village activity moves the characters into a more intimate location and provides a change in mood, the sea surge taking on emotional connotations like the cascade in *The Mended Lute*. Making use of culturally stereotyped imagery—lovers along the seashore—Griffith composes an archetypal image of love's promises. But like the images of family bliss which open *The Country Doctor*, this image is more than a visual cliché. The meaning of the stretch of strand changes as the story progresses.

Bill's departure to sea inspires Bitzer and Griffith to a composition drawn from late-nineteenth-century paintings of women watching at the shore for distant ships created by such painters as Robert Henri, George Innes, and Winslow Homer.[2] In fact, the shot deviates from the narrative arrangement of space Griffith most often employs. Instead of using the foreground for narratively important action and restricting the background to environmental detail, compositional and narrative interest stretches into the depth as Bill's boat puts out to sea in the background. The women are placed on the shore with care, and Emily actually stands in midground rather than foreground. A nameless woman with no role in the plot stands closer to the camera, although her position off to the right never interferes with the viewer centering on Emily.

In the next shot, Emily stands on the porch of her cabin, a location used in five shots, and searches the horizon for some sign of Bill's return. Searching the horizon becomes an emblematic action for Emily, the acting compliment of the compositional leitmotif of the sea. Excluding her deathbed scenes, she is shown looking out to sea in each shot in which she appears from this shot on. The sea has become a signifier of Bill, or rather of his absence, of love's failed promise, rather than a picture postcard backdrop for a romantic moment. Through repetition and transposition of connotations into a minor key, the image of this woman standing against the sea, searching for some sign of her faithless lover, carries strong emotional meaning. The juxtaposition of human form against the monumental form of nature, of human faith and desire questioning a vast and silent sea, creates an image of uncommon power reflecting—but exceeding—the consciousness of the character.

Omniscient parallel editing lets the audience know Bill's real activities. Griffith cuts from the first shot of Emily's vigil to Bill flirting with girls in another port. Alternating Bill's rakish progress with Emily's steadfast patience, we see Bill's courtship and marriage to a girl in a distant village. Ironically, this new love affair is also framed against the sea. The cut to Emily from Bill's marriage carries a poignant irony as Emily enters slowly from the right to an isolated stretch of shore. She stands with her back to the camera, her attention riveted on the horizon. Griffith turns the irony of Emily's faith to pathos, as two couples pass by in the foreground and laugh at Emily, her devotion making her a figure of ridicule to the community.

The next shot not only continues Emily's vigil before the sea, but also brings her to the exact location of Bill's pledge to her and gift of the bracelet. This location is framed from the exact camera placement of the earlier scene, a stretch of beach with a sea wall and the surf foaming white in the distance. Griffith obviously intended that the audience recognize this repetition of location because Emily performs a gestural soliloquy in which she raises her wrist and taps the bracelet, recalling the gift and its promise. She then gazes fixedly out to sea. Joe, her faithful suitor, approaches her from behind and begins to reach out and touch her. But before contact is made, he stops himself and leaves without distracting Emily's gaze from the horizon. Emily is left alone in the frame, fixed in her emblematic posture, waiting for her faithless lover's return.

At this point the shot fades. As in the only previous fade in a Griffith Biograph film, in *Fools of Fate*,[3] the fade is not to black. Rather, the image darkens so that Emily becomes a silhouette against the brighter background of sea and sky, the pearls of surf shining white against the darkened sea. The fade abstracts the image to a basic compositional opposition between figure and ground. The fade precedes an intertitle: "Six years later. Sick unto death with waiting," and so signifies a temporal elipsis—the role that fades will most often play in the later syntax of film transitions. In addition to signifying an elipsis, the fade also fixs and abstracts this central image of the film at an archetypal moment. This image of Emily stationed with her love token at the site of her unfulfilled betrothal stands for all the unseen moments of faithful vigil indicated by the intertitle. The original release print of the film further marked the emblematic nature of this shot by tinting it, probably either blue or gold.[4] All of these devices—the recurring action, the repetition of location and composition, the tinting, the fade, and the image of sea—tend to lift this image out of a simple realistic diegesis, endowing it with esthetic weight and emotion significance. The directing function of voice surrounds the access to character allowed through mood.

The film returns to the shore for its final shot after Emily's death in the arms of her masquerade lover. This concluding shot reworks the lyrical postscript. Instead of presenting the principal characters in a composition expressive of their emotional state, neither Emily, Joe, nor Bill appear. Instead, a group of anonymous fishermen gather about their boats on the shore, like the figures who filled the backgrounds of previous shots of the fishing village. They remove their hats and bow their heads in tribute to Emily's faithful life and death. Recalling the end of *The Country Doctor*, Griffith ends the film with an image stripped of the narrative foreground of major characters and action.

Recurring patterns of imagery, and particularly recurring camera positions and location, played an essential role not only in the narrative structure of later Griffith Biograph films but also, in his production methods. The thirteen shots of *The Adventures of Dollie* were photographed from twelve different camera set-ups, with the shot of the father's fight with the gypsy and the shot of the rescue of Dollie from the barrel filmed in the same riverside location and from the same camera position. In August 1909, the forty-three shots of *Fools of Fate* represent an increase of nearly 300 percent over the number of shots in *Dollie*, but only eleven camera positions are used in the film, one fewer than in Griffith's first film.

The large increase in the number of shots that made up a film and allowed the dramatic articulations in mood, tense, and voice was made possible by this creation of many shots out of footage shot from one setup. This production system preceded Griffith (Pathé and, particularly, Vitagraph exploited it in 1907 and early 1908), but Griffith's use of intercutting increased its effectiveness. The strictly linear narrative pattern of the earlier film genres—chase film such as *Personal* or linked vignettes like *Une dame vraiment bien*—did not allow much repetition. In contrast, the suspenseful parallel editing of *The Lonely Villa* yielded fifty-two shots from its twelve camera set-ups. Other forms of alternation could also generate a large number of shots out of a limited number of camera positions. The intercutting of Wharton and the stage play in *A Drunkard's Reformation* consists of some twenty shots, with thirty-two shots in the film as a whole and only five camera positions. In production terms these figures represent a sort of maximum return on investment, and the actual economy of the system made Griffith's hyper-editing viable.

Cutting up footage filmed from one camera setup entailed shooting out of sequence. It also demanded considerable preparation before shooting: breaking action into shots, distributing shots over locations, and keeping track of the interdependence of shots when filming over several locations—in other words, some form of shooting script. Whatever Griffith's role might have been in developing this method of shooting, by 1909 it was nearly universal. Vitagraph and Essany shot films out of sequence by 1909 and others must have also.[5] The system can be related to the rationalization of labor processes being introduced to industry about this time by Frederick W. Taylor.[6] It can also be seen as the logical outcome of the MPPC's demand for an increase in production. With greater elaboration supplied within a few years by Thomas Ince—the true father of industrial filmmaking in America—pre-shooting planning formed the basis of the rationalization of studio filmmaking in the United States, with careful shooting scripts giving the production company control over all aspects of filmmaking.[7]

But methods designed for production efficiency have esthetic implications and results. The use of a radical discontinuity in the shooting, which would yield a coherent whole when the shots were assembled, created a new attitude to the individual shot. It became clear that each shot took its meaning largely from its place in a syntagmatic chain. In Griffith's editing style every shot was interdependent. Shots assembled simply in the order in which they were filmed had severely limited, or potentially unlimited, meaning. This discontinuous process of shooting carries important consequences for film's narrative form and for screen acting. Film performances were strongly differentiated from those on stage by this discontinuity of filming. The final effect of a performance was not only determined by its filming, but also by the editor's hand.

In a number of films from late 1909, Griffith began to use recurring locations as a structuring element. More than simply a pragmatic plan for shooting, recurring locations became a narrative device, with the film's narrative discourse calling attention to the repetition of camera set-ups by endowing them with emotional associations. *Lines of White on a Sullen Sea* is a prime example, with the seaside location where Bill gave Emily the bracelet repeated during Emily's vigil. In numerous other films locations are repeated and the spectator's attention is drawn to the repetition as significant and thematic.

In *Comata, the Sioux* (August 6, 7), for example, Griffith seems to repeat locations in order to underscore the ironies of this story of an Indian girl, Clear Eyes (Linda Arvidson), seduced then abandoned by her white lover, Bud Watkins (Arthur Johnson). In the final shots of the film, as Clear Eyes returns to the hills of her people after her betrayal by Watkins, she is shown in the precise locations of their earlier courtship. In the final shot of the film she sinks down wearily beside a tall pine, the same location that had served to introduce her faithful Indian lover, Comata (James Kirkwood). At the end of this shot Comata discovers her and takes her back to her village. These repetitions may simply be practical, deriving from Griffith's desire to make full use of particularly pictorial views of Cuddebackville landscapes. But the principle of economy in filmmaking and the investing of locations with emotional associations through repetition are mutually reinforcing.

In some films the repetition is marked by a gestural soliloquy by the actors, as in *Lines of White*, when Leonard draws attention to her bracelet in order to recall that she was given this token at the same location. In *The Dancing Girl of Butte* (December 2, 4), a public park is used in four different shots. Howard Raymond (Owen Moore) and Bella the dance hall girl (Florence Barker) meet here when she twists her ankle and he comes to her aid. When Raymond passes through the location soon after, he pauses and performs a gestural soliloquy, happily recalling for himself and the audience the previous meeting. Later he crosses the park again, just after proposing to Bella. Again, he pantomimes their first meeting, this time pointing to his ankle. The final use of the location brings it full cycle, as Raymond and Bella move through the park wheeling a baby carriage.

Frequently, as in *Lines of White*, such repetitions are used to build up a sense of duration. In these instances the repetition shows some relation to tense. Through recurring locations an image of time is created, marked by human losses and desires. In *Two Women and a Man* (September 25, October 2, 4), shots of the entrance of the couple's cottage mark the different phases of their life: their first entrance after their wedding; leaving the cottage for New York after the husband's (Frank Powell) financial success; and the wife (Kate Bruce) returning after her husband has left her for a show girl. These repetitions mark key transition points in the story, creating, in a film of short running time, a sense of time and change, a sort of history of a place. In themselves they become emblematic of the stages that mark the story: the humble cottage in which happiness begins, which is abandoned when wealth is gained, and which is returned to when illusions fail.

Certain films depend on such recurring location and their emotional associations for their basic narrative structure. In 1909, the strongest example is *The Open Gate* (October 9, 12). A single location, the eponymous gate, appears in twelve shots of the thirty-shot film. The composition is picturesque—a white picket gate in a rural setting surrounded by bushes, trees, and vines—with lush foliage that rustles in the wind. The gate is imbued with transforming connotation through its pivotal role in the story: Hetty (Kate Bruce) and George (George Nichols) are engaged and later break their engagement at this gate. Its recurrence also marks the passage of time in the fifteen-minute film which covers more than a decade.

Images of the gate punctuate the successive stages of the story. It is Hetty's gate, and we first see it as George—an anxious young lover—arrives and beckons to her. It next appears when George gives Hetty a ring (the familiar exchange of a token) and the couple embrace in front of the gate. After a brief shot of Nichols returning to the gate and beckoning again to Hetty, the gate serves as background when Hetty breaks their engagement, explaining she cannot marry because of the new responsibility of raising her dead sister's child, Mary. The couple stands by the gate as Hetty returns the ring. George reacts angrily and, swinging the gate wide in fury, breaks it. This action takes on a symbolic overtone, as the gate is broken along with the couple's love affair. This symbolic role is fully acknowledged in the next shot of the gate. After an intertitle, "The Gate Never to be Closed," Hetty is shown at the gate, telling a worker not to repair it. The gate stands gaping open, hanging from its hinges. After the repairman exits, Hetty leans against it sadly. Like the scenes by the sea in *Lines of White,* the location is emblematic of the crucial event of the story, as well as the character's reaction to it.

An intertitle follows which marks a temporal elipsis: "Fifteen Years Later—Mary Grown to Young Womanhood." The next shot of the gate revives its old associations but brings them into a new generation, with a theme of eternal recurrence and cyclical repetition. Following an intertitle ("At the Gate—The Old Story"), we see Hetty's niece Mary (Gertrude Robinson) at the broken gate with her lover Jack, George's nephew (Owen Moore). Jack gives Mary a bouquet and then a ring. After she accepts his proposal, the two of them run in through the gate.

Soon after the engagement, the young couple quarrel and Mary returns Jack's ring. Immediately after the quarrel, Griffith returns to the gate, as Moore rushes out of it, furious over his rejection. The next shot at the gate specifically recalls its relation to the past. Following the intertitle "Be Reasonable. A Hasty Quarrel at this Gate Blighted my Life," Hetty brings her niece to the gate and advises her to reconsider the broken engagement.

The resolution of the narrative comes with the return of George, who has been wandering about the world since Hetty's rejection. Meeting his nephew Jack, he agrees to intercede for him and bring Jack's ring back to Mary, unaware that she is Hetty's niece. However, when he arrives at the gate, he pantomimes his sudden recognition of the place and its significance. Griffith articulates this memory and George's reaction to it with a cut-away to the young lovers. When we return to George, it seems he has reconsidered his mission, since he is coming back out of the gate. Hetty rushes into the shot to join him. After they talk excitedly, it is clear that the old love still lives. George slams the open gate shut, expressing the resolution of the narrative through this symbolic action.

Griffith continues intercutting the love stories of two generations as we cut away to the young couple settling their differences by themselves. Mary pantomimes for Jack to give her back his ring. A dialogue title follows: "Where is My Ring?" The intercutting is artfully brought together with this question, as we return to the older couple at the gate, George placing Jack's ring on Hetty's finger. The youngsters arrive, asking for their ring and the situation is explained. Embraces and handshakes all around, as George opens the gate and the two pairs of lovers go through.

As the title indicates, the film is the open gate; the recurring location and image stitch the film together. The gate provides structural unity and clarity, as well as crystalizing the emotional crux of the film. Through it, Griffith creates access to characters' emotions (that Hetty's love for George still lives as long as the gate remains open) and memory (George's sudden recognition). Throughout the film, a tone of nostalgia lingers; a narrative structure of loss, and recovery, of the object of desire. From overdetermined emotional images such as this broken gate, Griffith fashions a film which is not only comprehensible and coherent, but which solicts an investment of empathy and fantasy.

The structuring of a film around key images combines with an advanced use of parallel editing to create one of Griffith's Biograph masterworks, A Corner in Wheat, which he never surpassed in sophistication of construction and cohesion between social message and filmic form. Traditional treatments of Griffith's Biograph films universally accord A Corner in Wheat (November 3, 14) a key position. The devices of parallel editing reach a new abstraction in the film, creating Griffith's crowning work in the fashioning of an imagistic narrative structure. Further, the film's use of voice reaches into the extratextual space of social issues and discourse. No other Biograph film provides as clear a lesson in the necessity of interrelating esthetic structure and social context. This film exists in a welter of intertextuality that includes populist political rhetoric, the fiction of Frank Norris, and the art of Francois Millet.[8] The genre of the film was unprecedented at Biograph. Stretching narrative form farther than it had been before, Griffith used filmic discourse to present a social argument as much as a story. The Spectator of the New York *Dramatic Mirror* immediately recognized the innovative and experimental nature of this film:

> This picture is not a picture drama, although it is presented with dramatic force. It is an argument, an editorial, an essay on a subject of deep interest to all. The theme is the rising cost of living, the inability of the masses to meet the increase and the part played by the speculator in bringing about this unfortunate condition. No orator, no editorial writer, no essayist could so strongly and effectively present the thoughts that are conveyed in this picture. It is another demonstration of the force and power of motion pictures as a means of conveying ideas. It was a daring step for the Biograph producers to take to step out of the domain of picture drama as they have done in this film. . . .[9]

A *Corner in Wheat* works as a film "editorial" on several levels. Not surprisingly, the basic rhetorical figure of its argument is contrast expressed through parallel editing. Griffith had used this fundamental device of the narrator system to make social arguments since *The Song of the Shirt.* In A *Corner in Wheat* it is these contrasts, rather than the linear development of the story, that form the center of the film, substituting a paradigmatic axis of comparison for the syntagmatic axis of story development.

The film presents its most basic contrast in the first three shots, and with this rhetorical figure propells the viewer into the arguments of populist ideology. The opening shots of A *Corner in Wheat* show wheat farmers wearily setting out to their fields and then at labor sowing their grain. The third shot introduces the first contrast edit. Following an intertitle ("The Wheat King. Engineering the Great Corner"), Griffith cut from the fields to a grain specula-tor in his office, instructing his minions before they descend to the commodi-ties pit to buy up wheat and allow him to set prices.

This contrast between the staunch yeomen farmers sowing the wheat the nation needs and the millionaire grain speculator who profits from and exploits both farmer and consumer visualizes familiar images of populist rhetoric. One need look no further than William Jennings Bryan's famous "Cross of Gold" speech before the Democratic Convention in 1896 for a description of the opening characters of Griffith's film. Bryan contrasted "The farmer who goes forth in the morning and toils all day, who begins in Spring and toils all Summer, and who by the application of brain and muscle to the natural resources of the country creates wealth" with "the man who goes upon the Board of Trade and bets upon the price of grain."[10] But Bryan was only bringing to the politics of a national party an issue the populist movement had raised for more than a decade: the exploitation of the actual producers of a commodity by speculators who manipulated and fixed prices.

Throughout the 1890s the Populist party had tried to convince the nation of the severity of this economic injustice. In 1897–98 the attempt of Joe Leitner to corner the wheat market on the Chicago Board of Trade not only convinced many of the urgent nature of the populist's warning, but also provided Griffith, somewhat indirectly, with the basis for his character of the Wheat King. Leitner first made a fictional detour through literature and theater, inspiring Frank Norris's Curtis Jadwin, the major character in the second novel of Norris's proposed trilogy of wheat, *The Pit*.[11] The relation between Norris and Griffith is worth exploring beyond the confines of this film. Griffith's interest in literary and theatrical naturalism must have drawn him to the works of this "American Zola" who provided a model for the transformation of turn-of-the-century muckraking journalism into narrative form.

Griffith, having come to maturity during the heyday of muckraking journalists, was strongly impressed by their revelations of the gritty realities of American life and the new social consciousness that motivated them.[12] The denouement of the Griffith's play *A Fool and a Girl* undercut the apparently proper background of its hero with a muckraking expose of the actual source of his family's wealth:

> My money, you know my money, it was all made by Uncle Jim in the grocery business. Now I happen to know the truth. He had a lot of scales in his stores that told more lies every day than you ever told in all your life before. You know what my money is—dirt in the sugar, marble dust that eats people up at that, walnut shells in the coffee, railroad shares and stocks, paying double dividends by keeping down the working force and knocking people on their heads with carelessness and killing two or three every day, that's my money.[13]

As early as *The Song of the Shirt*, Griffith brought this muckraking sensibility to his films. Christy Cabanne, Griffith's assistant at Biograph, recalled him describing film as a "great medium to bring out truth about unjust social and economic conditions," a perfect outlet for muckraking themes.[14]

A *Corner in Wheat*'s initial contrast between farmer and speculator reappears in *The Pit*, as Cressler, a reformed speculator, denounces the Chicago speculator who stands between "the fellows who raise the grain and the other fellows who eat it, raises or lowers the price out of all reason, for the benefit of his pocket."[15] Norris's short story "A Deal in Wheat" (1903), as George C. Pratt has pointed out, directly inspired *A Corner in Wheat*.[16] By interweaving the fate of a Kansas farmer, Sam Lewiston, with the activities of grain speculators Hornung and Truslow, Norris shows the results of the extreme fluctuations of the market. Lewiston is forced to sell his farm because of the low price his wheat fetches when Truslow, "the great bear," dominates the market. Migrating to Chicago and unemployed, Lewiston is then refused bread in the bread line because the corner in wheat engineered by Hornung, "the unknown bull," has driven up the price of flour. As Norris concludes, "The farmer—he who raised the wheat—was ruined upon one hand; the working man—he who consumed it—was ruined upon the other," while the speculators profited.[17]

Populist politicians attempted to expand beyond a midwestern agricultural base by revealing grain speculators as common enemies to rural producers and urban consumers. *A Corner in Wheat* adopts this argument by expanding its simple opening contrast into a tripartite structure. The Wheat King moves from his office to the pit and then to a lavish party celebrating his financial victory. The dinner party is introduced with the intertitle "The Gold of the Wheat." The next shot follows the intertitle "The Chaff of the Wheat," cutting to the interior of an urban bakery, where the rise in wheat prices has led to a doubling in the price of bread. The Wheat King is now contrasted with the consumers of the wheat, poor urban customers, some of whom can not afford the higher price and leave hungry.

This triple contrast—weary farmer producers, hungry urban consumers, and fat-cat speculator between them—determines the narrative structure of *A Corner in Wheat* as a whole, giving it an abstraction that appears in no previous fiction film. Instead of cutting between two basic lines of action, the film circulates among the three centers of farmers, speculators, and bakery customers. The shots of the film are strung on these three narrative threads with the following distribution: thread 1: the farmers, shots one, two, eleven, and twenty-three; thread 2: the bakery, shots seven, nine, twelve, and eighteen; and thread 3: the story of the Wheat King, shots three through six, eight, ten, thirteen through seventeen, and nineteen through twenty-two.

While this structure certainly develops from patterns of parallel editing, the motives for the intercutting are new. In Griffith's previous films, cross-cutting was motivated by the actions and concerns of the characters. This is clearest in the race-to-the-rescue found in such films as *The Guerrilla, The Drive for a Life,* and *The Lonely Villa,* where the parallel editing is first based on the exchange of information from one line of action to another, for example, the messenger in *The Guerrilla,* the Widow Lebrun's confession in *The Drive for Life,* and the telephone call in *The Lonely Villa.* The climactic rush-to-the-rescue of these films then brings denouement as the two lines of action converge. Even the omniscient effects of parallel editing when the narrator system reveals more information to the audience than the characters possess, such as the shot of the unfaithful Bill following a shot of Emily's vigil in *Lines of White,* depend on a previous relationship within the story between the two lines of action.

A discussion of *The Song of the Shirt,* the closest predecessor to *A Corner in Wheat,* demonstrates this. The earlier film used a number of strong contrast cuts interrelating three locations: the sweat shop, the restaurant where the management eat and entertain chorus girls, and the tenement apartment where Florence Lawrence sews and her sister dies. However, the three locations are connected by the characters' movement between them. Lawrence travels from tenement to sweat shop; the boss moves from sweat shop to restaurant. Lawrence circulates among all the characters. At a few points the cuts between locations do not follow the path of a character (e.g., the cut from the boss at the restaurant with his chorus girl to Lawrence sewing feverishly next to her sick sister in the tenement apartment). It is in these cuts that an ideological contrast operates most strongly. But this contrast functions within a geography previously established by character movement.

In *A Corner in Wheat*, cutting patterns become more radical and the relations between shots more abstract. Instead of a geography unified by the movement of characters and the interrelation of separate characters via a character who communicates with them all, we see a series of disparate scenes of American life, brought together only by their economic relation. There is no communication between the characters of the three threads. The farmers do not appear at the bakery, nor does the Wheat King go out to inspect the farmer's crop. The only connection between them is the economic one of producer, consumer, and speculator. The structure of *A Corner in Wheat* goes beyond the occasional ideological contrast found in *The Song of the Shirt*. Structurally, the film is more than a melodrama with a social underpinning.

Parallel editing becomes in this film a form of economic analysis, linking elements in an economic chain dispersed in time and space. On an elementary level, Griffith shows the first stirrings of the great interrelation between montage and economic analysis which finds its complete expression in Eisenstein's *October* and Vertov's *The Man with a Movie Camera*. In some ways Griffith's film is more radical than its source, Norris's "A Deal in Wheat," in which the economic relation is narrativized by the ironic presence of Lewiston at both ends of the economic circuit, as farmer-producer and breadline consumer. Through his editing, Griffith coordinates the disparate points of the economic system in what is certainly one of the strongest examples of the narrator system at work, coordinating images and producing meanings.

The intercutting among the three threads reveals the sophistication Griffith achieved in employing parallel editing in different modes and situations. Thread 3, the narrative of the Wheat King, provides the spine of the film. The four shots of the farmers which make up thread 1 present something of a story, but a minimal one. Thread 2 of the bakery is less a story with continuous characters than a location with a series of situations. These two threads do not really function as independent stories, but provide contrasts and associations, based on economic relations, to the central story of the Wheat King.

The pattern of intercutting becomes most intense in the sequence which revolves around the lavish party given for the Wheat King after he has engineered his great corner, in which every cut switches to an alternate thread. The inspiration for this intercutting certainly comes, as George C. Pratt has shown, from the end of chapter 8 of Norris's *The Octopus*.[18] This section of the novel alternates Mrs. Hoover and her daughter Hilda, as they wander desperately through the streets of San Francisco searching for food, with the extravagant dinner party given by Gerard, the vice president of the railroad which dispossessed the Hoovers of their farm. In Norris's novel the alternation begins with sections of several pages each, and then builds to an alternation of brief paragraphs, as Mrs. Hoover dies of starvation while the cream of San Francisco society consumes stuffed artichokes, candied chestnuts, and glasses of Madiera.

But Griffith's tripartite structure goes beyond Norris's single contrast. With the contrasting intertitles mentioned previously, the party sequence introduces the first shot of the bakery. At the party the Wheat King is toasted by men in formal dress and women in lavish gowns as he enters the dining room. The stark set of the bakery is dominated by a large sign next to the bread counter, which announces, "Owing to the advance in the price of flour, the usual 5 cent loaf will be 10 cents." A series of customers buys bread and are reminded of the increased price. The last customer, an old woman (Kate Bruce) with a young girl, cannot afford the new price and leaves without her bread. The next shot returns to the dinner party, as guests eat and drink, the Wheat King sitting in the foreground.

At the bakery, customers have cleared out, and a breadline awaits the doling out of loaves to those who cannot afford to pay. The shot is a tableau vivant, with all the actors posed in a fixed position for the duration of the shot; the men and women of the breadline wait expectantly, the bakers are behind their counters (fig. 39). This frozen action seems to lift the image out of the narrative flow, to emphasize its paradigmatic role as comparison image for the dinner party.

In the dining room, the party is ending and the Wheat King stands surrounded by young women in white, who give him their devoted attention (fig. 40). The guests start to leave. The next shot switches to the first thread of the film, the wheat farmers. We see a farmyard where a woman and child await the men's return. They trudge into the farmyard, weary and forlorn. The younger farmer pantomimes that he has nothing, and it seems that they are returning from the market empty-handed (fig. 41). The film then cuts to the bakery as the tableau vivant comes to life and men shuffle forward to be handed their loaves. The supply runs out long before the line ends, and the remaining men walk off, empty-handed and dazed. These three shots draw the various threads together to form an economic nexus which produces want and despair for the masses and plenty for a few.

39, 40, and 41: The three threads of imagery in *A Corner in Wheat* (1909) come together as Griffith intercuts the tableau vivant of the breadline with the Wheat King's (Frank Powell) ball and the farmers (James Kirkwood, W. Chrystie Miller) returning home from market empty-handed. Frame enlargements from 35mm prints, courtesy of the Museum of Modern Art.

39

40

41

The sequence differs sharply from the cutting motivated by the actual physical movements of characters in *The Song of the Shirt.* Economic relations alone determine the cutting pattern within *A Corner in Wheat.* The geography of the film conceivably stretches across the whole nation. Even the time relations between shots are of little importance. Although it is possible that the dinner party, the actions at the bakery, and the farmers' return from the market are simultaneous, these temporal relations are of less importance than their structural role as relations on the economic level. Such theoretically motivated editing makes the film less a conventional, character-based story than what the Spectator termed a film "editorial," channeling the power of filmic codes into the expression of ideas. Here the ability of the narrator system to comment on action and characters through the aspect of voice reaches its furthest development.

The final cut into the Wheat King thread consists of a single but dramatic shot. After exulting over a telegram which informs him that he now controls the world's market in wheat, the Wheat King suddenly slips and falls into a grain elevator. Unable to get out, he is overwhelmed by a torrent of his own wheat as it fills the elevator. Griffith interrupts the violent fate of the specula-tor with a final return to the bakery. A group of men rush in angrily, gesturing violently at the baker. Two policemen enter and hit the group's leader over the head with a club. The crowd rushes the police, who then draw their revolvers and force them back. We then return to the grain elevator. Only the Wheat King's hand emerges from the heap of grain and flutters vainly before being covered. The cut-away to the bread riot articulates the Wheat King's death in much the same manner as the suspense cuts discussed earlier, delaying for a moment its resolution. But the cut also works on a metaphorical axis, comparing the violent death of the Wheat King to the violence he has unleashed in society.

The film ends with a return to the farmers who opened the film. In shot twenty-one James Kirkwood sows the grain as he did in the film's second shot (fig. 42). Although the action and location are the same as the earlier shot, a number of important contrasts are set up. Kirkwood now works alone; the older man who sowed alongside him is gone, as is the man with horse and harrow. It is possible that in the compressed narrative of this thread (a total of four shots), Griffith is conveying that the old man is dead, the horse and equipment sold. The circular pattern created by this closing shot invokes not only the narrative closure of the film, but also the agricultural cycle of sowing and reaping. One might see this image as an optimistic representation of nature's renewal after the death of the Wheat King. However, the melancholy quality to this closing shot, emphasized by Kirkwood's weary and oppressed motions as he sows the wheat, seems to indicate that the cycles of nature

42. The final image of the film, reproducing the composition of Millet's "The Sower."

revolve without consideration for humanity, as did the economic manipulations of the Wheat King.

The *Biograph Bulletin* interprets the film in a manner less threatening to genteel ideology, "There is no vengeance possible here but the hand of God," for "one of the sins that cries to heaven for vengeance is denying food to the hungry."[19] However, the imagery of the film and the logic of its editing—particularly the intercutting of the Wheat King's suffocation with the bread riot and the return to the farmers that ends the film—are closer to the determinism of Norris and other naturalists than to the *Bulletin*'s "vengeance is mine, sayeth the Lord" homily.

Although *A Corner in Wheat* draws primarily upon the resources of parallel editing, the compressed narratives of the farm and bakery threads and their primary role as contrasts create images with an emblematic and almost allegorical tone. The tableau vivant of the breadline stands out as a particularly excessive moment in which the frozen gestures of the actors draw attention to the shot as an image pregnant with meaning. Although Griffith's films occasionally use acting tableaux, usually at the end of film (e.g., *1776, or The Hessian Renegades* and *In Old Kentucky*), this shot in which there is no motion for the entire duration (it has even been mistaken by some viewers for a freeze frame) has no parallel in any other Griffith Biograph film.[20]

The reason that Griffith used this unusual technique is unclear. The shot shows the men waiting for the breadline to open. In Norris's "A Deal in Wheat," this takes four hours, so the frozen position may represent the anguished expectation of a meal, an expectation that will be disappointed for most of the people on the breadline. On a formal level the stillness of the breadline intervenes between two shots of the Wheat King's dinner party, both characterized by a flurry of activity, the well-dressed guests moving freely as they talk, eat, and drink. John Belton has pointed out that this tableau vivant recalls a number of other frozen moments in the film, all associated with the life-denying power of the Wheat King: the rapt attention of his assistants as they take his orders; the brief tableau of the farmer returning from the market; the frozen position of the bakery mob, hands up, as the police threaten them with pistols; and the brief tableau at the end of the film as the Wheat King's companions discover his body. But the breadline tableau has an excessive quality that no interpretation seems to exhaust, and which draws attention to the shot as image.

Like the circular images from earlier films, the image of the sower which appears in the second and final shot of the film gathers resonances from its encapsulating role. In addition to its place in a circular structure, the image also calls attention to itself through a sort of visual quotation. The *Biograph Bulletin* describes it as "an animated reproduction of Jean Francois Millet's masterpiece, 'The Sowers'."[21] The reproduction of a famous painting recalls the cultural ambition which led Biograph to the adaptation of literary master-pieces. At the same time, it also derives from the theatrical tradition of "Living Pictures," in which actors would be posed to recreate a famous painting. In accord with what Vardac calls the "pictorial sensibility" of the nineteenth-century theater, these reproductions were included in certain stage produc-tions, such as the reproduction of Leonardo's "The Last Supper" in Belasco's production of the *Passion Play* in San Francisco in 1879, or the reproduction of David Wilkie's painting "Rent Day" which began Jerrold's melodrama of the same title.[22] Reproduction of paintings could also be found in a number of popular arts, including wax museums and vaudeville, appearing in films as early as Lumìere and often providing an esthetic excuse for nudity.[23]

Among the most popular mass-reproduced paintings in the late nineteenth and early twentieth century were works by Millet, whose work, on first appearance, had been considered scandalous. A reproduction of "The An-gelus" had even penetrated the boyhood parlor of Biograph cameraman Billy Bitzer, who admitted in his memoirs that in his Biograph days he did "study closely the lights and shadows of reverse-light pictures, like 'The Gleaners' with the foreshadows on the field of stubble," even though he "didn't know much about art."[24]

Millet's composition and use of light, explicitly cited in this film, shaped many of Bitzer's compositions in rural settings. However, a direct comparison of Millet's painting and the second shot of *A Corner in Wheat* shows the somewhat off-hand nature of this "reproduction." Other than the action of the figure in the foreground, there is little that recalls the versions of Millet's original painting from 1850 or 1851.[25] The source for Bitzer's composition is most likely a crayon drawing by Millet from 1865, based on his earlier paintings, which was frequently engraved and reproduced.[26] In this version the figure of the sower is placed in a landscape, rather than dominating the frame as does the almost threatening figure in the painting. Behind him is the man with horse and harrow who appears in Griffith's film as well; the second sower, who also disappears in the film's last shot, is not present in either the painting or the drawing. Most strikingly, in the drawing Millet has substituted a high horizon line for the hillside of the painting. This is perhaps the shot's most important compositional debt to Millet, and one with strong connotations. As in many of Millet's compositions, such as "The Angelus," "The Man with the Hoe," and "The Gleaners," this high horizon line roots the farm laborers in the earth, silhouetting them against the land. From this point on in his Biograph career, Bitzer tended to film exteriors from a slightly high angle, framing characters against land and soil.

Millet's composition is also transformed by being put into motion. Vlada Petric has described the perceptual pattern of masking, revealing, and disappearing which occurs in this shot.[27] The sowers walk toward the camera, followed by the horses pulling the harrow and another farmhand. Coming very close to the camera, the sowers exit the frame as the titanic figure in Millet's painted version seemed to threaten to do. Freed from the immobility of the canvas, Griffith's figures disappear from the frame into off-screen space. They then reenter the frame, having completed a turn along the furrows off-screen. The horses follow the same trajectory, pirouetting off-screen so that when they reenter the frame their direction has switched from a movement toward the camera to a movement into the depth of the image, although the harrow and farmhand complete this turn within view of the camera. These exits and reentrances with a change of direction create one of the most dramatic uses of off-screen space thus far at Biograph. One wonders if this use of off-screen space was inspired by the thrust of the sower figure in Millet's painting out beyond the circumscribed space of the canvas.

The use of Millet undoubtedly carries connotations other than the reproduction of a famous painting. From their first appearance, Millet's work had been seized upon by socialist and agrarian reform movements, somewhat in spite of Millet's own intentions, as a plea for the wretched of the earth, stark images of the oppression of rural labor. This association had been particularly strong in the United States, where "The Man with the Hoe" inspired a populist poem by Edwin Markham in 1899. Pulling the web of intertextual references tighter, this poem, and its source in Millet's painting, is the basis for a major incident in Norris's *The Octopus*: the publication of Presley's "socialistic poem," "The Toilers." The film's "quotation" of Millet's painting, then, relates to the fabric of the film's social argument and possibly forms another complex reference to Norris.

The film's final image of the sower, the solitary presence of a lone farmer, in many ways invokes the "somber and desolate aspect" of Millet's original more strongly than the rather busy second shot.[28] In the last shot, the farmer's turn in the furrow is not made off-screen. Rather, he wearily turns his back to the audience and then trudges into the background of the shot. As he moves away from the camera, the shot fades. This fade is made in the camera and does not end in total blackness. A recent addition to Griffith's cinematic vocabulary, fades had ended Biograph films only twice before. In both cases the fade closes tragic stories, following the suicide of the husband in *The Expiation* (September 15, 16) and the death of the mountaineer brother in *The Mountaineer's Honor*. In *A Corner in Wheat* the fade closes down on a similarly pessimistic image, the exploited farmer sowing another crop that will be harvested for the profit of others. As in *Lines of White*, the fade eternalizes the image, fixing it as an emblem for the film.

"A Deal in Wheat" was published in 1903 (after Norris's death), *The Pit* in October 1902, and *The Octopus* in 1901. The period of their publication also marks the end of a decade of effort by populist reformers to control grain speculation. In fact, after 1893, the beginning of an era of relative prosperity for farmers undercut anti-speculator agitation, as attention of progressive reformers turned to Wall Street. When legislation to control speculation in commodity futures was introduced in Congress in 1910, it was attacked by one opponent as "the echo of the dying wail of populism."[29] In 1909, then, *A Corner in Wheat* was taking up a social battle cry more than a decade old and in some ways a dead issue.

Although the film's roots in populist rhetoric and muckraking journalism are vital to its innovative form, in its contemporaneous context it was not an intensely radical political statement. It is somewhat amusing that this attack on the evils of a monopoly in wheat was produced by a leading member of a newly formed film trust, but the social argument of *A Corner in Wheat* can actually be related to the purposes of the MPPC. The Wheat King, as the anti-speculator rhetoric always stressed, was a middle-man, standing between producers and consumers and extorting profit to the detriment of both. This attack corresponds in many ways to the MPPC's view of the exchangeman, who stood between production companies and the public and, according to the MPPC, thought only of his own profit, not the betterment of the film business. Whether or not Biograph president J. J. Kennedy was aware of the congruence of the message of *A Corner in Wheat* with the plans he was evolving for the MPPC to take over the exchange business, there was nothing in the film's social message to disturb him.

But one should not entirely discount the film's alignment with progressive themes, or its ambitions in entering into a political debate. When the New York *Dramatic Mirror* declared that *A Corner in Wheat* was "not a picture drama" but an "argument, an editorial, an essay," it recognized that the film's most radical aspect lay not in its message but in its decision to express a message, and the form it used to do so. The film's editing recurringly makes editorial comment on the events portrayed, displaying strong elements of voice. More than any other Biograph film, *A Corner in Wheat* addresses its spectator through a rhetoric of juxtaposition and contrast. It demands less that the spectator follow the story than that he or she respond to the economic contrasts offered. The mass of cultural material that the film works over—from speeches to novels to paintings—shows both Biograph's cultural ambitions and Griffith's ability to draw formal inspiration from a large range of sources. The narrator system resulted from pressures and influences from all sides, forging a system of filmic narration which opened onto the horizons of other discourses as well as determining the internal rules of tense and access to characters. Through the resources of both editing and the enframed image, the narrator system could create a realm of reference that went beyond the actions of

individual characters, or even their psychological motivations, to the world
of economic relations and the processes of history.

Notes

1. An unpublished essay by Maureen Turim treats this motif in painting, literature, and film and centers on Griffith's adaptations of "Enoch Arden," "Layers of Meaning: 'Enoch Arden' and an Historically Wrought Semiotics"; I am grateful for having access to it.

2. Turim's essay, drawing partly on P. G. Scott's *Tennyson's "Enoch Arden": A Victorian Best-Seller* (Lincoln: The Tennyson Society, 1970) summarizes this visual tradition.

3. The fade in *Fools of Fate* a few weeks earlier is quite curious. It does not seem to indicate a temporal elipsis, but rather serves as an ersatz lighting effect, indicating the coming of twilight as two hunters bed down at their campsite for the night. The fade is introduced to film extremely early, occasionally, as in *Fools of Fate*, to indicate a diegetic darkening, for example, Porter's *What Happened in the Tunnel* (1903). Tracing the history of this device is obfuscated by the occasional appearance in the films made from the Paper Print Collection of a fade clearly not in the original print but made during the printing process in the 1950s. For example, there seems to be a fade at the end of *A Rude Hostess* (March 3), but it is clear that it is actually a later addition.

4. New York *Dramatic Mirror*, Nov. 6, 1909, p. 13.

5. Ibid., May 1, 1909, p. 37; George Pratt, ed., *Spellbound in Darkness: A History of the Silent Film* (Greenwich: New York Graphic Society, 1973), p. 129.

6. The rational and scientific organization of film production is detailed in David Bordwell, Janet Staiger, and Kristin Thompson, *The Classical Hollywood Cinema: Film Style and Mode of Production to 1960* (New York: Columbia University Press, 1985), pp. 113–73. The systematic application of Taylor's "scientific management" to film production actually came later than the period under discussion, around 1914–15 (pp. 134–35). Shooting out of order is discussed on p. 125. These chapters were written by Janet Staiger.

7. Pratt, *Spellbound*, pp. 143–73; Bordwell, Staiger, and Thompson, *Classical Hollywood*, p. 138.

8. The version of the film on which my analysis is based is that found in the original negative now in the archive of the Museum of Modern Art, rather than the paper print which lacks the essential tableau vivant shot. For a detailed discussion of the textual problems of this film, see Eileen Bowser, "The Reconstruction of *A Corner in Wheat*," *Cinema Journal* 15 (Spring 1976): 45–52, and "Addendum to 'The Reconstruction of *A Corner in Wheat*,' " *Cinema Journal* 19 (Fall 1979): 101–2, as well as my Ph.D. dissertation, "D. W. Griffith and the Narrator System," New York University, 1986, pp. 641–44.

9. New York *Dramatic Mirror*, Dec. 25, 1909, p. 15.

10. William Jennings Bryan, "Cross of Gold," in *Myth and Reality in the Populist*

Revolt, ed. Edwin C. Rozwenc and John C. Matten (Lexington: D.C. Heath, 1967), p. 25.

11. Clipping in Robinson Locke Scrapbooks, Library of the Performing Arts, Lincoln Center, New York City, p. 71.

12. On the literary influence of muckrackers, see Richard Hofstader, *The Age of Reform: From Bryan to FDR* (New York: Vintage Books, 1955), pp. 186–214.

13. *A Fool and a Girl,* D. W. Griffith Papers, Museum of Modern Art Film Library, New York City.

14. Cabanne interview in Braverman material, D. W. Griffith Papers, Film Library, Museum of Modern Art, New York City.

15. Frank Norris, *The Pit: A Story of Chicago* (New York: Modern Library, 1934), p. 121.

16. Pratt, *Spellbound,* p. 67.

17. Norris, "A Deal in Wheat," in ibid., pp. 74–76.

18. Ibid., pp. 77–80.

19. Eileen Bowser, ed., *Biograph Bulletins, 1908–1912* (New York: Farrer, Straus and Giroux, 1973), p. 150.

20. See Seymour Stern, "The Birth of a Nation," *Film Culture* no. 36 (Spring–Summer 1965):83.

21. Bowser, *Biograph Bulletins,* p. 150.

22. A. Nicholas Vardac, *From Stage to Screen: Theatrical Method from Garrick to Griffith* (1949, repr. New York: Benjamin Blom, 1968), pp. 109–10.

23. Georges Sadoul, *Histoire géneral du cińema,* vol. 2: *Les pionniers du cińema 1897–1909* (Paris: Denoel, 1951), p. 77.

24. Billy Bitzer, *His Story: The Autobiography of D. W. Griffith's Master Cameraman* (New York: Farrar, Strauss and Giroux, 1973), pp. 83–84.

25. See Robert Herbert, *Jean Francois Millet Catalogue* (London: Arts Council of Great Britain, 1976), p. 78.

26. Herbert, *Millet,* p. 157.

27. Vlada Petric, "A Corner in Wheat: Griffith's Earliest Masterpiece," *University Film Study Center Newsletter* 5, no. 2 (1974):4.

28. Herbert, *Millet,* p. 78.

29. See Cecil B. Cowing, *Populists, Plungers, and Progressives: A Social History of Stocks and Commodity Speculation* (Princeton: Princeton University Press, 1965), pp. 27, 37, 43.

9

The Narrator System Beyond 1909

THE PERIOD of Griffith's work at Biograph presents an elegant symmetry. His directorial premiere came at a time of industry transformation that would be embodied in the formation of the MPPC. His departure in 1913 came at a time when the MPPC was being sued by the U.S. government under antitrust laws and forces within the industry were preparing for a new transformation based on the triumph of the feature film. Once again, trade journals recognized that the film industry was in a "period of transition,"[1] and this industry transformation would have strong effects on the forms of film narration. The triumph of the feature film changed the American film industry, both internally and externally. As the theatrical film industry is still founded on the production, distribution, and exhibition of feature films, it inaugurated an era that in many ways still continues, exiling Griffith's Biograph films to the "pre-feature" era.

The basic forces within the film industry remained fairly constant from 1909 to 1913, although approaching changes were being incubated. Throughout the period the "uplift" of the film industry formed a long and ongoing process, the Motion Picture Patents Company maintained the same basic practices and goals, and battles continued against local censorship movements, as did industry campaigns to raise the social respectability of film.

From 1909 on, the MPPC faced a major challenge to its hegemony of American production and distribution from the newly formed independent production companies. However, detailing these legal, economic, and sometimes nearly physical battles is beyond the scope of this work.[2] The independent faction gained strength steadily from 1910 to 1913. By 1913 the independents had become at least an opponent equal to the MPPC. The patents by which the MPPC had sought to guarantee their monopoly crumbled one by one, as the tide of the patents battles gradually turned against the trust.

Perhaps the most far-reaching change in the film industry during the period was the fulfillment of one of the basic motivations behind the formation of the MPPC: the control of film distribution by the production companies. In 1910 the MPPC began to set up its own system of distribution, General Film. Although the MPPC and General Film were legally separate, they were intimately interconnected in their economic goals and the strategies to achieve them, and the term *General Film* became synonymous with the licensed forces. The wholesale engulfing of licensed exchanges by General Film was accomplished by 1912. By 1913 the output of the American film industry was abundant and stable; *Moving Picture World* put weekly releases at two hundred reels a week, including multireel features.[3] This is a striking achievement when one recalls that in 1908, when Griffith began as a director, barely a dozen domestic reels were issued each week. Although the two-hundred-reel figure certainly includes some imports, foreign films had progressively become less important.[4]

The era of the small-time nickelodeon was ending, and the harbingers of the picture palace had arrived by 1913. More elaborate theaters and higher admission prices indicated growing middle-class acceptance of film as entertainment. Motion picture exhibiting, a business that during the era of the store show had required a minimum of investment, began to involve substantial capital.

Trade journals urged exhibitors to create a comfortable environment for patrons. The importance of proper ventilation was stressed, and many theaters publicized their achievements. Uniformed attendants were frequent in "well-conducted" theaters and provided such services as bringing glasses of ice water to patrons, as well as showing them to their seats. But the central difference from theaters of the later era and typical nickelodeons was capacity. By 1913, theaters seating several hundred, and even some with capacities of more than a thousand, had appeared.

How successful was the industry's courtship of the middle-class audience? Unbiased information on the makeup of film audiences in 1909 is hard to come by. The only information on class backgrounds based on any sort of statistical survey comes from 1910, when the Russell Sage Foundation conducted a survey of audiences in New York City theaters, finding that 25 percent of the audience fell into the category they termed "clerical," indicating white-collar, lower-middle class.[5] This indicates that at least by 1910 exhibitors had succeeded in attracting enough middle-class patrons to constitute a quarter of their audience, while the great majority of motion picture patrons remained working class. The middle-class proportion of the audience seems to have steadily increased until 1913, but only with the coming of feature films and picture palaces did the middle class completely give in to the seduction of cinema.

If well-regulated theaters with snappily dressed attendants who catered to the patrons' needs were an idealized image of film theaters in 1909, there is no doubt that the nightmare end of the spectrum still existed. An investigation of New York City motion pictures shows published in 1911 by the commissioner of accounts described a theater on Pitkin Avenue in Brooklyn, which it found among the most offensive: "Seats full and about 250 standing in the rear and in the aisles. . . . The crowd was surging back and forth, pushing and shoving for vantage points of view. Quarrels were frequent. The air was fetid and stifling."[6] Ventilation problems were widespread. The report described one common solution: "In many places attendants went through the room with an atomizer, spraying perfume on the crowd to allay the odor."[7]

The audience's interest in actors had been institutionalized through studio-controlled, or at least abetted, publicity by 1913, although huge star salaries did not begin until 1914. Even Biograph finally gave in to public pressure and released actors' names in 1913, after acrimonious complaints in the newly issued fan magazines. For example, in 1911 the Spectator had answered a reader's request for the name of a Biograph actor with the response "Biograph actors have no names. When the director speaks to them it is by number."[8] However, stars had not yet become the major method of product differentiation they became with the triumph of features.

The rise of feature films was the major innovation of the period, and began to dominate the industry by the end of 1913, causing sweeping changes. Its appearance had been gradual. As early as 1909, Edison, Pathé, Biograph, and Vitagraph had all produced multireel films. By 1911, both licensed and independent producers released occasional two- or three-reelers, but the phenomenon of the multireel spectacle film came from Europe. From 1911 through 1913, Italian films in particular raised standards in length and production values.

It was not the occasional production of longer films that transformed the film industry at the end of 1913, however, but the features' displacement of single-reel films as the standard product of the industry. This transformation posed a major challenge to the system of production, distribution, and even exhibition that the MPPC had founded, and which had formed a context for Griffith's work at Biograph. The system of weekly releases and standing orders with exchanges did not adapt itself immediately to the appearance of multireel films. The MPPC had to make feature films without dismantling its already existing production and distribution system based on single-reel films. As Janet Staiger has shown, the policy of standing orders and maintaining price schedules based on single-reel films created economic disadvantages for trust features.[9]

The arrival of feature films gives the period that ends Griffith's Biograph career a sense of déjà vu. Once again, the industry had to redefine its commodity, and this redefinition showed again the interrelation between the narrative form of films and the industrial system. The introduction of features provoked another crisis in narrative form, as viewer interest and narrative clarity had to be maintained over a longer period. The first wave of features even sparked a renewed call for film lecturers as narrative aids because "there are at least three films out of ten which are difficult to understand without some sort of explanation." Further, in the longer feature format the lecturer could relieve the "natural tension and impatience" the new length would bring.[10]

Longer films also allowed more extensive and complete film drama, different from the compression necessary in the single reel film. Once again, film's increased narrative ambitions led to invoking the stage as a model. Ingevald Oes of Great Northern, pioneer in multireel features with its imports from Denmark, felt that feature films brought films closer to the stage ideal.[11] Recalling 1908–9, the ambition of the *films d'art* reappeared in 1912–13 with an extended film length allowing closer approximations of stage plays. It is at this point that the bifurcation Jean Mitry makes between narrativity and theatricality represents radical alternatives for filmmakers.

But once again, the theatrical influence on early features should not be viewed monolithically. If certain features seemed to return to an earlier approach to space and time, and further stylistic analysis is needed of these films, they also extended the ambitions of length and narrative complexity introduced in 1908–9. These challenges were answered by further developments in filmic discourse, as a feature such as Griffith's *The Birth of a Nation* (1915) showed. Further, the refinements in mise-en-scène offered by both French and Italian features of the period made important contributions to film's narrative discourse. The ambition of feature films could not be fulfilled by a return to theatricality of the *films d'art* sort, but rather called on the combined compositional resources of the Italian films and the control of space and time offered in Griffith's spectacle films from his late Biograph period. It is precisely such a synthesis that is sketched in *Judith of Bethulia* (1913) and fulfilled by *The Birth of a Nation*.

Stylistic development and experiment continued in Griffith's Biograph films during the later years. The excitement in studying his Biograph career lies in the fact that his style continued to develop, with new approaches attempted and old ones abandoned. However, by the end of 1909, the basis for later stylistic development had been laid. The changes that occurred in 1910–13 had roots in the earlier developments. While the possibilities of the narrator system were far from exhausted, its future evolution had been charted.[12]

Lasting changes came to Biograph in 1910. It was in December of 1909 that Biograph added a second production unit. Although Griffith's contract with the company makes it clear that he supervised these productions, Biograph releases began to appear that were not personally directed by Griffith. How much control he exerted over these films remains a subject for further research. Although there are indications about which films Griffith directed from this period, the director could be disputed for a few.

In the beginning of 1910 the Biograph Company made their first voyage to the West Coast. Spurred on by the success of the Cuddebackville films and the new popularity of Westerns, which led a number of production companies to trek West in search of authentic and picturesque locations, Griffith led the company to the Los Angeles area. Profiting by their escape from New York winters, the company stayed until mid-April, shooting films in genres which took advantage of the varied terrains the area offered. The trip was a harbinger of the eventual shift of American film production from the East to the West Coast and became a yearly pilgrimage for Griffith and company, stretching in 1913 into a seven-month stay.

But the films themselves claim chief focus; aspects of Griffith's later style developed from approaches laid out in the films of 1909. The triumph of the verisimilar style of acting marks one of the biggest differences between the films of 1909 and those of 1912–13. While fully underway by 1909, its complete development only came in the later years. Some Griffith actors (e.g., Wilfred Lucas) never completely abandoned the conventional or exaggerated gestures of the histrionic style, but versimilar performances dominated the later films. Pickford hit her stride in 1910, and continued to turn in outstanding performances on her return to Biograph in 1912 after her brief stay at IMP. Her performances in In the Seasons of Buds, An Arcadian Maid, Simple Charity, A Plain Song (all 1910), Home Folks, The New York Hat, and My Baby (all 1912) still astonish with the intimacy they achieve, conveying a maximum of emotional revelation with a minimum of codified gesture. This is not to slight the contribution of such members of the Biograph stock company as Claire McDowall, Mack Sennett, Marion Sunshine, W. Chrystie Miller, Blanche Sweet, Joseph Graybill, Lionel Barrymore, Harry Carey, Elmer Booth, or Lillian Gish—all of whom have at least one extraordinary performance to their credit, while several (such as Blanche Sweet) have dozens. Both Robert Harron and Mae Marsh had no stage experience, yet supplied some of the most spontaneous and unmannered performances at Biograph. "Restraint in expression" often became literal in these late films, as in Lillian Gish's and Lionel Barrymore's almost motionless reaction to the impending foreclosure on their store in The Lady and the Mouse (1913).

Russell Merritt has offered the most complete analysis of a late Biograph performance in his treatment of Blanche Sweet's powerful portrayal of The Painted Lady (1912). In this detailed and subtle reading Merritt isolates two performance elements which frequently appear in the late films. The first is a development of the verisimilar technique Roberta Pearson calls "byplay with props." As Merritt shows, Sweet in this film creates a vertible interior monologue by drawing the spectator's attention to psychologically loaded objects.[13] But this reliance on props to express psychology was supported by a new stress on facial expressions. In a single medium shot, Sweet's face goes through a range of transformations revealing her conflicting emotions and gradual realizations.[14]

This focus on the face did not close off naturalist attention to the actors' total bodies. But in a place of the athletic movements of the histrionic style, late Biograph actors created performances that reflected character and states of mind through gait, posture, and pace. Pickford's performance in *An Arcadian Maid* (1910) shows a mastery of this physical style. This unsentimental drama portrays the seduction and betrayal of a simple-minded and unattractive rural domestic drudge by an itinerate peddlar (Mack Sennett), who manipulates her into stealing her master's savings. She agrees to the crime, thinking they will start a new life on the money, only to find herself abandoned by the peddlar once he has the loot.

Pickford's weary gait as she trudges through the fields in the film's opening shots expresses the toil and monotony of her life. In a direct contrast, Sennett is introduced moving through the same locations, his step springy, with a jaunty sway to his arms and shoulders. His snappy gestures as he displays his trinkets to the mistress of the farm provoke Pickford's open-mouthed fascination. After the mistress reenters the house, Sennett approaches Pickford, bent over her wash at the farmyard well. She notices him and does an embarrassed, clumsy curtsy. Sennett twists his moustache and presents Mary with a small box of rings from which to choose. She turns away shyly and then, turning back, quickly points to one. As Sennett lifts it out, she wipes her soapy hands on her apron. He slips the ring on her finger as she wipes her brow with her other hand and drops another awkward curtsy. Sennett examines her, gives his moustache another quick twist, and turns to trot off at his jaunty pace. Mary turns her back to the camera as she watches him leave. He pauses and turns back to her, doffing his hat, which elicits a final curtsy from Mary, before he waves and leaves the frame. Mary turns back toward the camera, her mouth hanging open. She shakes her head as if to dispel her amazement and returns to her scrubbing. Stopping suddenly, she takes off her new ring and places it carefully inside her blouse before she resumes her chore.

Both Sennett and Pickford have created fullbodied characters with a variety of gestures and interactions. The contrast between Pickford's slow-paced gestures and bashful reactions and Sennett's energy and confidence creates a dramatic encounter long before the intrigue begins. Even Sennett's twisting of his moustache does not read as a conventional sign of villainy, but as the flirting gesture of a small-time dandy. This physical characterization allows subtle motivations to guide the plot.

It becomes clear, for example, that Pickford does not agree to the theft simply because of a sexual seduction. She is attracted to Sennett's energy and zest,—the contrast he presents to her wearisome environment and oppressed physical being. After their first clandestine meeting and kiss, Pickford again watches Sennett as he leaves. Alone, she then turns to the camera, hikes up her belt, and walks forward, swinging her arms in an awkward imitation of Sennett's gait. This private moment, with its humor and pathos, reveals to the audience a hidden and repressed side to the maid, conveyed not by a gestural soliloquy, but by individualized behavior.

Griffith turns resolutely away from the histrionic mode and its exhibitionist scenography by exploring these private moments witnessed only by the camera. In his late Biograph films, as well as in his features, Griffith parlayed the voyeuristic scenography of the cinema of narrative intergration into a new conceptualization of the relation between the actor and the camera. Although founded on the verisimilar style's rejection of conventional gestures and the self-conscious theatricality they involved, Griffith's use of the camera to penetrate a character's privacy conceives of the actor as only one part of a film performance. The camera's effect on the actor and the spectator's identification with the camera are also powerful components.

This aspect of Griffith's style is difficult to pin down, and some theoretical consideration of early film acting is needed. The performers in the cinema of attractions greeted the camera's gaze with gusto, employing glances, winks, and nods. With the establishment of a coherent diegesis, any acknowledgment of the camera became taboo, condemned by critics as destructive of the psychological effect essential for an involved spectator. But the actor in the cinema of narrative integration had to be both aware of the camera and yet seem not to be aware.

The camera is no longer the stand-in for the responsive audience of vaudeville theater. It becomes a more spectral presence, whose power forces the actor not to address or look at it directly. In the late Biograph films Griffith created a new relationship between performer and camera, one based on an understanding of the camera, and therefore the cinema spectator, as a powerful voyeur with the ability to penetrate into the character's most private reaches. Griffith used the camera's undeviating stare to extract a depth of characterization from his actors, almost in spite of them. In a powerful performance by Pickford, Harron, Marsh, or Gish, one senses that Griffith and the camera have wrested something from them, going beneath the surface of a conscious performance.

This performance style rests very much on the strictures that emerging film critics, such as Frank Woods of the *Dramatic Mirror,* laid down against the actor consciously displaying himself or herself. "The good director," Woods had intoned in his weekly column on films, "is constant and persistent in his instruction to his players to keep their eyes away from the camera and the good players try to obey this injunction."[15] The actor must not greet the camera's gaze because that act would not only make the spectator aware of the camera, but also aware of the actor acting and aware of the act of watching. As Woods put it; "When the movement or attitude of the player is obviously unnatural in turning his face towards the camera, he betrays by the act the fact that he is acting—that there is someone in front unseen by the spectators to whom the actor is addressing himself. Immediately the sense of reality is destroyed and the hypnotic illusion that has taken possession of the spectator's mind, holding him by the power of visual suggestion, is gone."[16]

Woods describes an essential aspect of classical cinema which Christian Metz has described as the voyeuristic position of the film spectator: "The cinema's voyeurism must (of necessity) do without any very clear mark of consent on the part of the object." For Metz, and this accords with Woods's description of the process, the relation between film and spectator is founded upon a spectacle which "*lets* itself be seen without *presenting* itself to be seen."[17] In his late Biograph films Griffith pushed this relation to an extreme, creating a new confrontation between camera and actor, one based on the invisible power of the viewer as voyeur. In Griffith's cinema, the spectator is in a position of visual mastery because he or she can never be seen by the spectacle being watched. The actor, as long as he or she does not greet the camera's gaze, appears vulnerable because of being visible. The spectator can identify with the camera's power to unmask and penetrate into the hidden feelings of the figure on the screen.

Griffith uses this probing voyeur camera to create an extraordinary sense of intimacy with his actors and particularly his actresses—the phallic metaphors are not accidental. Inspired by the ideal of acting "that appears not to be acting," a phrase used by Woods in his columns on film acting, Griffith evokes subtle gestures from his actors that make it appear we are discovering moments of revelation rather than having them presented to us.[18] The sequence from *The Lady and the Mouse* (pp. 266–67) exemplifies this; at a moment when she believes she is alone, we watch Lillian Gish's reluctance to drown a mouse caught in a trap. The tenderness which underlies her determined character is revealed by this private moment, which is witnessed by an intradiegetic voyeur as well, a young boarder who watches her secretly from the doorway.

The powerful voyeur camera, stripping away both presence and pretense, destroyed the histrionic style as much as any other factor. The conscious self-presentation of the histrionic style stressed the power of the actor. The voyeur camera empowers the spectator as it seemingly catches the actor in a moment of self-revelation. The extreme development of the powerful camera comes—paradoxically—in moments in which Biograph actors actually do acknowledge the presence of the camera, but in a diametrically different manner than the cocky salutes and saucy winks shared with the camera by performers in the cinema of attractions. Rather than exhibiting themselves, Griffith's actors seem at these moments to hide from the camera, as if from a sense of shame.

The most frequent form of this concealment later became a filmic convention, one which inscribes the voyeuristic conception of the cinema of narrative integration—the kiss that is hidden from the camera. But before it became a cliche, Griffith endowed it with formal invention, such as the close-up of hands which displace the kiss in *The Lady and the Mouse* or the shadow kiss in *The School Teacher and the Waif* (1912). *A Timely Interception*, (1913) shows the contrasting emotional situations which prompted this game of visual hide and seek. First, Griffith conceals a kiss as Lillian Gish hides behind a door after she and Bobby Harron have been given her father's permission to marry. Harron sticks his head behind the door to kiss her, and Gish's hand appears on his shoulder pulling him entirely into her concealed space. Later in the film, this hiding from the camera takes on a different emotional tone. Financial disaster cancels Harron and Gish's wedding, and Gish enters the same location as the earlier shot, weeping. Then, as if ashamed of her tears, she hides again behind the door, even though there is no one to witness her emotion—except the camera. Rather than denying the spectator's fantasy of visual mastery, Gish's actions acknowledge it by defending herself against it.

The Biograph actors' technique was to play key emotional scenes with their back to the camera, very different from the Vitagraph practice of actors having their backs to the camera at undramatic moments. For example, Wilfred Lucas sits with his back to the camera as he beholds the charred ruins of his plantation on his return from the Civil War in *Swords and Hearts* (1911). The practice indirectly acknowledges the pressure exerted by the voyeur camera. The most extended sequence of hiding emotion from the camera comes in *Her Mother's Oath* (1913). When Dorthy Gish returns home after being publicly shamed in church, she hides her face behind a prayer book as she enters her parlor. Again, it is the camera's gaze from which the book shields her; she puts it down after she turns away from the camera. In the next shot she enters her bedroom, rather awkwardly, with her back turned to the camera. She kneels before her bed and covers her face with her hands. Then, to further hide her shame, she buries her face in the bedclothes, pulling the quilt over her head.

At such extreme moments Griffith makes the spectator aware of his or her voyeuristic position without, however, undermining visual mastery of the scene or invisible invulnerability. One almost feels like averting one's eyes. If there is a sadism implicit in the camera's voyeurism, it is balanced in these moments by a rush of sympathy and concern. These private moments solicit audience involvement, in part by blocking it. Exerting pressure on what it films, the camera has stripped the character bare, puncturing the public facade and revealing intimate emotions. The secret of this late acting style lies in sensitizing performers to the role of camera as voyeur and witness. The camera is not a communal public audience with which the actor can share a joke, but a single probing eye. Individually, each member of the audience can identify with this isolated viewpoint, capable of evoking both intimacy and shame. But in contrast to the cinema of attraction, whose exhibitionist address punctures the diegetic world of the film, these probes directed at the actors increase the spectator's involvement with the characters and world of the story. Like ink into a blotter, we become absorbed into this diegetic world through our act of voyeurism.[19]

Perhaps even more than the change in acting style, one can immediately differentiate a later Biograph film from a 1908–9 film by the increase in the number of shots. The average number of shots per thousand-foot reel—rather than film, because some films were "split reels," two on one reel and some later films were two-reelers, although the vast majority of films were one-reelers—increased steadily during Griffith's Biograph career (table 1).[20] The number of shots per reel not only increases over the years, but it also accelerates sharply in 1910. Melodramas with races to the rescue or chases frequently have the most shots, but such comedies as *When a Man Loves* or *The Lady and the Mouse* also generated large numbers of shots.

Although parallel editing continued to provide the royal road of the narrator system, overlapping cuts and analytical editing began to play a role in 1912 and 1913. Only in these years did Griffith begin to break a single space into separate shots, achieving the syntagm that Christian Metz calls the scene. A sequence from a film from January of 1912, *The Girl and Her Trust*, which reworks the plot of Biograph's *The Lonedale Operator* (1911), expands

Table 1. Shots per Reel, Griffith's Biograph Files, 1908–13

Year	Average Number Shots (per 1,000 feet)	Film Viewed with Largest Number of Shots	Number of Shots
1908	16.6	*The Guerrilla*	45
1909	24.8	*The Lonely Villa*	52
1910	44.4	*When a Man Loves*	85
1911	71.4	*A Terrible Discovery*	122
1912	82	*The Girl and Her Trust*	126
1913	87.8	*The Lady and the Mouse*	118

the explanatory insert close-ups found in 1908 and 1909 into an extended sequence. Grace (Dorothy Bernard), a telegraph operator in an isolated train station, is threatened by tramps attempting to steal a payroll. Intercutting dominates the film, cutting from Grace to her engineer boyfriend, or from Grace within the office to the tramps on the other side of the door. But when Grace decides to frighten the tramps away by making them believe she has a gun, Griffith cuts together different shot sizes within a single overlapping location to convey her ingenuous scheme:

> Shot seventy-three: Long shot of interior office, framing Grace's entire standing figure. She is at the door listening to the tramps trying to force the lock on the other side. She moves to her desk and picks up a bullet and a pair of scissors, then returns to the door.
>
> Shot seventy-four: An extreme close-up of the doorknob and keyhole below it. Grace's hand enters and fits the bullet into the keyhole.
>
> Shot seventy-five: Return to the long shot as in shot seventy-three. Grace stands up and backs away from the door. She waves her scissors in nervous indecision.
>
> Shot seventy-six: Cutaway to a full figure framing of the tramps on the other side of the door as they try to force it.
>
> Shot seventy-seven: Long shot. Grace picks up a hammer from the desk and moves resolutely towards the door. She bends down.
>
> Shot seventy-eight: Medium close-up of doorknob (farther back than shot seventy-four). Grace's head and shoulders fill the frame as she kneels. She raises the scissors in one hand and the hammer in the other.
>
> Shot seventy-nine: Cut-in to the extreme close-up of shot seventy-four, as Grace raises the hammer and hits the end of the scissors. She slumps a bit as nothing happens, then raises the hammer again.
>
> Shot eighty: Return to the medium close-up as Grace hits the scissors again.
>
> Shot eighty-one: Cutaway to the tramps (as in shot seventy-six) as they back away in alarm as gunsmoke comes from the door. They gesture to each other.
>
> Shot eighty-two: Grace in medium closeup against doorknob as she relaxes in relief. Gunsmoke pours from the keyhole. She rises up.

This sequence simply expands the motive for earlier close-ups—the enlargement of a narratively small detail—into a sequence. However the close-ups no longer enlarge a single object such as Blanche Sweet's much more pragmatic monkey wrench, used for the same purpose in *The Lonedale Operator,* but portray a process. Because this process is so bizarre, its various stages need to be detailed in order to be understood. It becomes an analytical sequence, with almost seamless cutting on action from shot to shot, prefiguring later classical continuity.[21]

The sequence from *The Lady and the Mouse* develops scene cutting much further, with dramatic relations between characters supplying the motives for a spatial analysis.

Shot fifty-eight: In medium long shot Lillian Gish (framed below knee but with space above her head) stands in a kitchen, holding a mouse in a trap over the wooden bucket in which her aunt has ordered her to drown it. Behind her to the right stands Harry Hyde in a doorway. She is unaware that he watches her (fig. 43).

Shot fifty-nine: Cut-in to a closer view of Gish (framed at thigh and eliminating the space above her head) as she examines the mouse (the position of her face and arm slightly different from shot fifty-eight). Hyde is not visible in this framing. (fig. 44).

Shot sixty: The right half of shot fifty-eight, eliminated in shot fifty-nine is now shown, as Hyde (framed at hip) looks off-screen at Gish; the kitchen table at the left overlaps these last two shots (fig. 45).

Shot sixty-one: Return to Gish (framed as in shot fifty-nine), lowering the trap toward the bucket but averting her eyes from the mouse's fate.

Shot sixty-two: Return to Hyde (framed as in sixty) as he looks on sympathetically.

Shot sixty-three: Gish (as in shot fifty-nine) continues to lower the trap, unable to watch.

43, 44, and 45: In *The Lady and the Mouse* (1912), with Lillian Gish and Harry Hyde, Griffith breaks down the medium-long shot into two medium shots in a way that anticipates later classical scene breakdown. Frame enlargement from 35mm print, courtesy of the Museum of Modern Art.

43

44

45

Shot sixty-four: Cut-in to a close-up of the trap being lowered into the water, the mouse climbing to the top to avoid the water. Gish's hand holds the trap at the top of the frame. The camera shoots the bucket from slightly above so that we see into it.

Shot sixty-five: Cut-out to the closer framing of Gish (as in shot fifty-nine) as she pulls the trap out of the bucket.

Shot sixty-six: Return to Hyde (as in shot sixty) as he smiles at her reluctance to drown the mouse.

Shot sixty-seven: Return to Gish (as in fifty-nine), the close framing emphasizing her facial expression. Her lip pouts as she comes to a decision.

Shot sixty-eight: Return to Hyde (as in sixty), laughing with pleasure. He leaves the frame.

Shot sixty-nine: Gish (as in fifty-nine) opens the mousetrap and bends out of the frame.

Shot seventy: Close-up of Gish's hand placing mousetrap on the floor, allowing the mouse to scamper out. This high-angle close-up also shows the hem of Gish's skirt and the toe of her foot in the corner of the screen. After the mouse escapes, Gish's hand enters again and picks up the empty trap.

Shot seventy-one: Return to the medium long shot of the kitchen (as in shot fifty-eight) as Gish's aunt (Kate Toncray) enters the kitchen. Gish tells her off and exits carrying the bucket.

The closer shot of Gish in shot fifty-nine does enlarge the small detail of the mouse scurrying in its trap, but equally important is its enlargement of Gish's face, cueing her reluctance to drown the mouse and allowing the audience to empathize with her problem. The cut-in to Hyde provides a nearly classical reaction shot and sets up a clear sight link between the two characters. Shot fifty-eight therefore functions as a master shot, which is then subdivided into smaller areas of narrative interest prefiguring the classical method of scene analysis. Within the context of a single location, Griffith continues to use alternation as he intercuts Gish's dilemma with Hyde's sympathetic reactions.

However, the sight link between Gish and Hyde differs from a classical point-of-view structure. The shots of Gish are by no means filmed from Hyde's perspective, in fact he really could not have a good view of her actions. Rather, both Gish, Hyde, and the medium-long shot of the kitchen are filmed from a frontal position that angles itself a bit in the shots that isolate each character (fig. 46). The spatial analysis of this sequence has no parallel in the films from 1908–9. The cut-ins direct attention to characters' decisions and reactions, providing a dramatic and psychological analysis. It inaugurates the scene breakdown of classical editing, with its establishing master shot, cut-ins to shots of characters and key details, and then the return to the master shot after the action is completed.[22] However, the frontal position of the camera in all shots still seems to derive from the frontality of a theatrical

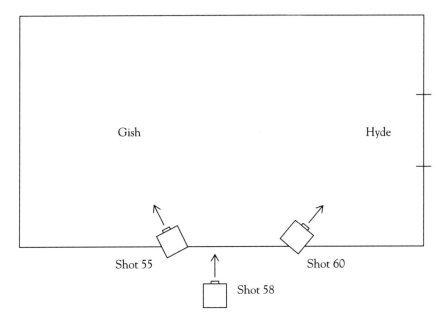

46. Camera positions in shots 55, 58 and 60 of *The Lady and the Mouse* (1912).

tableau shot. As opposed to the 180-degree axis which organizes the classical scene breakdown around the position of the characters in relation to each other, the fragmentation of this scene is unified by a frontal authorial view with a fixed orientation to an unmoving set. Sadoul's "le Monsieur de l'orchestre" has been divided rather than abolished.

The climax of this film also plays with fragmentation and character point of view, although more eccentrically. Hyde finally confesses his love for Gish and asks her to marry him. Griffith visualizes this proposal and its acceptance through a series of close-ups:

> Shot 108: A stairway landing. Gish and Hyde stand with Lionel Barrymore (her father). Hyde takes Gish out of the frame to the left, leaving Barrymore in the frame looking after them, somewhat shyly.
>
> Shot 109: A close shot framing Hyde and Gish's shoulders and arms as they face each other in a doorway. Gish waves her hand about, and Hyde takes it in his.
>
> Shot 110: Cut back to Barrymore, looking away from the scene, stroking his chin. As the shot ends, he slowly glances to the left.
>
> Shot 111 (framed as in 109): Hyde places Gish's hand on his shoulder. She pulls it away, and he drops his hand and arm resignedly.
>
> Shot 112: Return to Barrymore, looking left. He turns his head away, as if in reaction to this scene.

Shot 113 (same framing as 109): Gish coyly walks her fingers up Hyde's arm and on his shoulder. He grabs her hand.

Shot 114: Return to Barrymore rubbing his chin, with his eyes averted from the left. Gish and Hyde enter the landing from the left and inform him of their decision.

This sequence alternates between Barrymore and the synecdotally framed lovers. It is rooted in Barrymore's oblique point of view, which somewhat motivates the curious framing. The intercutting performs the familiar task of dramatically articulating the action (shot 109, proposal; shot 111, apparent rejection; shot 113, acceptance). However, Barrymore's point of view does not fully explain the framing, particularly because Barrymore's attention is apparently averted during some of the most important actions. The oblique framing comes as much from a playful narrator as from the limited perspective of a character. Griffith images this scene of erotic acceptance indirectly, drawing attention to the audience's voyeurlike position. With its defamiliarized framing, it becomes another estheticized Biograph image.

While the camera in the later Biograph films comes closer more frequently than it did in 1908–9, it also withdraws farther, expanding the frame with vistas of landscapes and expansive action, creating what Griffith called "distant views" in his 1913 *Dramatic Mirror* advertisement. This landscape pictorialism was well advanced in 1909 in such films as *The Mended Lute,* but the western landscapes offered by the first California trip inspired Griffith to panoramic compositions that explode theatrical framing. *Ramona* (1910), which Griffith cited in the *Dramatic Mirror* as the first film with "distant views," provides the model for all later panoramic shots, as the Indian Allessandro (Henry Walthall) witnesses the burning of his village from a mountainside aerie. The contrast in scale between Allessandro (framed full figure in the foreground) and the they tiny figures seen scurrying below as smoke rises from the conflagration introduces a planar tension Griffith had not achieved before. A number of later films particularly spectacle films such as *The Massacre* (1912), which reproduces this composition in another raid on an Indian village, also use these distant views to create dramatic planes of action.

But these extreme long shots were not limited to scenes of expansive action such as battles or wagon trains. Beginning in 1911, Griffith drew psychological connotations from placing characters within vast spaces. *The Failure* frames Wilfred Lucas in an extreme long shot as he leaves town after the collapse of his business, his small scale in the shot expressing his overwhelming despair. Expanding upon the pictorial composition of the lovers in *The Mended Lute,* Griffith shot seaside lovers from mountainside vistas, producing lyrical images in *A Lodging for the Night* and *The Sands of Dee* (both from 1912).

The effects of the closer or more distant framings cannot be described fully outside of their place in edited sequences. This is particularly true in the spectacle films that Griffith began to turn out after 1909. Undoubtedly, the ambition to make films with crowds of extras and "sensation scenes" of expansive action had long been an ambition the author of *War*, with its portrayal of the course of the American Revolution and its debt to the spectacle stage of Belasco and Steele McKay. As budgets increased at Biograph, Griffith began to expand the horizons of the action film. A remarkable Civil War film from the end of 1909, *The Honor of His Family*, shows the first stirrings of this impulse in its elaborate battle scenes. Throughout 1910, both Westerns and Civil War films included "sensation scene" battles. In 1911, *The Last Drop of Water* was accompanied by pre-release publicity which announced the film under the title *Crossing the Plains in the 1840's*, uncommon for Biograph, which declared the production used two hundred cowboys, eleven prairie schooners, and a hundred horses.[23] This may exaggerate the facts a bit, but the film does exceed any previous Biograph production in spectacular outfittings. Civil War films from 1911, such as *Swords and Hearts* and *The Battle*, also add to Griffith's pro-filmic elaborations, with battle sequences and house burnings.

In 1912, Griffith's spectacular productions reached a new height that the 1913 spectacles, the three-reel *The Battle of Elderbush Gulch* and the four-reel *Judith of Bethulia*, could only expand upon by breaking out of the one-reel format. Griffith's naturalist's interest in the environment took on the recreation of vanished civilizations in his caveman film *Man's Genesis* and his masterpiece of Indian civilization before Columbus, *A Pueblo Legend*, filmed on location at the Iseleta pueblo in New Mexico. The sensational battle sequence was given definitive form through Griffith's masterful editing in three spectacle films set in different periods: *A Feud in the Kentucky Hills* (a hillbilly mountaineer film), *The Informer* (a Civil War film whose climax resembles *The Birth of a Nation*), and *The Massacre* (a Western).

The editing in these battle sequences are demonstrations of the narrator system's control of space and tempo, weaving dramatic action from a range of shot sizes and perspectives. The battle that ends *The Massacre* intercuts close-ups and distant views of the action, as a series of four shots from this nearly fifty-shot sequence shows:

> Shot 128: A view from a mountainside of the Indian attack in the valley below. Indians and besieged settlers appear as tiny figures as they swarm in frenzied motion (fig. 47). The settlers have grouped together in a small knot, as the Indians, mounted on horses, ride around them. The screen is dotted with small puffs of gunfire.
>
> Shot 129: Cut-in to a medium long shot of the settlers, filmed from ground level (fig. 48). Gunsmoke nearly obscures them at the end of the shot.
>
> Shot 130: Cut-in to an even closer view of the settlers, a medium shot focusing on two fancily dressed gamblers who fire revolvers at the Indians. Other

settlers are visible behind them, and in the background the circling Indians can be glimpsed.

Shot 131: Cut-in again to a medium-close shot of the main character of the film, a settler woman (Blanche Sweet). She is framed at the waist as she cowers at the center of the group, sheltering her baby (fig. 49). She is placed between antithetical elements: a priest who reads his Bible in terror at the left and a hand firing a revolver, very large in the frame, on the right. With each recoil of the revolver, Sweet covers the ears of her crying baby.

This four-shot sequence moves steadily from a panoramic overview of the action to an intimate glimpse of a personal and empathetic moment. Such editing shows more than a mastery of space; Griffith's dramaturgy picks up both the sweep of action and the vulnerable human detail and interrelates them. As the battle continues, Griffith directly juxtaposes the extreme long shots and closer shots, the change in shot scale increasing dramatic intensity. This intra-scene cutting develops the syntagm of the scene, but without the theatrical frontality that appears in the interior action of *The Lady and the Mouse*.

47, 48, and 49: In the battle sequence from *The Massacre* (1912), Griffith cuts fluidly among panoramic views of the battle, to long shots of the action, to medium close-ups of details such as Blanche Sweet shielding her baby's ears from the noise of gunfire. Frame enlargements from prints made from Paper Print Collection, Library of Congress.

47

48

49

The response to California landscapes that inspired the distant views also brings a new imagistic sense of space and environment to the later Biograph films, a tendency begun in 1909 by the films shot in Cuddebackville. Griffith used the varied terrains and locations California offered. Deserts, mountains, mission settlements, seacoasts, as well as urban streets, railway stations, oilfields, and the gardens of Hollywood, appear in the California films. The desert provided an environment unlike anything in Griffith's previous films and inspired dark naturalistic treatments of humanity's battle against the elements. A strong series of films set in the desert—*Over Silent Paths* (1910), *The Last Drop of Water, Under Burning Skies, The Female of the Species, Man's Lust for Gold* (all 1912), and *Just Gold* (1913)—pit greed, jealousy, and endurance against a hostile environment. Lush pastoral landscapes (introduced in films like *The Country Doctor*) continue to appear in Biograph films, however. *Just Gold*, in fact, intercuts the green and blossoming farm the characters leave with the arid desert in which they search for gold and find madness and death.

Likewise, the nearly documentary detailing of urban environments begun in 1908 continues as a recurring element in later Biographs filmed in New York. A shot of Rivington Street in *A Child of the Ghetto* (1910) appears to film Biograph actress Dorthy West from a hidden position as she moves among peddlars' carts, bearded Orthodox Jews, and unceasing streams of women and children, some of whom seem to glimpse the camera. A fight which breaks out in the background of a slum street scene in *Bobby the Coward* (1911) seems to be a distraction Griffith has arranged, as he had in 1908, to keep the attention of the crowd away from the camera.

However, by 1912 Griffith was creating his own street scenes, as the presence of familiar Biograph extras on the street and stoops of *The Inner Circle* reveals. But this is all that gives them away, as Griffith models these scenes on his earlier candid shots. The extras are positioned casually across the frame, and each is given a specific activity, like a little girl in the foreground who picks, first, her nose, and then, her teeth. Griffith's masterpiece of this realist arrangement is *The Musketeers of Pig Alley* (1912). In compositions that show careful observation of the vitality and spontaneity of the Lower East Side, Griffith orchestrates the textures of glass, fruit, paper, skin, fabric, hair, and brickwork in a constantly changing clash of surfaces; one can almost hear and smell the close-packed, turn-of-the-century urban world. Throughout the film, Griffith and Bitzer's images recall the New York slum photographs of Jacob Riis which may well have supplied a direct inspiration for the film.

Movement within the frame formed an early aspect of Griffith and Bitzer's composition. This sometimes took on a special dramatic effect, as in exits toward the camera. Bitzer and Griffith were well aware of the often-startling effect of enlargement that movement toward the camera could create, and had, in fact, featured it in a melodrama about escaped lunatics, *Where the Breakers Roar* (1908). In the later films this movement is more deliberate, slower, and often expresses psychological intensity. In *Conscience* (1910), a hunter (Joseph Graybill) who has accidentally shot a woman flees through the woods. He finally slows down and approaches the camera, moving into a facial close-up. Graybill pauses, his face filled with guilt and terror, before he exits the frame. Although Graybill in effect "moves toward the front" to convey his emotion, he by no means acknowledges the camera with an aside. Rather the camera captures a private moment of oppressive guilt.

In a madhouse drama from 1913, *The House of Darkness*, Griffith mines this technique for its threatening and suspenseful effects. The shot begins with a grove of trees in slightly soft focus. An escaped lunatic (Charles Mailes) appears in the background of the shot peering through the branches and seemingly playing peek-a-boo with the camera. He then disappears off left. After a moment, his head pops suddenly into view around a tree trunk in close-up and sharp focus. Slowly, he emerges from behind the tree, then finally exits left. This shot shows the increased sophistication of Griffith and Bitzer's camerawork at the end of the Biograph period. To the basic effect of enlargement with its threatening overtones, the shot adds an element of interruption (the exit off-screen) and surprise (the sudden reentry, now much larger).

Griffith's most famous use of this technique, and the most technically controlled, appears in *The Musketeers of Pig Alley*. The show-down between rival gangs in this slum melodrama is portrayed by a series of shots of the gangsters maneuvering through streets and alleyways. Many of these shots end with the gangsters exiting into close-up. But in the climactic shot of this sequence, Griffith pushes the technique further. The Snapper Kid (Elmer Booth) emerges from the edge of a wall and inches his way toward the camera until his face fills the right half of the frame. His eyes shift back and forth, then he exits right, followed by his cohorts. Not only is this movement toward the camera closer than the previous examples, but there is also an obvious adjustment of focus as the Kid moves into close-up. The shot from *The House of Darkness* (made six months later) avoids this by setting the focus for Mailes's close-up appearance so that the background appears in soft focus throughout the shot, even when the lunatic lurks in this area. But in *Musketeers*, Booth remains in sharp focus while in the mid-ground at the beginning of the shot, and in close-up at the end; his companions become blurred a bit as focus shifts to the foreground. The clarity of this focus change is a tribute to Bitzer's skill as an operator in a period when changing focus while shooting was a difficult and often risky business.[24]

The emblematic images, crystalizations of emotional overtones in late 1909 films, continue to appear in later Biograph films, with pictorial compositions heightening their expressivity. But as in *The Country Doctor* or *Lines of White*, the power of these images comes as much from their place in the film's narrative structure as their composition. The opening and closing shots of *The Inner Circle* (1912) recall *The Country Doctor*'s circular structure. The first shot introduces a poor Italian widower and establishes his love for his daughter and devotion to the memory of his wife. Fading in on a rather bare tenement parlor, the composition is dominated by a large table on which a framed picture (presumably of his dead wife) is set. On the left a little girl sleeps in a chair. The widower (Adolph Lestina) enters from the right, holding a flower. He places the flower before the picture, then kisses his daughter before he goes out. At the film's end the widower has been killed while saving his daughter from a bomb placed by a "black hand" extortion gang. The final shot returns again to the tenement parlor, now empty; the picture of the dead wife remains on the table. The shot fades out. As in *The Country Doctor*, Griffith gives this emptiness a voice, converting objects into signs of absent characters and recalling their loss.

In some films this emblematic quality is pushed toward allegory. With these images, composition no longer simply supplies a realist environment but becomes a symbolic horizon reflecting the significance of the story. A film constructed around such resonant imagery is *The Sands of Dee* (1912), adapted from Charles Kinglsey's poem. Of all Griffith's adaptations of narrative poems, this seems the most poetic, with its recurring use of pictorial composition to form emotional images. In perhaps the most powerful of Griffith's many sea films, the sea's symbolic presence threads its way throughout the film, attaining an ironic climax at the end. In the opening scenes the sea forms a graceful pictorial background to the introduction of Mary (Mae Marsh) and her young suitor Bobby (Bobby Harron). The Santa Monica locations provide Bitzer with his most picturesque landscapes. Beach, sea-worn rocks, and cliffs provide an environment in which the characters seem to become one with their surroundings. A deliberate pictorial posing of the actors characterizes this film, carefully integrating human forms with those of nature. Few Griffith films so strongly recall the composition of late-Victorian or pre-Raphaelite paintings as *The Sands of Dee*.

As the mood of the film darkens, the surroundings continue to echo the postures and evoke the emotions of the characters. At points, Griffith depends more on the emotional resonance of the image, and particularly the landscape, than the expressivity of the actors, who are greatly restrained. After seeing Mary flirting with a seaside painter on holiday, Bobby wanders off to a formation of sea rock by the shore. As he slumps sadly against the rocks, his back turned to the camera, his posture echoes the rocky forms that surround him. Later in the film, after being abandoned by her painter-seducer and banished by her puritanical father, Mary—in despair—comes to the shore and stands against the surf-pounded rocks, handling her false engagement ring (fig. 50). As she throws it over her shoulder into the ocean, the background of the shot is filled with cascades of white water, the surf running over the rocky ledges that jut into the sea. She turns her back to the camera and watches the foam-dripping rocks, then walks off. It is as though these drenched and streaming rocks do her weeping for her.

The final shot of Mary, before she drowns herself, finds her perched on a sea rock, already surrounded by surf. She sits motionless in one of the film's most pictorial poses. Her knees are drawn up, her head sloped down, her back forming a graceful arc against the sea, her arms dangling down limp towards the water. This image of her, cut off from the land, foreshadows her watery death.

The sea has gradually moved in the film from a picturesque overtone to an increasingly dramatic and even malevolent, although still strikingly beautiful, dominant. This movement reaches its apogee in one of Griffith's strongest "empty" shots, in which the sea seems to sweep the screen free of characters. Shot from a somewhat high camera angle and rather close camera position,

50. Mae Marsh about to throw her false engagement ring into the sea, images of which dominate *The Sands of Dee* (1912). Frame enlargement from 16mm print, courtesy of Museum of Modern Art.

it shows a strip of beach, with lines of foam curving gently onto it as the waves glide in and retreat. No living thing stirs, and the frame shuts out the horizon. This graceful and strongly pictorial image serves as a replacement for Mary's suicide. It is introduced by an intertitle, a quote from Kingsley's poem, for which Griffith and Bitzer provide a precise visual equivalent:

> The creeping tide came up along the sea
> And o'er and o'er the sea
> And round and round the sea
> And never home came she.

The following shot, again from a somewhat high camera angle but close camera position, shows Mary's body floating lifelessly in the sea.

The sea also dominates the end of the film. After Bobby pulls Mary's body from the sea, the shot fades as he carries her along the shore, followed by her grieving parents. The three shots that follow form a ghostly epilogue, an extended lyrical postscript. First, two fishermen, their nets slung over their backs, stand in the same seaside location at which Mary earlier tossed her ring into the ocean. Watching off-screen, one of them cups his hand to his ear as if hearing something in the distance. The other points off right. An intertitle follows, "But still the boat men hear her call the cattle home across the sands o'Dee." There follows a haunting, pictorially conceived shot. Mary stands in the distance on the sea cliffs. She appears as a small, ghostlike white figure, her hand raised to her mouth as if calling. The cliffs surround her with eerily jagged shapes while the sea rushes in below her. The next shot returns to the fishermen who walk slowly off to the right, as if drawn by her phantom call. After they leave the frame, the camera holds on the ocean and begins a very slow fade on this empty space. The surf crashes on the rocks in the background, sending up plumes of spray, and the lapping of the waves on the shore in the foreground ends the film. Again, emptiness provides an echo chamber for the emotions accumulated by the film.

A shot without any characters also ends the 1913 Western *The Yaqui Cur*. Kira (Bobby Harron) is a Christian Indian abandoned by his tribe and murdered by white men. Kira's death is a Christian sacrifice; he takes the blame for the death of a white man actually killed by his friend Ocalla (Walter Miller). After Kira's death, the film follows Ocalla and his wife as they camp for the night. The shots of setting up their camp are backlit by the setting sun, as earlier a key shot of Kira had been. The last four shots of the film cut between the couple as they sit sadly in the tent interior, meditating on their friend's sacrifice, and exterior views of the landscape as the sun sinks behind the mountainous cliffs. The film ends with a shot of the sun disappearing below the horizon, a symbolic image of Kira's sacrifice, emphasizing its religious overtones.

The most allegorical use of an empty finale occurs in another 1913 Western, *Just Gold*. The film contrasts the fates of three brothers who head West searching for gold (Charles West, Alfred Paget, and Joseph McDermott) with a fourth brother (Lionel Barrymore), who obeys his mother's wish and stays on the family's midwestern farm. Although initially disconsolate, Barrymore finds love and contentment at home, while his brothers all die, killed over gold claims.

The two final shots of the film follow the deaths the last two brothers, who have shot each other in the interior of their gold diggings. Griffith slowly fades in on the entrance to the excavation. No character is seen; the only movement within the frame comes from wind-blown dust. As has been true in most of the examples cited from Griffith's late Biograph films, this emptiness becomes a sign of death. The shot fades out. The final shot of the film fades in. The use of the fade in these images, like the fades in *The Sands of Dee*, recalls their prototype in *Lines of White on a Sullen Sea;* they stress the significance of the shots as much as indicating the passage of time. In the interior of the diggings lie two skeletons, the brothers' remains, the hand of one extending toward the gold ore. The only movement comes from the grass growing among the dry bones, rustled by the wind (fig. 51). In this emblem of Griffith's pessimistic naturalism, natural forces have triumphed over human,

51. The final image in *Just Gold* (1913), skeleton hands reaching for gold ore.

reducing the men to their mineral elements. But the human remains frozen in a gesture of greed also compose a classical allegorical image. This *momento mori* stands as an archetype of allegory's frozen significance. As Walter Benjamin states, "In allegory the observer is confronted with the *fancies hippocratia* of history as a petrified, primordial landscape. Everything about history that, from the very beginning, has been untimely, sorrowful, unsuccessful, is expressed in a face—or rather in a death's head. . . . The greater the significance, the greater the subjection to death, because death digs most deeply the jagged line between physical nature and significance."[25]

Although these "empty" shots are not frequent in Griffith's later films, they are exemplary of Griffith's use of images within the narrator system. The shots can function without characters because their significance has become fully defined within the story. Yet their narrative role is complex, precisely because they add no further information to the story. The death and absences they mark are portrayed more directly in other shots. In their role as final images they brake the flow of events and confirm the completeness of the story by reflecting back on events and emotions within the film via signs—emblems or metaphors such as the widower's portrait of his wife, the sunset representing Kira's sacrifice, the brothers' dry bones.

In this way, they direct the viewer's attention to the structure of the film, its final economy and closure, relating, as in the pans in *The Country Doctor*, to the "directing function," of voice, its concern with the internal organization of the text.[26] And yet at the same time, like all of Griffith's instances of voice, they are not metadiegetic. These images present the world of the story in the process of emptying itself and thereby accomplishing its completeness. If the characters have disappeared from these shots, it is because the film's significance has reached a point of clarity which no longer has need of them. These shots are empty of characters and action because they are replete with meaning.[27]

If, as in *The Country Doctor*, the directing gestures of the narrator system lead into the world of a story rather than deflecting attention away from it with a diegesis puncturing alienation effect, nonetheless this leading gesture is strongly felt and has a determinate effect on the way the film is received. Griffith's style bends discourse to the exigencies of story, but this does not mean that discourse is discarded or lost along the way. We return again to the central duality of narrative art: the telling of a story, the act and process of narrating which brings the story into being. The most seemingly classical of Griffith's uses of filmic discourse, the creation of narrative suspense, supplies a clear example of the essential part that the narrator, or the structuring narrative discourse, plays in our involvement with the story.

Buried in the Library of Congress's paper print collection Griffith has left a film (never to my knowledge discussed before) that contains a brief sequence that seems designed to call attention to the power of the narrator in creating suspense. This sequence comes from *His Lesson* (1912), which re-works a familiar Biograph triangle. An overworked and neglected country wife (Dorothy Bernard) becomes enamoured with a holiday fisherman from the city (Charles West). Learning of the flirtation, the husband (Edwin August) sets out to kill his would-be rival. The sequence covers this encounter between the two men, after the farmer has trailed the fisherman through the woods.

> Shot sixty: August confronts West at the edge of a clearing, trees visible behind them (fig. 52). As the two men stand arguing, the camera pans away from them to the right, passing over a grove of trees (fig. 53), coming to rest on one tree as the breeze rustles its leaves (fig. 54).
>
> Shot sixty-one: A parallel cut back to Bernard in her kitchen (fig. 55). She rises wearily and moves toward the camera.
>
> Shot sixty-two: Cuts back to the framing of the trees that ended shot sixty (fig. 56). Slowly the camera now pans to the left, reversing its previous trajectory, until it reveals West and August still arguing, although at a somewhat further distance from the camera than in shot sixty (fig. 57).

The pan in shot sixty jolted me when I first saw it at the Library of Congress, an experience repeated each time I have looked at it since. One assumes at first that it is going to reveal a new element of the situation, but it reveals—nothing. At least nothing of narrative interest—merely trees catching the breeze in their leaves. Is this like the preeminently nonclassical moment in *Two or Three Things I Know About Her* in which Godard on the soundtrack wonders whether to concentrate on his main character or on the October foliage of a nearby tree?

As extraordinary as this moment is, Griffith is not making the anti-narrative gesture of digression that Godard considers. Rather, Griffith is experimenting with the style of interruption so crucial to his editing, particularly his use of suspense. But this sequence is unique in its use of a combination of camera movement and editing to accomplish the interruption of story action. Although unusual, the sequence is obviously not an accidental anomaly, irrelevant to Griffith's style, but a strongly intentional stylistic elaboration of usual practice. Rather than contradicting the narrativization central to Griffith's style, it "lays bare the device," strikingly displaying a technique normally less obvious. The camera movement bares the hold Griffith's narrative discourse asserts both over story events and spectator attention. Griffith toys with the spectator's interest in the unfolding of the events by blocking visual access to them, briefly exiling the characters to the realm of off-screen space. What this pan reveals is viewer involvement in this suspenseful situation, and the narrator system's power to satisfy or frustrate it.

The next three shots continue the suspense, and resolve it through the more common interrupting technique of parallel editing:

52, 53, 54, 55, 56, and 57: Three shots from *His Lesson* (1912). Griffith pans right from the jealous farmer (Edwin August) confronting the city visitor (Charles West) in the woods, ending by framing leaves rustling in the breeze. He then cuts to the farmer's wife (Dorothy Bernard) at home. Returning to the woods, he pans left from the trees to reveal the men still arguing.

52

53

54

55

56

57

Shot sixty-two (whose beginning was described previously): West walks away from August, exiting right. As he leaves, August raises his rifle, aiming off-screen as if he were going to shoot.

Shot sixty-three: Another parallel edit back to Bernard in the kitchen as she brings in the wash and begins her laundry tasks.

Shot sixty-four: A return to August, his rifle still aimed off-screen. Slowly, he lowers the barrel and exits in the opposite direction, leaving his rival unharmed.

The cut between shots sixty-three and sixty-four is a rich example of the many narrative roles such interrupting cuts can play. The cut suspensefully interrupts August's act of firing the gun (will he shoot West?). In addition, the cut to Bernard provides a causal link: she is the subject of the men's enmity. Finally, the cut provides subjective motivation for August because it articulates August's decision whether or not to shoot. Bernard's washing plays a role as well because the family disharmony that sets this story in motion came from August treating his wife as a household drudge. The articulation of August's decision not to shoot indicates that he realizes his own fault in the matter: his neglect and overwork of his wife have led to her flirtation with the fisherman.

While these three shots focus their narrative meanings more clearly than the previous triad (shot sixty-two, of course, operates in both groups), the pans in shots sixty and sixty-two perform essentially the same role, albeit in a more flamboyant and experimental manner. The narrator system displays its force here precisely by removing attention from the center of the story. However, by asserting this power, Griffith only reminds the audience of his ultimate bonding with the story. As a suspense technique, it increases involvement with the fictional happenings, making us, like Scheherazade's auditor, Shariar, impatient for its resolution. Like Griffith's "empty" shots, this movement away from the characters is not a movement away from narrativization.

Rather, the camera movement celebrates the narrator's role in creating a story, calling attention to its control over discourse. Unlike the apparently, and often beautifully, aimless camera movement sometimes encountered in pre-Griffith cinema, the narrative intention of this pan is never in doubt. However, it does more than simply direct attention to an important element previously off-screen. It draws spectators' attention to the expectations they have invested in the story and its unfolding, an unfolding controlled by the narrator system. Unlike an anti-narrative technique in the middle of an apparently narrative film, such as the interpolation of documentary footage in the beginning of *L'Age d'or*, this is not a deconstructive moment aimed at short-circuiting conventional expectations. Like all the devices of the narrator system, these pans assert the film's control over significance.

Griffith's late films at Biograph develop and intensify the methods of the narrator system. He further elaborates the elements of filmic discourse on all three levels to shape and communicate narrative meanings. If all these elements are at the service of narrativization—the use of film images to tell stories—they also assert the act of the filmic narrator in telling the story. The increase in the number of shots; the variety in spatial distance and intra-scene cuttings, the new control of elements within a shot, both in arrangement and movement, and the creation of intensified significant imagery—all these developments reveal the hand of the filmic narrator, its control of the means of mediation by which the story is told. If the filmic narrator exists only in the way it highlights and intensifies the story, if it is visible only through its storytelling, we can also say that the story is visible only through the filmic discourse that tells it.

Notes

1. *Moving Picture World*, July 12, 1912, p. 208.

2. For a detailed presentation of rise of the independent production companies see my dissertation, "D. W. Griffith and the Narrator-System," New York University, 1966, pp. 682–95, with a consideration of the later struggle in pp. 799–806, as well as Eileen Bowser, *History of American Cinema*, vol. 2: *1907–1915* (New York: Scribner's, 1990), passim.

3. *Moving Picture World*, June 21, 1913, p. 1237.

4. The take-over of the domestic market is discussed in detail and with insight in Kristin Thompson, *Exporting Entertainment: America in the World Film Market, 1907–1934* (London:British Film Institute, 1985), pp. 1–27.

5. The survey is summarized in Michael Davis, *The Exploitation of Pleasure: A Study of Commercial Recreations in New York City* (New York: Russell Sage Foundation, 1911), see particularly, pp. 21, 25, 30. Historical studies that have investigated the nickelodeon in terms of urban environments include the Merritt and Allen studies mentioned earlier and, for a later period, Douglas Gomery, "Movie Audiences, Urban Geography, and the History of the American Film," *Velvet Light Trap*, no. 19 (1982): 23–29.

6. Raymond B. Fosdick, *A Report on the Condition of Motion Picture Shows in New York* (New York: Office of the Commissioner of Accounts, City of New York, 1911), p. 14.

7. Fosdick, *A Report*, p. 12.

8. New York *Dramatic Mirror*, Feb. 8, 1911, p. 30.

9. Janet Staiger, "Combination and Litigation: Structures of U.S. Film Distribution, 1896–1917," *Cinema Journal* 23 (Winter 1983): 56; Robert Anderson, "The Role of Western Film Genre in Industry Competition, 1907–1911," *Journal of the University Film Association* (Spring 1979): 19–26.

10. *Moving Picture World*, March 16, 1912, p. 940; June 22, 1912, p. 1105; Nov. 2, 1912, p. 429; Aug. 5, 1911, p. 275.

11. Ibid., Nov. 23, 1912, p. 759.

12. An excellent treatment of Griffith's later Biograph films emphasizing their difference from the earlier films highlighted by this book can be found in Charles Keil, "Transition through Tension: Stylistic Diversity in the Late Griffith Biographs," *Cinema Journal* 28 (Spring 1989): 22–40.

13. Russell Merritt, "Mr. Griffith, *The Painted Lady* and the Distinctive Frame," in *Image on the Art and Evolution of the Film Photographs and Articles from the Magazine of the International Museum of Photography,* ed. Marshall Deutelbaum (New York: Dover Publications, 1979), p. 149.

14. Merritt, "Mr. Griffith," pp. 51–152.

15. New York *Dramatic Mirror,* July 10, 1909, p. 19.

16. Ibid., May 14, 1910, p. 18. This review, along with several other columns by Woods, is reprinted in its entirety in *American Film Criticism from the Beginning to Citizen Kane: Reviews of Significant Films at the Time They First Appeared,* ed. Stanley Kauffman (New York: Liveright, 1972).

17. Christian Metz, *The Imaginary Signifier: Psychoanalysis and the Cinema,* trans. Celia Britton et al. (Bloomington: Indiana University Press, 1982), p. 63.

18. New York *Dramatic Mirror,* May 22, 1909, p. 17.

19. My concept of absorption in film is indebted to Michael Fried's treatment of eighteenth-century French painting, *Absorption and Theatricality: Painting and the Beholder in the Age of Diderot* (Berkeley: University of California Press, 1980).

20. The figures given here for 1908 and 1909 represent a nearly complete sample for those years. The figures for 1910 are drawn only from those Biograph films Griffith is believed to have directed. From 1911–13, the survey represents only the Griffith-directed films for which projection prints exist, well over 50 percent of his work for those years. In contrast to the methods of David Bordwell, Janet Staiger, and Kristin Thompson in *The Classical Hollywood Cinema: Film Style and Mode of Production to 1960* (New York: Columbia University Press, 1985), I have excluded intertitles from these counts. Because intertitles from 1908 and most of 1909 have not been preserved, their sudden inclusion in the later film would have skewed the figures.

21. However, the last two shots of the film cut in from a longer shot of Grace and her engineer sweetheart seated on the cow-catcher of a locomotive and somewhat surprisingly show a pre-*Dollie* repetition of action, as the engineer twice places his lunchbox in front of Grace. This the only pronounced repeated action I have found in a late Griffith Biograph film.

22. David Bordwell and Kristin Thompson, *Film Art: An Introduction* (Reading: Addison Wesley, 1979), pp. 163–71.

23. *Moving Picture World,* June 3, 1911, p. 1244.

24. See Frederick A. Talbot, *Moving Pictures: How They Are Made and Worked* (1912, repr. New York: Arno Press, 1970), p. 255.

25. Walter Benjamin, *The Origins of German Tragic Drama,* trans. John Osborne (London: NLB, 1977), p. 166.

26. Gérard Genette, *Narrative Discourse: An Essay in Method,* trans. Jane E. Lewin (Ithaca: Cornell University Press, 1980), p. 255.

27. It is interesting to contrast these "empty" shots in Griffith with Noel Burch's discussion of the similarly unpeopled "pillow shots" in the films of Yasujiro Ozu, *To the Distant Observer: Form and Meaning in the Japanese Cinema,* rev. and ed. Annette Michelson (Berkeley: University of California Press, 1979), pp. 160–85. Ozu, as

interpreted by Burch, "suspends the diegetic flow" (p. 160) by his recurrent use of shots which "focus for a moment, often a long one, on some inanimate aspect of Man's environment" (p. 161). Such shots often provide a "paradigm of de-centering and meaningless" (p. 172). In contrast, Griffith's "empty" shots are paradigms of meaning-fulness. However, the confrontation with death that is common to the shots cited from Griffith and to the concluding pillow shots in such Ozu films as *The Only Son* (1936), *Late Spring* (1947), *Tokyo Story* (1952), and *End of Summer* (1961) may call into question Burch's absolute opposition between significance and meaninglessness in narrative film.

Conclusion: Griffith,
Film History, and Us

I N THIS work I have sought to develop a historical approach to Griffith's Biograph films, concentrating on the period 1908–9. At the same time, looming over this more circumscribed concern has been an attempt to define the film historian's task, the nature of its parameters and methods. Although the theoreticalization of film history is beyond the scope of this volume, these films and this period of the American film industry raise basic issues which need to be brought into focus. As a film historian, one not only interrogates a period of production or a corpus of films, but one must also respond to them, uncovering the questions they address.

I have therefore paid attention to these films not only as evidence of the industrial practices of the American film industry in 1908–9, but also as works of art that still address us and whose destiny goes beyond the immediate horizons of their initial production and reception. However, any historical transcendence of the original horizon of these films must be founded on an initial understanding of how they were produced and understood. Therefore I have tried to integrate the insights of textual analysis into a historical understanding of film, and vice versa. Although the methods of industrial history and textual analysis diverge, a true historical approach demands their interrelation. The task is delicate because historical analysis develops a sense of general practices, whereas esthetic analysis approaches a film as a unique work. Defining the territory where the historical and the particular intersect requires a shifting focus. I will focus first on the background of general context.

David Bordwell's term *modes of film practice* provides a rubric for the general stylistic context for any period of film production.[1] These modes are historically defined norms which provide the background against which individual texts can be studied. Because they are constantly changing, an analyst must determine the specific mode relevant for individual films and periods. Without determining this historical context, Bordwell points out, film analysis will unconsciously use its own contemporary context as the background against which a film is discussed. This is particularly dangerous when dealing with early film. Therefore one of the first tasks of film historians must be to determine the relevant succession of film styles (or "modes of film practice"), such as the movement from the cinema of attractions to one of narrative integration.

Here, too, the dynamic nature of the individual work of art asserts its claim. Such a diachronical series never provides authoritarian definition of the film style of a particular period, overwhelming and determining the creative energies of individual works. Jan Mukarovsky's concept of the "aesthetic norm" provides a dynamic approach to the context of artistic works, in which the power of norms come from their violation as much as their preservation.[2] The modes of film practice do not define individual works, but rather provide a background against which they can be understood, defining both elements of conformity and divergence in specific films.

This involves a circular relationship in which the norms are constructed from individual works, and individual works are then analyzed by reference to these norms. This work on Griffith has tried to maintain a shifting focus, examining both the individuality of Griffith's films and their relation to a broader mode of film practice. Future detailed work on the surviving films of Griffith's contemporaries will define more clearly which elements of the narrator system are unique and which are shared with the norm of the cinema of narrative integration. Narrativization clearly defines the motive force of filmmaking in this period and provides the shared area between the cinema of narrative integration and the narrator system. However, the unique elements in Biograph films do not necessarily contradict their historical norms. For example, a preliminary overview of the period indicates that Griffith's films contain a larger number of shots than other films. Such emphasis on editing hardly contradicts the thrust toward narrativization that defines the period, rather, it intensifies and directs it toward one particular element of filmic discourse—editing.

The cinema of narrative integration defines the mode of film practice of one specific slice of film history. The essence of this slice is its development of filmic discourse for the purpose of storytelling. All levels of filmic discourse become organized around the narrative task: pro-filmic elements such as acting, costuming, and settings; the arrangements of elements within the film frame; and the elements of editing. The cinema of narrative integration can be distinguished from the cinema of attractions, exemplified by Porter and

Méliès, in which the task of storytelling has not yet asserted absolute dominance over the free play of filmic discourse.

The contrast the narrator system, Griffith's individual response within the cinema of narrative integration, poses to the succeeding period, the introduction of feature films, is less hard-edged. The dominant of narrativization provides a strong element of continuity between Griffith's filmmaking and this later period. The narrator system stands as a transitional period from earlier, less narrativized cinema to later periods of filmmaking which are its heirs. This transitional role is what makes Griffith's Biograph films so useful as the role of narrative in film is now being theorized. In the narrator system, the process of narrativization is particularly visible; the process of creating a fictional world is revealed. In semiological terms, we could say that the marks of enunciation are not effaced, at least in comparison to the later classical style. As Jacques Aumont says, discussing the matching of shots in Griffith's Biograph film, *Enoch Arden* (1911): "Griffith does nothing to conceal the white threads that stitch the shots together: On the contrary, he displays them, parades them, insists heavily on them, pointing them out with the whole signifying apparatus."[3] This marked visibility of the narrative process in Griffith's early films makes them both historically and theoretically invaluable.

Beyond relating a film to its contemporaneous mode of film practice and period norms lies the immense task of placing films within the horizons of social history, to relate as Hans Robert Jauss describes it, "special history" of an art form to "general history."[4] Bordwell again provides a concise way to conceptualize this in his study of Yasujiro Ozu.[5] A filmmaker's work can be viewed as the core of a series of concentric circles, with specific working constraints, the situation of the film industry, and the broader historical and social context ringing it round. But the outer circles can only be related to the core through a series of mediations. Thus the industrial situation would be mediated by Biograph's specific place in the film industry and Griffith's position within Biograph's production scheme. Likewise, the elements of a broader social history are mediated through the filter of the film industry's needs and projects. This book does not attempt a complete treatment of the social and ideological material contained in the Biograph films. However its focus on narrative form has shown that Griffith's style of narration fulfilled a number of desiderata of the film industry during this period: narrative coherence, an emulation of the psychology found in other socially respectable narrative forms (such as drama and the novel), and the creation of a moral rhetoric for film. The change in the narrative form found in Griffith's first films at Biograph responded to the challenge posed by the new economic organization represented by the MPPC.

However, we must not lose sight of the "special" history of film; this is a history of an art form, as the emphasis herein on film analysis indicates. This means that we are dealing with a particularly complicated process of signification, one that cannot be understood as a simple decoding, but through interpretation. Therefore, the address of these films extends beyond their original historical horizons to our own contemporary reception of them. It is an historicist illusion to believe that previous stylistic norms can be reconstructed "objectively"—"the phantom of an historical object which is the object of progressive research," as Gadamer puts it.[6] By acknowledging our own role in the historical interpretation of works of art, we define the hermenuetic task involved in film history. This means recognizing the temporal distance these films have from us, and our own historical position in reaching across that gap to understand them.

This historical understanding is based on both an understanding of the difference of the past from the present—"the tension between text and present," as Gadamer puts it[7]—and an assertion of a continuity between the two. In the attempt to understand its otherness from the past, the historian forges a sense of tradition, of history which relates the present to the past through the text.

Our understanding of Griffith's films remains incomplete, therefore, if it limits itself to a reconstruction of the historical context of his filmmaking. As contemporary film viewers, we are addressed directly by these films from the past, and their relation to us must be part of our historical understanding. Griffith's Biograph films are at the beginning of a certain historical tradition in film. The nature of this tradition has rarely been sufficiently explored by either its partisans or its detractors. We can not approach it simply as an objectified "past," but as a force that has already influenced us. In a historical understanding we are not simply uncovering a past but attempting to understand ourselves. But this does not mean that this past is immediately accessible, simply a form of self-exploration. The reconstruction of past horizons reveals our difference and distance from the past, its often-alien nature. But at the same time, we are not its prisoners. As history consists of a series of changes, historical understanding can be a means of change as well, with revolutionary implications found precisely in what seems most alien.

Griffith's Biograph films address us as contemporaries through laying bare the narrative processes of the cinema. For film viewers nurtured in a cinema that classically conceals its narrative operations through an "invisible" style, Griffith's films reveal the encounter of filmic discourse with narrative purposes. In Griffith what is rendered "invisible" in later cinema still remains visible. We witness in these early films the transformation of filmic discourse into figures of narrative significance. This historical spotlighting of the narrative process in Griffith's films comes into focus by contrasting them with modes of film practice that precede and follow them. But allowing them to address us as contemporary viewers also reveals their uniqueness, their bearing on issues dealing with film narrative that are contemporarily relevant to both historians and filmmakers.

The title of this concluding section, "Griffith, Film History and Us," emphasizes through a homage to Eisenstein's seminal, critical essay on Griffith, "Dickens, Griffith and We" (translated by Jay Leyda as "Dickens, Griffith and the Film Today") that these films still address us. Jacques Aumont has responded to this address in his essay, "Griffith, le cadre, le figure" (which also carries a subtitle "Griffith et nous" for its concluding section). Aumont is particularly aware of the ability of Griffith's Biograph films to make visible narrative processes which the later classical style labors to conceal. However, Aumont's work has been criticized by David Bordwell as being ahistorical. Bordwell faults Aumont for ignoring the relevant contemporary "modes of film practice," particularly in his discussion of Griffith's 1911 Biograph film *Enoch Arden*.[8] But I would assert the value of Aumont's analysis. A comparison of his essay with Bordwell's criticism shows that in some ways Aumont's discussion of Griffith and Biograph comes closer to what I see as a true historical understanding, while Bordwell's criticism verges on historicism.

Aumont's observations on Griffith's Biograph films center on the way in which these films are different from the classical filmmaking that Griffith traditionally is seen as inaugurating. Elements of Griffith's Biograph films appear to Aumont "as the antithesis of the tendency towards the cinema of transparence." Aumont is well aware that it would be an error to dismantle the understanding of Griffith as the "necessary patriarch" of the later classical style.[9] But his perception of the deviation of Griffith's films from classical practice opens a historical understanding of the Janus-headed role played by the narrator system, looking not only toward the later classical style, but also back at the less narrativized practices of earlier film.

Much of Griffith's filmic discourse reveals this transitional role. A good example would be an element I have frequently discussed, the use of a detailed background environment in exterior shots, with a careful arrangement of extras engaged in a variety of tasks, but who have no direct involvement with the narrative action occurring in the foreground. I have discussed this practice, particularly in contrast to earlier films, in terms of Griffith's naturalist ambitions: the desire to create a complex and detailed environment in which the narrative can take place. Aumont acknowledges this aspect of Griffith's treatment of the depth of the shot, its role in anchoring the drama in an illusion of real life in which events are not dissociated from their background.[10]

But, at the same time, Aumont notes the arranged quality of these backgrounds, the way they announce their own artificial composition, the careful placing of principle action over secondary action (which remains restricted to the background), so that the extras serve less as human figures than "a swarming and motley section of the decor."[11] This division between the narrative zone of the foreground and the atmospheric role of the background shows that naturalist purposes within the narrator system may be expressed in a way that appears artificial, compared to later realist styles.

Likewise, the close-up, which is the locus classicus of Griffith's nomination as the father of narrative cinema as the "inventor of the close-up," is often disruptive in Griffith's early films. This is due to—again in comparison to later practice—the relative lack of continuity devices which in classical filmmaking would render the joins between shots less noticeable and the enlargement of the close-up less jolting and excessive. Although Griffith's use of the close-up plays an important role in the narrativization of filmic discourse and sketches the foundations of the later decoupage, as discussed in relation to *The Lady and the Mouse,* it, too, plays a double role, pre-figuring the later classical style but violating its principle of "invisibility."

Bordwell's criticism of Aumont centers on his treatment of two shots from *Enoch Arden,* which Aumont describes as forming an ambiguous figure.[12] According to Aumont, the cut seems paradoxically to assert (through a false eyeline match) that two spaces that are diegetically distant—Annie Lee in England and Enoch's shipwreck on a desert island—are somehow contiguous. Bordwell criticizes Aumont for not understanding this sequence in terms of the proper "mode of film practice." According to Bordwell, this is not a false eyeline match because, he claims, such eyeline matches are rare in Griffith's work in this period. Rather, it is a "switchback," an editing figure which combines a character's mental operations (Annie is thinking of Enoch . . .) with a parallel cut to another actual happening (. . . while Enoch is shipwrecked). This figure has been discussed previously, particularly in dealing with *Enoch Arden*'s predecessor *After Many Years.* On the one hand, Bordwell offers a good historical analysis; instead of referring the shots to a familiar classical practice (the point-of-view shot), Bordwell invokes a contemporaneous convention which is unfamiliar to modern viewers but presumably understood by Griffith's 1911 audience.

On the other hand, although the classical point-of-view shot was rarely used in Griffith's films, cuts based on a character's off-screen look were important figures in Griffith's style, and increasingly so in 1911. Further, the pronounced off-screen look and reaction which Linda Arvidson provides in this sequence would most probably be read as involving a sight link because it precisely follows a pattern of other sight links in Griffith's work. (The sequence described from *The Redman and the Child* is an early example.) In fact, the sequence exemplifies a curious phenomenon in Griffith's narrative discourse, an indication of a character's premonition which is immediately confirmed by the editing pattern. Aumont's description of the sequence as a paradoxical sight link is not a misleading understanding.

My rereading basically affirms Bordwell's principle of the relevant "mode of film practice," simply indicating the careful research needed to determine what modes, in fact, are relevant. But it also shows how past modes of film practice may involve apparent paradoxes. Noting such anomalies in relation to contemporary practice can provide an opening to a historical analysis. Bordwell's conclusion of his criticism of Aumont seems practically prey to historicism: "In sum, the *Enoch Arden* cut may well instantiate a minor but clear convention of the American silent cinema of a certain period; if so, the cut cannot display the arbitrariness of Griffith's *écriture*, no matter how odd it may seem to us today."[13]

Whether Aumont has really claimed an arbitrary *écriture* seems debatable; rather, he claims a particular visibility of the signifying process contrasted with the seamless matching of the classical film. In whatever way this sequence is analyzed, it reveals an ambiguity compared to later practice. The switchback, as Bordwell defines it, is not a familiar figure today, precisely because it maintains an ambiguity between subjective and objective shots that is not tolerable to the later classical cinema. It is, of course, an error if Aumont describes this sequence as a transgressive device in 1911 which would confuse a contemporaneous spectator, becoming a "de-constructive" moment in Griffith's work. But Aumont expresses his own contemporary surprise at the sequence. His surprise maintains the tension between this film and the contemporary classical modes of filmmaking, an insight open to further development as a historical understanding.

Bordwell's analysis of the sequence threatens to close down a comparison between different periods of film style, although I am sure this is not the intention of one of the most subtle of recent film historians, as his work on Japanese cinema demonstrates. It goes beyond the important task of constructing the horizon of expectation of the film's original audience, and risks succumbing to a historicism that founds the reconstruction of past expectations on the suppression of our own historical situation. But although Aumont's "against the grain" reading of Griffith could potentially be misunderstood, it emphasizes that the contrast between Griffith's filmmaking and the classical model can strike us with a contemporary force. This provides a powerful historical understanding of the Biograph films.

Griffith's work cuts both ways, and a historical understanding must be aware of this. As a transitional moment in film history, the narrator system must be understood both as a founding moment of the later classical system, as well as an approach in some respects at odds to later practice. In this way these films participate in what Walter Benjamin termed the "dialectic which is inherent in origin."[14] The phrase "origins of American narrative film" in the title of this volume does not simply refer to the fact that these films come from an early period of film history. Nor is it a biological metaphor, indicating all later American narrative film as the descendants of Griffith. In a Benjaminian sense, I mean to indicate that the investigation of these early Biograph films reveal the dynamics which will be set into play in the subsequent history of narrative film. And in this sense the unique aspects of Griffith's Biograph films gains historical significance.

Pushing the methods of narrativization to an extreme, Griffith's first films lay bare the dynamics of the period in a way the more conventional productions of the period might not allow. Griffith's Biograph films are rich contradictory objects which in some sense display both the foundations of the later classical style (its narrativization), as well as alternatives to that style through their flaunting of the rhetorical presence of the filmic narrator. The narrator system, therefore, stands less as an indication of the typical approach to filmmaking of the cinema of narrative integration than as one of its extremes—a focal point in which its dynamic dialectic is revealed.

If the narrator system crystalizes the move from a scenography of exhibitionism as found in the earlier cinema of attractions to one of voyeurism in which films are no longer a direct display of the body of the actors, or the magical possibilities of the cinematic apparatus, but the witnessing of a self-contained story within a coherent diegesis, nonetheless the spectator remains the object of a clearly defined address. The audience is invited to look beyond the individual image and its possibilities of display to the story expressed by filmic discourse. The spectator is still addressed, but this address channels his or her attention toward the story. This defines the roles of the narrator system in directing the spectator's attention to the story: intensifying impact; interrupting the flow of action; allowing access to a character's motivation; and drawing moral conclusions. Instead of Méliès bowing to the spectator directly, the spectator becomes lost in a fictional world, but his or her access to this world is constantly shaped by the filmic narrator.

Once again the issue of suspense, traditionally an important element in all discussions of Griffith's style, and later equally identified with one of Griffith's most important heirs in the realm of filmic discourse—Alfred Hitchcock, steps into the spotlight. Griffith's suspense involves a complex game with the spectator, raising narrative expectations and then suspending them, creating a flow of action and then interrupting it. As *His Lesson* shows, the power of the narrator system lies in its control over a story; it never abdicates from its shaping and commanding power over both the story and the spectator who follows it.

The Biograph films open up an investigation of the narrative form of film that need not situate itself in the crux of a dilemma between a transparent classical style and instances of deconstructive *écriture*. Instead, Griffith's first films reveal a field of teeming energy and multiple possibilities within the process of filmic narration. These possibilities and the still-to-be-explored potentials of narrative in film are liberated through a historical understanding of how films have been narrated and how these narratives have been understood. In this ongoing project the Biograph films offer guidance and inspiration; their formal beauty provides a spur.

Notes

1. David Bordwell, "Textual Analysis, Etc.," *Enclitic* 5–6 (Fall 198 Spring 1982): 125–36.

2. See Jan Mukarovsky, "The Aesthetic Norm" in *Structure, Sign, and Function,* ed. and trans. John Burbank and Peter Steiner (New Haven: Yale University Press, 1978); Victor Erlich, *Russian Formalism* (New Haven: Yale University Press, 1981), pp. 251–71.

3. Jacques Aumont, "Griffith, le cadre, le figure," in *Le cinéma Americain: Analyses de films,* vol. 1, ed. Raymond Bellour (Paris: Flammarion, 1980), p. 59.

4. Hans Robert Jauss, *Towards an Aesthetic of Reception,* trans. Timothy Bahti (Minneapolis: University of Minnesota Press, 1982), p. 39.

5. David Bordwell, *Ozu and the Poetics of Cinema* (Princeton: Princeton University Press, 1988), p. 17.

6. Hans Georg Gadamer, *Truth and Method* (New York: Seabury Press, 1975), p. 267.

7. Gadainer, *Truth and Method,* p. 273.

8. Bordwell, "Textual Analysis, Etc.," pp. 128–29. Aumont himself, in a later essay that somewhat revises his earlier work, submitted his work to a similar auto-critique for its lack of historical grounding, but also maintains the value of certain of his insights, Jacques Aumont, "L'Ecriture Griffith-Biograph," in *David Wark Griffith: Études sous la direction de Jean Mottet* (Paris: L'Harmattan, 1984), pp. 234, 247.

9. Aumont, "Griffith" pp. 54, 52.

10. Ibid., p. 62.

11. Ibid., pp. 62–63. My translation.

12. Bordwell, "Textual Analysis," pp. 128–29.

13. Ibid., p. 129.

14. Walter Benjamin, *The Origins of German Tragic Drama,* trans. John Osborne (London, NLB, 1977), p. 46.

Bibliography

1. Books

Allen, Robert C. *Vaudeville and Film, 1895–1915: A Study in Media Interaction.* New York: Arno Press, 1980.

———, and Douglas Gomery. *Film History: Theory and Practice.* New York: Alfred A. Knopf, 1985.

Anti-Saloon League Yearbook 1910. Columbus: Anti-Saloon League of America, 1910.

Arvidson, Linda. [Mrs. D. W. Griffith]. *When the Movies Were Young.* 1925. Reprint. New York: Dover Publications, 1969.

Aumont, J., A. Gaudreault, and M. Marie, ed. *Histoire du cinéma: Nouvelles approaches.* Serie Langues et Langages, vol. 19. Paris: Publications de la Sorbonne, 1989.

Bakhtin, M. M., *The Dialogic Imagination: Four Essays by M. M. Bakhtin.* Edited by Micheal Holquist, and translated by Caryl Emerson and Micheal Holquist. Austin: University of Texas Press, 1981.

Bakhtin, M. M., and P. M. Medvedev. *The Formal Method in Literary Scholarship: A Critical Introduction to Sociological Poetics.* Translated by Wlad Godzich. Cambridge: Harvard University Press, 1985.

Balio, Tino, ed. *The American Film Industry.* Madison: University of Wisconsin Press, 1976.

Balshofer, Fred, and Arthur Miller. *One Reel a Week.* Berkeley: University of California Press, 1967.

Barthes, Roland. *Image Music Text.* Edited and translated by Stephen Heath. New York: Hill and Wang, 1977.

———. *Empire of Signs.* Translated by Richard Howard. New York: Hill and Wang, 1982.

Becker, George. *Documents of Modern Literary Realism.* Princeton: Princeton University Press, 1963.

Bellour, Raymond, ed. *Le Cinéma Americain: Analyses des films.* Vol. 1. Paris: Flamma-rion, 1980.

Belton, John. *Cinema Stylists.* Metuchen: Scarecrow Press, 1983.

Benjamin, Walter. *Origins of German Tragic Drama.* Translated by John Osborne. London: NLB, 1977.

———. *Understanding Brecht.* Translated by Ana Bostock. London: NLB, 1977.

Bergala, Alain. *Initiation à la sémiologie du récit en images.* Paris: Ligue francais de l'enseignement et de l'éducation permanente, n.d.

Benveniste, Emile. *Problems in General Linguistics.* Coral Gables: University of Miami Press, 1970.

Bitzer, Billy. *His Story: The Autobiography of D. W. Griffith's Master Cameraman.* New York: Farrar Straus and Giroux, 1973.

Booth, Michael. *English Melodrama.* London: Herbert Jenkins, 1965.

Booth, Wayne C. *The Rhetoric of Fiction.* Chicago: University of Chicago Press, 1961.

Bordwell, David. *The Films of Carl-Theodore Dreyer.* Berkeley: University of California Press, 1981.

———. *Narration in the Fiction Film.* Madison: University of Wisconsin Press, 1985.

———. *Ozu and the Poetics of Cinema.* Princeton: Princeton University Press, 1988.

———, and Kristin Thompson. *Film Art: An Introduction.* Reading: Addison Wesley, 1979.

———, Janet Staiger, and Kristin Thompson. *The Classical Hollywood Cinema: Film Style and Mode of Production to 1960.* New York: Columbia University Press, 1985.

Bowser, Eileen, ed. *Biograph Bulletins, 1908–1912.* New York: Farrar Straus and Giroux, 1973.

———. *History of American Cinema.* Vol. 2, *1907–1915.* New York: Scribners, 1990.

Branigan, Edward R., *Point of View in the Cinema: A Theory of Narration and Subjectivity in Classical Film.* Amsterdam: Mouton Publishers, 1984.

Brooks, Peter. *The Melodramatic Imagination: Balzac, Henry James, Melodrama and the Mode of Excess.* New Haven: Yale University Press, 1976.

———. *Reading for the Plot: Design and Intention in Narrative.* New York: Random House, 1984.

Brown, Karl. *Adventures with D. W. Griffith.* Edited by Kevin Brownlow. New York: Farrar, Straus and Giroux, 1973.

Burch, Noel. *To The Distant Observer: Form and Meaning in the Japanese Cinema.* Revised and edited by Annette Michelson. Berkeley: University of California Press, 1979.

Caughie, John. *Theories of Authorship: A Reader.* British Film Institute Readers in Film Study. London: Routledge and Kegan Paul, 1981.

Chatman, Seymour. *Story and Discourse: Narrative Structure in Fiction and Film.* Ithaca: Cornell University Press, 1978.

Chinoy, Helen Kritch, and Toby Cole. *Directors and Directing: A Source Book of the Modern Theater.* Indianapolis: Bobbs-Merrill, 1976.

Cochrane, Thomas C., and William Miller. *The Age of Enterprise: A Social History of Industrial America.* Revised edition. New York: Harper and Row, 1961.

Cowing, Cedric B. *Populists, Plungers, and Progressives: A Social History of Stocks and Commodity Speculation, 1890–1930*. Princeton: Princeton University Press, 1965.

Cross, Gilbert. *Next Week—East Lynn: Domestic Drama in Performance, 1820–1874*. Lewisburg: Bucknell University Press, 1977.

Davis, Michael. *The Exploitation of Pleasure: A Study of Commercial Recreations in New York City*. New York: Russell Sage Foundation, 1911.

Deslandes, Jacques, and Jacques Richard. *Histoire comparée du cinéma*. Vol. 2, *Du cinématographe au cinéma, 1896–1906*. Paris: Casterman, 1968.

Deutelbaum, Marshall, ed. *Image on the Art and Evolution of the Film: Photographs and Articles from the Magazine of the International Museum of Photography*. New York: Dover Publications, 1979.

Dickens, Charles. *Oliver Twist*. New York: New American Library, 1961.

Dyer, Richard. *Stars*. London: British Film Institute, 1979.

Eisenstein, Sergei. *Film Form*. Edited and translated by Jay Leyda. San Diego: Harcourt Brace Jovanovich, 1942.

Erlich, Victor. *Russian Formalism: History-Doctrine*. 3d edition. New Haven: Yale University Press, 1981.

Fell, John L. *Film and the Narrative Tradition*. Norman: University of Oklahoma Press, 1974.

———. ed. *Film Before Griffith*. Berkeley: University of California Press, 1983.

Fosdick, Raymond B. *A Report on the Condition of Motion Picture Shows in New York*. New York: Office of the Commissioner of Accounts, City of New York, 1911.

Foucault, Michel. *Language, Counter-Memory, Practice: Selected Essays and Interviews*. Edited by Donald F. Bouchard and translated by Donald F. Bouchard and Sherry Simon. Ithaca: Cornell University Press, 1977.

Fried, Michael. *Absorption and Empathy: Painting and the Beholder in the Age of Diderot*. Berkeley: University of California Press, 1980.

Gadamer, Hans Georg. *Philosophical Hermeneutics*. Edited and translated by David E. Linge. Berkeley: University of California Press, 1977.

———. *Truth and Method*. New York: Seabury Press, 1975.

Gaudreault, André. *Du littéraire au filmique: System du récit*. Paris: Meridiens Klincksieck, 1988.

———, ed. *Ce que je vois de mon ciné* Paris: Meridiens Klincksieck, 1988.

Genette, Gérard. *Figures of Literary Discourse*. Translated by Alan Sheridan. European Perspectives Series. New York: Columbia University Press, 1982.

———. *Narrative Discourse: An Essay in Method*. Translated by Jane E. Lewin. Ithaca: Cornell University Press, 1980.

Gilbert, Douglas. *American Vaudeville: Its Life and Times*. 1940. Reprint. New York: Dover Publications, 1963.

Gish, Lillian. *The Movies, Mr. Griffith and Me*. New York: Avon Books, 1970.

Grau, Robert. *The Theater of Science*. 1913. Reprint. New York: Benjamin Blom, 1966.

Griffith, D. W. *The Man Who Invented Hollywood: The Autobiography of D. W. Griffith*. Edited and annotated by James Hart. Louisville: Touchstone Publishing, 1972.

Guibbert, Pierre. ed. *Les premier ans du cinéma francais*. Perpignan: Institute Jean Vigo, 1985.

Gutman, Herbert G. *Work, Culture and Society in Industrializing America: Essays in American Working Class and Social History.* New York: Vintage Books, 1966.

Hampton, Benjamin. *History of the American Film Industry, from Its Beginnings to 1931.* Reprint. New York: Dover Publications, 1970.

Handlin, Oscar. *The Uprooted: The Epic Story of the Great Migrations that Made the American People.* New York: Grosset and Dunlap, 1951.

Hansen, Miriam. *Babel and Babylon: Spectatorship in American Silent Film.* Cambridge: Harvard University Press, 1990.

Heath, Stephen. *Questions of Cinema.* Bloomington: Indiana University Press, 1981.

Henderson, Robert. M. *D. W. Griffith: The Years at Biograph.* New York: Farrar, Straus and Giroux, 1970.

Hendricks, Gordon. *Beginnings of the Biograph.* New York: Beginnings of the American Film, 1964.

———. *The Edison Motion Picture Myth.* Berkeley: University of California Press, 1961.

Herbert, Robert. *Jean Francois Millet.* London: Arts Council of Great Britain, 1976.

Hewitt, Barnard. *Theater USA, 1668–1957.* New York: McGraw-Hill, 1959.

Hofstader, Richard. *The Age of Reform: From Bryan to FDR.* New York: Vintage Books, 1955.

Holman, Roger, ed. *Cinema 1900–1906: An Analytical Study by the National Film Archives (London) and the International Federation of Film Archives.* Vol. 1 and Vol. 2, *Filmography.* Brussels: FIAF, 1982.

Jacobs, Lewis. *The Rise of the American Film: A Critical History, with an Essay, Experimental Cinema in America 1921–1947.* Studies in Culture and Communication. New York: Teachers College Press, 1968.

Jauss, Hans Robert. *Towards an Aesthetic of Reception.* Translated by Timothy Bahti. Theory and History of Literature, vol. 2. Minneapolis: University of Minnesota Press, 1982.

Jenkins, Stephen, ed. *Fritz Lang: The Image and the Look.* London: British Film Institute Publishing, 1981.

Jesionowski, Joyce E. *Thinking in Pictures: Dramatic Structure in D. W. Griffith's Biograph Films.* Berkeley: University of California Press, 1987.

Jowett, Garth. *Film: The Democratic Art.* American Film Institute Series. Boston: Little, Brown, 1976.

Kasson, John F. *Amusing the Million: Coney Island at the Turn of the Century.* American Century Series. New York: Hill and Wang, 1978.

Kauffman, Stanley, ed., with Bruce Henstall. *American Film Criticism from the Beginnings to Citizen Kane: Reviews of Significant Films at the Time They First Appeared.* New York: Liveright, 1972.

Lahue, Kalton C. *Motion Picture Pioneer: The Selig Polyscope Company.* South Brunswick: A. S. Barnes, 1973.

Lindsay, Vachel. *The Art of the Motion Picture.* 1915. Reprint. New York: Liveright, 1970.

Long, Robert. *David Wark Griffith: A Brief Sketch of His Career.* New York: D. W. Griffith Services, 1920.

Lounsbury, M. O. *The Origins of American Film Criticism.* New York: Arno Press, 1979.

Lyons, John. *Introduction to Theoretical Linguisitics.* Cambridge: Cambridge University Press, 1971.

Malthete-Méliès, Madeliene, ed. *Méliès et la naissance du spectacle cinématographique.* Paris: Meridiens Klincksieck, 1984.

Marker, Lise-Lone. *David Belasco: Naturalism in the American Theater.* Princeton: Princeton University Press, 1975.

May, Lary. *Screening Out the Past: The Birth of Mass Culture and the Motion Picture Industry.* New York: Oxford University Press, 1980.

Metz, Christian. *Film Language: A Semiotics of the Cinema.* Translated by Michael Taylor. New York: Oxford University Press, 1974.

———. *The Imaginary Signifier: Psychoanalysis and the Cinema.* Translated by Celia Britton et al. Bloomington: Indiana University Press, 1982.

Mitry, Jean. *Esthétique et psychologie du cinéma.* 2 vols. Paris: Éditions Universitaires, 1966.

———. *Histoire du cinéma: Art et industrie.* Vol. 1, *1895–1914.* Paris: Éditions Universitaires, 1967.

Mottet, Jean. *D. W. Griffith: Études sous la direction de Jean Mottet.* Publications de la Sorbonne. Paris: L'Harmattan, 1984.

Mukarovsky, Jan. *Structure, Sign, and Function.* Edited and translated by John Burbank and Peter Steiner. New Haven: Yale University Press, 1978.

Musser, Charles, *High Class Motion Pictures: Lyman H. Howe and the Traveling Exhibitor.* Princeton: Princeton University Press, 1989.

———, ed. *Motion Picture Catalogs by American Producers and Distributors 1894–1908: A Microfilm Edition.* Frederick, Md.: Thomas A. Edison Papers, 1985.

Niver, Kemp R., comp. *The Biograph Bulletins, 1896–1908.* Edited by Bebe Bergsten. Los Angeles: Locare Research Group, 1971.

———. *D. W. Griffith: His Biograph Films in Perspective.* Edited by Bebe Bergsten. Los Angeles: John D. Roche, 1974.

———. *Early Motion Pictures: The Paper Print Collection in the Library of Congress.* Edited by Bebe Bergstrom. Washington, D.C.: Library of Congress, 1985.

Norris, Frank. *The Octopus.* New York: Signet Classics, 1964.

———. *The Pit: A Story of Chicago.* New York: Modern Library, 1934.

Piess, Kathy. *Cheap Amusements: Working Women and Leisure in Turn-of-the-Century New York.* Philadelphia: Temple University Press, 1983.

Pratt, George, ed. *Spellbound in Darkness: A History of the Silent Film.* Rev. ed. Greenwich: New York Graphic Society, 1973.

Rahill, Frank. *The World of Melodrama.* University Park: Pennsylvania State University Press, 1967.

Ramsaye, Terry. *A Million and One Nights: A History of the Motion Picture Through 1925.* 1926. Reprint. London: Frank Cass, 1964.

Ricouer, Paul. *Interpretation Theory: Discourse and the Surplus of Meaning.* Fort Worth: Texas Christian University Press, 1976.

———. *The Rule of Metaphor: Multi-disciplinary Studies of the Creation of Meaning in Language.* Translated by Robert Czerny, Kathleen McLaughlin, and John Costello. Toronto: University of Toronto Press, 1977.

————. *Time and Narrative.* 3 vols. Translated by Kathleen Blamey and David Pellauer. Chicago: University of Chicago Press, 1984, 1985, 1988.

Rosenzweig, Roy. *Eight Hours for What We Will: Workers and Leisure in an Industrial City 1870–1920.* New York: Cambridge University Press, 1983.

Rozwenc, Edwin C., and John C. Matten, eds. *Myth and Reality in the Populist Revolt.* Lexington: D.C. Heath, 1967.

Sadoul, Georges. *Georges Méliès: Présentation et bio-filmography; choix de textes et propos de Méliès.* Series Cinema d'aujourd'hui. Paris: Seghers, 1961.

————. *Histoire général du cinéma.* Vol. 2, *Les pionniers du cinéma 1897–1909.* Vol. 3, *Le cinéma devient un art 1909–1920, premier volume: L'avant-guerre.* Paris: Denoel, 1951.

Salt, Barry. *Film Style and Technology: History and Analysis.* London: Starword, 1983.

De Saussure, Fernand. *Course in General Linguistics.* Edited by Charles Bally and Albert Sechehaye in collaboration with Albert Riedlinger, translated by Wade Baskin. New York: McGraw-Hill, 1966.

Schickel, Richard. *D. W. Griffith: An American Life.* New York: Simon and Schuster, 1983.

Scott, P. G. *Tennyson's "Enoch Arden": A Victorian Best-Seller.* Lincoln: The Tennyson Society, 1970.

Sklar, Robert. *Movie-made America: A Cultural History of American Movies.* New York: Vintage Books, 1975.

Smith, Albert. *Cricket on the Hearth; or, A Fairy Tale of Home.* New York: Samuel French, n.d.

Sternberg, Meir. *Expositional Modes and Temporal Ordering in Fiction.* Baltimore: John Hopkins University Press, 1978.

Talbot, Frederick A. *Moving Pictures: How They Are Made and Worked.* 1912. Reprint. New York: Arno Press, 1970.

Thompson, Kristin. *Exporting Entertainment: America in the World Film Market, 1907–1934.* London: British Film Institute, 1985.

Todorov, Tvetzan. *Introduction to Poetics.* Theory and History of Literature, vol. 1. Translated by Richard Howard. Minneapolis: University of Minnesota Press, 1981.

————. *The Poetics of Prose.* Translated by Richard Howard. Ithaca: Cornell University Press, 1977.

Tyler, Alice Felt. *Freedom's Ferment: Phases of American Social History from the Colonial Period to the Outbreak of the Civil War.* New York: Harper and Row, 1944.

Vardac, A. Nicholas. *From Stage to Screen: Theatrical Method from Garrick to Griffith.* 1949. Reprint. New York: Benjamin Blom, 1968.

Veyne, Paul. *Writing History.* Translated by Mina Moore-Rinvolucri. Middletown: Wesleyan University Press, 1984.

Wagenknecht, Edward. *The Movies in the Age of Innocence.* New York: Ballantine Books, 1971.

White, Hayden. *MetaHistory: The Historical Imagination in Nineteenth-Century Europe.* Baltimore: John Hopkins University Press, 1973.

Williams, Raymond. *Problems in Materialism and Culture: Selected Essays.* London: NLB, Verso Editions, 1980.

———. *The Sociology of Culture*. New York: Schocken Books, 1982.
Wilson, Garff. *A History of American Acting*. Bloomington: Indiana University Press, 1966.
Wilson, George M. *Narration in Light: Studies in Cinematic Point of View*. Baltimore: John Hopkins University Press, 1986.

2. Periodicals

A. Trade Journals

Billboard, 1908–10; *Film Index* (early issues, *Views and Film Index*), 1907–11; the *Edison Kinetogram*, 1909–11; *Moving Picture World*, 1908–13; the New York *Clipper*, 1908–10; the New York *Dramatic Mirror*, 1908–11; *Nickelodeon* (became *Motography* in 1911), 1909–11; *Show World*, 1908–10; *Variety*, 1908–11.

B. Articles

(Preference has been given to articles anthologized in book form. Such articles are not listed here, but have their bibliographic reference under section 1 and their full reference in individual footnotes.)

Anderson, Robert. "The Role of the Western Film Genre in Industry Competition, 1907–1911." *Journal of the University Film Association* (Spring 1979): 19–26.
Bordwell, David. "Textual Analysis, Etc." *Enclitic* 5–6 (Fall 1981-Spring 1982): 125–36.
———, and Kristin Thompson. "Linearity, Materiality and the Study of Early American Cinema." *Wide Angle* 5, no. 3 (1983): 4–15.
Bowser, Eileen. Addendum to 'The Reconstruction of *A Corner in Wheat*. *Cinema Journal* 19 (Fall 1979): 101–2.
———. "The Reconstruction of *A Corner in Wheat*." *Cinema Journal* 15 (Spring 1976): 45–52.
Brewster, Ben. "A Scene at the Movies." *Screen* 23 (July–Aug. 1982): 4–15.
Burch, Noel. "Film's Institutional Mode of Representation and the Soviet Response." *October* 11 (Winter 1979): 77–96.
———. "How We Got into Pictures." *AfterImage* 8/9 (Winter 1980–81): 24–38.
———. "Passion, poursuite: la linearisation." *Communication* 38 (1983): 30–50.
———. "Une Mode de representation primitif." IRIS 2 (Spring 1984): 113–23.
Camper, Fred, and Jonathan Shimkin. "Griffith's Composition and Recent American Cinema." *University Film Study Center Newsletter* 5 (Dec. 1974): 6–8.
Cassady, Ralph. "Monopoly in Motion Picture Production and Distribution, 1908–1915." *Southern California Law Review*, no. 32 (Summer 1959): 325–45.
Collier, John. "Cheap Amusements." *Charities and the Commons*, April 11, 1908, pp. 73–74.
Currie, Barton W. "Nickel Madness." *Harper's Weekly*, Aug. 24, 1907, pp. 1246–47.
Cushman, Richard B. "A Tribute to Mary Pickford." AFI, n.p. (program notes).
deCordova, Richard. "The Emergence of the Star System in America." *Wide Angle* 6, no. 4 (1985): 4–13.

Fell, John L. "Motive. Mischief and Melodrama: The State of Film Narrative in 1907." *Film Quarterly* 23 (Spring 1983): 30–37.

Fisher, Robert. "Film Censorship and Progressivist Reform: The National Board of Censorship of Motion Pictures, 1909–1922." *Journal of Popular Film* 4, no. 2 (1975): 143–56.

Gaudreault, André "Bruitage, musique at comentaires aux débuts du cinéma." *Protée* 12 (Summer 1985): 12–20.

Gessner, Robert. "Porter and the Creation of Cinematic Motion: An Analysis of *The Life of an American Fireman.*" *Journal of the Society of Cinematologists* 2 (1962): 1–13.

Gomery, Douglas. "Movie Audiences, Urban Geography, and the History of the American Film." *Velvet Light Trap*, no. 19 (1982): 23–29.

Gordon, Henry Stephen. "The Story of D. W. Griffith," *Photoplay* (June–Nov. 1916): no. 1, pp. 28–37, 162–166; no. 2, pp. 122–32; no. 3, pp. 78–88; no. 4, pp. 79–86, 146–48; no. 5, pp. 86–94; no. 6, pp. 27–40.

Gubern, Roman. "David Wark Griffith et l'articulation cinématographique." *Les Cahiers de la Cinémathèque*, no. 17 (Dec. 1975): 7–11.

Gunning, Tom. "The Cinema of Attraction: Early Film, Its Spectator and the Avant-Garde." *Wide Angle* 8, nos. 3, 4 (1986): 63–70.

———. "The Movies, Mr. Griffith, and Us." A review of Richard Schickel's *D. W. Griffith: An American Life. American Film* 9 (June 1984): 57–59, 70, 72.

———. "Non-continuity, Continuity and Discontinuity: A Theory of Genres in Early Film." IRIS 2 (Spring 1984): 101–12.

———. " 'Primitive Cinema'—A Frame-up? or, The Trick's on Us." 28 *Cinema Journal* (28 Winter 1988–89): 3–12.

———. "Weaving a Narrative: Style and Economic Background in Griffith's Biograph Films." *Quarterly Review of Film Studies* (Winter 1981): 10–25.

Gutman, Peter. "D. W. Griffith: The Rise of Film Art," part 6. *Classic Images* 89 (n.d.): 7–8.

Hammond, Paul. "George, This Is Charles." *AfterImage* 8/9 (Winter 1980–81): 39–48.

Hansen, Miriam. "Benjamin, Cinema and Experience: The Blue Flower in the Land of Technology." *New German Critique* 40 (Winter 1987).

Jenn, Pierre, and Michael Nagard. "L'Assasinat du duc de Guise." *L'Avant Scene Cinema* (Nov. 1984): 58.

Keil, Charles. "Transition through Tension: Stylistic Diversity in the Late Griffith Biographs." *Cinema Journal* 28 (Spring 1989): 22–40.

Lawrence, Florence. "Growing up with the Movies." *PhotoPlay* (Nov. 1914–Jan. 1915).

Lagny, Michele. "History, Cinema's Auxiliary." *Sub-Stance* 51 (December 1986): 12–21.

Loughney, Patrick. "In the Beginning Was the Word: Six Pre-Griffith Motion Picture Scenarios." IRIS 2, no. 1 (1984): 17–31.

Mast, Gerald. "Film History and Film Histories." *Quarterly Review of Film Studies* 1 (Aug. 1976): 297–314.

McNamara, Brooks. "The Scenography of Popular Entertainment." *The Drama Review,* March 1974, pp. 16–24.

Merritt, Russell. "Rescued from a Perilous Nest: D. W. Griffith's Escape from Theater into Film." *Cinema Journal* 2 (Fall 1981): pp?

Michelson, Annette, "Camera Lucida/Camera Obscura." *Art Forum,* January 1973, pp. 30–37.

Mitry, Jean. "Les Mésaventures d'un Pompier." *Cinématographe* 74 (Jan. 1982): 61–68.

Musser, Charles. "American Vitagraph 1897–1901." *Cinema Journal* 22 (Spring 1983): 4–46.

———. "The Nickleodeon Era Begins: Establishing the Framework for Hollywood's Mode of Representation." *Framework* 22–23 (Autumn 1983): 4–11.

———. "Another Look at the 'Chaser Theory'." *Studies in Visual Communications* 10, no. 4 (1984): 24–44.

Vlada, Petric. "A Corner in Wheat: Griffith's Earliest Masterpiece." *University Film Study Center Newsletter* 5, no. 2 (1974): 4.

Ropars-Wuilleumier, Marie-Claire. "Function du montage dans la constitution du récit au cinema." *Revue des Sciences Humaines* 36 (Jan.–March 1971): 33–52.

Salt, Barry. "The Physician of the Castle." *Sight and Sound* 54 (Winter 1985–86).

———. "What We Can Learn from the First Twenty Years of Cinema." IRIS 2, no. 1 (1984): 83–90.

Staiger, Janet. "Combination and Litigation: Structures of U.S. Film Distribution, 1896–1917." *Cinema Journal* 23 (Winter 1983): 41–71.

———. "The Eyes Are Really the Focus: Photoplay Acting and Film Form and Style." *Wide Angle* 6, no. 4 (1985).

———. "Seeing Stars" *Velvet Light Trap* 20 (Summer 1983): 14–23.

Stern, Seymour. "The Birth of a Nation." *Film Culture* 36 (Spring-Summer 1965).

Waters, Theodore. "Out with a Moving Picture Machine." *Cosmopolitan* (Jan. 1906): 251–59.

Whitney, John H. "The Pragmatic Artist." *Classic Film Collector* (New York, n.d.).

3. Unpublished Material

A. Archives

The Museum of Modern Art Film Library, New York City: The D. W. Griffith Collection includes Biograph Company records: Cameraman's Book, Author Book, the Barnet Braverman material, and the Billy Bitzer material.

Edison National Historic Site Archives, West Orange, N.J.: includes records and memos of MPPC and Edison Manufacturing Company, and National Board of Censorship Material.

Library of Performing Arts, New York City, Lincoln Center, Billy Rose Theater Collection: includes clipping files for play reviews and National Board of Censorship material.

B. Individual Works

Anderson, Robert Jack. "The Motion Picture Patents Company," Ph.D. diss., University of Wisconsin-Madison, 1983.

Gaudreault, André. "Récit scriptual, récit theatral, récit filmique: Prolegomenes à une theorie narratologique du cinéma," Ph.D. diss., Université de Paris-III, 1985.

Gunning, Tom. "D. W. Griffith and the Narrator-System: Narrative Structure and Industry Organization in Biograph Films, 1908–1909," Ph.D. diss., New York University, 1986.

Loughney, Patrick. "A Descriptive Analysis of the Library of Congress Paper Print Collection and Related Copyright Material," Ph.D. diss., George Washington University, 1988.

Merritt, Russell. "The Impact of D. W. Griffith's Motion Pictures from 1908 to 1915 on Contemporary American Culture," Ph.D. diss., Harvard University, 1970.

Pearson, Roberta. "The Modesty of Nature: Performance Style in the Griffith Biographs," Ph.D. diss., New York University, 1987.

Philips, M. B., and Howe, Francis T. "Memorandum for the MPPC and General Film Co. Concerning the Investigation of Their Business by the Department of Justice." Museum of Modern Art.

Turim, Maureen. "Layers of Meaning: 'Enoch Arden' and an Historically Wrought Semiotics."

4. Legal Documents

"Property of Motion Picture Patents Company" (volume of legal agreements relating to the MPPC bound with this title, on file at Museum of Modern Art under "MPPC").

United States v. Motion Picture Patents Company, 225 F. 800 (E.D. Pa., 1915) Record. 6 volumes.

Motion Picture Patents Company v. Independent Motion Picture Company, U.S. Circuit Court, (S.D. N.Y. 1910).

Motion Picture Patents Company v. New York Motion Picture Company (E.D., N.Y. 1910).

5. Filmographic

Thoroughly researched and accurate filmographic information for all the Griffith-directed Biograph films referred to herein can be found in Cooper C. Graham et al. *D. W. Griffith and the Biograph Company.* Filmmaker Series, no. 10. Metuchen: Scarecrow Press, 1985.

References to most of the early non-Griffith films referred to herein can be found in *Cinema 1900–1906*, vol. 2: *Filmography*, ed. Roger Holman. Brussels: FIAF, 1982.

Index

(Unless otherwise noted, films listed are directed
by D. W. Griffith, numbers in italics indicate
illustrations.)